MIKIYO TSUDA PRESENTS

THE DAY OF REVOLUTION

2

DMP

DIGITAL MANGA
PUBLISHING

THE DAY OF REVOLUTION 2

CONTENTS

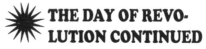

Translation	Sachiko Sato
Lettering	Melanie Lewis
Graphic Design	Wendy Lee/Fred Lui
Editing	Stephanie Donnelly
Editor in Chief	Fred Lui
Publisher	Hikaru Sasahara

English Edition Published by
DIGITAL MANGA PUBLISHING
A division of DIGITAL MANGA, Inc.
1487 W 178th Street, Suite 300
Gardena, CA 90248

www.dmpbooks.com

First Edition: December 2006
ISBN-10: 1-56970-889-4
ISBN-13: 978-1-56970-889-7

1 3 5 7 9 10 8 6 4 2

Printed in China

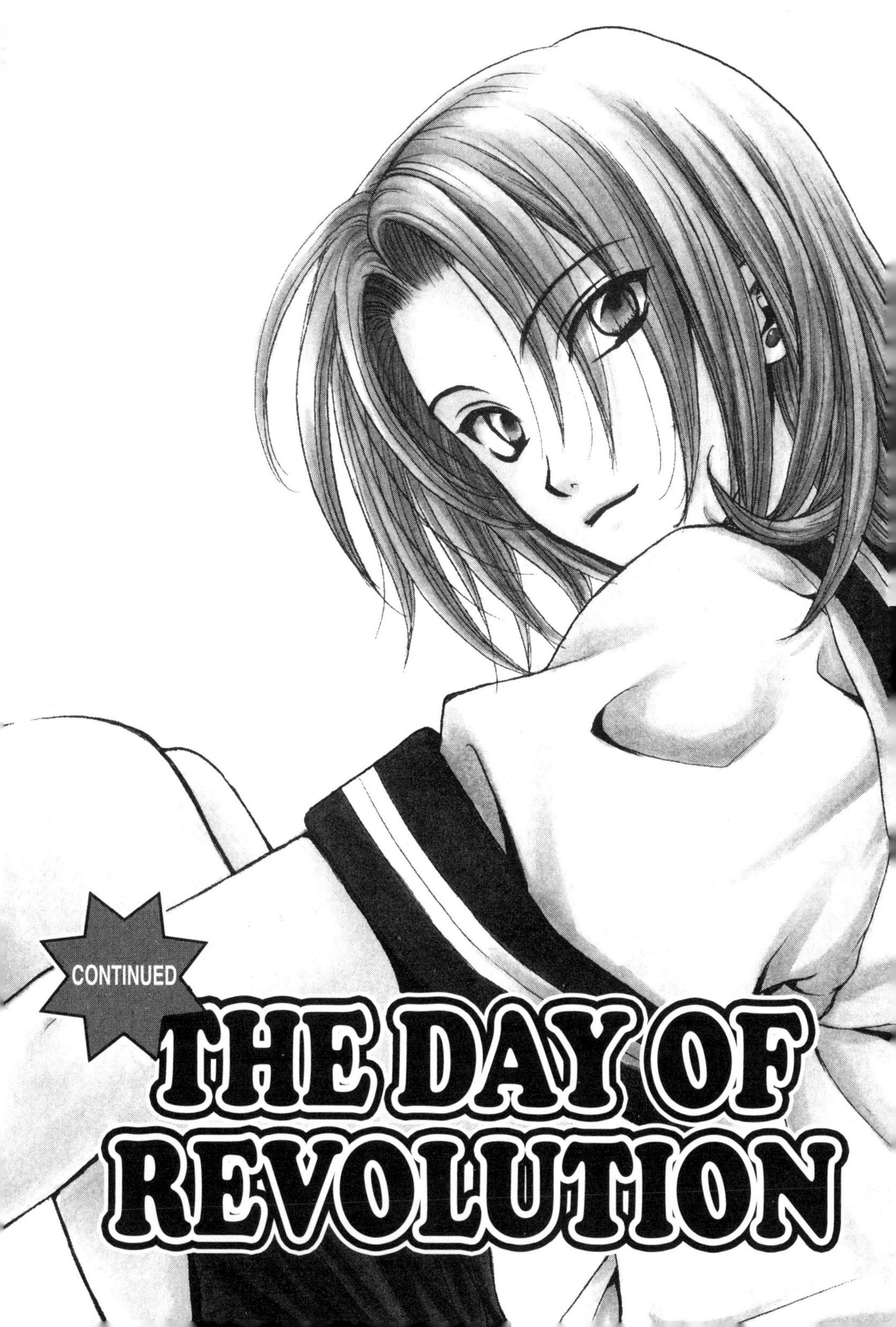
CONTINUED
THE DAY OF
REVOLUTION

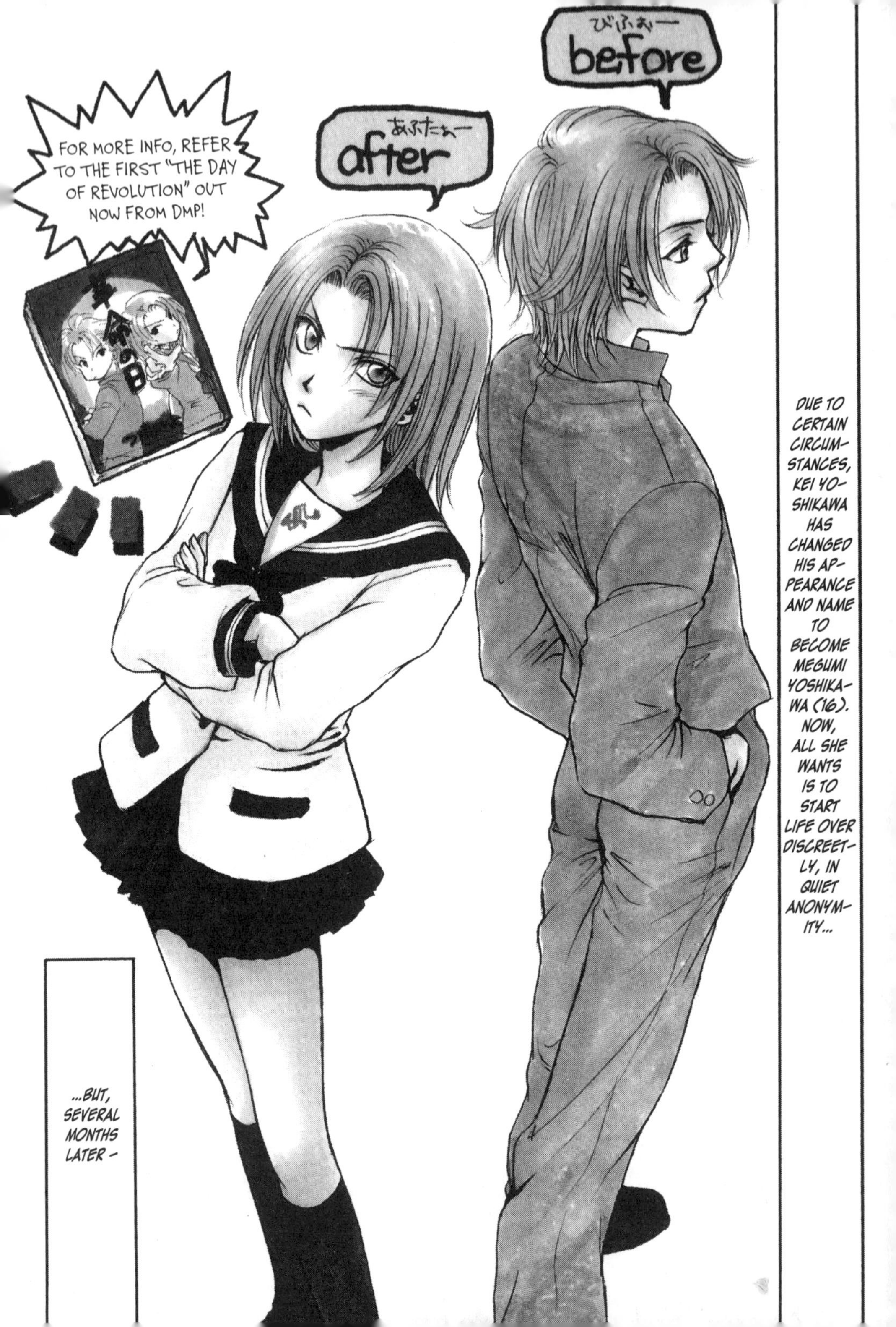
びふぉー
before
あふたぁー
after
FOR MORE INFO, REFER TO THE FIRST "THE DAY OF REVOLUTION" OUT NOW FROM DMP!
DUE TO CERTAIN CIRCUMSTANCES, KEI YOSHIKAWA HAS CHANGED HIS APPEARANCE AND NAME TO BECOME MEGUMI YOSHIKAWA (16). NOW, ALL SHE WANTS IS TO START LIFE OVER DISCREETLY, IN QUIET ANONYMITY...
...BUT, SEVERAL MONTHS LATER -

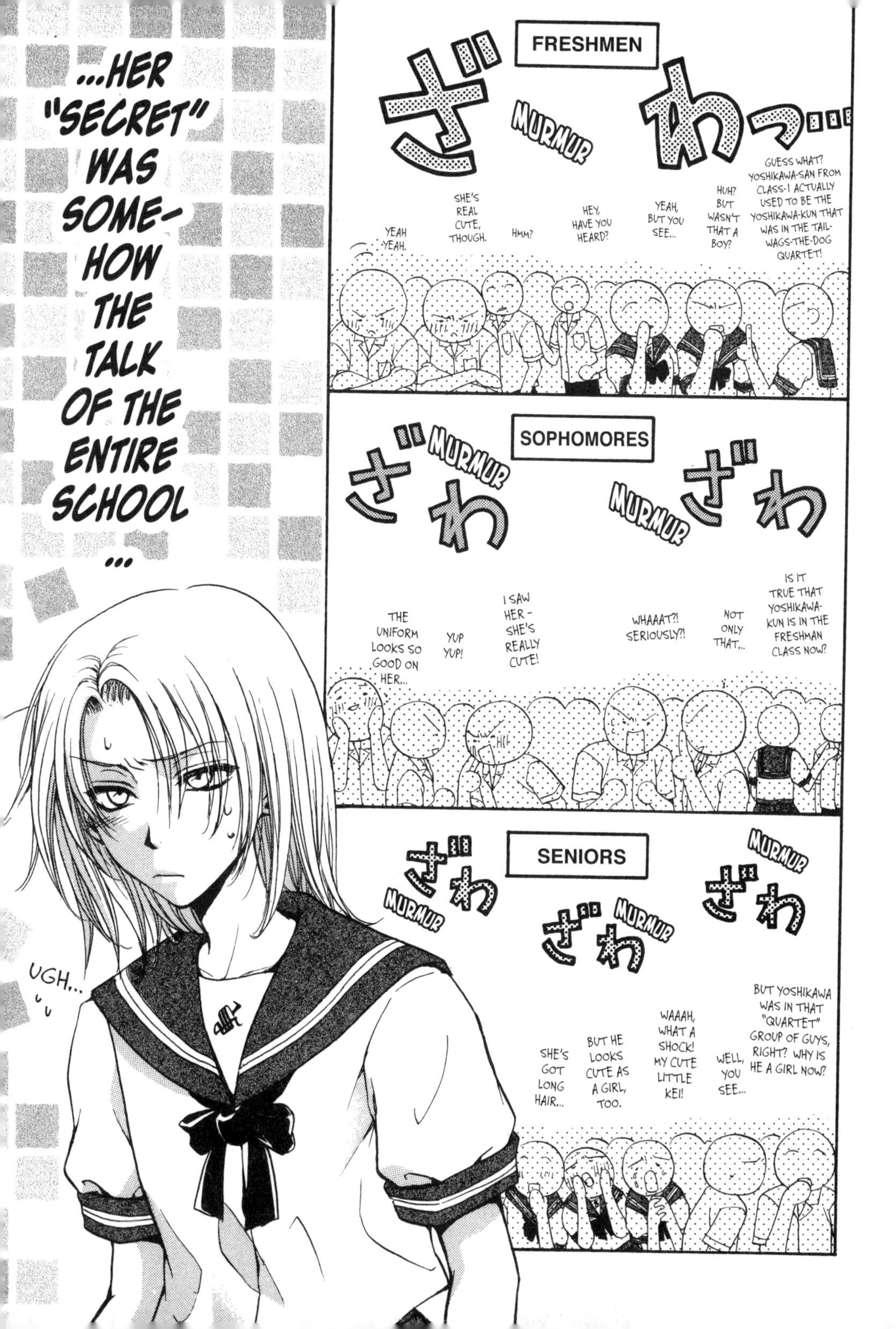

FRESHMEN
ざわっ…
MURMUR
GUESS WHAT? YOSHIKAWA-SAN FROM CLASS-1 ACTUALLY USED TO BE THE YOSHIKAWA-KUN THAT WAS IN THE TAIL-WAGS-THE-DOG QUARTET!
HUH? BUT WASN'T THAT A BOY?
YEAH, BUT YOU SEE...
HEY, HAVE YOU HEARD?
HMM?
SHE'S REAL CUTE, THOUGH.
YEAH YEAH.
SOPHOMORES
ざわ ざわ
MURMUR
MURMUR
IS IT TRUE THAT YOSHIKAWA-KUN IS IN THE FRESHMAN CLASS NOW?
NOT ONLY THAT...
WHAAAT?! SERIOUSLY?!
I SAW HER - SHE'S REALLY CUTE!
YUP YUP!
THE UNIFORM LOOKS SO GOOD ON HER...
SENIORS
ざわ ざわ ざわ
MURMUR
MURMUR
MURMUR
BUT YOSHIKAWA WAS IN THAT "QUARTET" GROUP OF GUYS, RIGHT? WHY IS HE A GIRL NOW?
WELL, YOU SEE...
WAAAH, WHAT A SHOCK! MY CUTE LITTLE KEI!
BUT HE LOOKS CUTE AS A GIRL, TOO.
SHE'S GOT LONG HAIR...
...HER "SECRET" WAS SOMEHOW THE TALK OF THE ENTIRE SCHOOL...
UGH...

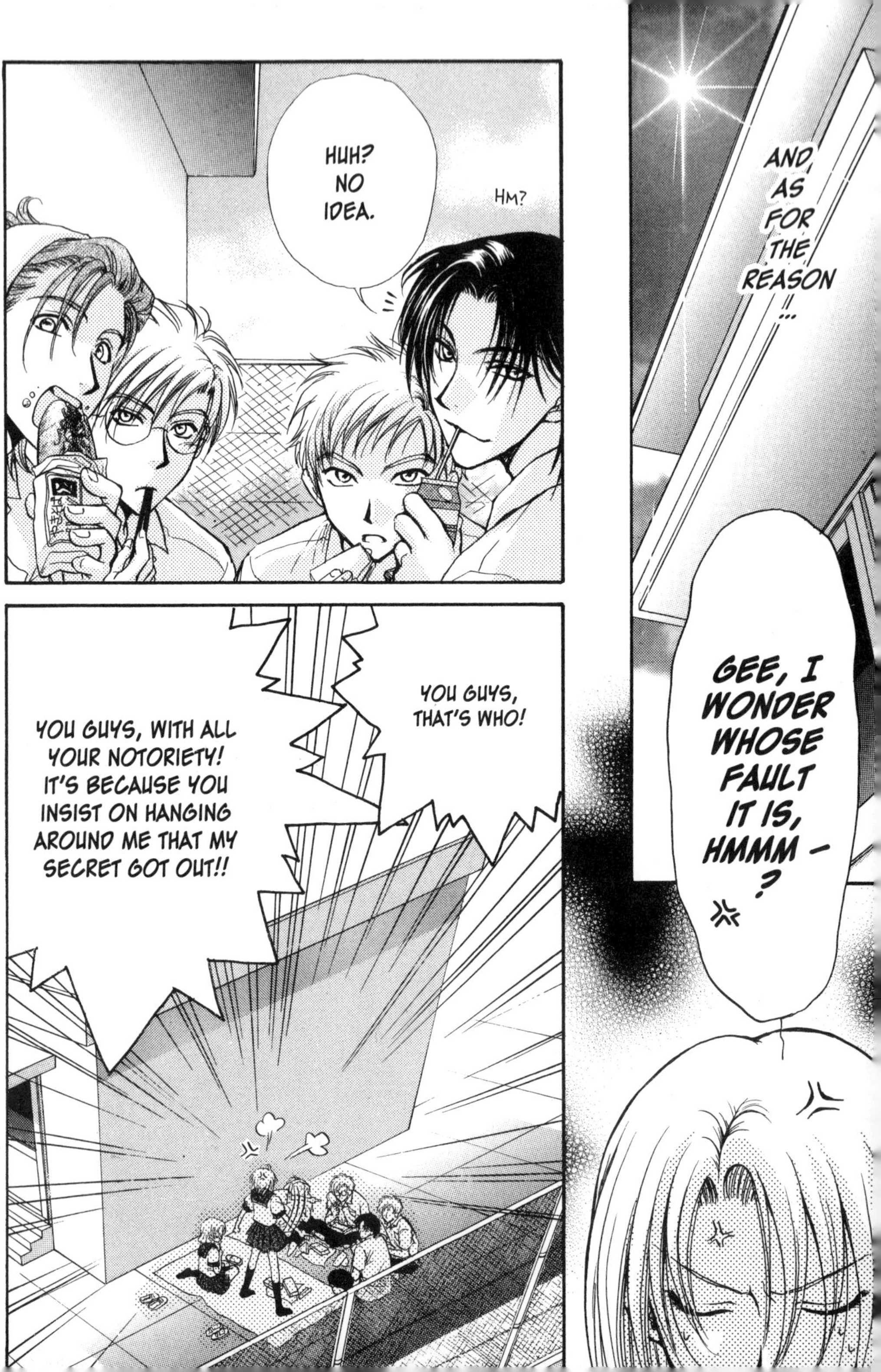
AND, AS FOR THE REASON ...
GEE, I WONDER WHOSE FAULT IT IS, HMMM — ?
HUH? NO IDEA.
HM?
YOU GUYS, THAT'S WHO!
YOU GUYS, WITH ALL YOUR NOTORIETY! IT'S BECAUSE YOU INSIST ON HANGING AROUND ME THAT MY SECRET GOT OUT!!

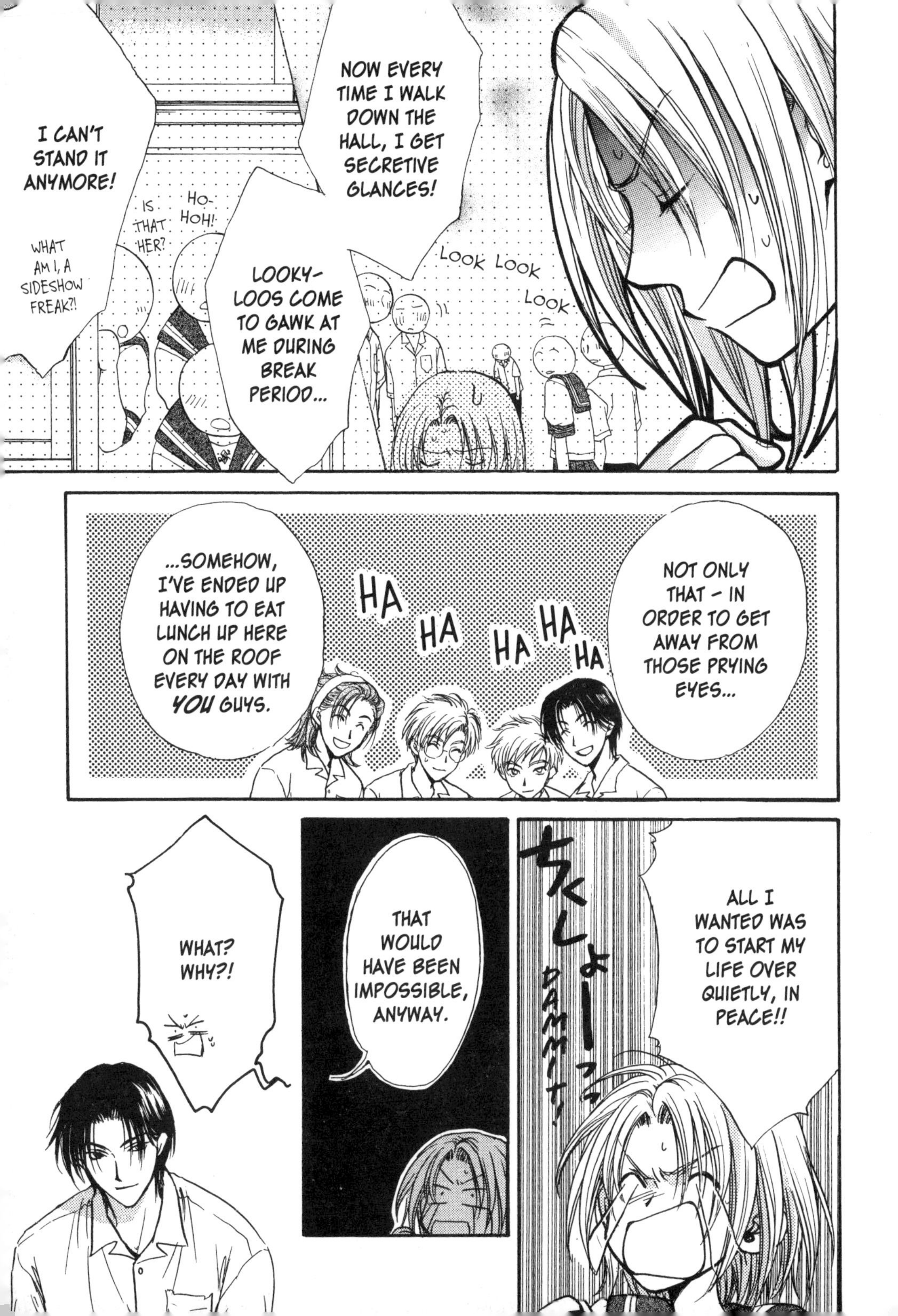
LOOK LOOK
LOOK
NOW EVERY TIME I WALK DOWN THE HALL, I GET SECRETIVE GLANCES!
I CAN'T STAND IT ANYMORE!
LOOKY-LOOS COME TO GAWK AT ME DURING BREAK PERIOD...
HO-HOH!
IS THAT HER?
WHAT AM I, A SIDESHOW FREAK?!
NOT ONLY THAT - IN ORDER TO GET AWAY FROM THOSE PRYING EYES...
HA HA HA HA HA
...SOMEHOW, I'VE ENDED UP HAVING TO EAT LUNCH UP HERE ON THE ROOF EVERY DAY WITH *YOU* GUYS.
ちくしょーっ
DAMMIT!
ALL I WANTED WAS TO START MY LIFE OVER QUIETLY, IN PEACE!!
THAT WOULD HAVE BEEN IMPOSSIBLE, ANYWAY.
WHAT? WHY?!

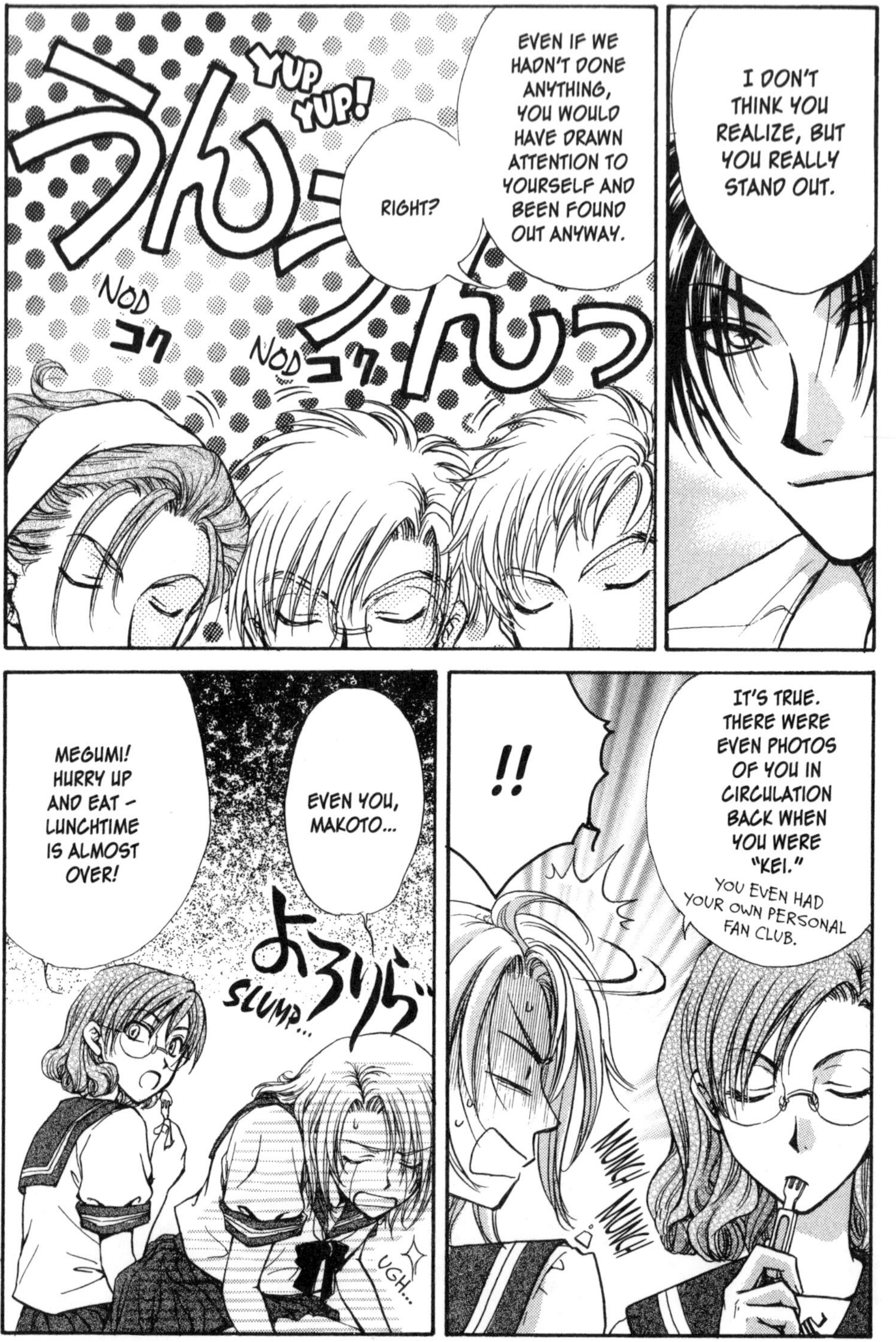
I DON'T THINK YOU REALIZE, BUT YOU REALLY STAND OUT.
EVEN IF WE HADN'T DONE ANYTHING, YOU WOULD HAVE DRAWN ATTENTION TO YOURSELF AND BEEN FOUND OUT ANYWAY.
RIGHT?
YUP YUP!
NOD コク
NOD コク
!!
IT'S TRUE. THERE WERE EVEN PHOTOS OF YOU IN CIRCULATION BACK WHEN YOU WERE "KEI."
YOU EVEN HAD YOUR OWN PERSONAL FAN CLUB.
MUNCH MUNCH
MEGUMI! HURRY UP AND EAT - LUNCHTIME IS ALMOST OVER!
EVEN YOU, MAKOTO...
SLUMP...
UGH...

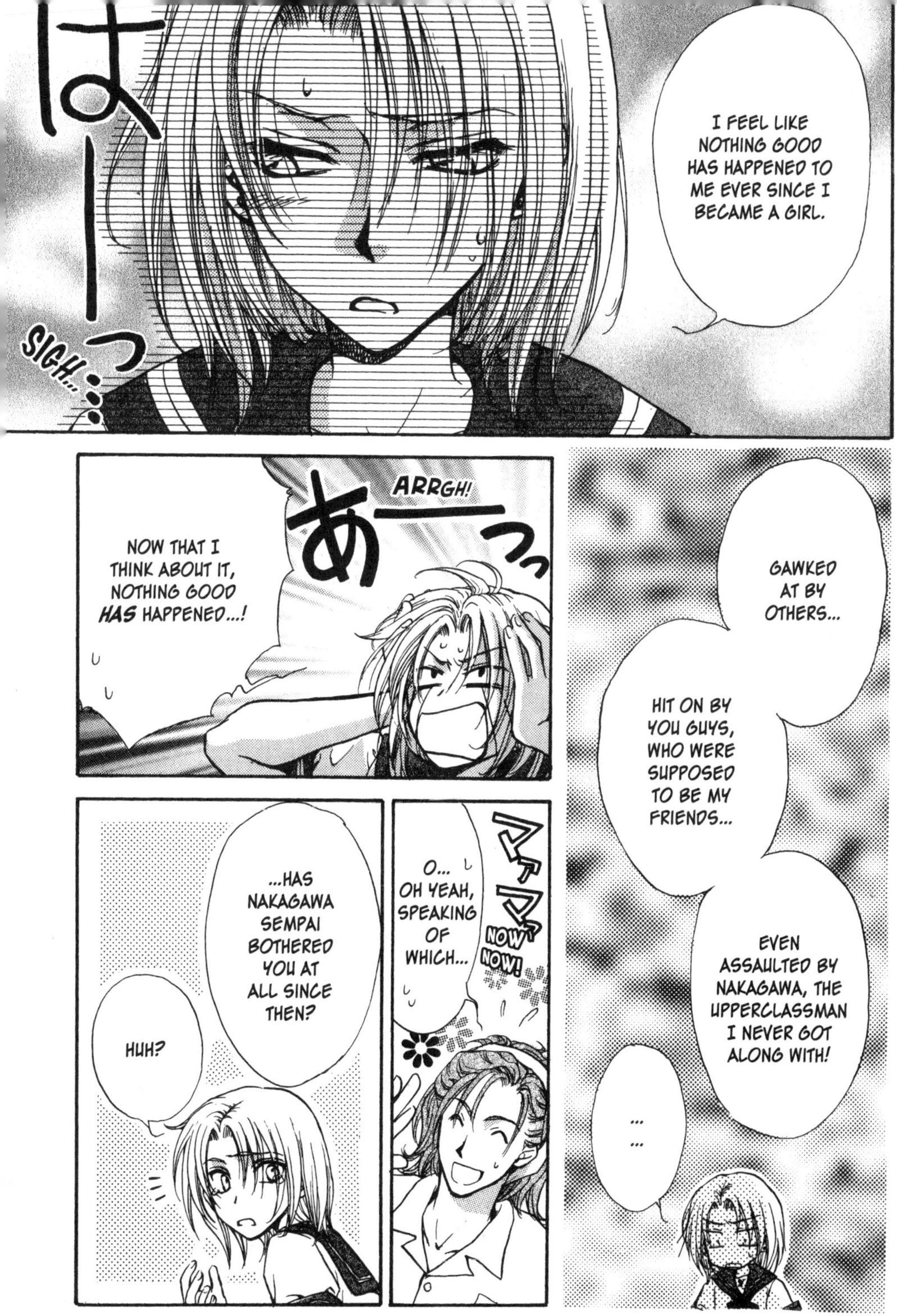
I FEEL LIKE NOTHING GOOD HAS HAPPENED TO ME EVER SINCE I BECAME A GIRL.
はーっ
SIGH...
GAWKED AT BY OTHERS...
HIT ON BY YOU GUYS, WHO WERE SUPPOSED TO BE MY FRIENDS...
EVEN ASSAULTED BY NAKAGAWA, THE UPPERCLASSMAN I NEVER GOT ALONG WITH!
... ...
あーっっ
ARRGH!
NOW THAT I THINK ABOUT IT, NOTHING GOOD ***HAS*** HAPPENED...!
マァマァ
NOW NOW!
O... OH YEAH, SPEAKING OF WHICH...
...HAS NAKAGAWA SEMPAI BOTHERED YOU AT ALL SINCE THEN?
HUH?

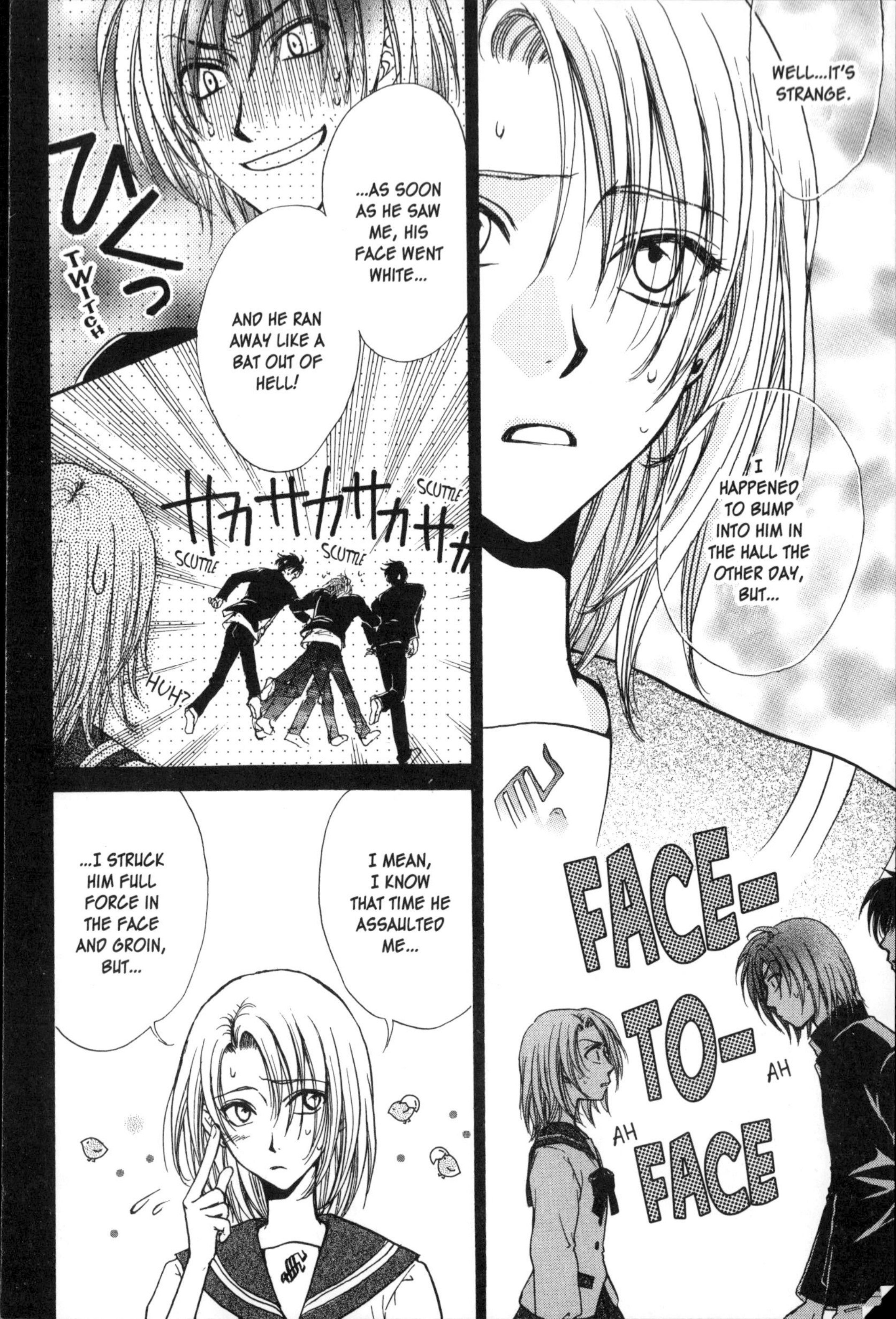
WELL...IT'S STRANGE.
I HAPPENED TO BUMP INTO HIM IN THE HALL THE OTHER DAY, BUT...
TWITCH
...AS SOON AS HE SAW ME, HIS FACE WENT WHITE...
AND HE RAN AWAY LIKE A BAT OUT OF HELL!
SCUTTLE
SCUTTLE
SCUTTLE
HUH?
FACE-TO-FACE
AH
AH
I MEAN, I KNOW THAT TIME HE ASSAULTED ME...
...I STRUCK HIM FULL FORCE IN THE FACE AND GROIN, BUT...

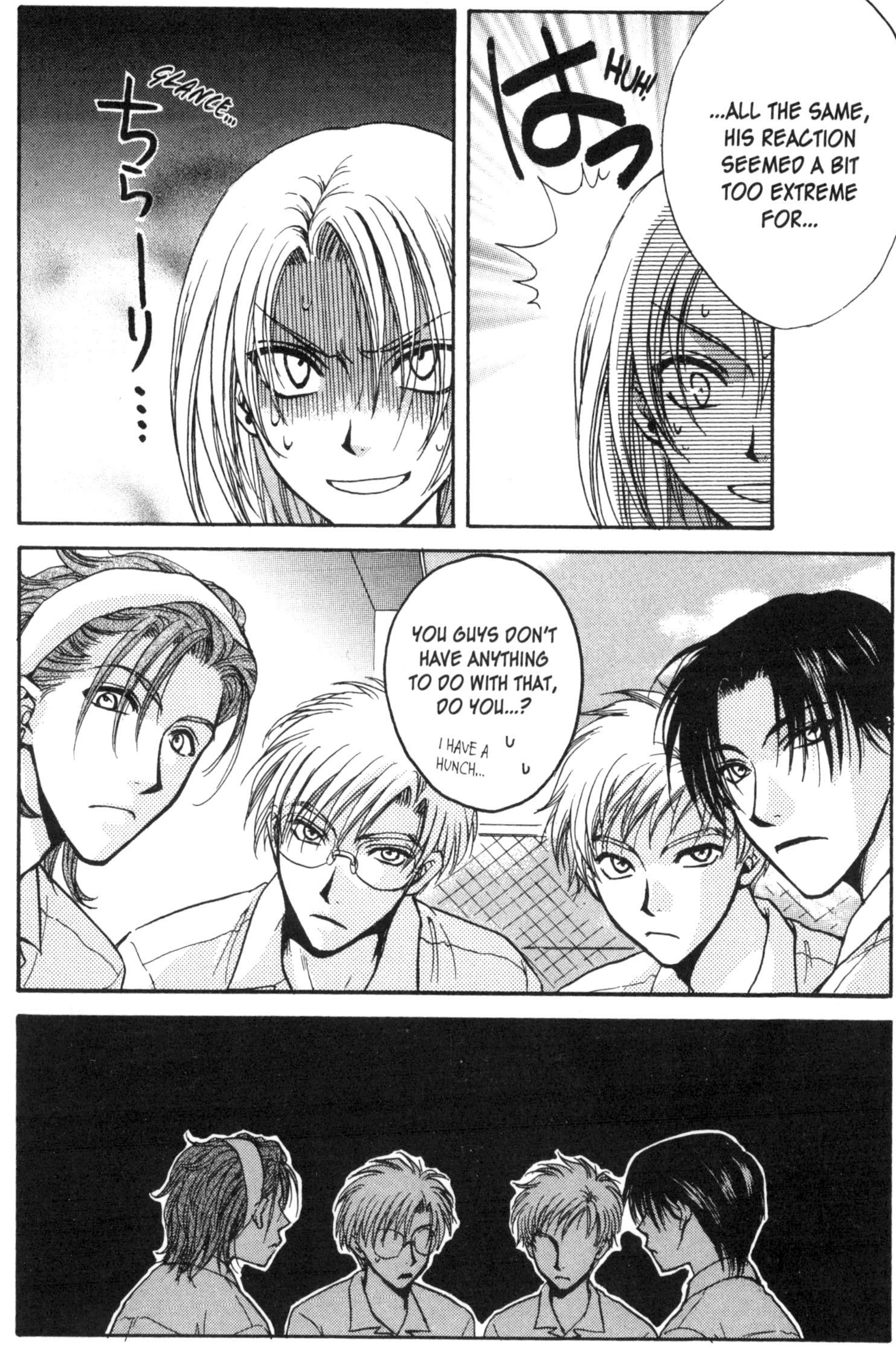

はっ
HUH!
...ALL THE SAME, HIS REACTION SEEMED A BIT TOO EXTREME FOR...
ちらーーり・・・
GLANCE...
YOU GUYS DON'T HAVE ANYTHING TO DO WITH THAT, DO YOU...?
I HAVE A HUNCH...

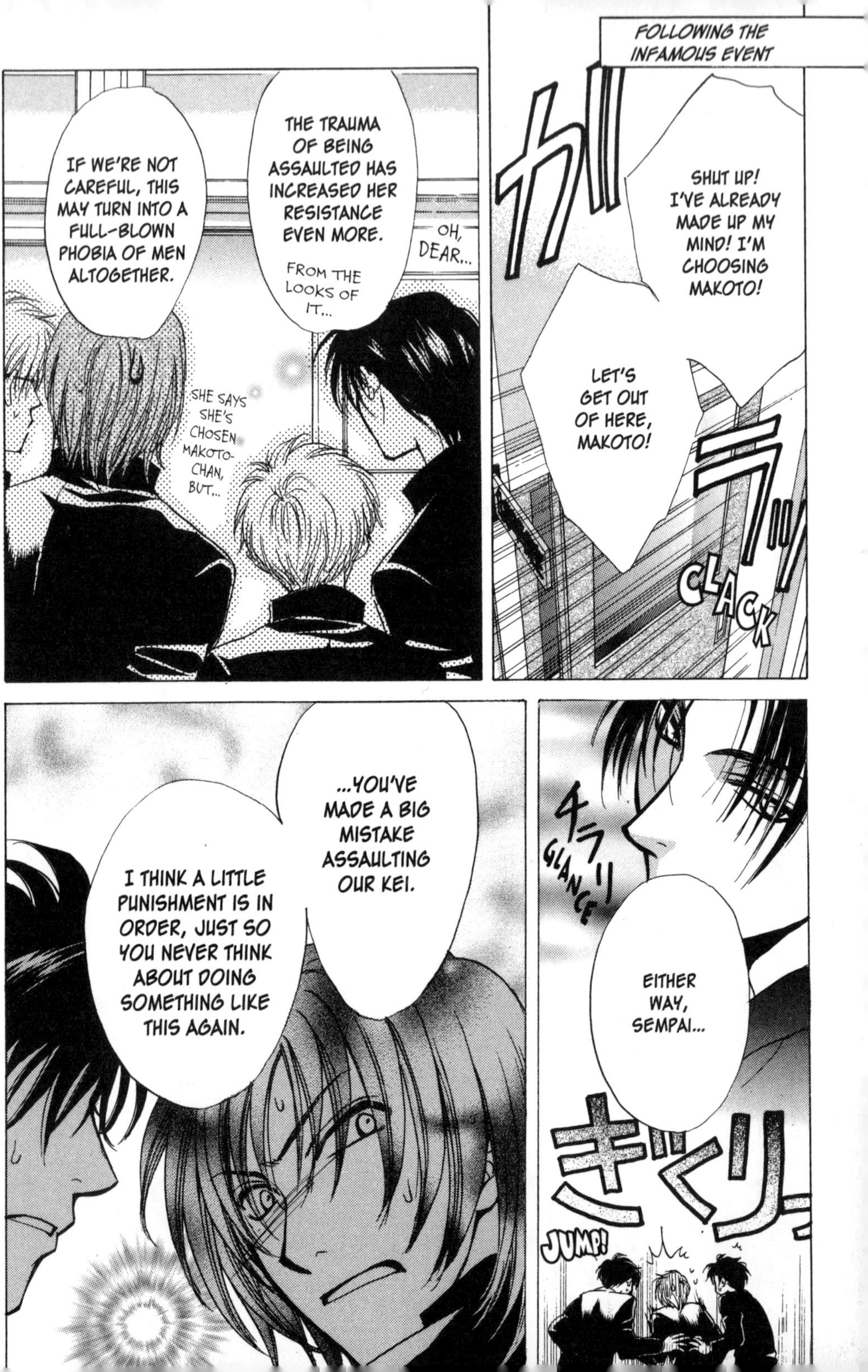
FOLLOWING THE INFAMOUS EVENT
SHUT UP! I'VE ALREADY MADE UP MY MIND! I'M CHOOSING MAKOTO!
LET'S GET OUT OF HERE, MAKOTO!
CLACK
OH, DEAR...
THE TRAUMA OF BEING ASSAULTED HAS INCREASED HER RESISTANCE EVEN MORE.
FROM THE LOOKS OF IT...
IF WE'RE NOT CAREFUL, THIS MAY TURN INTO A FULL-BLOWN PHOBIA OF MEN ALTOGETHER.
SHE SAYS SHE'S CHOSEN MAKOTO-CHAN, BUT...
GLANCE
EITHER WAY, SEMPAI...
JUMP!
...YOU'VE MADE A BIG MISTAKE ASSAULTING OUR KEI.
I THINK A LITTLE PUNISHMENT IS IN ORDER, JUST SO YOU NEVER THINK ABOUT DOING SOMETHING LIKE THIS AGAIN.

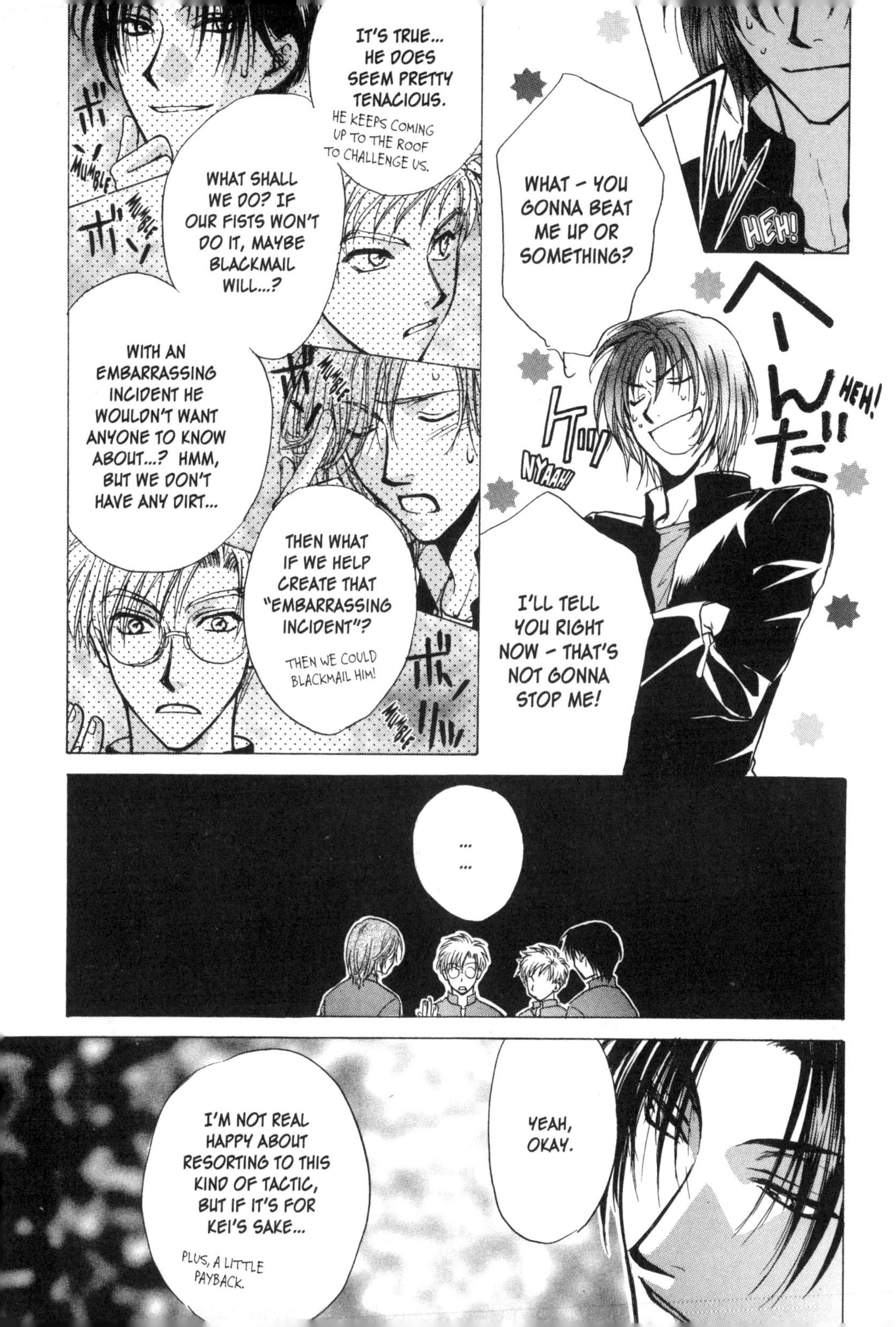
HEH!
WHAT - YOU GONNA BEAT ME UP OR SOMETHING?
HEH!
NYAAH!
I'LL TELL YOU RIGHT NOW - THAT'S NOT GONNA STOP ME!
IT'S TRUE... HE DOES SEEM PRETTY TENACIOUS.
HE KEEPS COMING UP TO THE ROOF TO CHALLENGE US.
MUMBLE
MUMBLE
WHAT SHALL WE DO? IF OUR FISTS WON'T DO IT, MAYBE BLACKMAIL WILL...?
MUMBLE
WITH AN EMBARRASSING INCIDENT HE WOULDN'T WANT ANYONE TO KNOW ABOUT...? HMM, BUT WE DON'T HAVE ANY DIRT...
THEN WHAT IF WE HELP CREATE THAT "EMBARRASSING INCIDENT"?
THEN WE COULD BLACKMAIL HIM!
MUMBLE
... ...
YEAH, OKAY.
I'M NOT REAL HAPPY ABOUT RESORTING TO THIS KIND OF TACTIC, BUT IF IT'S FOR KEI'S SAKE...
PLUS, A LITTLE PAYBACK.

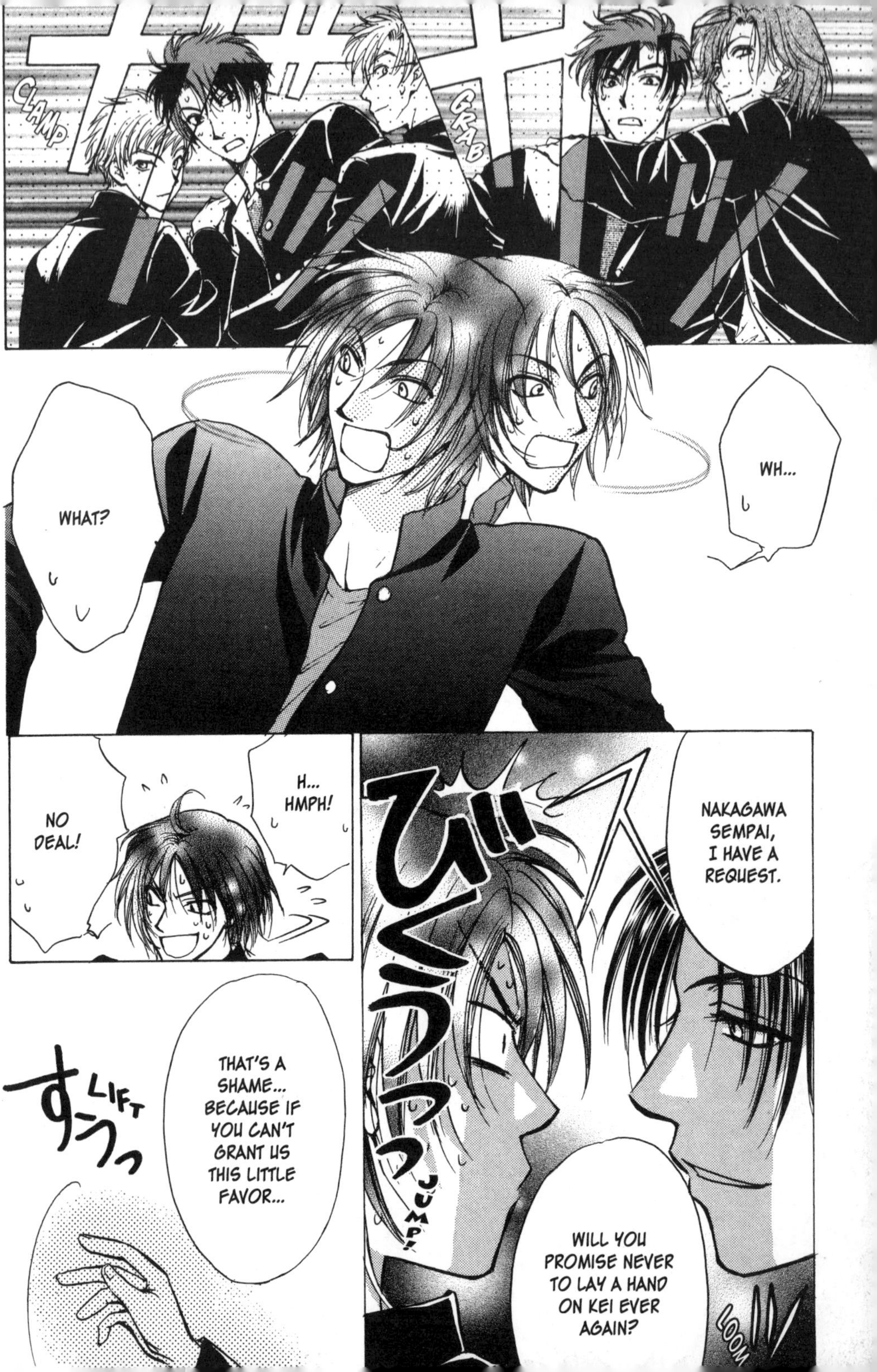
GRAB
CLAMP
WH...
WHAT?
NAKAGAWA SEMPAI, I HAVE A REQUEST.
びくうっ
JUMP!
WILL YOU PROMISE NEVER TO LAY A HAND ON KEI EVER AGAIN?
LOOM
H... HMPH!
NO DEAL!
THAT'S A SHAME... BECAUSE IF YOU CAN'T GRANT US THIS LITTLE FAVOR...
すーっ
LIFT

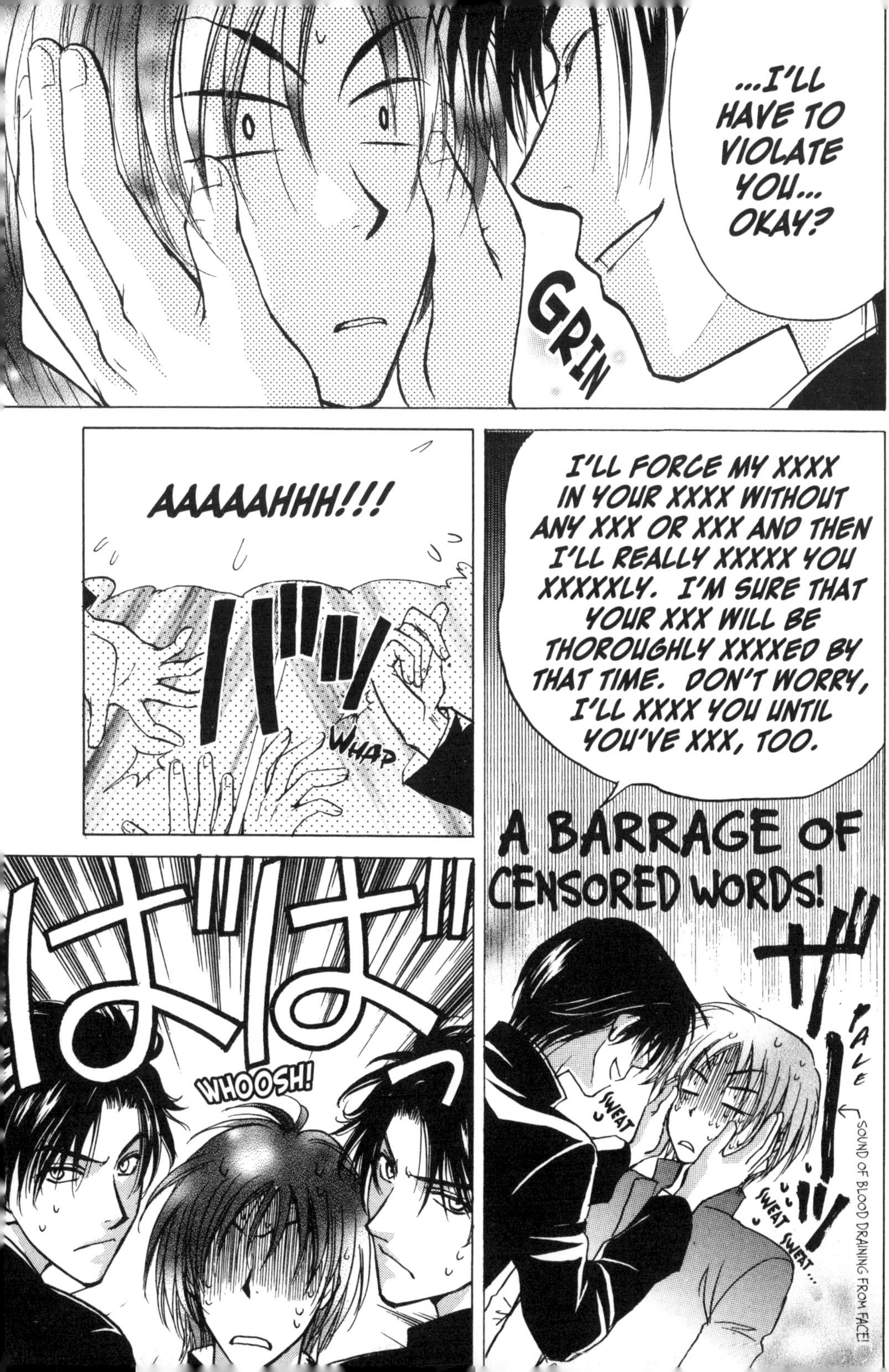
...I'LL HAVE TO VIOLATE YOU... OKAY?
GRIN
I'LL FORCE MY XXXX IN YOUR XXXX WITHOUT ANY XXX OR XXX AND THEN I'LL REALLY XXXXX YOU XXXXXLY. I'M SURE THAT YOUR XXX WILL BE THOROUGHLY XXXXED BY THAT TIME. DON'T WORRY, I'LL XXXX YOU UNTIL YOU'VE XXX, TOO.
A BARRAGE OF CENSORED WORDS!
PALE
SOUND OF BLOOD DRAINING FROM FACE!
SWEAT
SWEAT SWEAT...
AAAAAHHH!!!
バッ
WHAP
ばっばっ
WHOOSH!

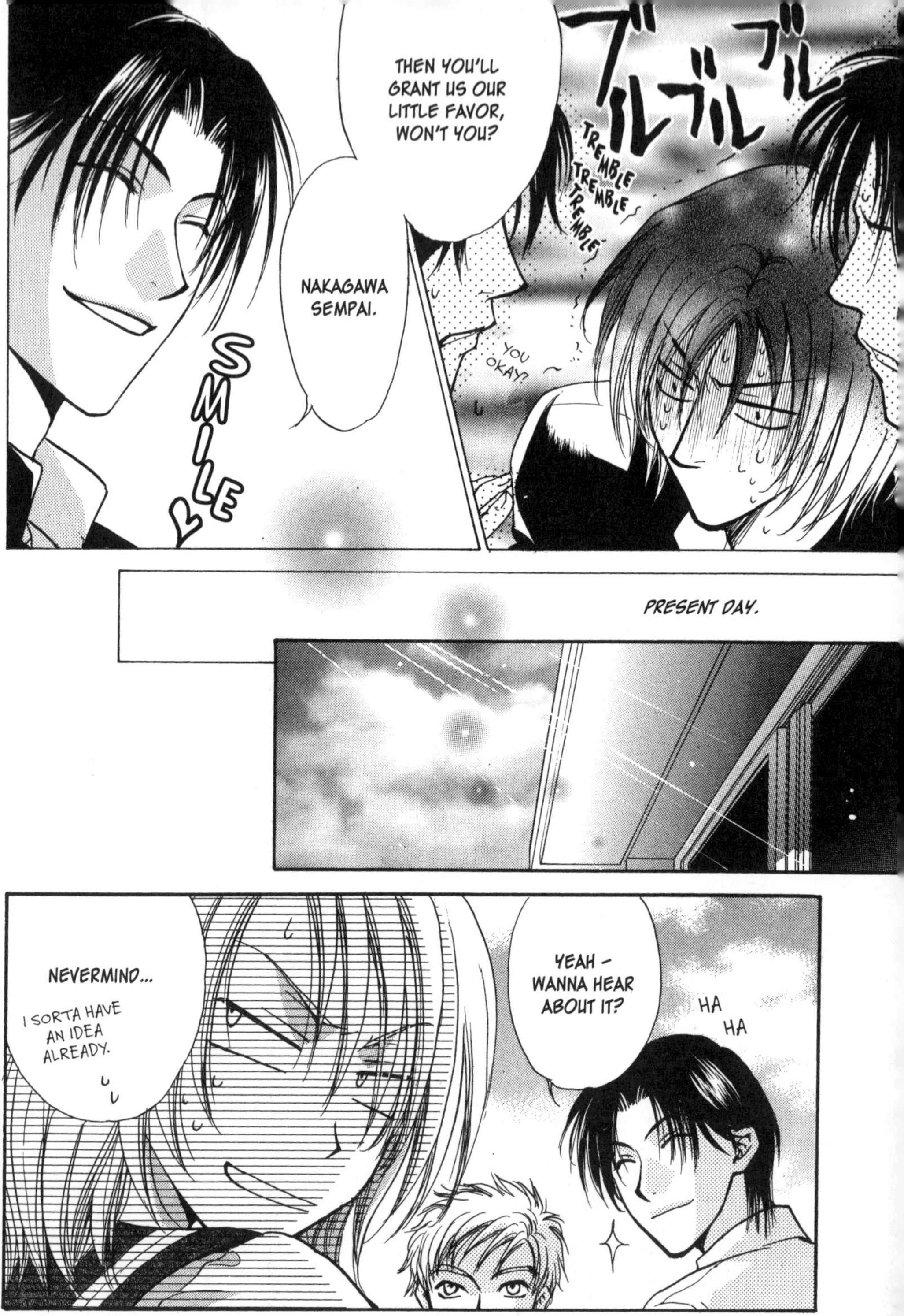
ブルブル
TREMBLE TREMBLE TREMBLE
YOU OKAY?
THEN YOU'LL GRANT US OUR LITTLE FAVOR, WON'T YOU?
NAKAGAWA SEMPAI.
SMILE
PRESENT DAY.
YEAH - WANNA HEAR ABOUT IT?
HA HA
NEVERMIND...
I SORTA HAVE AN IDEA ALREADY.

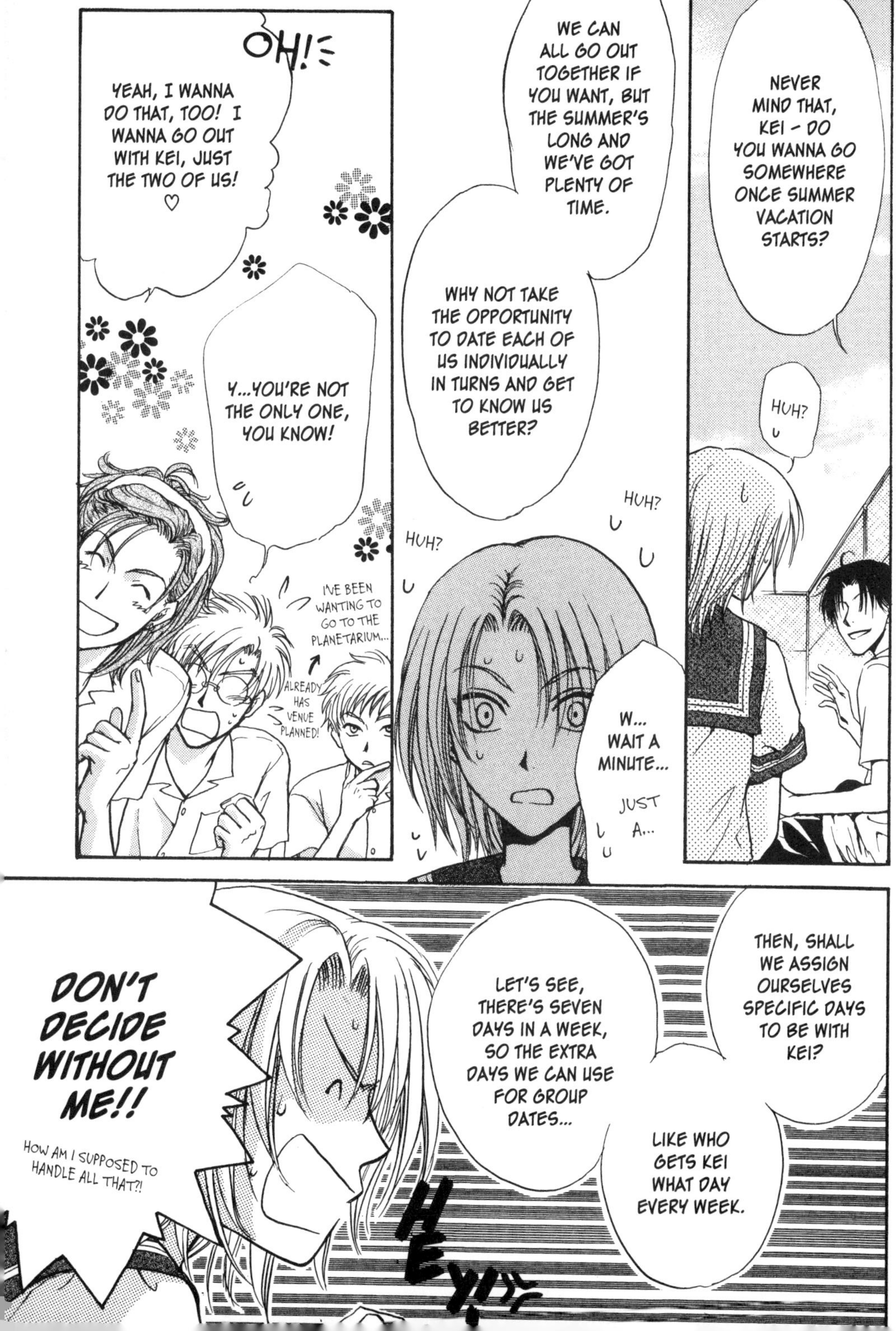

NEVER MIND THAT, KEI - DO YOU WANNA GO SOMEWHERE ONCE SUMMER VACATION STARTS?
HUH?
WE CAN ALL GO OUT TOGETHER IF YOU WANT, BUT THE SUMMER'S LONG AND WE'VE GOT PLENTY OF TIME.
WHY NOT TAKE THE OPPORTUNITY TO DATE EACH OF US INDIVIDUALLY IN TURNS AND GET TO KNOW US BETTER?
HUH?
HUH?
W... WAIT A MINUTE...
JUST A...
OH!
YEAH, I WANNA DO THAT, TOO! I WANNA GO OUT WITH KEI, JUST THE TWO OF US! ♡
Y...YOU'RE NOT THE ONLY ONE, YOU KNOW!
I'VE BEEN WANTING TO GO TO THE PLANETARIUM...
ALREADY HAS VENUE PLANNED!
THEN, SHALL WE ASSIGN OURSELVES SPECIFIC DAYS TO BE WITH KEI?
LET'S SEE, THERE'S SEVEN DAYS IN A WEEK, SO THE EXTRA DAYS WE CAN USE FOR GROUP DATES...
LIKE WHO GETS KEI WHAT DAY EVERY WEEK.
HEY!!
DON'T DECIDE WITHOUT ME!!
HOW AM I SUPPOSED TO HANDLE ALL THAT?!

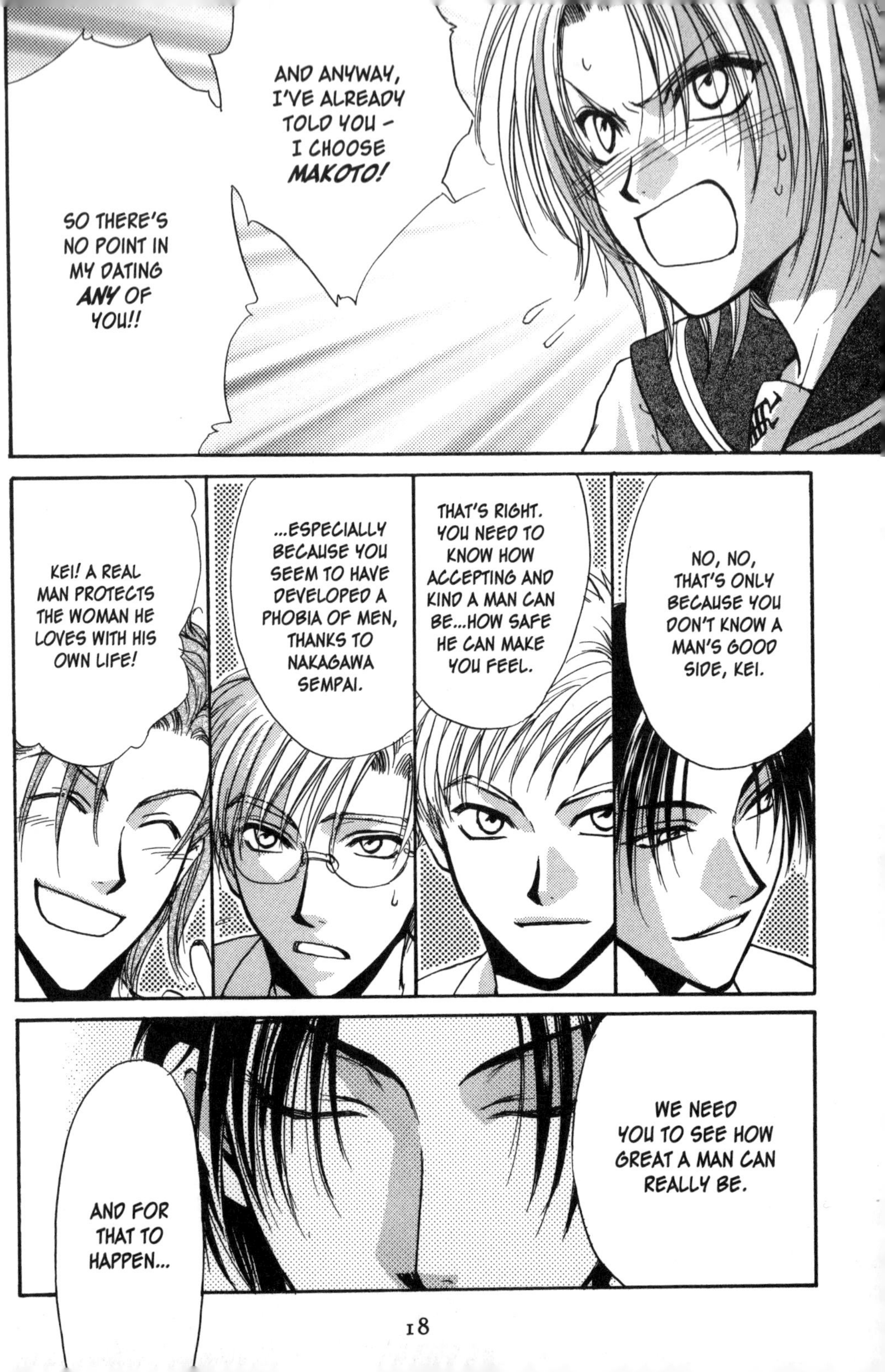
AND ANYWAY, I'VE ALREADY TOLD YOU - I CHOOSE MAKOTO!
SO THERE'S NO POINT IN MY DATING ANY OF YOU!!
NO, NO, THAT'S ONLY BECAUSE YOU DON'T KNOW A MAN'S GOOD SIDE, KEI.
THAT'S RIGHT. YOU NEED TO KNOW HOW ACCEPTING AND KIND A MAN CAN BE...HOW SAFE HE CAN MAKE YOU FEEL.
...ESPECIALLY BECAUSE YOU SEEM TO HAVE DEVELOPED A PHOBIA OF MEN, THANKS TO NAKAGAWA SEMPAI.
KEI! A REAL MAN PROTECTS THE WOMAN HE LOVES WITH HIS OWN LIFE!
WE NEED YOU TO SEE HOW GREAT A MAN CAN REALLY BE.
AND FOR THAT TO HAPPEN...

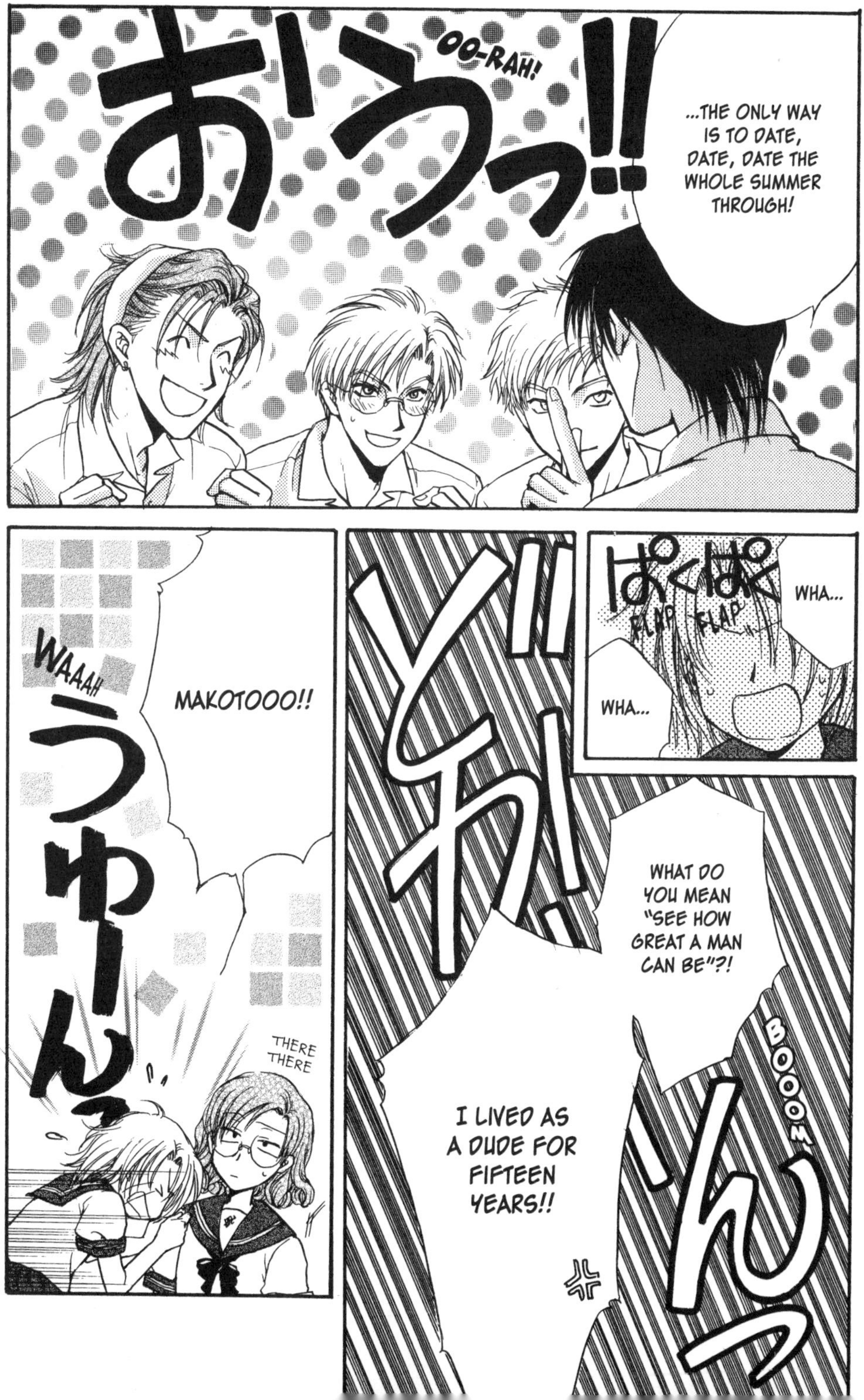
...THE ONLY WAY IS TO DATE, DATE, DATE THE WHOLE SUMMER THROUGH!
おうっ!!
OO-RAH!
ぱくぱく
FLAP FLAP
WHA...
WHA...
WHAT DO YOU MEAN "SEE HOW GREAT A MAN CAN BE"?!
んっ
BOOOOM
I LIVED AS A DUDE FOR FIFTEEN YEARS!!
どわ!
MAKOTOOO!!
うゅーんっ
WAAAH
THERE THERE

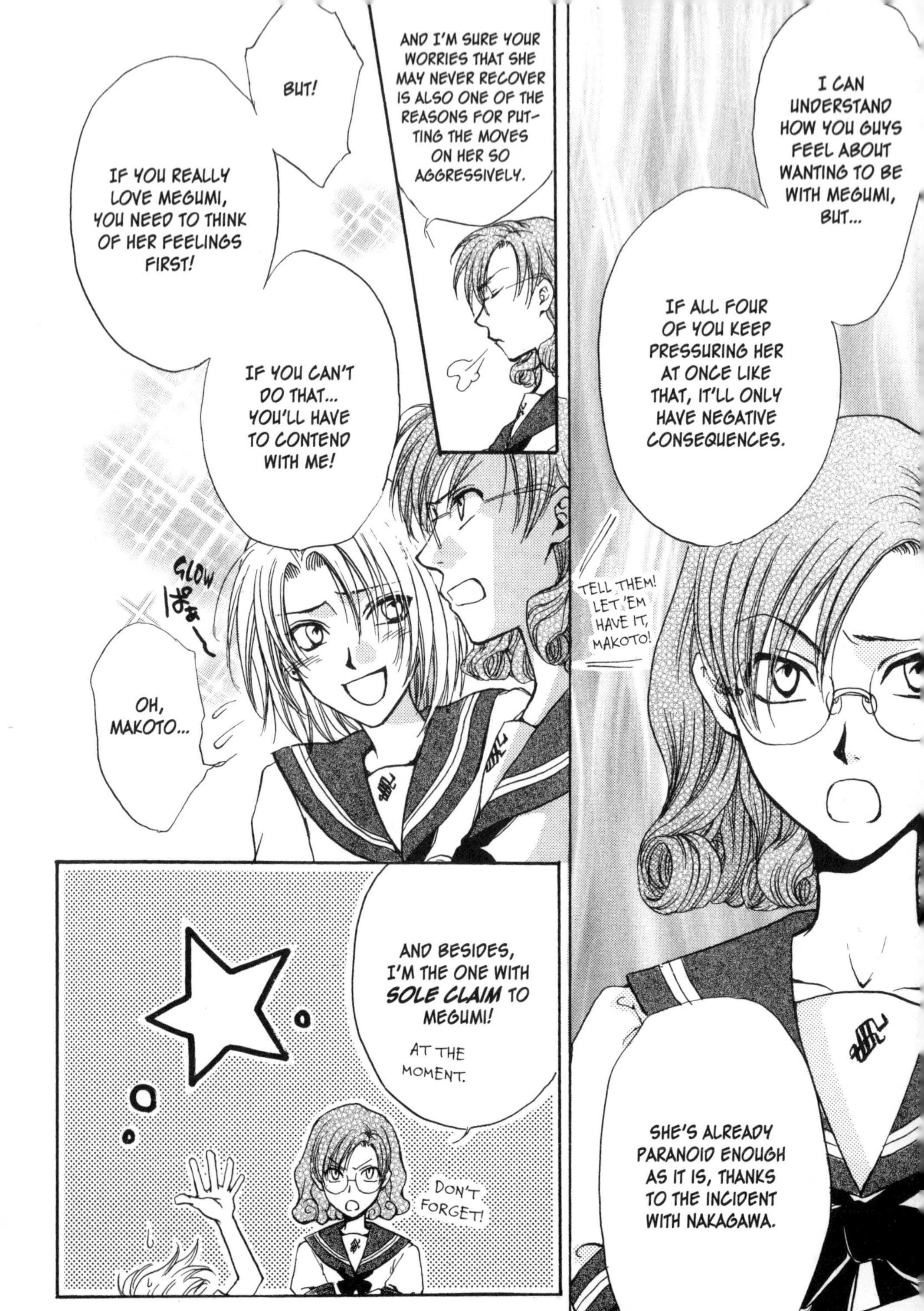
I CAN UNDERSTAND HOW YOU GUYS FEEL ABOUT WANTING TO BE WITH MEGUMI, BUT...
IF ALL FOUR OF YOU KEEP PRESSURING HER AT ONCE LIKE THAT, IT'LL ONLY HAVE NEGATIVE CONSEQUENCES.
TELL THEM! LET 'EM HAVE IT, MAKOTO!
SHE'S ALREADY PARANOID ENOUGH AS IT IS, THANKS TO THE INCIDENT WITH NAKAGAWA.
AND I'M SURE YOUR WORRIES THAT SHE MAY NEVER RECOVER IS ALSO ONE OF THE REASONS FOR PUTTING THE MOVES ON HER SO AGGRESSIVELY.
BUT!
IF YOU REALLY LOVE MEGUMI, YOU NEED TO THINK OF HER FEELINGS FIRST!
IF YOU CAN'T DO THAT... YOU'LL HAVE TO CONTEND WITH ME!
GLOW
ぽぉ～
OH, MAKOTO...
AND BESIDES, I'M THE ONE WITH SOLE CLAIM TO MEGUMI!
AT THE MOMENT.
DON'T FORGET!

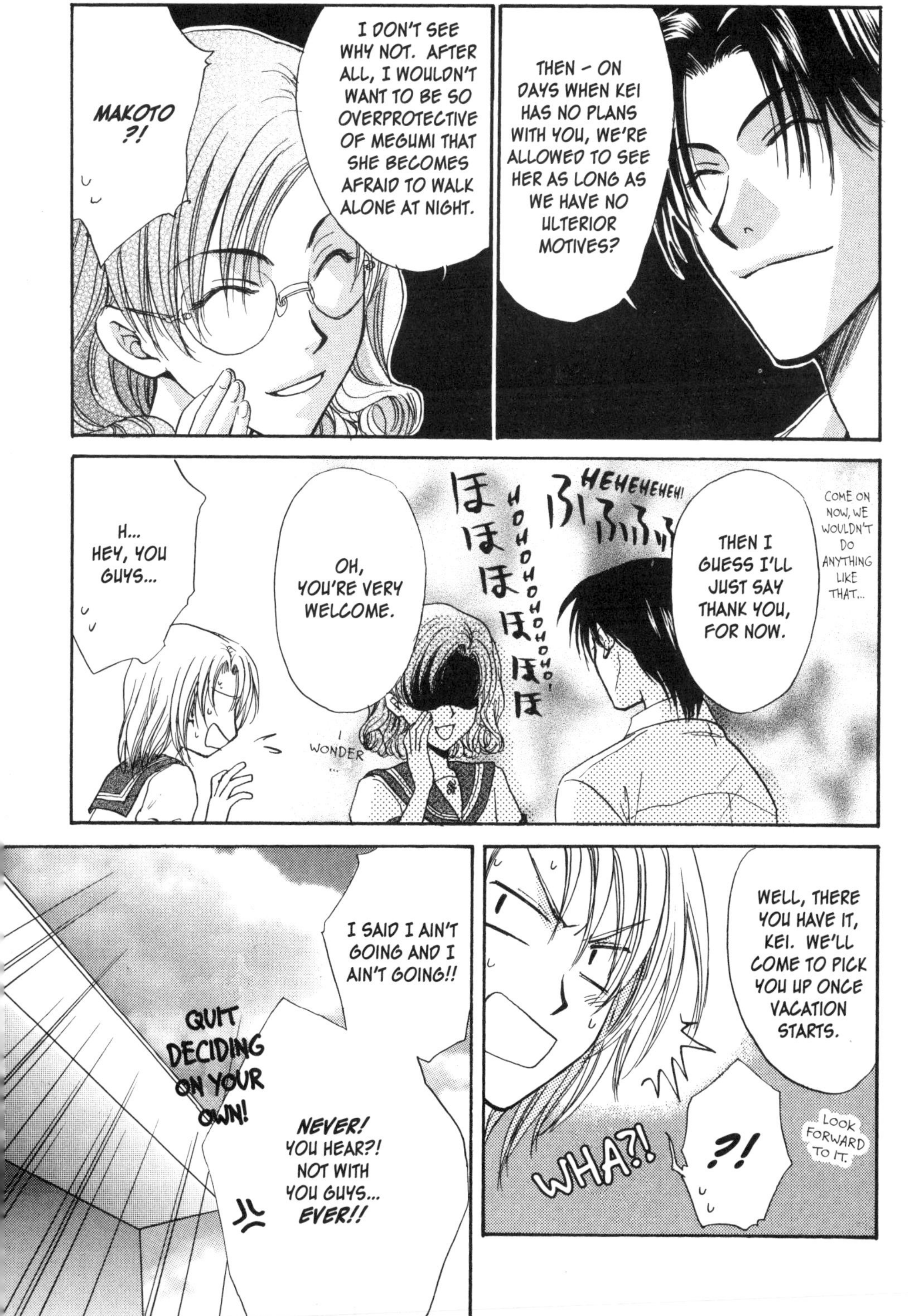

THEN - ON DAYS WHEN KEI HAS NO PLANS WITH YOU, WE'RE ALLOWED TO SEE HER AS LONG AS WE HAVE NO ULTERIOR MOTIVES?
I DON'T SEE WHY NOT. AFTER ALL, I WOULDN'T WANT TO BE SO OVERPROTECTIVE OF MEGUMI THAT SHE BECOMES AFRAID TO WALK ALONE AT NIGHT.
MAKOTO ?!
COME ON NOW, WE WOULDN'T DO ANYTHING LIKE THAT...
THEN I GUESS I'LL JUST SAY THANK YOU, FOR NOW.
ふふっ
HEHEHEHEH!
ほほほほほほ
HOHOHOHOHOHOHO!
OH, YOU'RE VERY WELCOME.
I WONDER...
H... HEY, YOU GUYS...
WELL, THERE YOU HAVE IT, KEI. WE'LL COME TO PICK YOU UP ONCE VACATION STARTS.
LOOK FORWARD TO IT.
?!
WHA?!
I SAID I AIN'T GOING AND I AIN'T GOING!!
QUIT DECIDING ON YOUR OWN!
NEVER! YOU HEAR?! NOT WITH YOU GUYS... EVER!!

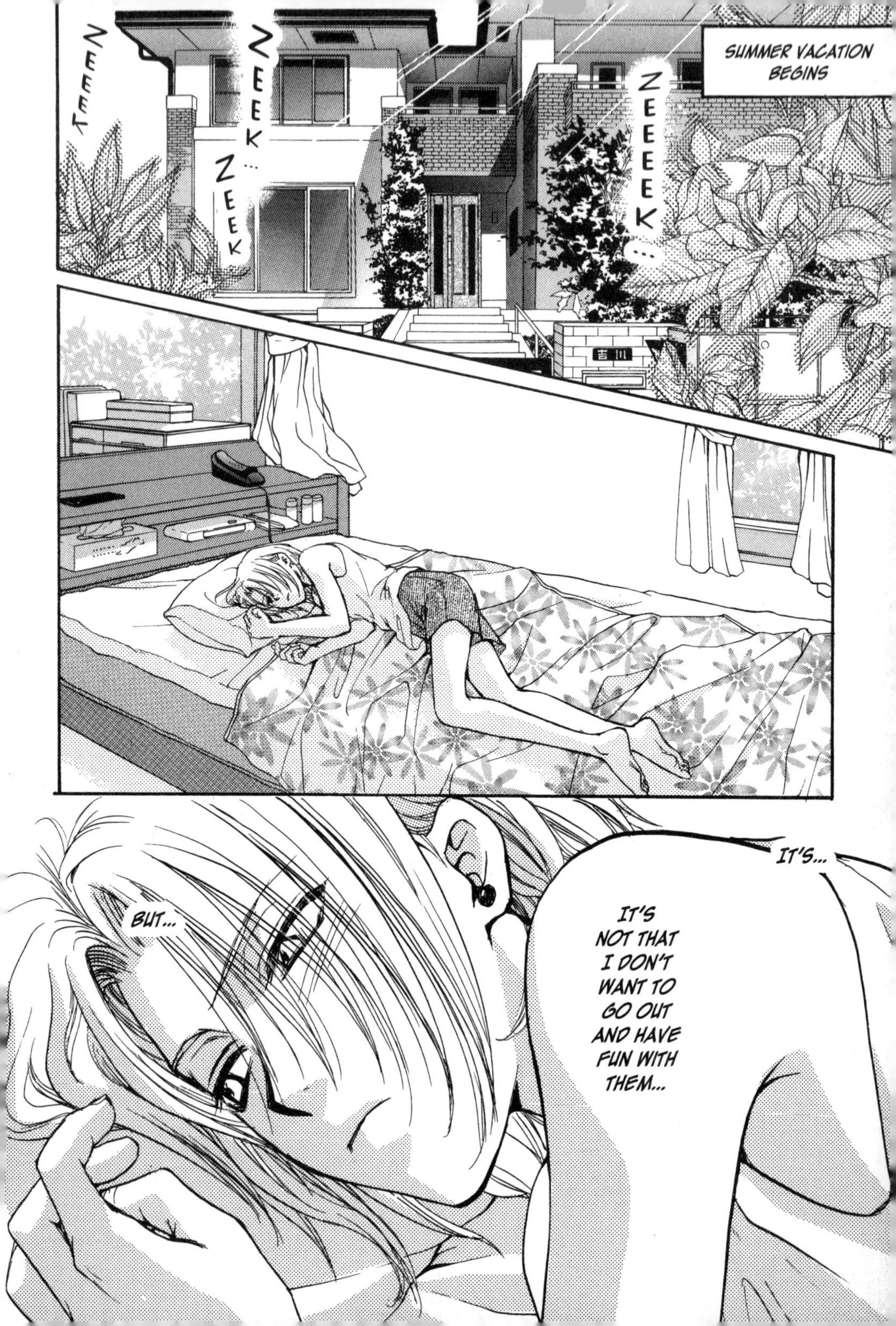
SUMMER VACATION BEGINS
ZEEEEK...
ZEEK... ZEEK
ZEEEK
吉川
IT'S...
IT'S NOT THAT I DON'T WANT TO GO OUT AND HAVE FUN WITH THEM...
BUT...

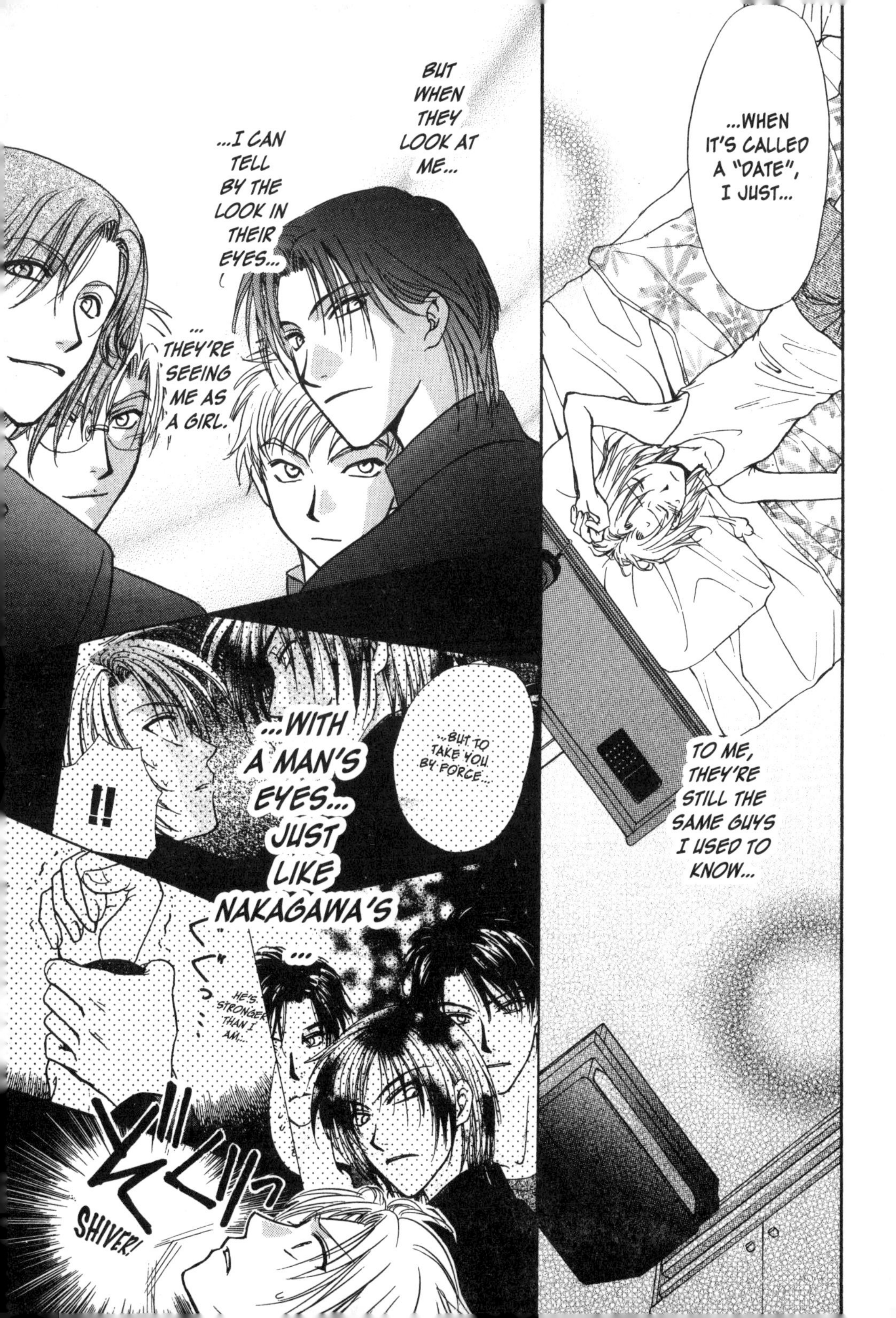
...WHEN IT'S CALLED A "DATE", I JUST...
TO ME, THEY'RE STILL THE SAME GUYS I USED TO KNOW...
BUT WHEN THEY LOOK AT ME...
...I CAN TELL BY THE LOOK IN THEIR EYES...
...THEY'RE SEEING ME AS A GIRL.
...BUT TO TAKE YOU BY FORCE...
...WITH A MAN'S EYES... JUST LIKE NAKAGAWA'S ...
!!
HE'S STRONGER THAN I AM...
SHIVER!

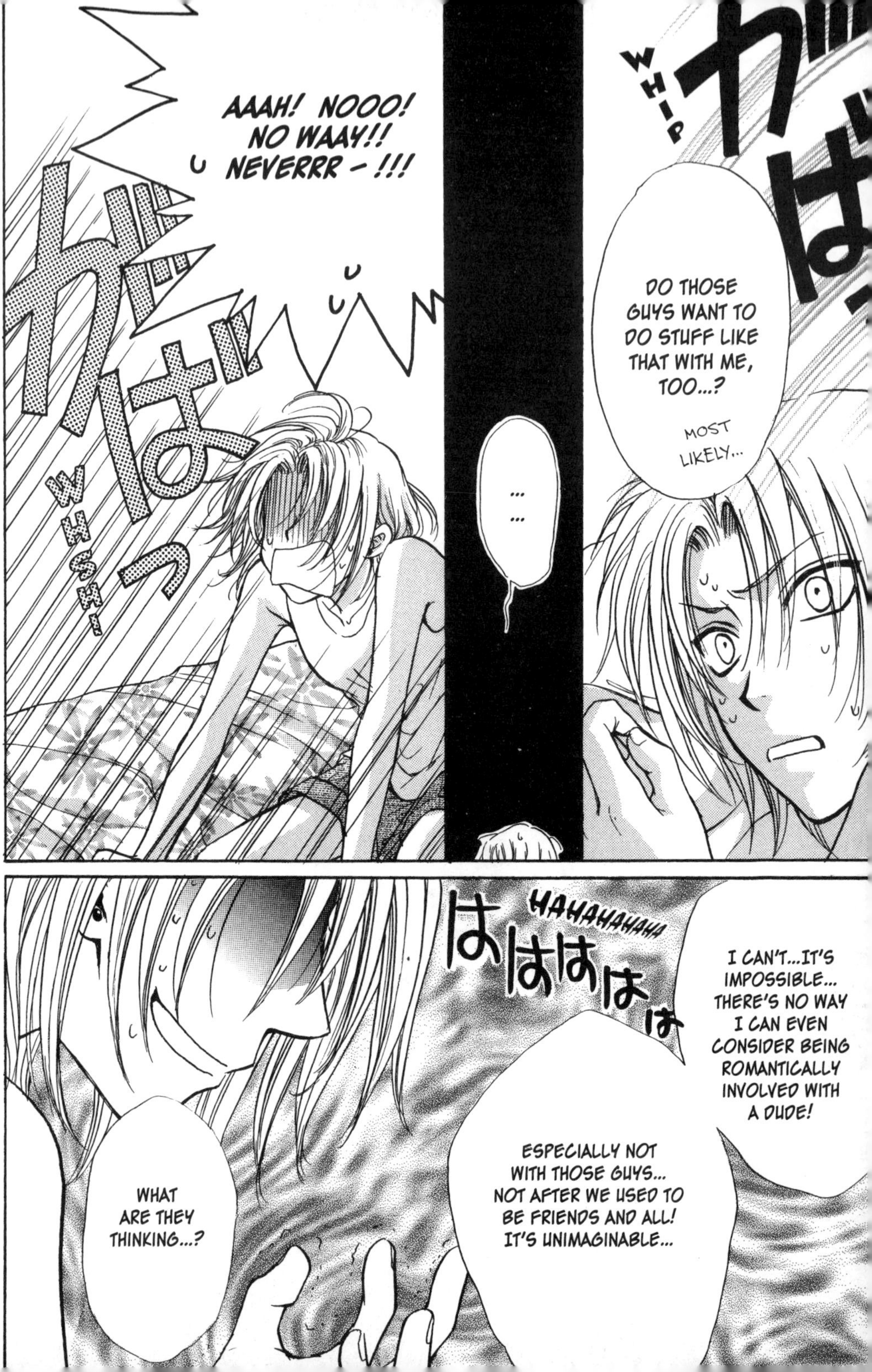
WHIP
DO THOSE GUYS WANT TO DO STUFF LIKE THAT WITH ME, TOO...?
MOST LIKELY...
... ...
AAAH! NOOO! NO WAAY!! NEVERRR - !!!
WHSH
ははははは
HAHAHAHAHA
I CAN'T...IT'S IMPOSSIBLE... THERE'S NO WAY I CAN EVEN CONSIDER BEING ROMANTICALLY INVOLVED WITH A DUDE!
ESPECIALLY NOT WITH THOSE GUYS... NOT AFTER WE USED TO BE FRIENDS AND ALL! IT'S UNIMAGINABLE...
WHAT ARE THEY THINKING...?

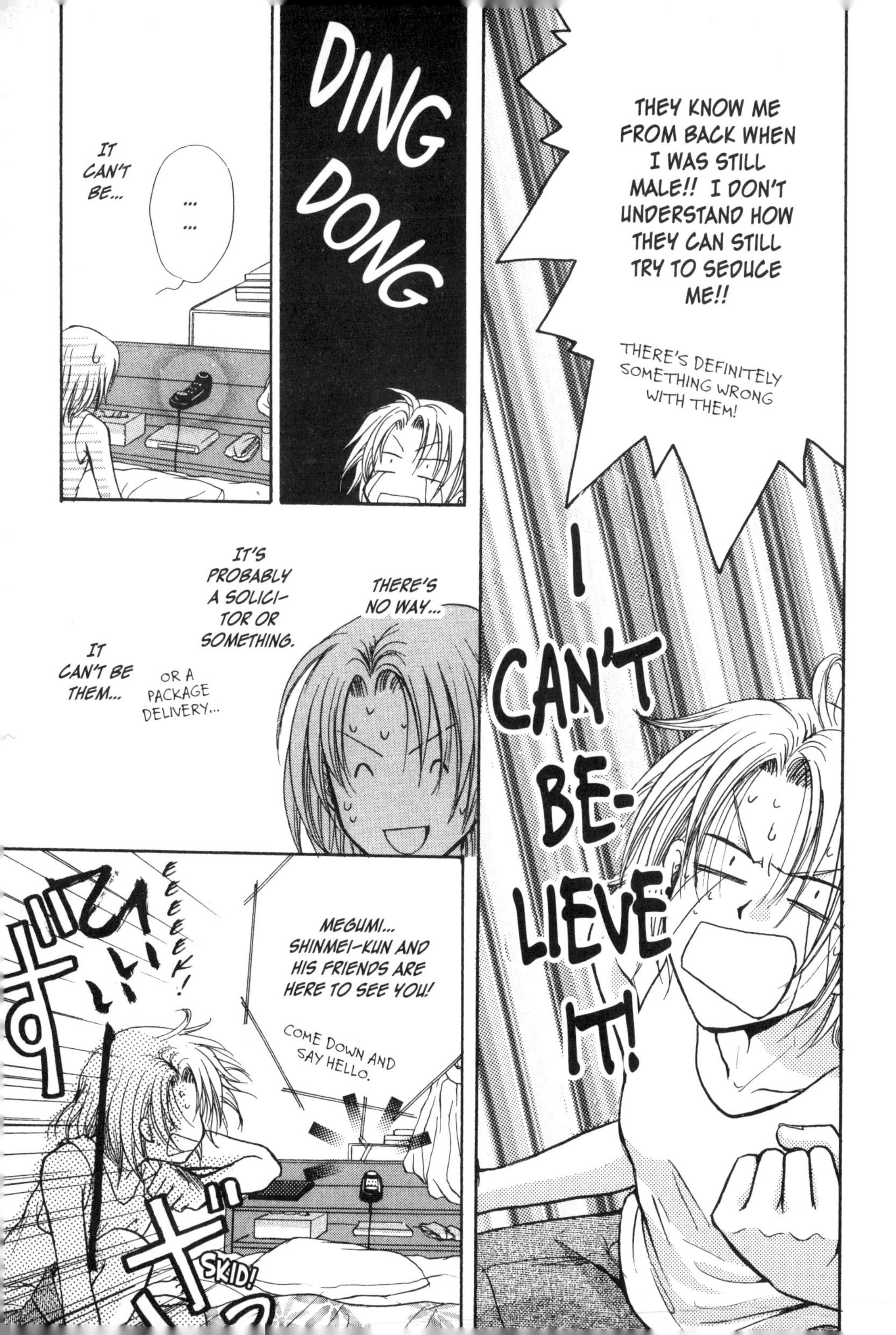
THEY KNOW ME FROM BACK WHEN I WAS STILL MALE!! I DON'T UNDERSTAND HOW THEY CAN STILL TRY TO SEDUCE ME!!
THERE'S DEFINITELY SOMETHING WRONG WITH THEM!
I CAN'T BE-LIEVE IT!
DING DONG
...
...
IT CAN'T BE...
THERE'S NO WAY...
IT'S PROBABLY A SOLICI-TOR OR SOMETHING.
OR A PACKAGE DELIVERY...
IT CAN'T BE THEM...
MEGUMI... SHINMEI-KUN AND HIS FRIENDS ARE HERE TO SEE YOU!
COME DOWN AND SAY HELLO.
EEEEEEK!
SKID!

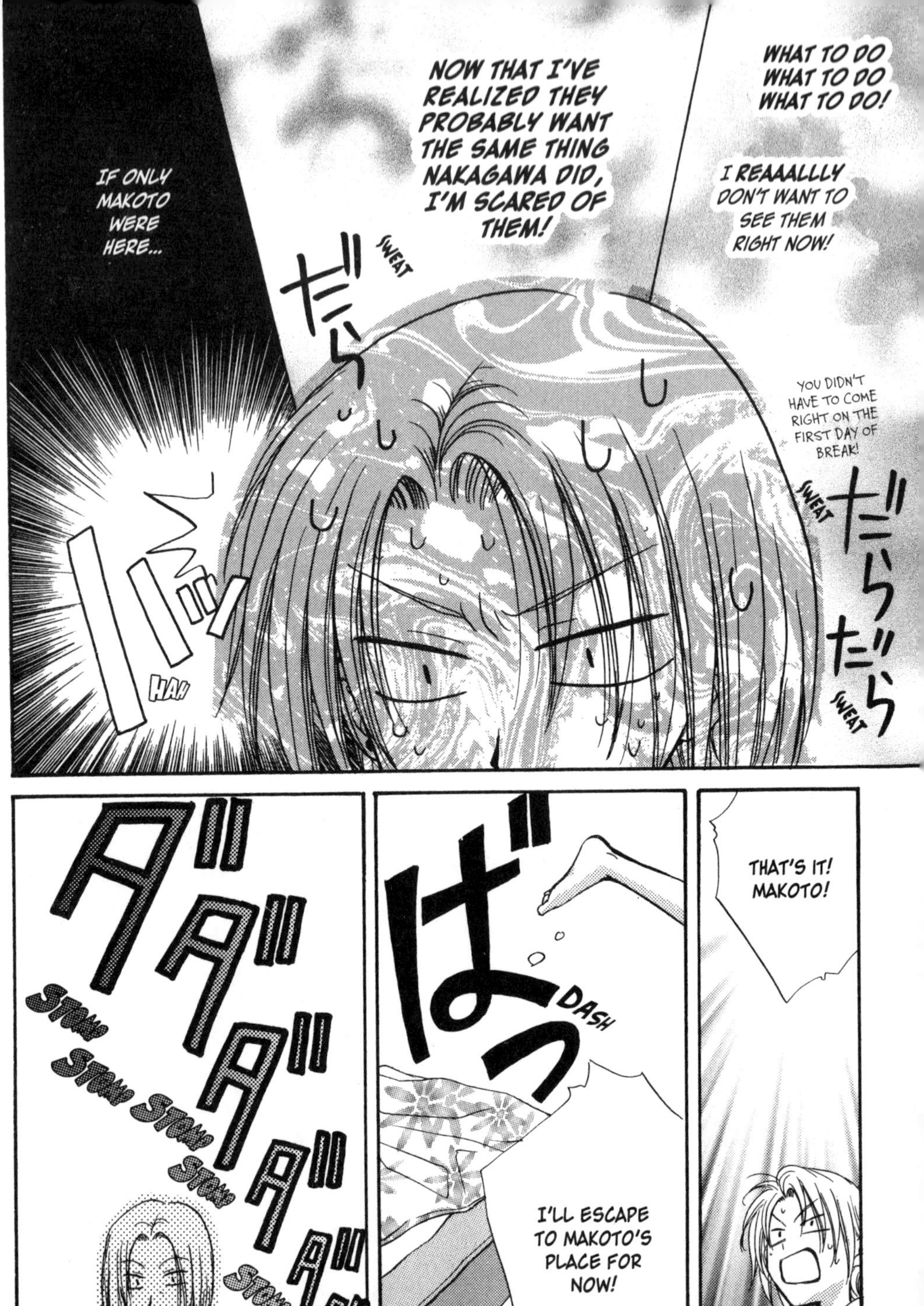
WHAT TO DO WHAT TO DO WHAT TO DO!
I REAAALLLY DON'T WANT TO SEE THEM RIGHT NOW!
NOW THAT I'VE REALIZED THEY PROBABLY WANT THE SAME THING NAKAGAWA DID, I'M SCARED OF THEM!
IF ONLY MAKOTO WERE HERE...
だら
SWEAT
YOU DIDN'T HAVE TO COME RIGHT ON THE FIRST DAY OF BREAK!
だらだら
SWEAT
SWEAT
ハッ
HAH
THAT'S IT! MAKOTO!
ばっ
DASH
I'LL ESCAPE TO MAKOTO'S PLACE FOR NOW!
ダダダダダダ
STOMP STOMP STOMP STOMP STOMP STOMP STOMP

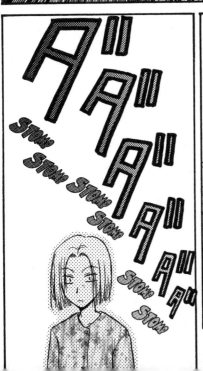

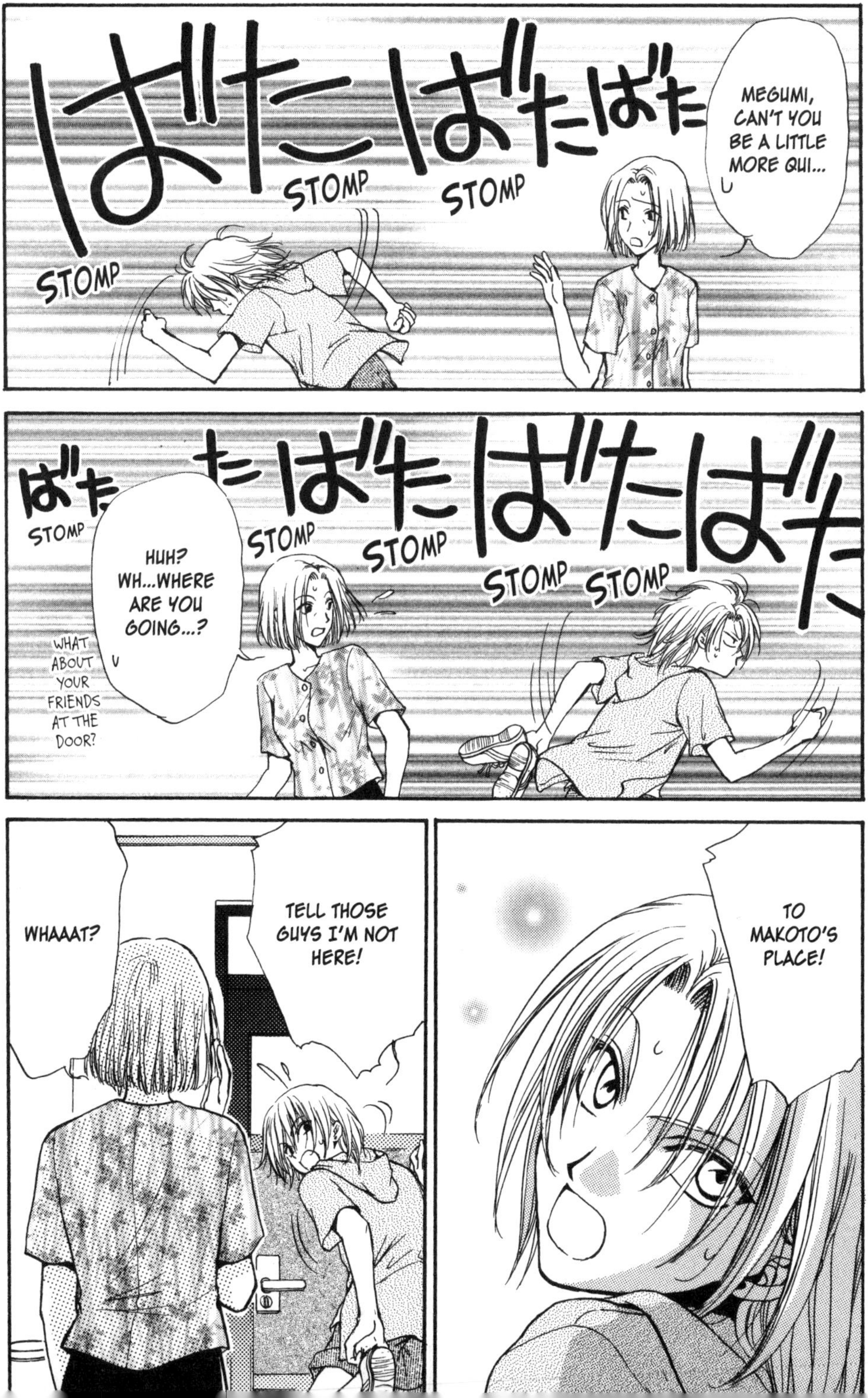

MEGUMI, CAN'T YOU BE A LITTLE MORE QUI...
ばたばたばた
STOMP
STOMP
STOMP
ばたばたばたばた
STOMP
STOMP
STOMP
STOMP
STOMP
HUH? WH...WHERE ARE YOU GOING...?
WHAT ABOUT YOUR FRIENDS AT THE DOOR?
TO MAKOTO'S PLACE!
TELL THOSE GUYS I'M NOT HERE!
WHAAAT?

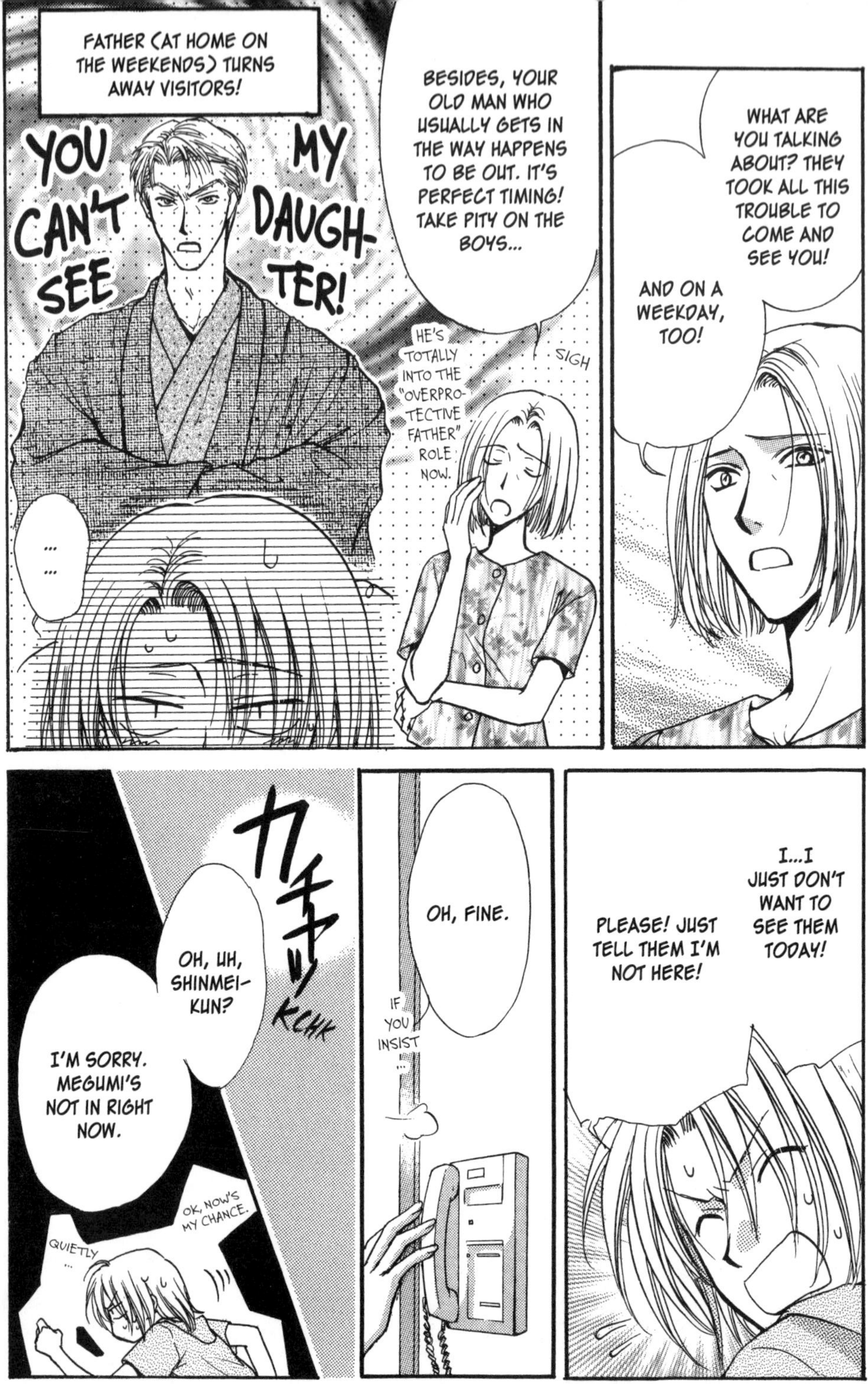

WHAT ARE YOU TALKING ABOUT? THEY TOOK ALL THIS TROUBLE TO COME AND SEE YOU!
AND ON A WEEKDAY, TOO!
BESIDES, YOUR OLD MAN WHO USUALLY GETS IN THE WAY HAPPENS TO BE OUT. IT'S PERFECT TIMING! TAKE PITY ON THE BOYS...
SIGH
HE'S TOTALLY INTO THE "OVERPROTECTIVE FATHER" ROLE NOW.
FATHER (AT HOME ON THE WEEKENDS) TURNS AWAY VISITORS!
YOU CAN'T SEE MY DAUGHTER!
......
I...I JUST DON'T WANT TO SEE THEM TODAY!
PLEASE! JUST TELL THEM I'M NOT HERE!
OH, FINE.
IF YOU INSIST...
KCHK
OH, UH, SHINMEI-KUN?
I'M SORRY. MEGUMI'S NOT IN RIGHT NOW.
OK, NOW'S MY CHANCE.
QUIETLY...

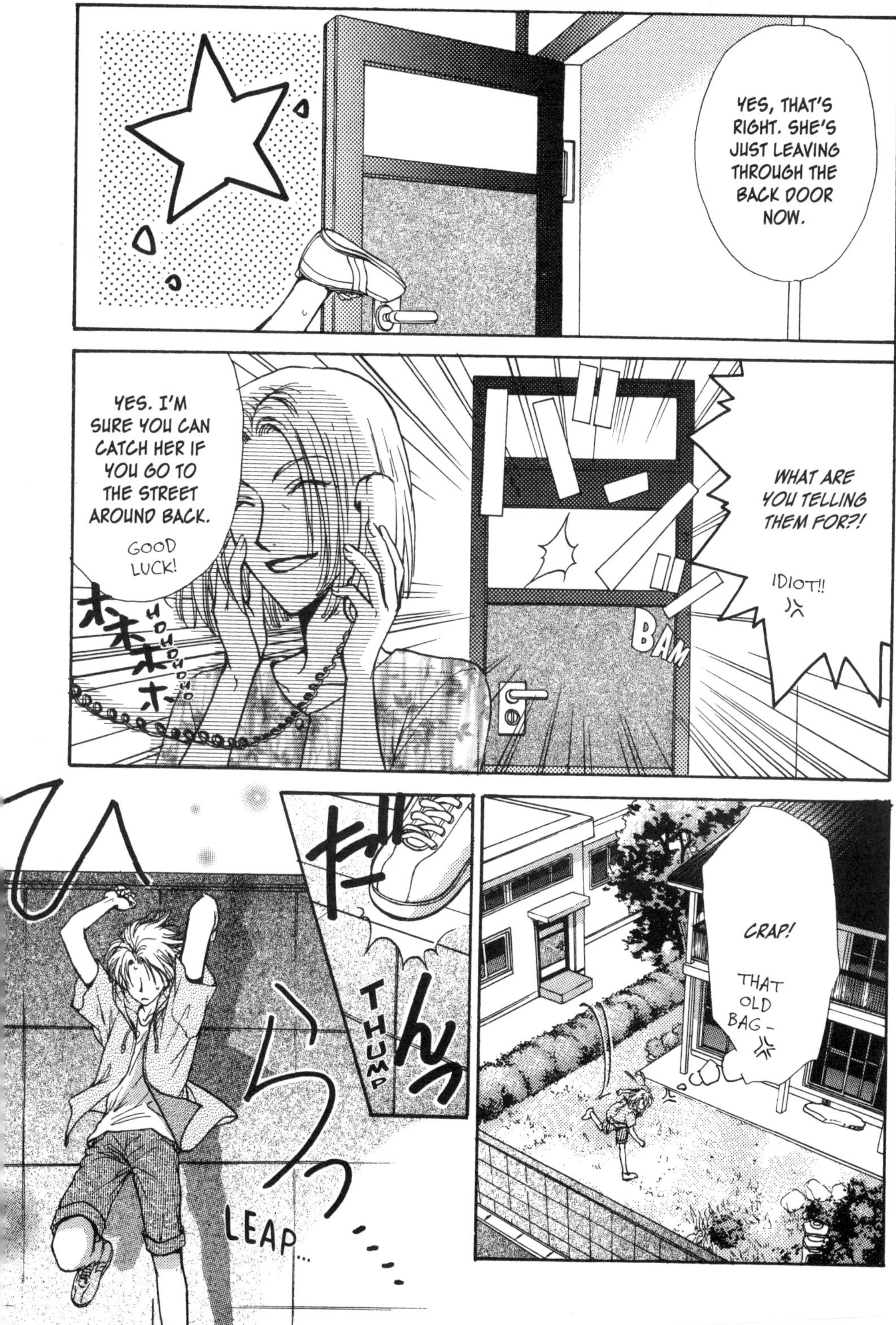
YES, THAT'S RIGHT. SHE'S JUST LEAVING THROUGH THE BACK DOOR NOW.
WHAT ARE YOU TELLING THEM FOR?!
IDIOT!!
BAM
YES. I'M SURE YOU CAN CATCH HER IF YOU GO TO THE STREET AROUND BACK.
GOOD LUCK!
ホホホホ
HOHOHOHOHO
CRAP!
THAT OLD BAG-
THUMP
LEAP...

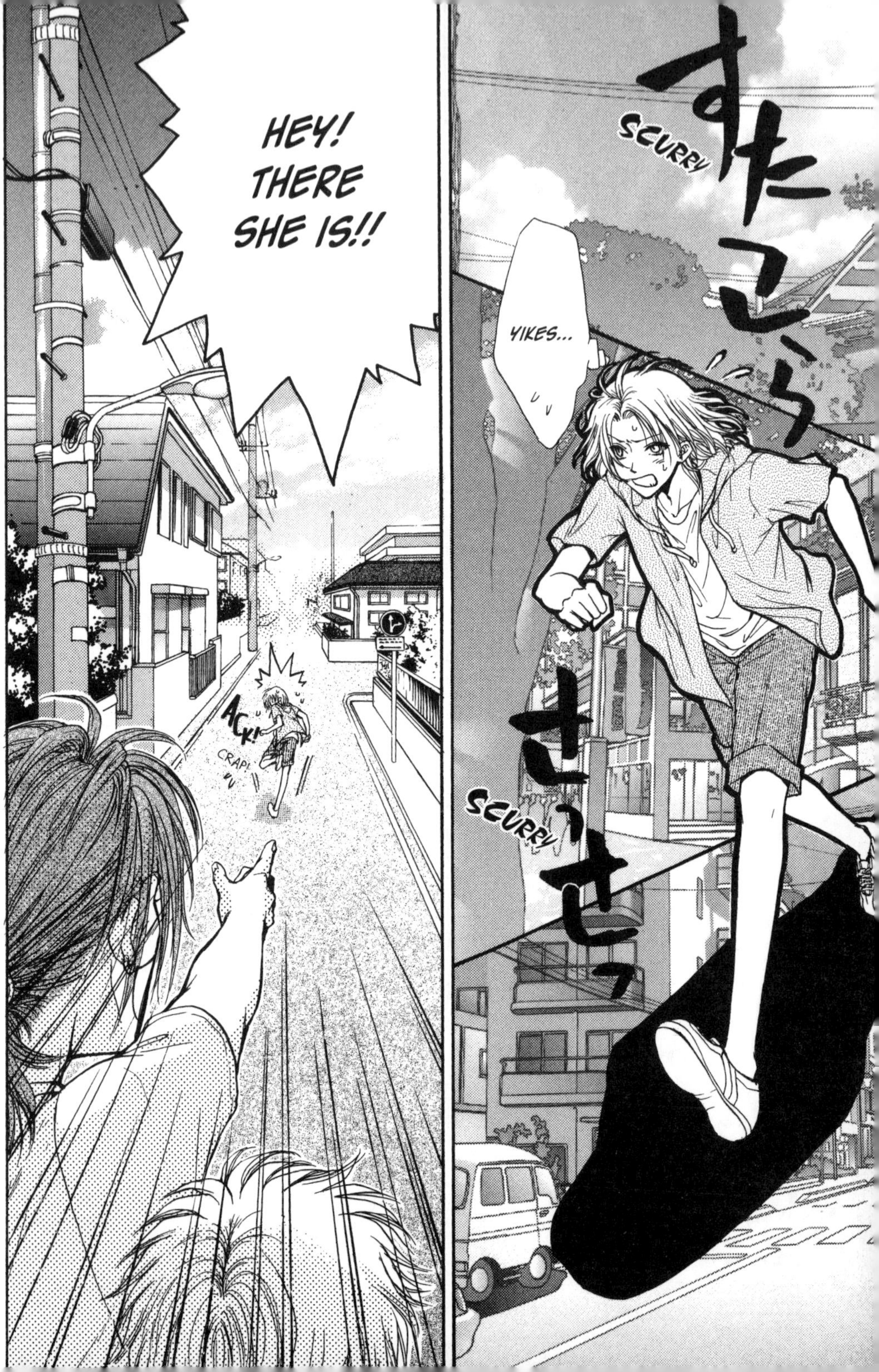
すたこら
SCURRY
YIKES...
さっさっ
SCURRY
HEY! THERE SHE IS!!
ACK!
CRAP!

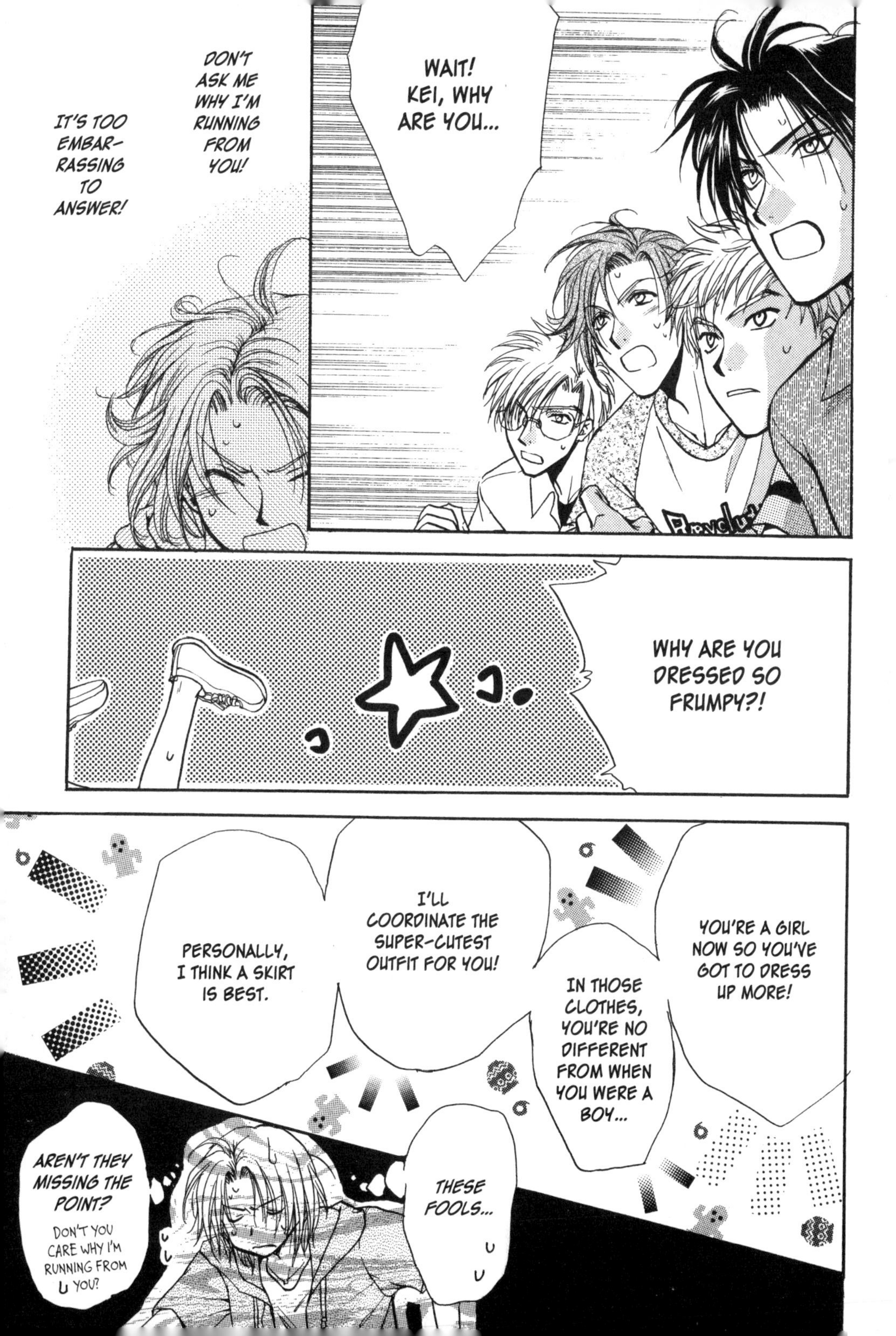
WAIT! KEI, WHY ARE YOU...
DON'T ASK ME WHY I'M RUNNING FROM YOU!
IT'S TOO EMBAR-RASSING TO ANSWER!
WHY ARE YOU DRESSED SO FRUMPY?!
YOU'RE A GIRL NOW SO YOU'VE GOT TO DRESS UP MORE!
IN THOSE CLOTHES, YOU'RE NO DIFFERENT FROM WHEN YOU WERE A BOY...
I'LL COORDINATE THE SUPER-CUTEST OUTFIT FOR YOU!
PERSONALLY, I THINK A SKIRT IS BEST.
THESE FOOLS...
AREN'T THEY MISSING THE POINT?
DON'T YOU CARE WHY I'M RUNNING FROM YOU?

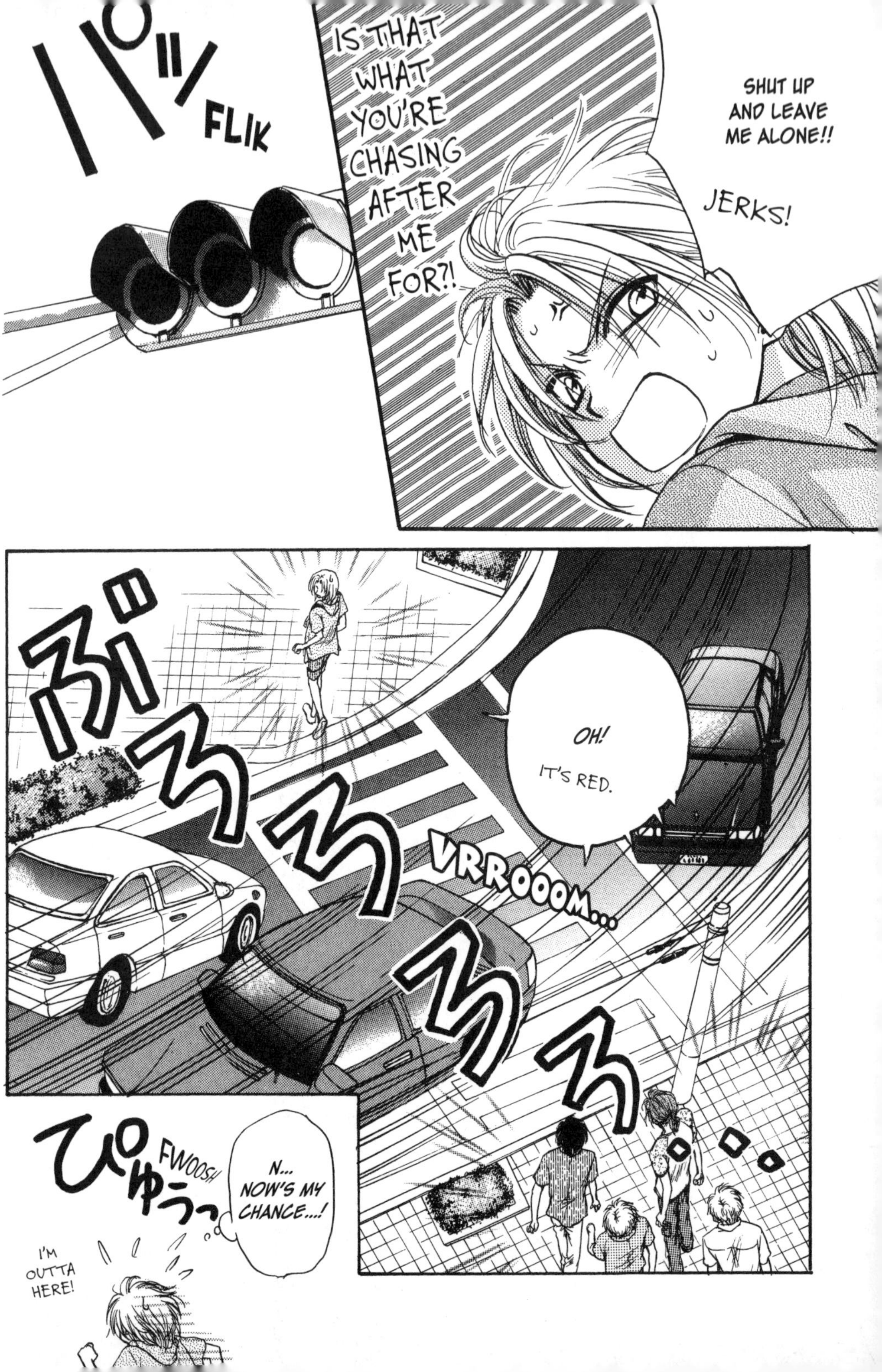
IS THAT WHAT YOU'RE CHASING AFTER ME FOR?!
SHUT UP AND LEAVE ME ALONE!!
JERKS!
パッ
FLIK
OH!
IT'S RED.
ぶろろろろろ
VRROOOM...
N... NOW'S MY CHANCE...!
ぴゅうっ
FWOOSH
I'M OUTTA HERE!

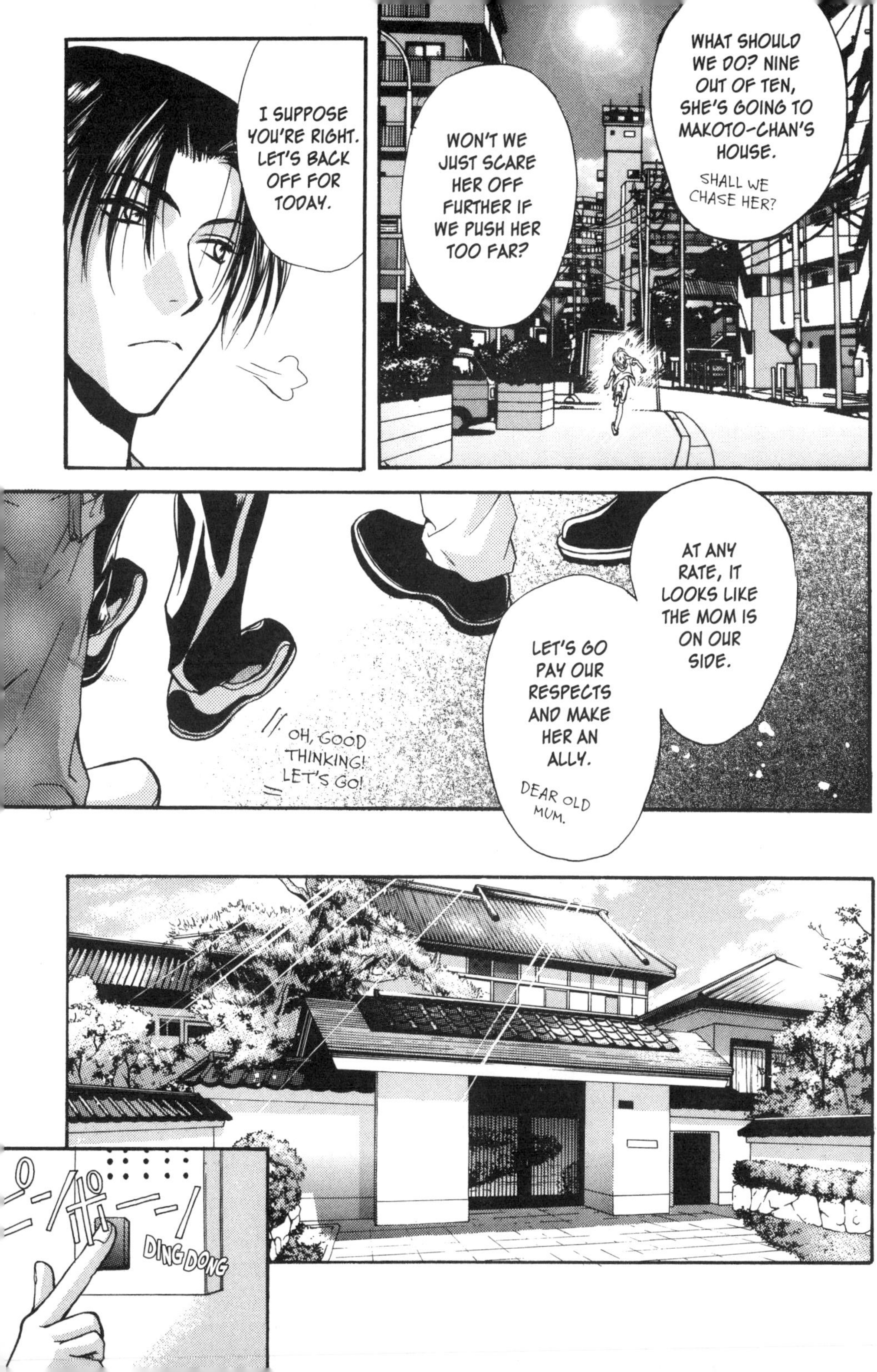
WHAT SHOULD WE DO? NINE OUT OF TEN, SHE'S GOING TO MAKOTO-CHAN'S HOUSE.
SHALL WE CHASE HER?
WON'T WE JUST SCARE HER OFF FURTHER IF WE PUSH HER TOO FAR?
I SUPPOSE YOU'RE RIGHT. LET'S BACK OFF FOR TODAY.
AT ANY RATE, IT LOOKS LIKE THE MOM IS ON OUR SIDE.
LET'S GO PAY OUR RESPECTS AND MAKE HER AN ALLY.
DEAR OLD MUM.
OH, GOOD THINKING! LET'S GO!
DING DONG

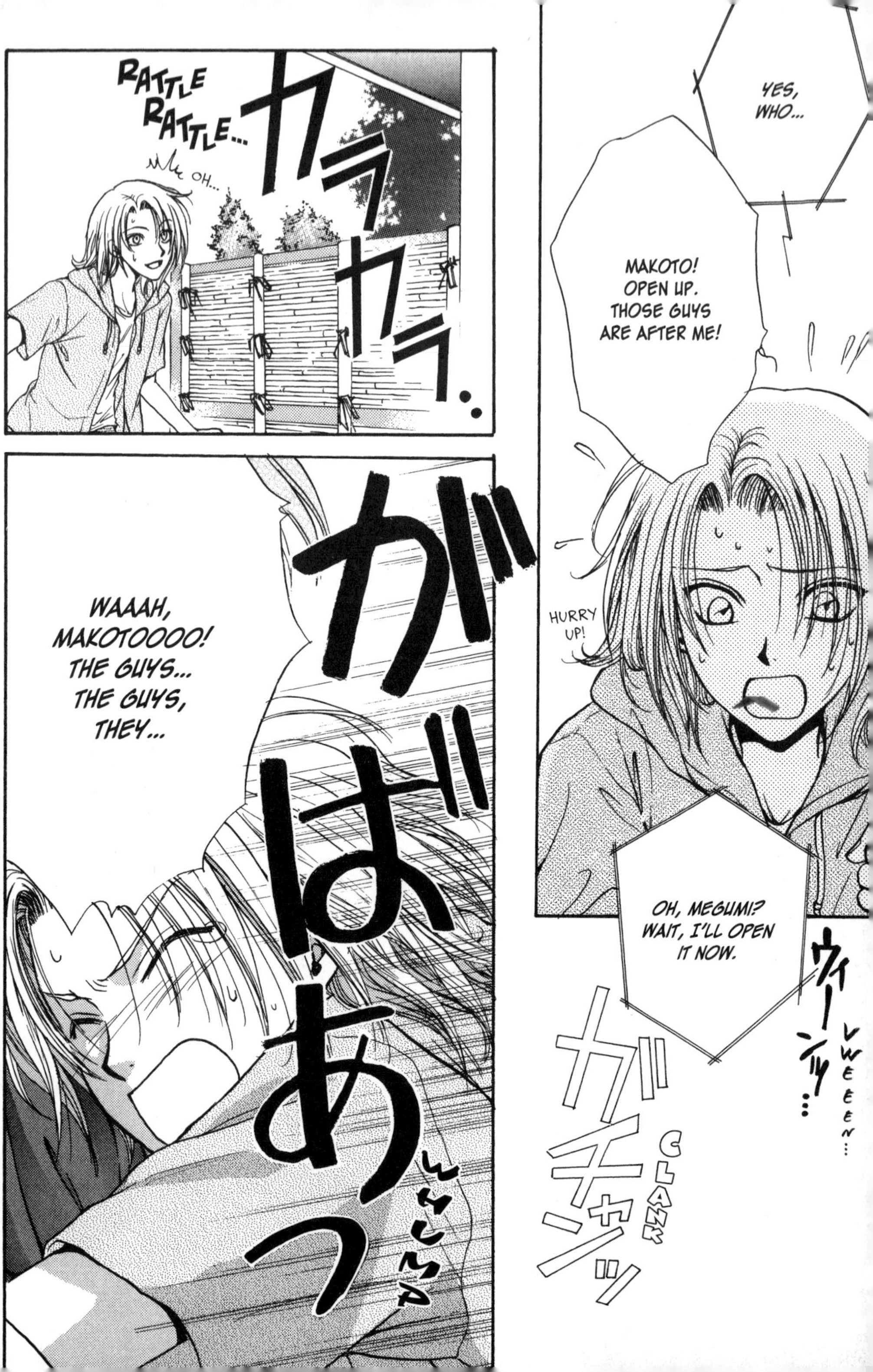
YES, WHO...
MAKOTO! OPEN UP. THOSE GUYS ARE AFTER ME!
HURRY UP!
OH, MEGUMI? WAIT, I'LL OPEN IT NOW.
ウィーンッ…
VWEEEN...
ガチャンッ
CLANK
RATTLE RATTLE...
カラカラ..
OH...
WAAAH, MAKOTOOOO! THE GUYS... THE GUYS, THEY...
がばあっ
WHUMP

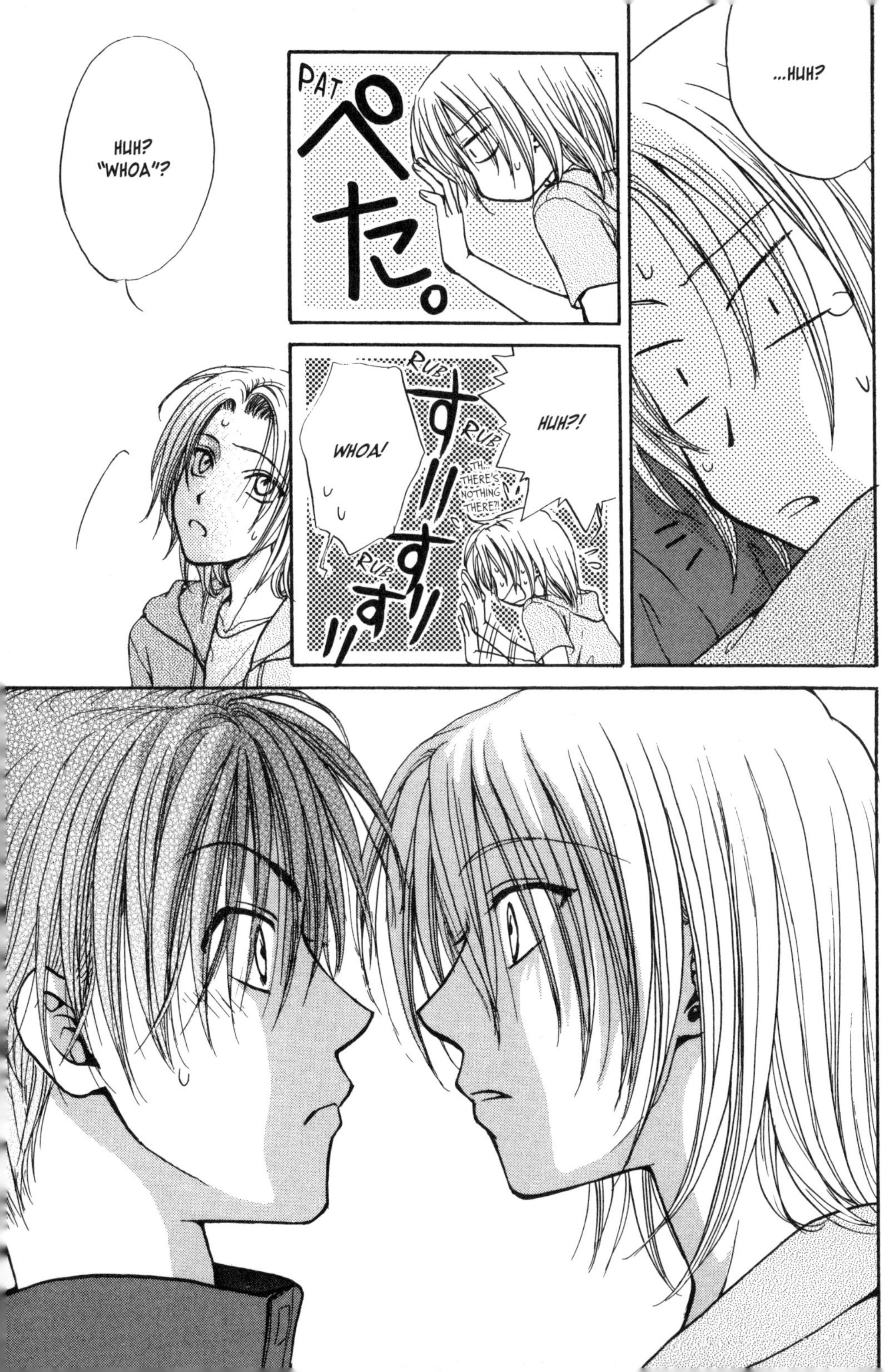
...HUH?
PAT
ぺた。
RUB RUB RUB
すりすりすり
HUH?!
WHOA!
TH... THERE'S NOTHING THERE?!
HUH? "WHOA"?

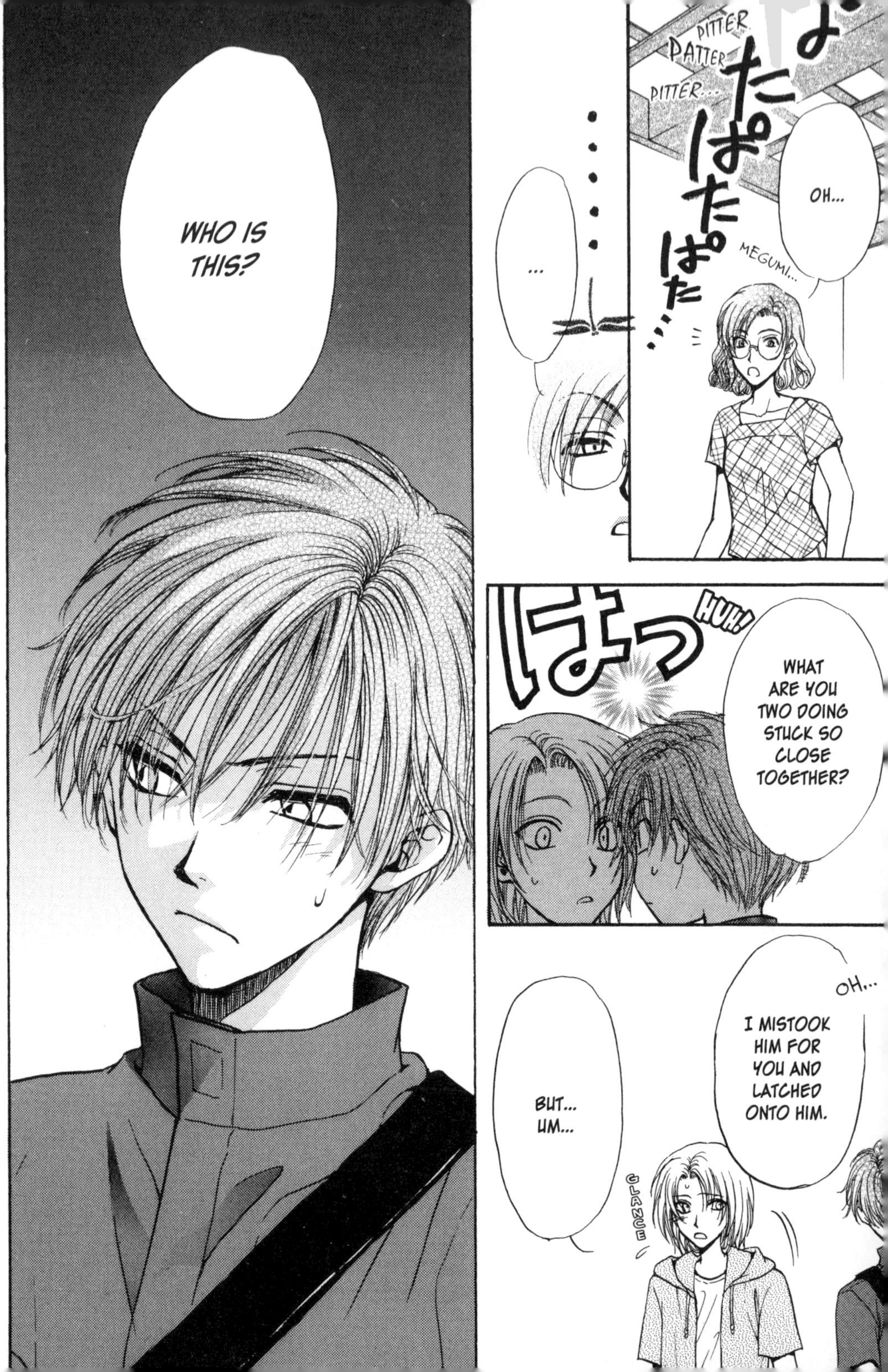
ぱたぱたぱた…
PITTER PATTER PITTER...
OH...
MEGUMI...
...
はっ
HUH!
WHAT ARE YOU TWO DOING STUCK SO CLOSE TOGETHER?
OH...
I MISTOOK HIM FOR YOU AND LATCHED ONTO HIM.
GLANCE
BUT... UM...
WHO IS THIS?

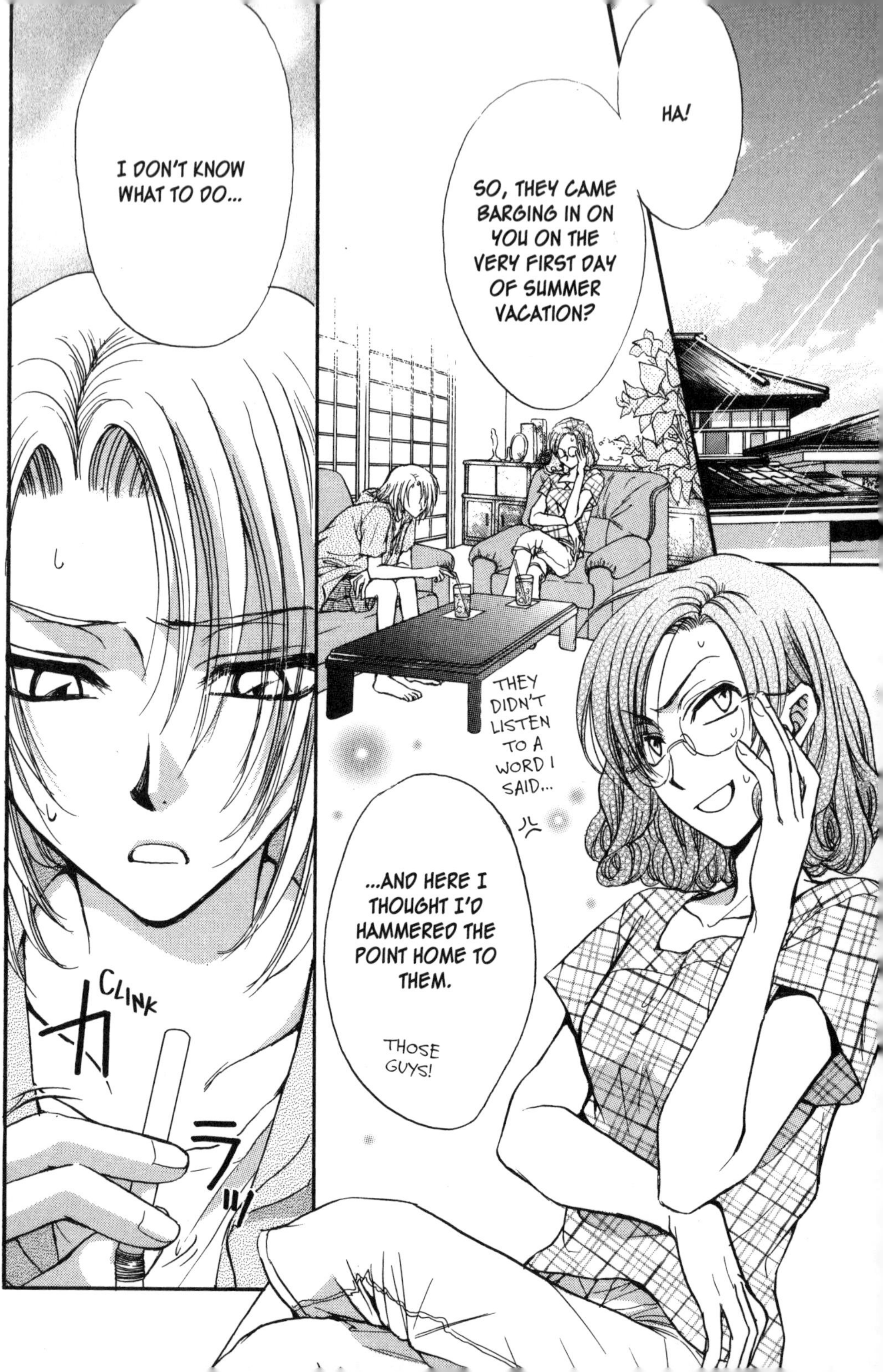
HA!
SO, THEY CAME BARGING IN ON YOU ON THE VERY FIRST DAY OF SUMMER VACATION?
THEY DIDN'T LISTEN TO A WORD I SAID...
...AND HERE I THOUGHT I'D HAMMERED THE POINT HOME TO THEM.
THOSE GUYS!
I DON'T KNOW WHAT TO DO...
CLINK

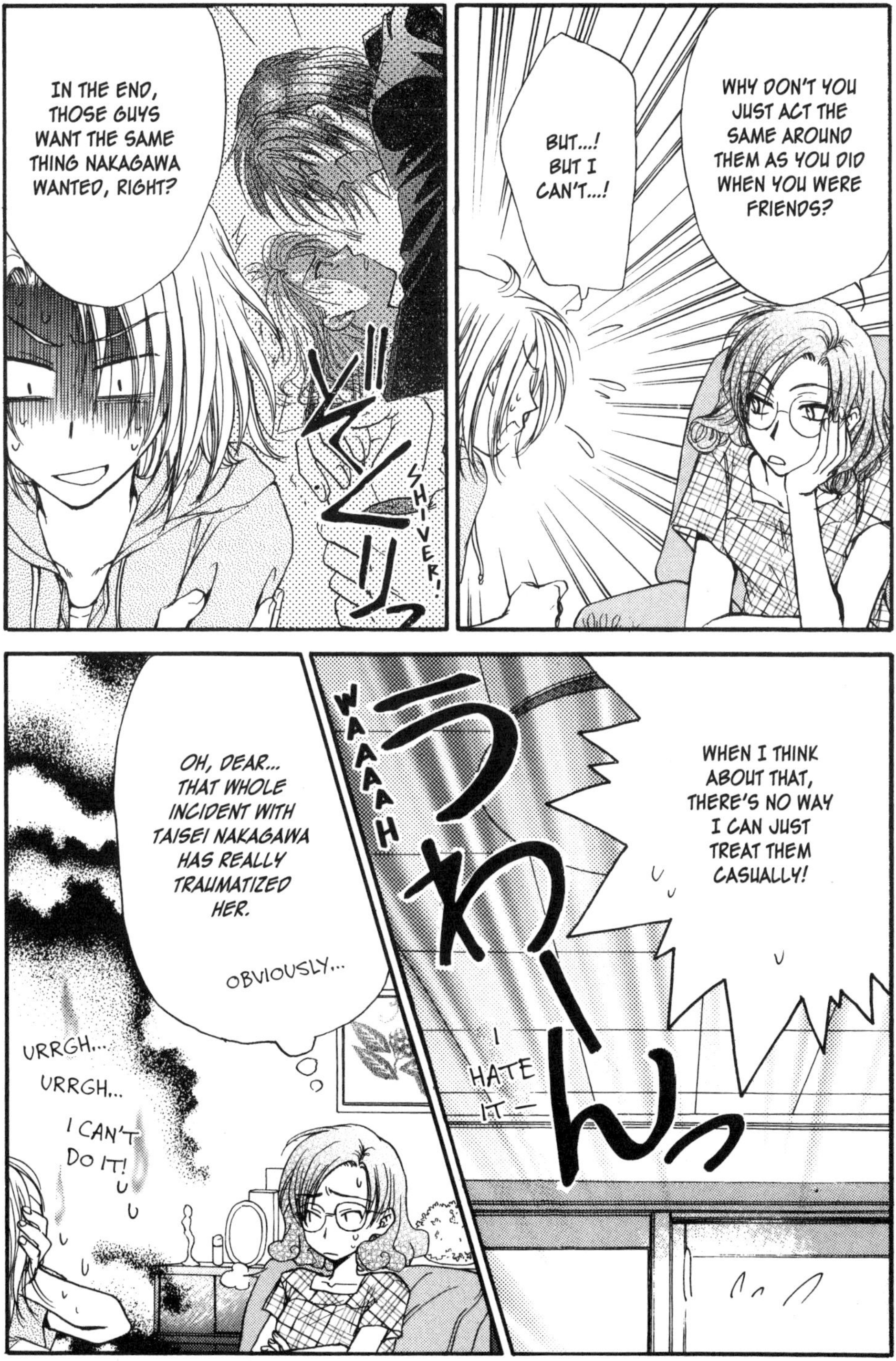
WHY DON'T YOU JUST ACT THE SAME AROUND THEM AS YOU DID WHEN YOU WERE FRIENDS?
BUT...! BUT I CAN'T...!
IN THE END, THOSE GUYS WANT THE SAME THING NAKAGAWA WANTED, RIGHT?
ぞくりっ
SHIVER!
WHEN I THINK ABOUT THAT, THERE'S NO WAY I CAN JUST TREAT THEM CASUALLY!
うわーんっ
WAAAAAH
I HATE IT—
OH, DEAR... THAT WHOLE INCIDENT WITH TAISEI NAKAGAWA HAS REALLY TRAUMATIZED HER.
OBVIOUSLY...
URRGH...
URRGH...
I CAN'T DO IT!

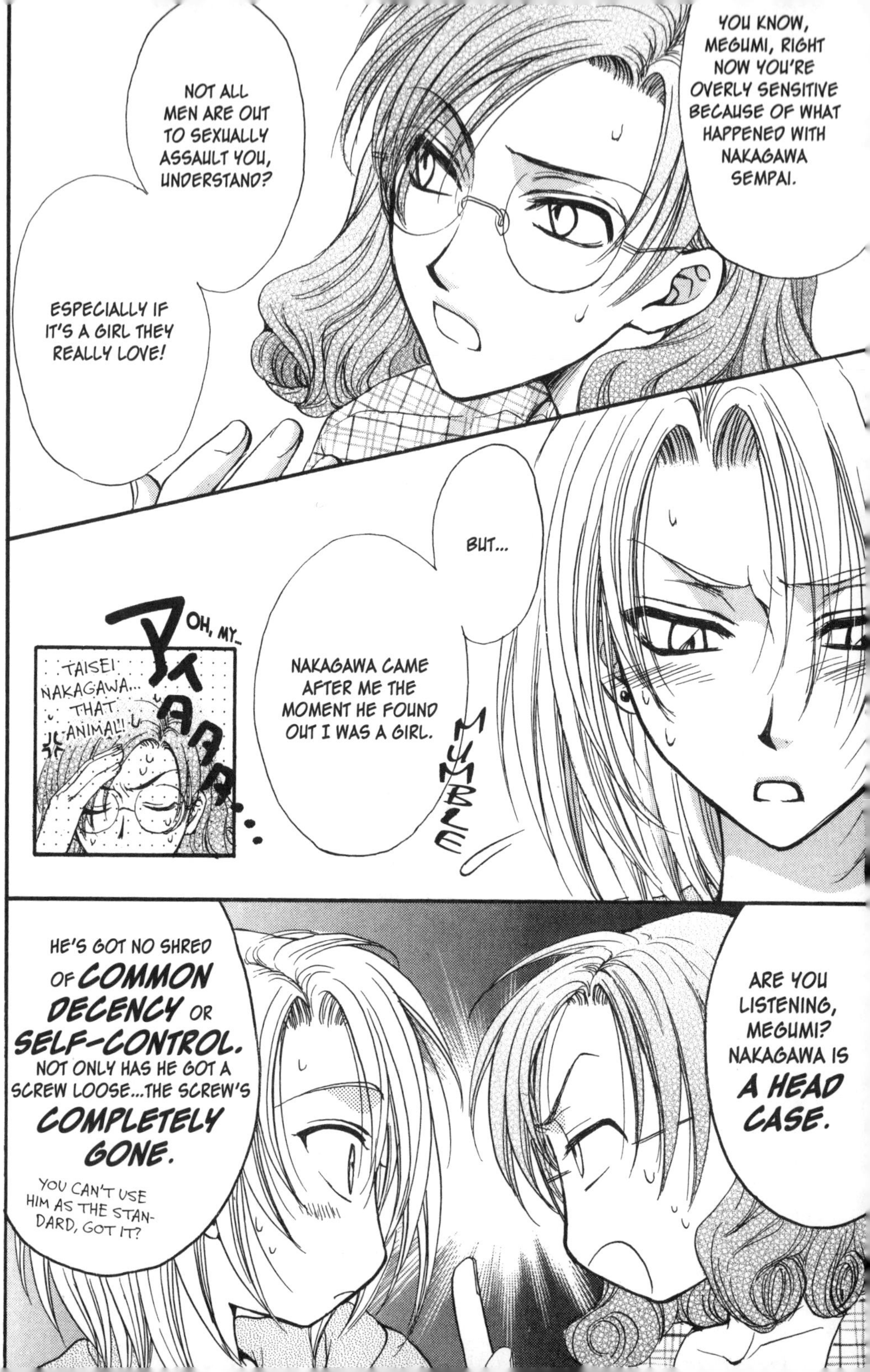
YOU KNOW, MEGUMI, RIGHT NOW YOU'RE OVERLY SENSITIVE BECAUSE OF WHAT HAPPENED WITH NAKAGAWA SEMPAI.
NOT ALL MEN ARE OUT TO SEXUALLY ASSAULT YOU, UNDERSTAND?
ESPECIALLY IF IT'S A GIRL THEY REALLY LOVE!
BUT...
NAKAGAWA CAME AFTER ME THE MOMENT HE FOUND OUT I WAS A GIRL.
MUMBLE
OH, MY...
TAISEI NAKAGAWA... THAT ANIMAL!!
ARE YOU LISTENING, MEGUMI? NAKAGAWA IS A HEAD CASE.
HE'S GOT NO SHRED OF COMMON DECENCY OR SELF-CONTROL. NOT ONLY HAS HE GOT A SCREW LOOSE...THE SCREW'S COMPLETELY GONE.
YOU CAN'T USE HIM AS THE STANDARD, GOT IT?

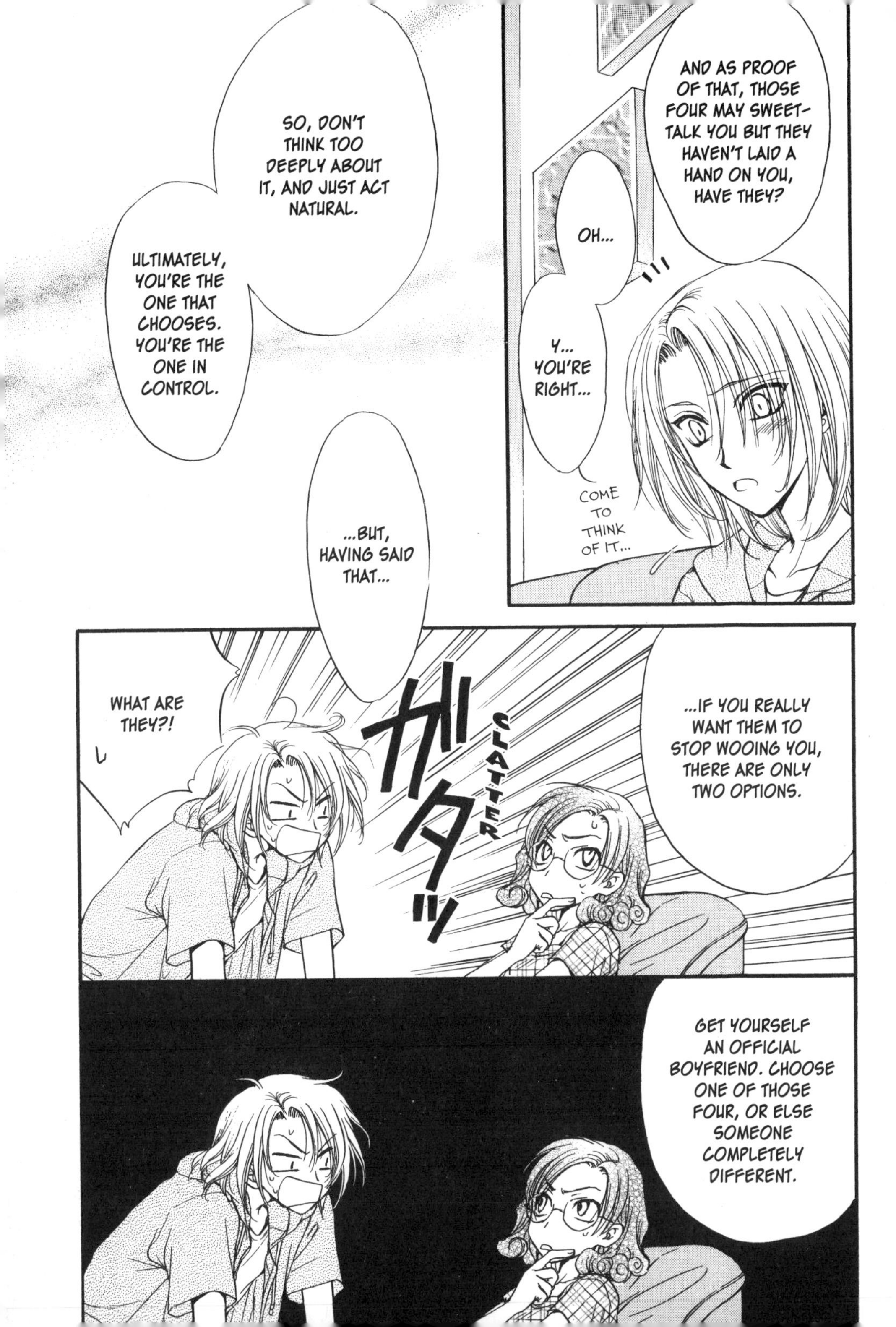
AND AS PROOF OF THAT, THOSE FOUR MAY SWEET-TALK YOU BUT THEY HAVEN'T LAID A HAND ON YOU, HAVE THEY?
OH...
Y... YOU'RE RIGHT...
COME TO THINK OF IT...
SO, DON'T THINK TOO DEEPLY ABOUT IT, AND JUST ACT NATURAL.
ULTIMATELY, YOU'RE THE ONE THAT CHOOSES. YOU'RE THE ONE IN CONTROL.
...BUT, HAVING SAID THAT...
...IF YOU REALLY WANT THEM TO STOP WOOING YOU, THERE ARE ONLY TWO OPTIONS.
ガタッ
CLATTER
WHAT ARE THEY?!
GET YOURSELF AN OFFICIAL BOYFRIEND. CHOOSE ONE OF THOSE FOUR, OR ELSE SOMEONE COMPLETELY DIFFERENT.

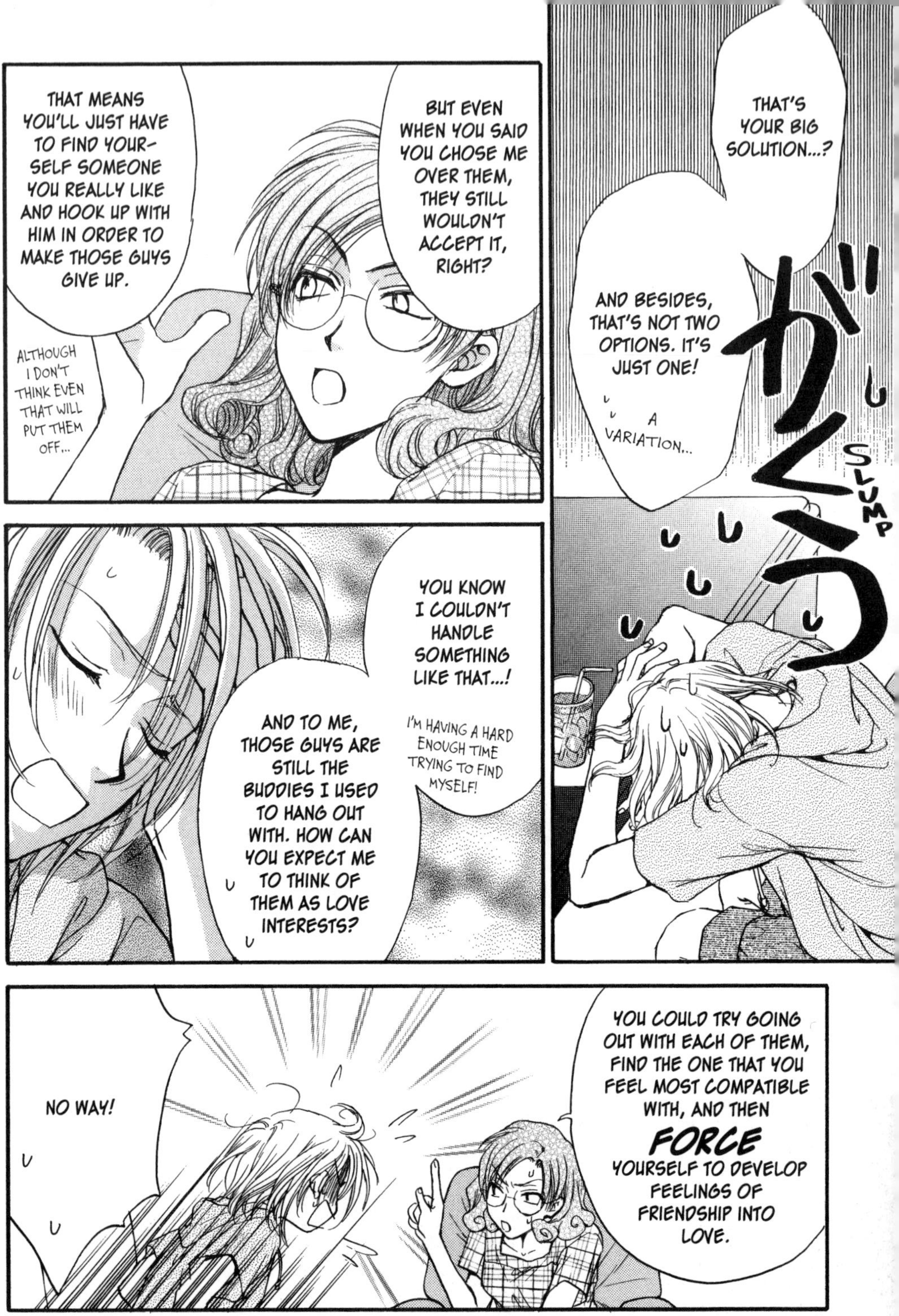
THAT'S YOUR BIG SOLUTION...?
AND BESIDES, THAT'S NOT TWO OPTIONS. IT'S JUST ONE!
A VARIATION...
がくっ
SLUMP
BUT EVEN WHEN YOU SAID YOU CHOSE ME OVER THEM, THEY STILL WOULDN'T ACCEPT IT, RIGHT?
THAT MEANS YOU'LL JUST HAVE TO FIND YOURSELF SOMEONE YOU REALLY LIKE AND HOOK UP WITH HIM IN ORDER TO MAKE THOSE GUYS GIVE UP.
ALTHOUGH I DON'T THINK EVEN THAT WILL PUT THEM OFF...
YOU KNOW I COULDN'T HANDLE SOMETHING LIKE THAT...!
I'M HAVING A HARD ENOUGH TIME TRYING TO FIND MYSELF!
AND TO ME, THOSE GUYS ARE STILL THE BUDDIES I USED TO HANG OUT WITH. HOW CAN YOU EXPECT ME TO THINK OF THEM AS LOVE INTERESTS?
YOU COULD TRY GOING OUT WITH EACH OF THEM, FIND THE ONE THAT YOU FEEL MOST COMPATIBLE WITH, AND THEN FORCE YOURSELF TO DEVELOP FEELINGS OF FRIENDSHIP INTO LOVE.
NO WAY!

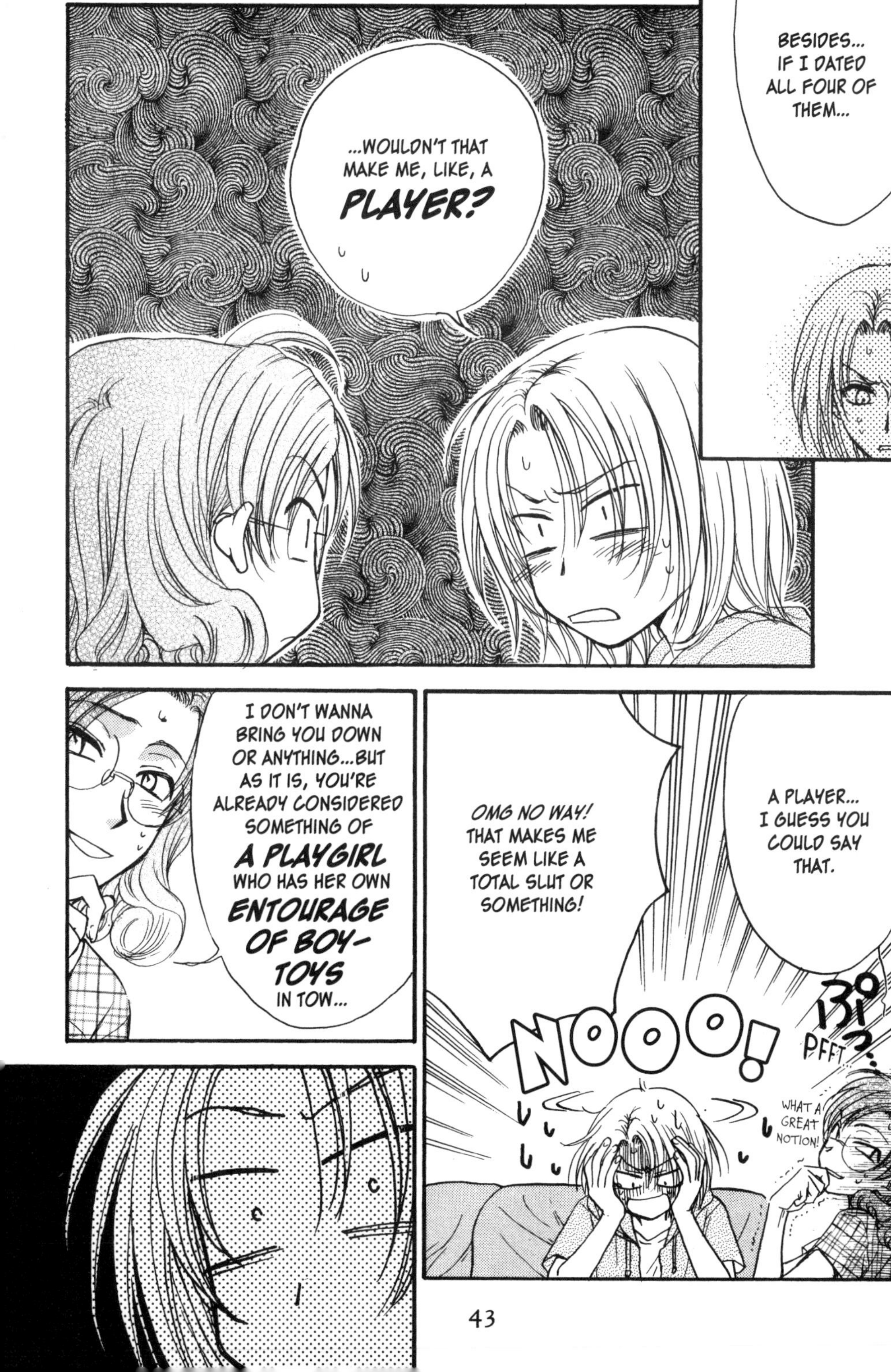
BESIDES... IF I DATED ALL FOUR OF THEM...
...WOULDN'T THAT MAKE ME, LIKE, A PLAYER?
A PLAYER... I GUESS YOU COULD SAY THAT.
PFFT
WHAT A GREAT NOTION!
OMG NO WAY! THAT MAKES ME SEEM LIKE A TOTAL SLUT OR SOMETHING!
NOOO!
I DON'T WANNA BRING YOU DOWN OR ANYTHING...BUT AS IT IS, YOU'RE ALREADY CONSIDERED SOMETHING OF A PLAYGIRL WHO HAS HER OWN ENTOURAGE OF BOY-TOYS IN TOW...

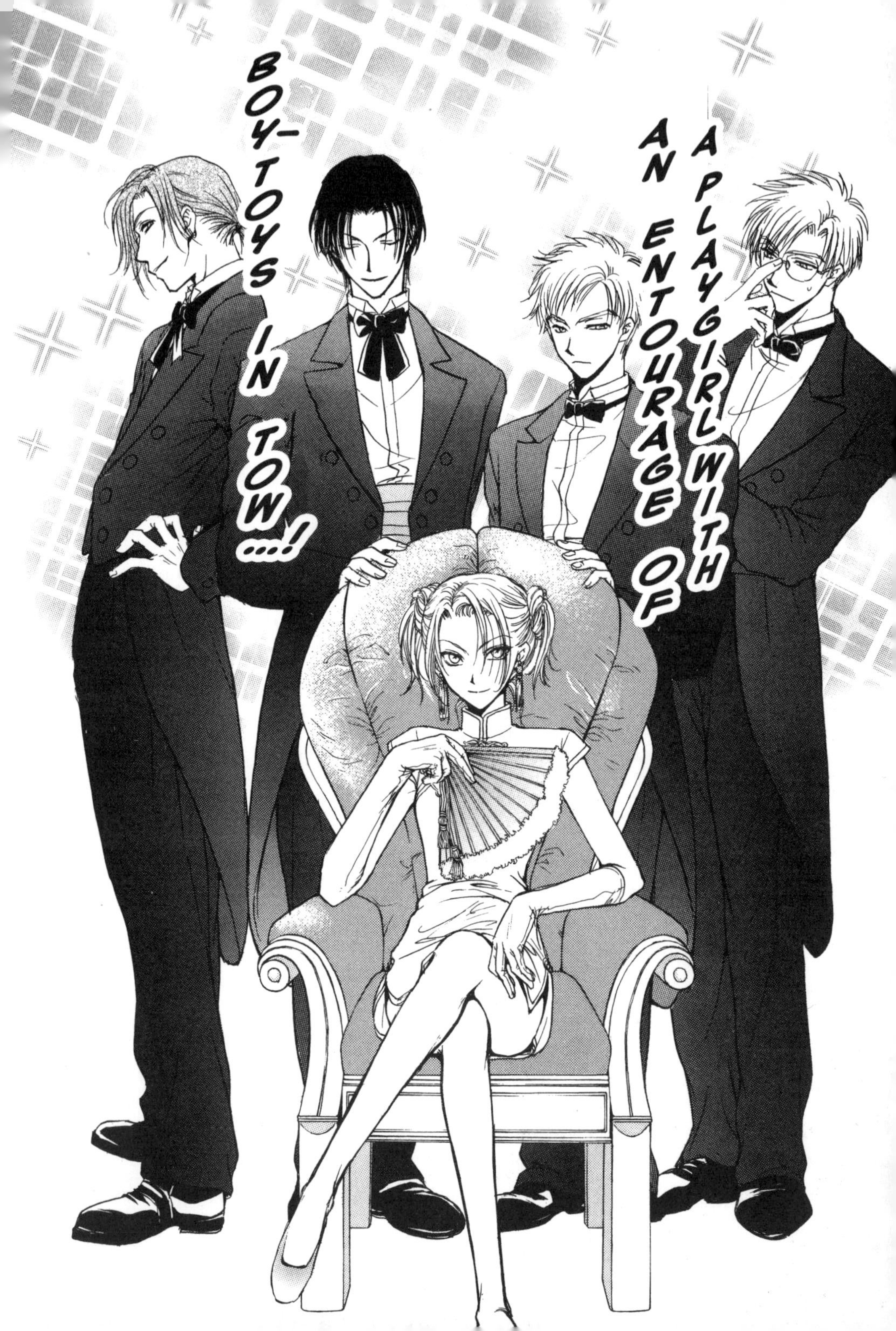
A PLAYGIRL WITH
AN ENTOURAGE OF
BOY-TOYS IN TOW...!

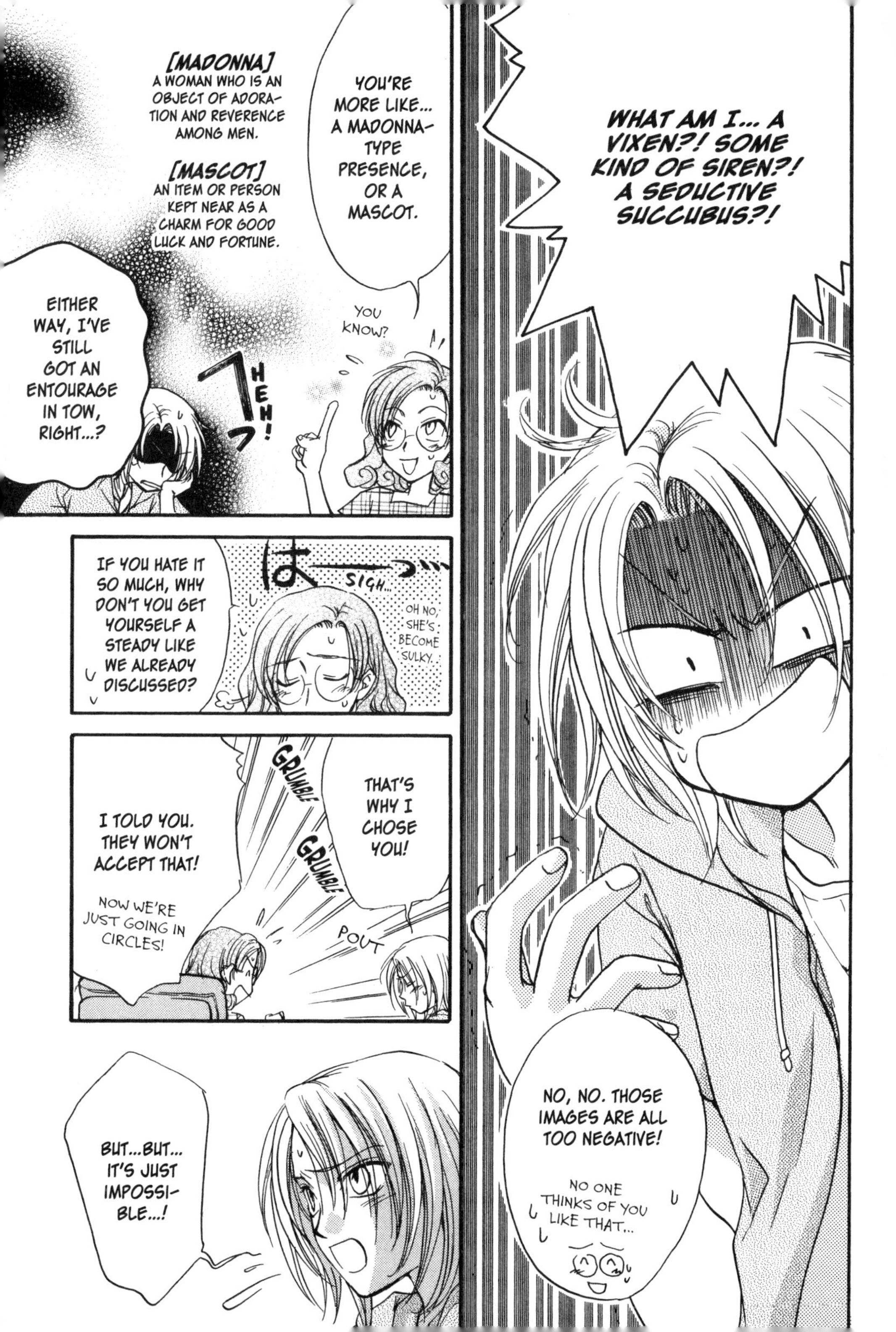

WHAT AM I... A VIXEN?! SOME KIND OF SIREN?! A SEDUCTIVE SUCCUBUS?!
NO, NO. THOSE IMAGES ARE ALL TOO NEGATIVE!
NO ONE THINKS OF YOU LIKE THAT...
YOU'RE MORE LIKE... A MADONNA-TYPE PRESENCE, OR A MASCOT.
YOU KNOW?
[MADONNA] A WOMAN WHO IS AN OBJECT OF ADORATION AND REVERENCE AMONG MEN.
[MASCOT] AN ITEM OR PERSON KEPT NEAR AS A CHARM FOR GOOD LUCK AND FORTUNE.
HEH!
EITHER WAY, I'VE STILL GOT AN ENTOURAGE IN TOW, RIGHT...?
SIGH...
OH NO, SHE'S BECOME SULKY.
IF YOU HATE IT SO MUCH, WHY DON'T YOU GET YOURSELF A STEADY LIKE WE ALREADY DISCUSSED?
THAT'S WHY I CHOSE YOU!
GRUMBLE
GRUMBLE
I TOLD YOU. THEY WON'T ACCEPT THAT!
NOW WE'RE JUST GOING IN CIRCLES!
POUT
BUT...BUT... IT'S JUST IMPOSSI-BLE...!

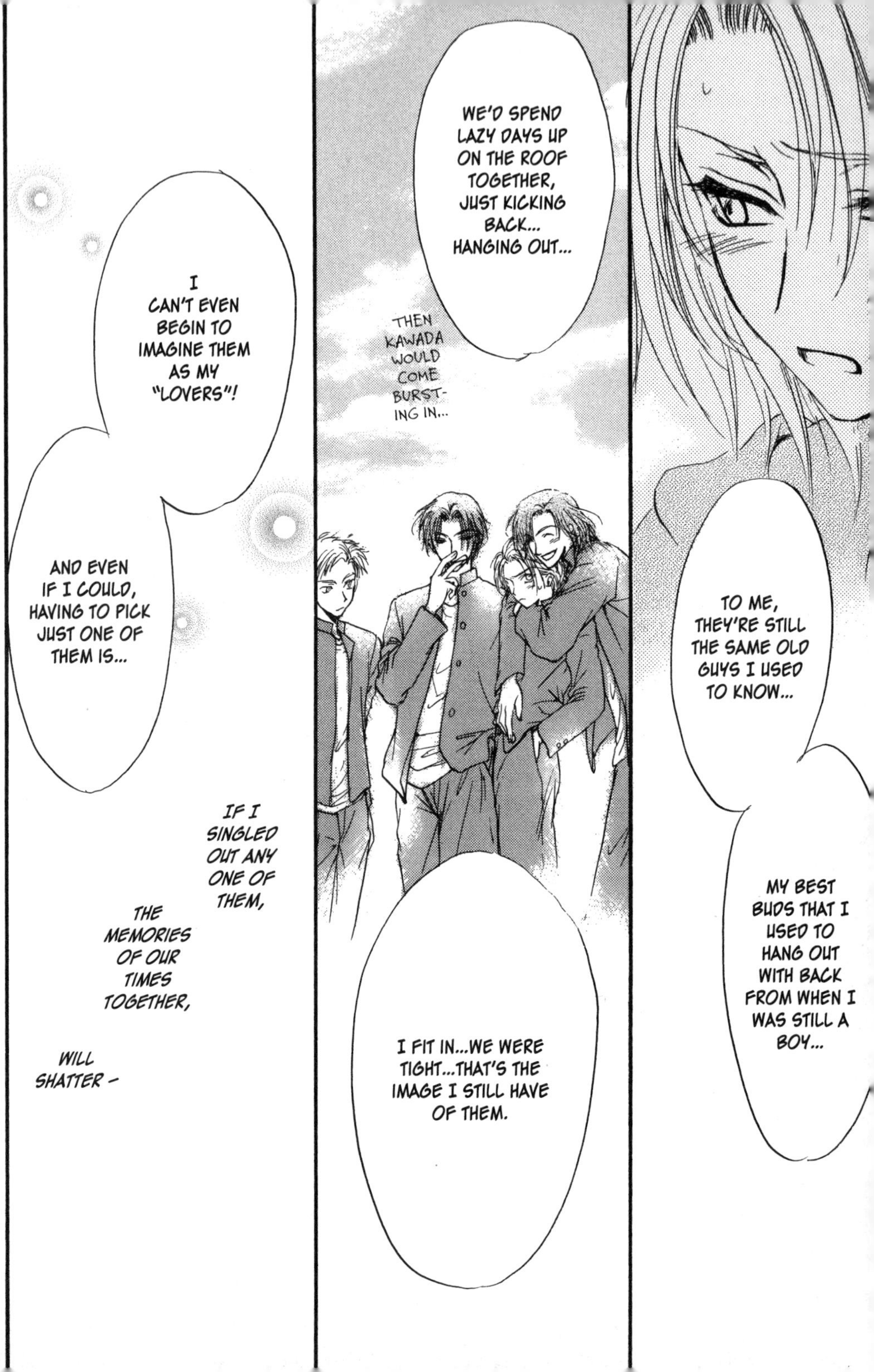
TO ME, THEY'RE STILL THE SAME OLD GUYS I USED TO KNOW...
MY BEST BUDS THAT I USED TO HANG OUT WITH BACK FROM WHEN I WAS STILL A BOY...
WE'D SPEND LAZY DAYS UP ON THE ROOF TOGETHER, JUST KICKING BACK... HANGING OUT...
THEN KAWADA WOULD COME BURST-ING IN...
I FIT IN...WE WERE TIGHT...THAT'S THE IMAGE I STILL HAVE OF THEM.
I CAN'T EVEN BEGIN TO IMAGINE THEM AS MY "LOVERS"!
AND EVEN IF I COULD, HAVING TO PICK JUST ONE OF THEM IS...
IF I SINGLED OUT ANY ONE OF THEM,
THE MEMORIES OF OUR TIMES TOGETHER,
WILL SHATTER –

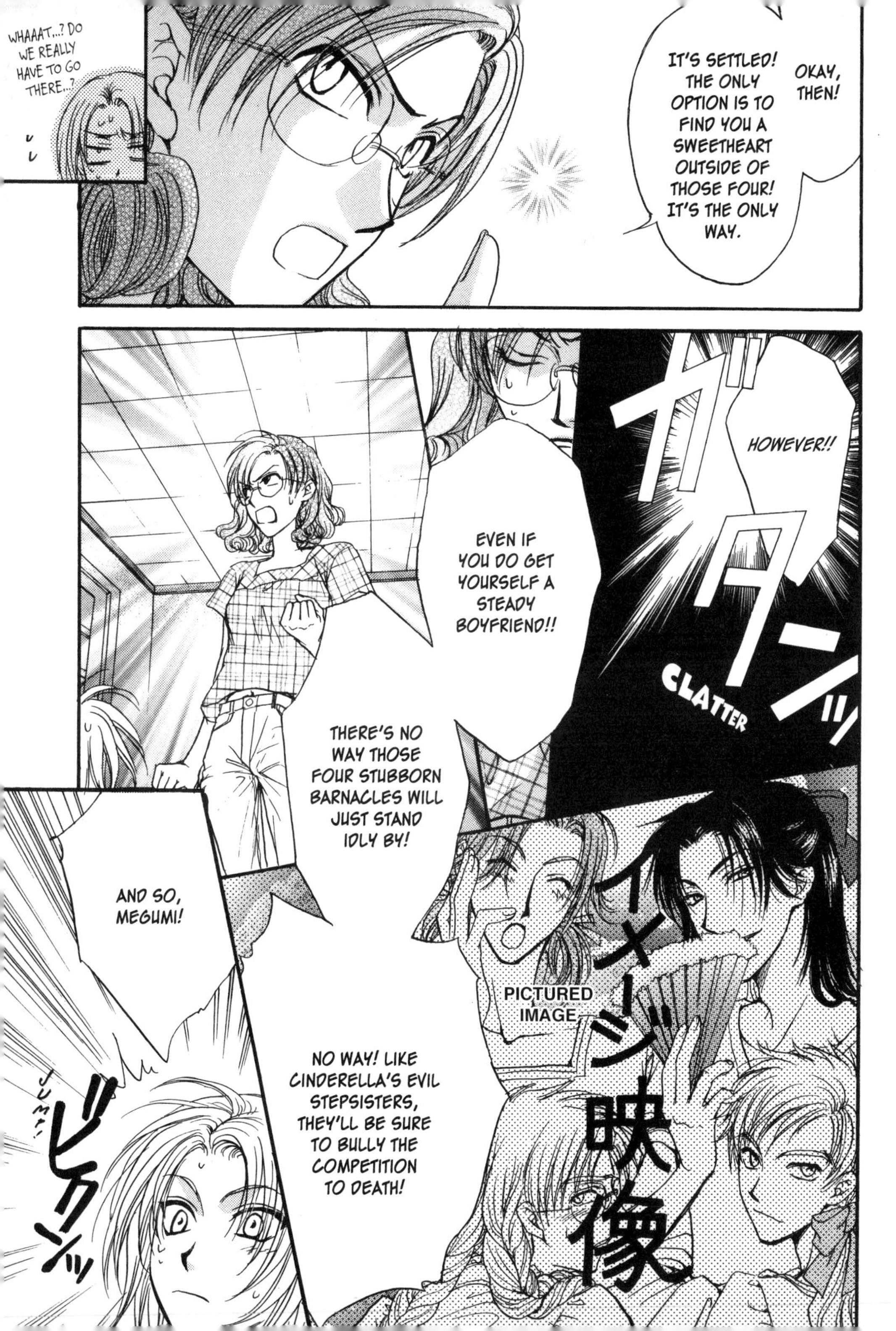

OKAY, THEN!
IT'S SETTLED! THE ONLY OPTION IS TO FIND YOU A SWEETHEART OUTSIDE OF THOSE FOUR! IT'S THE ONLY WAY.
WHAAAT...? DO WE REALLY HAVE TO GO THERE...?
HOWEVER!!
ガターンッ
CLATTER
EVEN IF YOU DO GET YOURSELF A STEADY BOYFRIEND!!
THERE'S NO WAY THOSE FOUR STUBBORN BARNACLES WILL JUST STAND IDLY BY!
イメージ映像
PICTURED IMAGE
NO WAY! LIKE CINDERELLA'S EVIL STEPSISTERS, THEY'LL BE SURE TO BULLY THE COMPETITION TO DEATH!
AND SO, MEGUMI!
ビクンッ
JUMP!

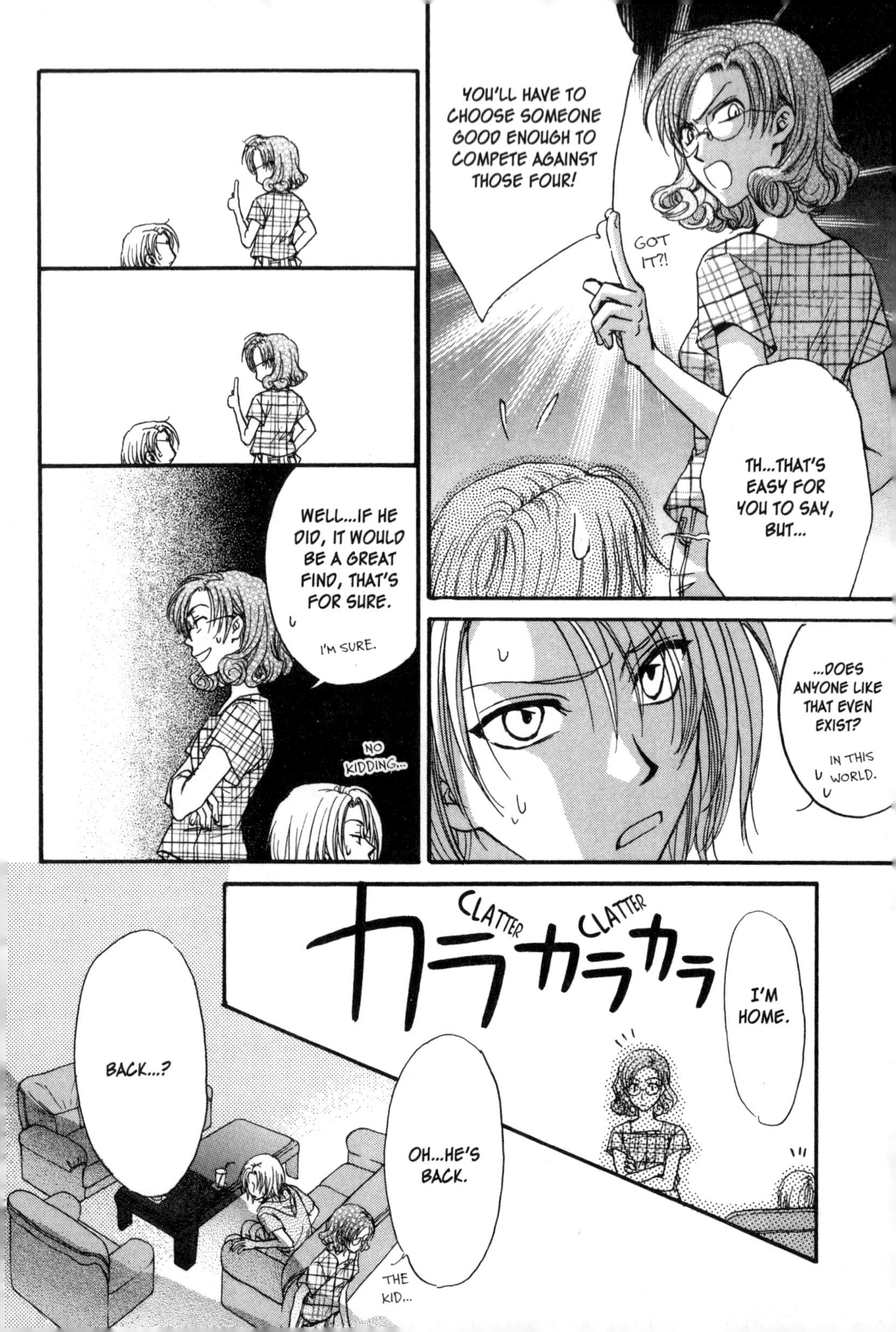
YOU'LL HAVE TO CHOOSE SOMEONE GOOD ENOUGH TO COMPETE AGAINST THOSE FOUR!
GOT IT?!
TH...THAT'S EASY FOR YOU TO SAY, BUT...
...DOES ANYONE LIKE THAT EVEN EXIST?
IN THIS WORLD.
WELL...IF HE DID, IT WOULD BE A GREAT FIND, THAT'S FOR SURE.
I'M SURE.
NO KIDDING...
カラカラカラ
CLATTER CLATTER
I'M HOME.
OH...HE'S BACK.
THE KID...
BACK...?

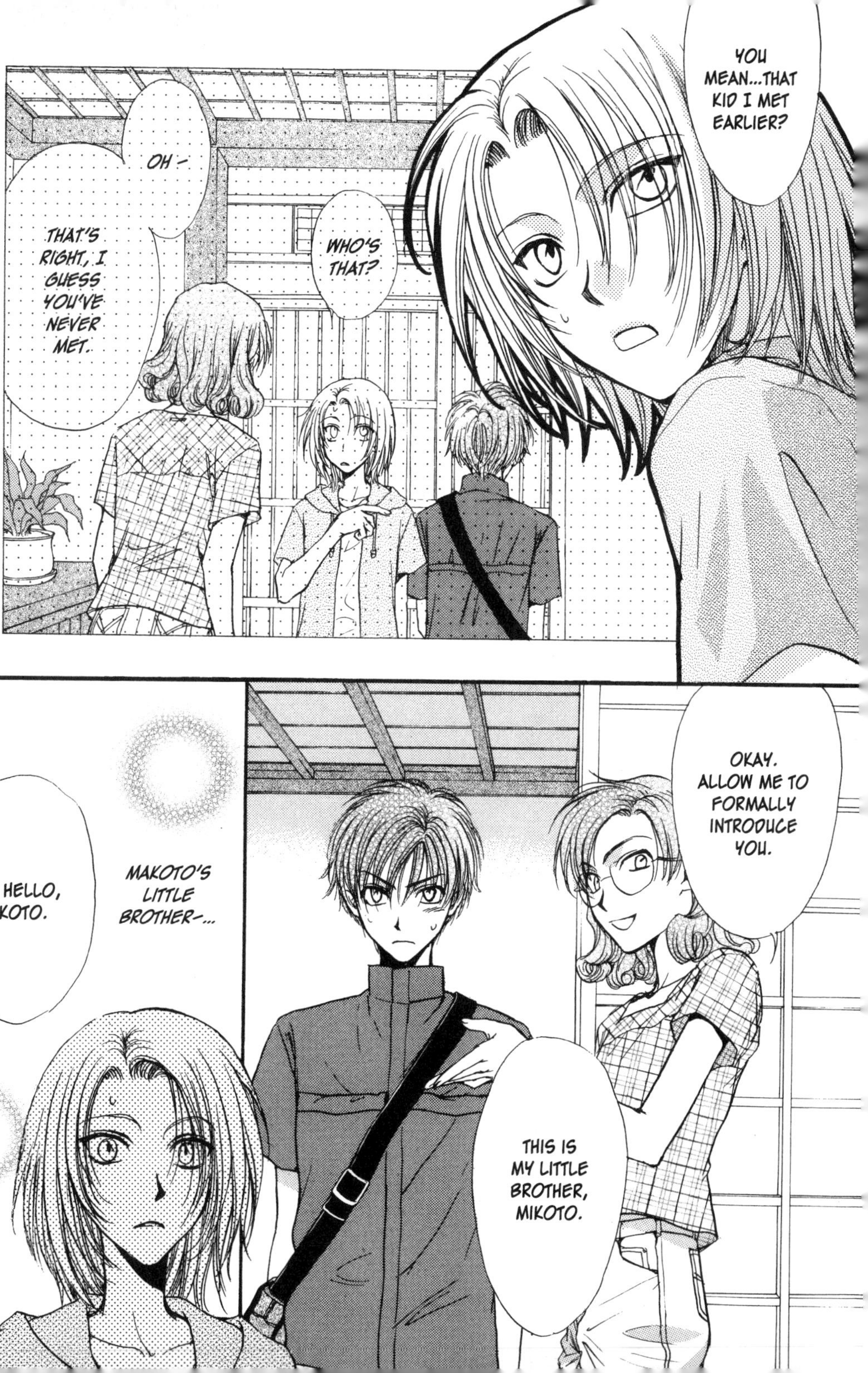
YOU MEAN...THAT KID I MET EARLIER?
WHO'S THAT?
OH -
THAT'S RIGHT, I GUESS YOU'VE NEVER MET.
OKAY. ALLOW ME TO FORMALLY INTRODUCE YOU.
THIS IS MY LITTLE BROTHER, MIKOTO.
MAKOTO'S LITTLE BROTHER-...
SAY HELLO, MIKOTO.

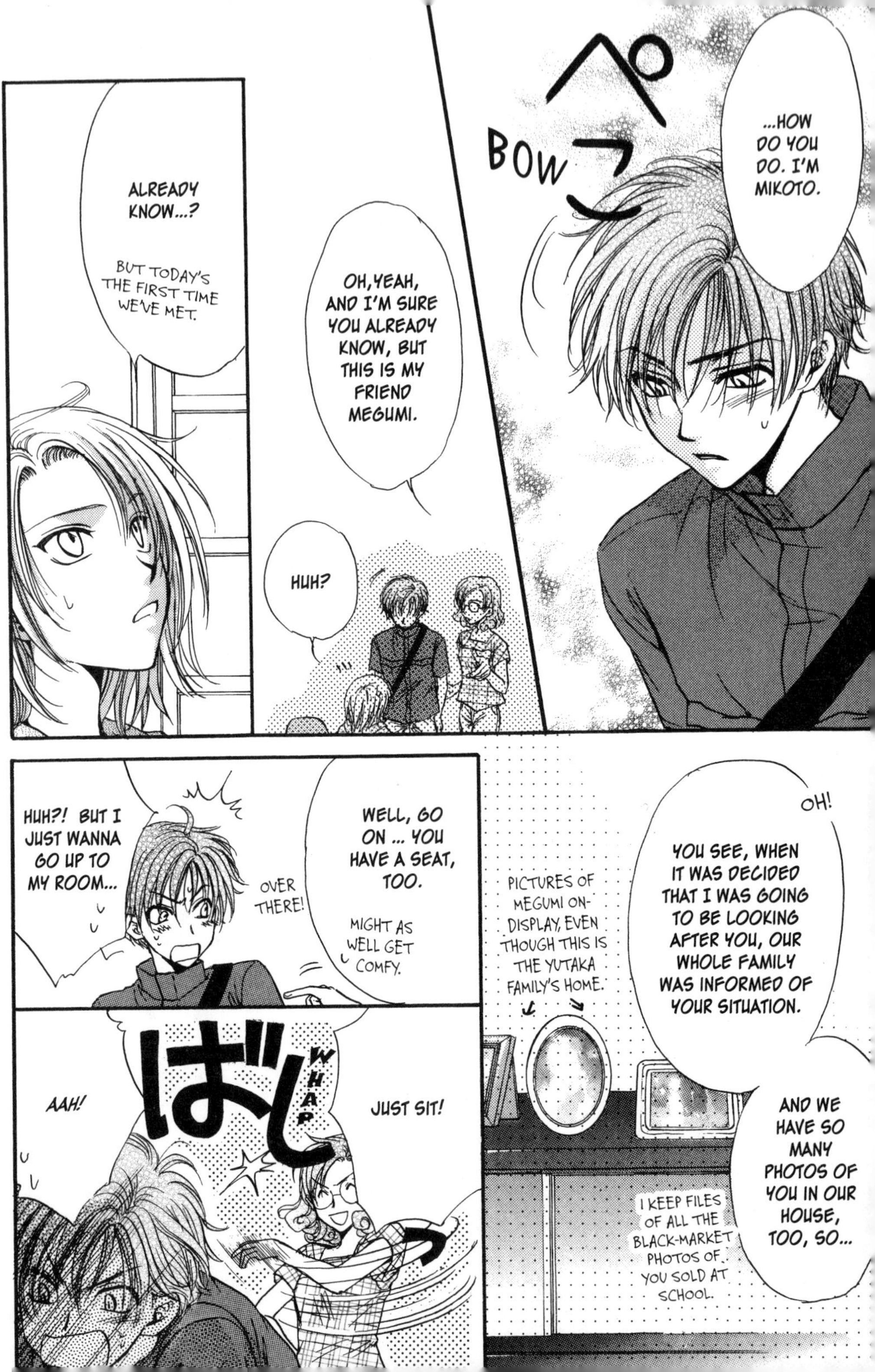
ペこ
BOW
...HOW DO YOU DO. I'M MIKOTO.
OH, YEAH, AND I'M SURE YOU ALREADY KNOW, BUT THIS IS MY FRIEND MEGUMI.
HUH?
ALREADY KNOW...?
BUT TODAY'S THE FIRST TIME WE'VE MET.
OH!
YOU SEE, WHEN IT WAS DECIDED THAT I WAS GOING TO BE LOOKING AFTER YOU, OUR WHOLE FAMILY WAS INFORMED OF YOUR SITUATION.
PICTURES OF MEGUMI ON-DISPLAY, EVEN THOUGH THIS IS THE YUTAKA FAMILY'S HOME.
AND WE HAVE SO MANY PHOTOS OF YOU IN OUR HOUSE, TOO, SO...
I KEEP FILES OF ALL THE BLACK-MARKET PHOTOS OF YOU SOLD AT SCHOOL.
WELL, GO ON ... YOU HAVE A SEAT, TOO.
OVER THERE!
MIGHT AS WELL GET COMFY.
HUH?! BUT I JUST WANNA GO UP TO MY ROOM...
ばし
WHAP
JUST SIT!
AAH!

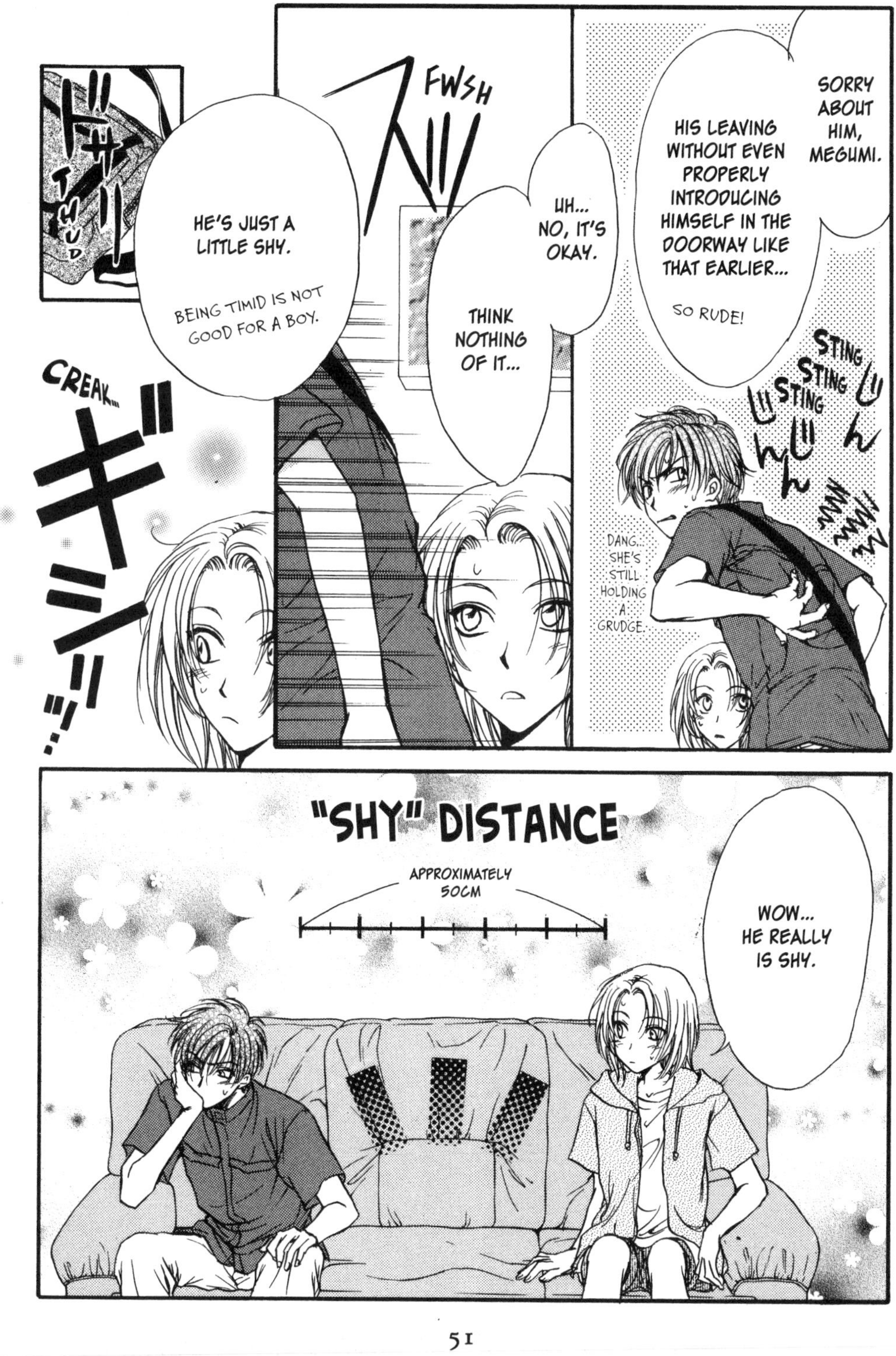
SORRY ABOUT HIM, MEGUMI.
HIS LEAVING WITHOUT EVEN PROPERLY INTRODUCING HIMSELF IN THE DOORWAY LIKE THAT EARLIER...
SO RUDE!
STING STING STING
DANG... SHE'S STILL HOLDING A GRUDGE.
FWSH
UH... NO, IT'S OKAY.
THINK NOTHING OF IT...
HE'S JUST A LITTLE SHY.
BEING TIMID IS NOT GOOD FOR A BOY.
THUD
CREAK...
WOW... HE REALLY IS SHY.
"SHY" DISTANCE
APPROXIMATELY 50CM

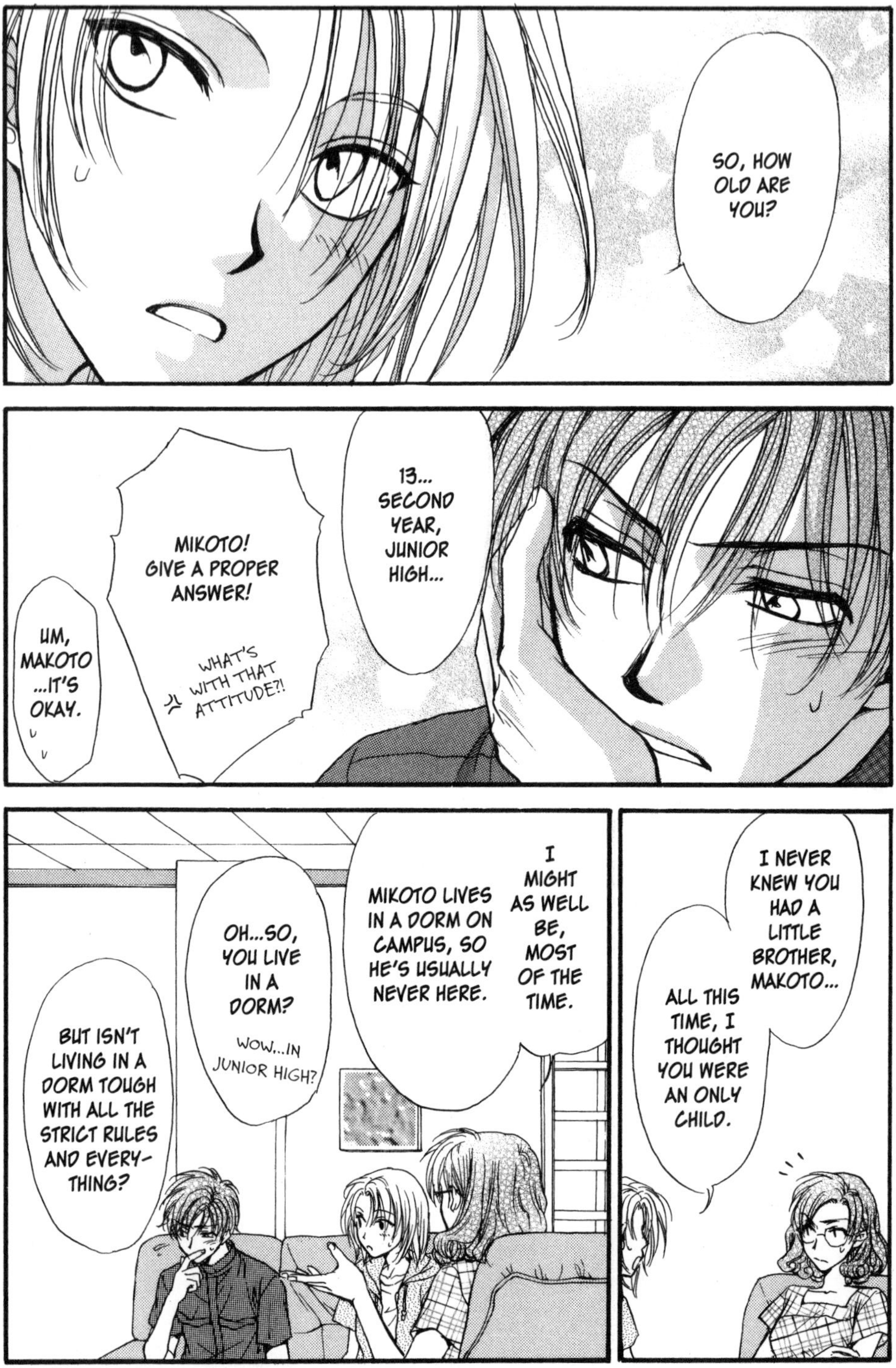
SO, HOW OLD ARE YOU?
13... SECOND YEAR, JUNIOR HIGH...
MIKOTO! GIVE A PROPER ANSWER!
WHAT'S WITH THAT ATTITUDE?!
UM, MAKOTO ...IT'S OKAY.
I NEVER KNEW YOU HAD A LITTLE BROTHER, MAKOTO...
ALL THIS TIME, I THOUGHT YOU WERE AN ONLY CHILD.
I MIGHT AS WELL BE, MOST OF THE TIME.
MIKOTO LIVES IN A DORM ON CAMPUS, SO HE'S USUALLY NEVER HERE.
OH...SO, YOU LIVE IN A DORM?
WOW...IN JUNIOR HIGH?
BUT ISN'T LIVING IN A DORM TOUGH WITH ALL THE STRICT RULES AND EVERY-THING?

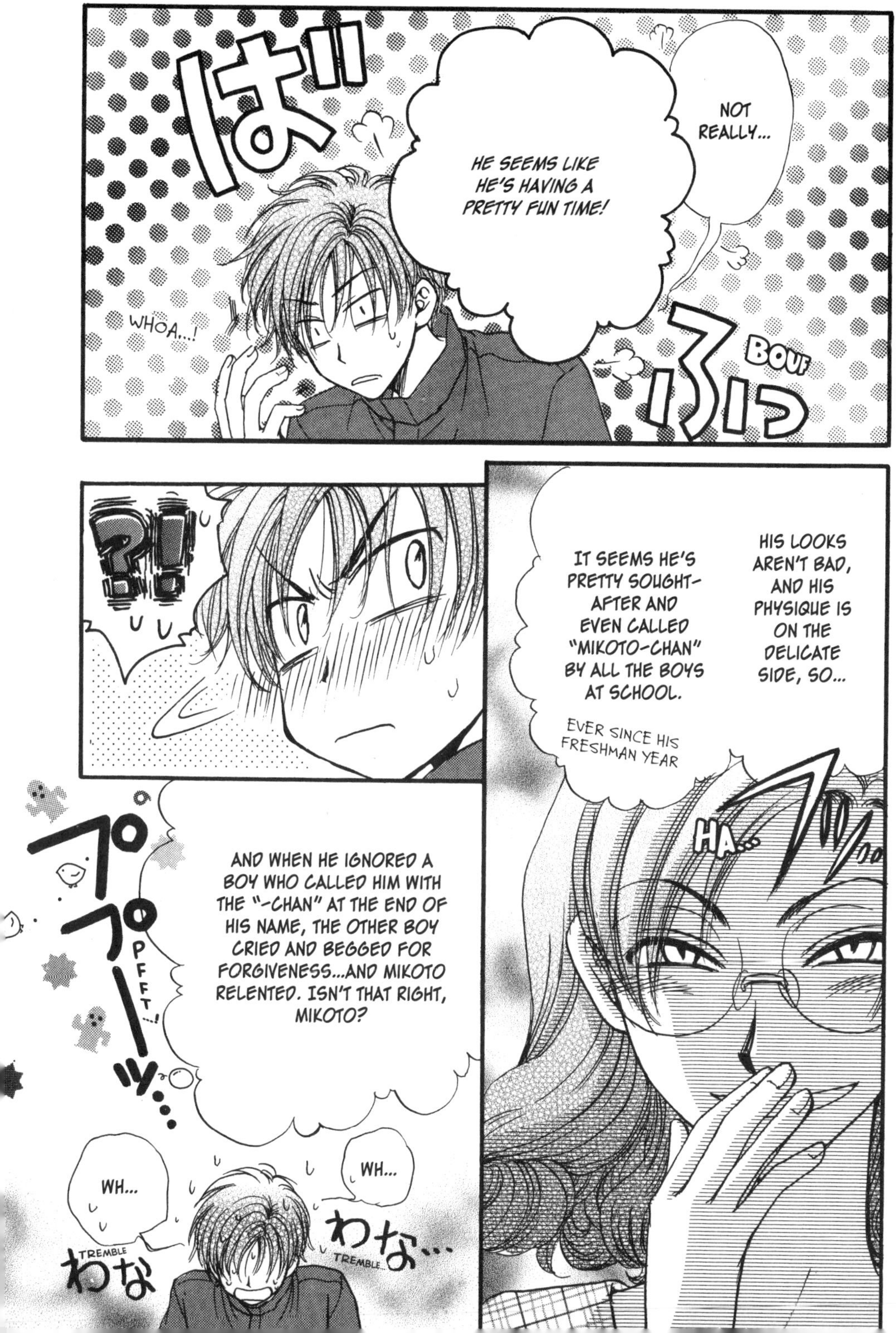
NOT REALLY...
HE SEEMS LIKE HE'S HAVING A PRETTY FUN TIME!
ば
ふっ
BOUF
WHOA...!
HIS LOOKS AREN'T BAD, AND HIS PHYSIQUE IS ON THE DELICATE SIDE, SO...
IT SEEMS HE'S PRETTY SOUGHT-AFTER AND EVEN CALLED "MIKOTO-CHAN" BY ALL THE BOYS AT SCHOOL.
EVER SINCE HIS FRESHMAN YEAR
HA...
?!
AND WHEN HE IGNORED A BOY WHO CALLED HIM WITH THE "-CHAN" AT THE END OF HIS NAME, THE OTHER BOY CRIED AND BEGGED FOR FORGIVENESS...AND MIKOTO RELENTED. ISN'T THAT RIGHT, MIKOTO?
ププーッ...
PFFT...!
WH...
WH...
わな...
TREMBLE...
わな
TREMBLE

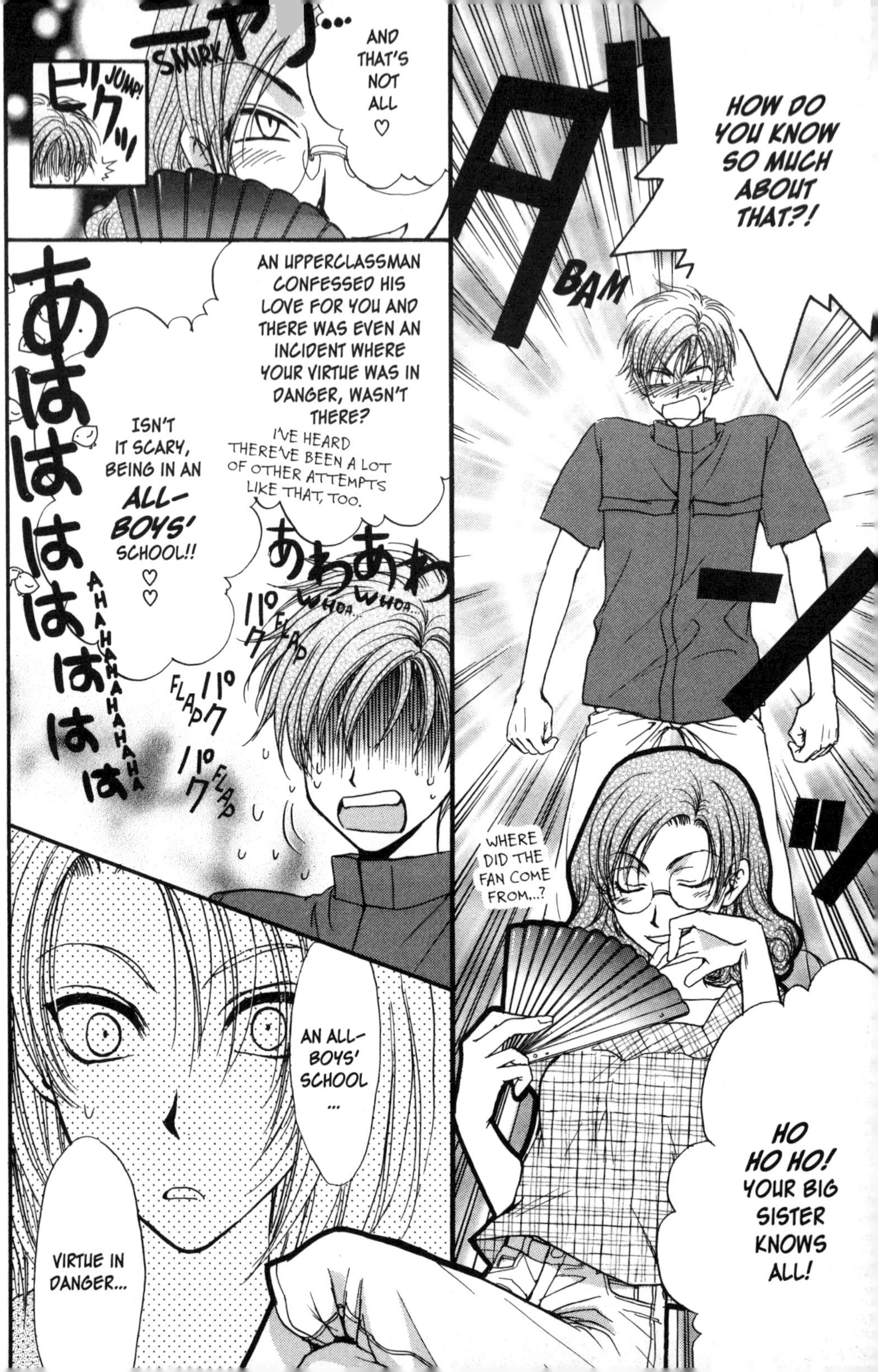
HOW DO YOU KNOW SO MUCH ABOUT THAT?!
BAM
WHERE DID THE FAN COME FROM...?
HO HO HO! YOUR BIG SISTER KNOWS ALL!
SMIRK
JUMP!
AND THAT'S NOT ALL ♡
AN UPPERCLASSMAN CONFESSED HIS LOVE FOR YOU AND THERE WAS EVEN AN INCIDENT WHERE YOUR VIRTUE WAS IN DANGER, WASN'T THERE?
I'VE HEARD THERE'VE BEEN A LOT OF OTHER ATTEMPTS LIKE THAT, TOO.
ISN'T IT SCARY, BEING IN AN ALL-BOYS' SCHOOL!! ♡ ♡
あははははは
AHAHAHAHAHAHA
あわあわ
WHOA... WHOA...
FLAP
FLAP
FLAP
AN ALL-BOYS' SCHOOL ...
VIRTUE IN DANGER...

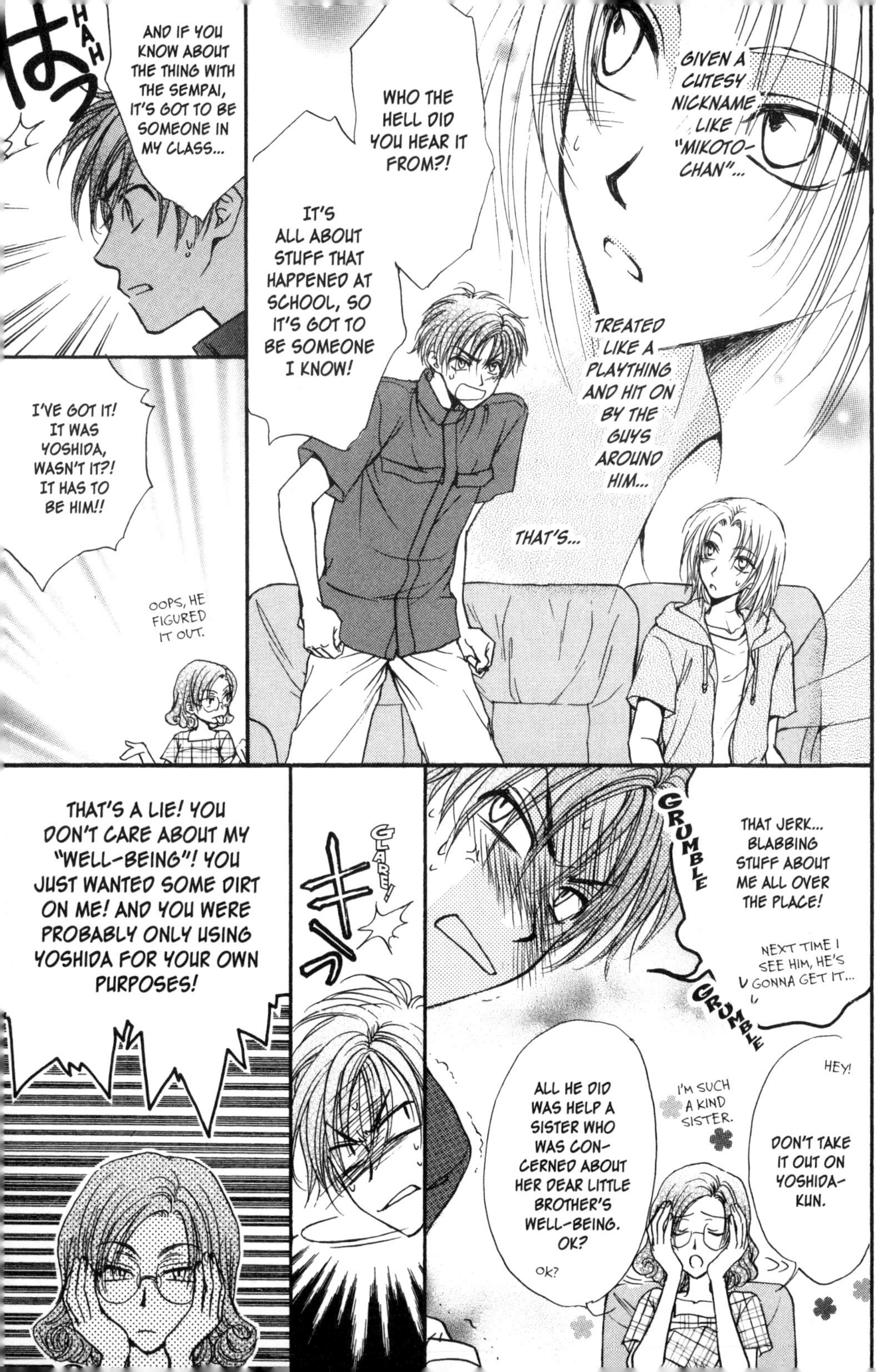

GIVEN A CUTESY NICKNAME LIKE "MIKOTO-CHAN"...
TREATED LIKE A PLAYTHING AND HIT ON BY THE GUYS AROUND HIM...
THAT'S...
WHO THE HELL DID YOU HEAR IT FROM?!
IT'S ALL ABOUT STUFF THAT HAPPENED AT SCHOOL, SO IT'S GOT TO BE SOMEONE I KNOW!
HAH
AND IF YOU KNOW ABOUT THE THING WITH THE SEMPAI, IT'S GOT TO BE SOMEONE IN MY CLASS...
I'VE GOT IT! IT WAS YOSHIDA, WASN'T IT?! IT HAS TO BE HIM!!
OOPS, HE FIGURED IT OUT.
GRUMBLE
THAT JERK... BLABBING STUFF ABOUT ME ALL OVER THE PLACE!
NEXT TIME I SEE HIM, HE'S GONNA GET IT...
GRUMBLE
HEY!
DON'T TAKE IT OUT ON YOSHIDA-KUN.
ALL HE DID WAS HELP A SISTER WHO WAS CONCERNED ABOUT HER DEAR LITTLE BROTHER'S WELL-BEING. OK?
I'M SUCH A KIND SISTER.
OK?
GLARE!
THAT'S A LIE! YOU DON'T CARE ABOUT MY "WELL-BEING"! YOU JUST WANTED SOME DIRT ON ME! AND YOU WERE PROBABLY ONLY USING YOSHIDA FOR YOUR OWN PURPOSES!

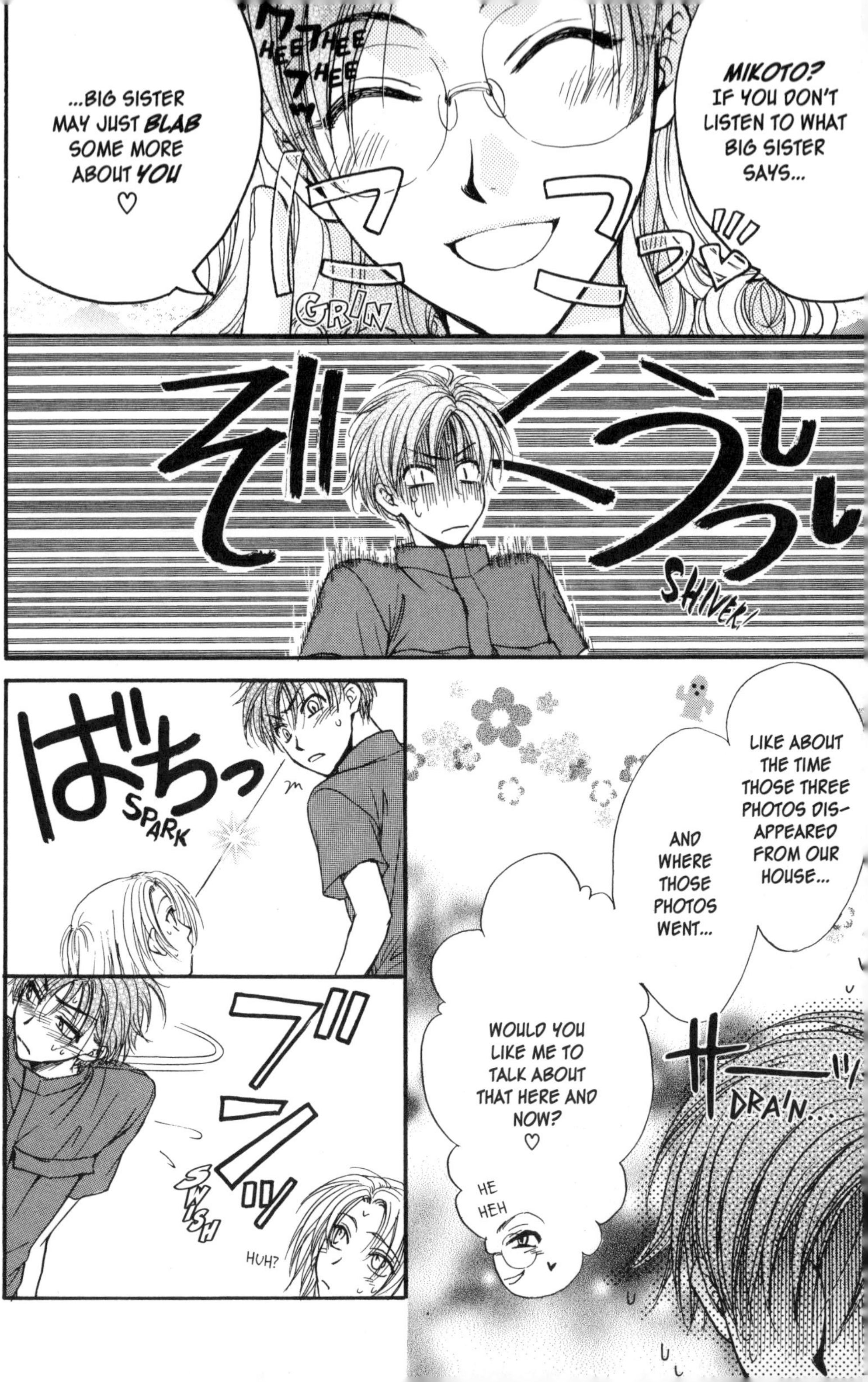
HEE HEE HEE
MIKOTO? IF YOU DON'T LISTEN TO WHAT BIG SISTER SAYS...
...BIG SISTER MAY JUST BLAB SOME MORE ABOUT YOU ♡
GRIN
SHIVER!
LIKE ABOUT THE TIME THOSE THREE PHOTOS DIS-APPEARED FROM OUR HOUSE...
AND WHERE THOSE PHOTOS WENT...
WOULD YOU LIKE ME TO TALK ABOUT THAT HERE AND NOW? ♡
HE HEH
DRAIN...
SPARK
SWISH
HUH?

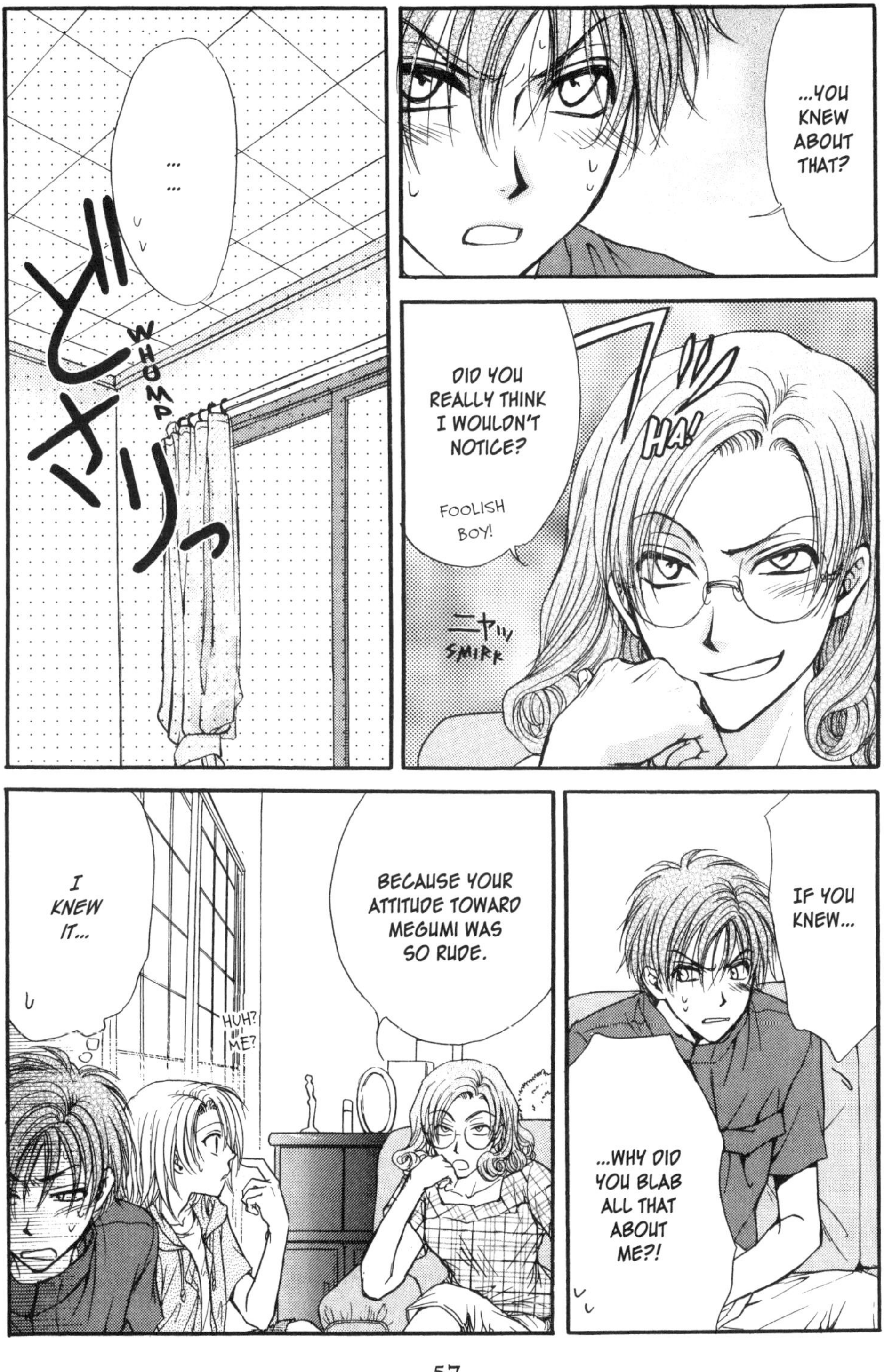
...YOU KNEW ABOUT THAT?
DID YOU REALLY THINK I WOULDN'T NOTICE?
FOOLISH BOY!
HA!
ニヤッ
SMIRK
...
...
どさりっ
WHUMP
IF YOU KNEW...
...WHY DID YOU BLAB ALL THAT ABOUT ME?!
BECAUSE YOUR ATTITUDE TOWARD MEGUMI WAS SO RUDE.
HUH? ME?
I KNEW IT...

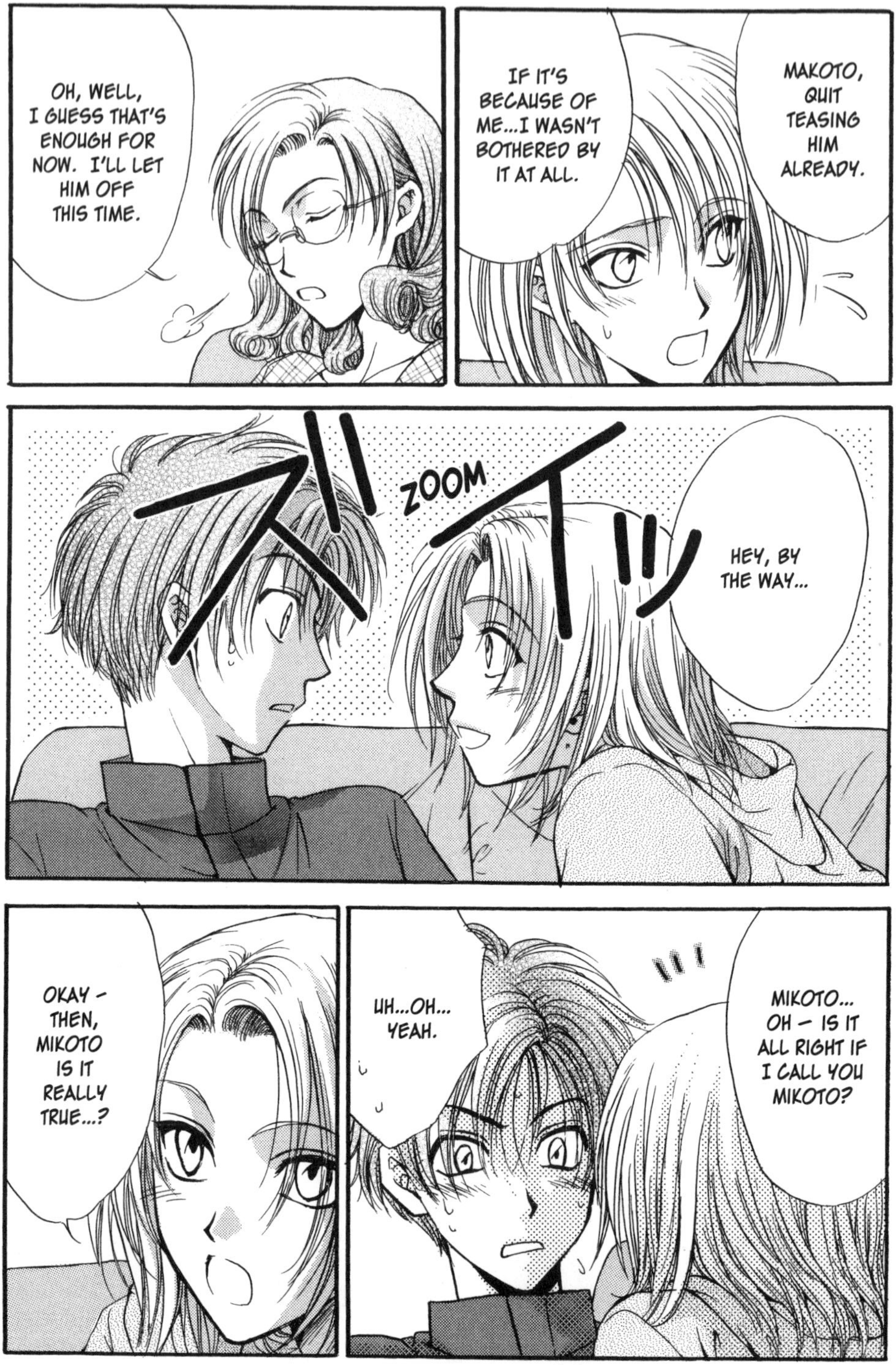
MAKOTO, QUIT TEASING HIM ALREADY.
IF IT'S BECAUSE OF ME...I WASN'T BOTHERED BY IT AT ALL.
OH, WELL, I GUESS THAT'S ENOUGH FOR NOW. I'LL LET HIM OFF THIS TIME.
ZOOM
HEY, BY THE WAY...
MIKOTO... OH — IS IT ALL RIGHT IF I CALL YOU MIKOTO?
UH...OH... YEAH.
OKAY — THEN, MIKOTO IS IT REALLY TRUE...?

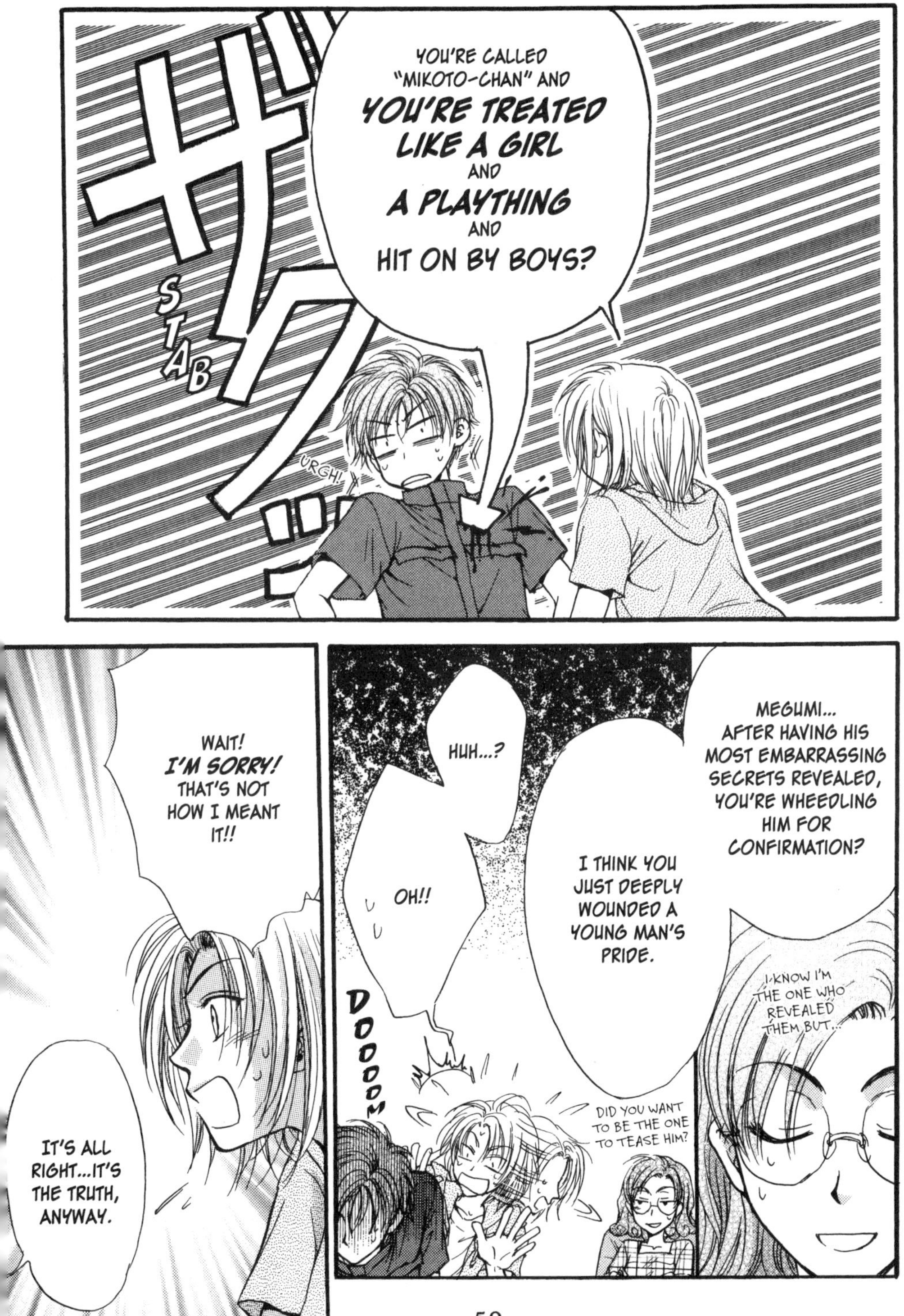

YOU'RE CALLED "MIKOTO-CHAN" AND YOU'RE TREATED LIKE A GIRL AND A PLAYTHING AND HIT ON BY BOYS?
STAB
URGH!
...
MEGUMI... AFTER HAVING HIS MOST EMBARRASSING SECRETS REVEALED, YOU'RE WHEEDLING HIM FOR CONFIRMATION?
I THINK YOU JUST DEEPLY WOUNDED A YOUNG MAN'S PRIDE.
HUH...?
OH!!
I KNOW I'M THE ONE WHO REVEALED THEM BUT...
DID YOU WANT TO BE THE ONE TO TEASE HIM?
DOOOOOM
WAIT! I'M SORRY! THAT'S NOT HOW I MEANT IT!!
IT'S ALL RIGHT...IT'S THE TRUTH, ANYWAY.

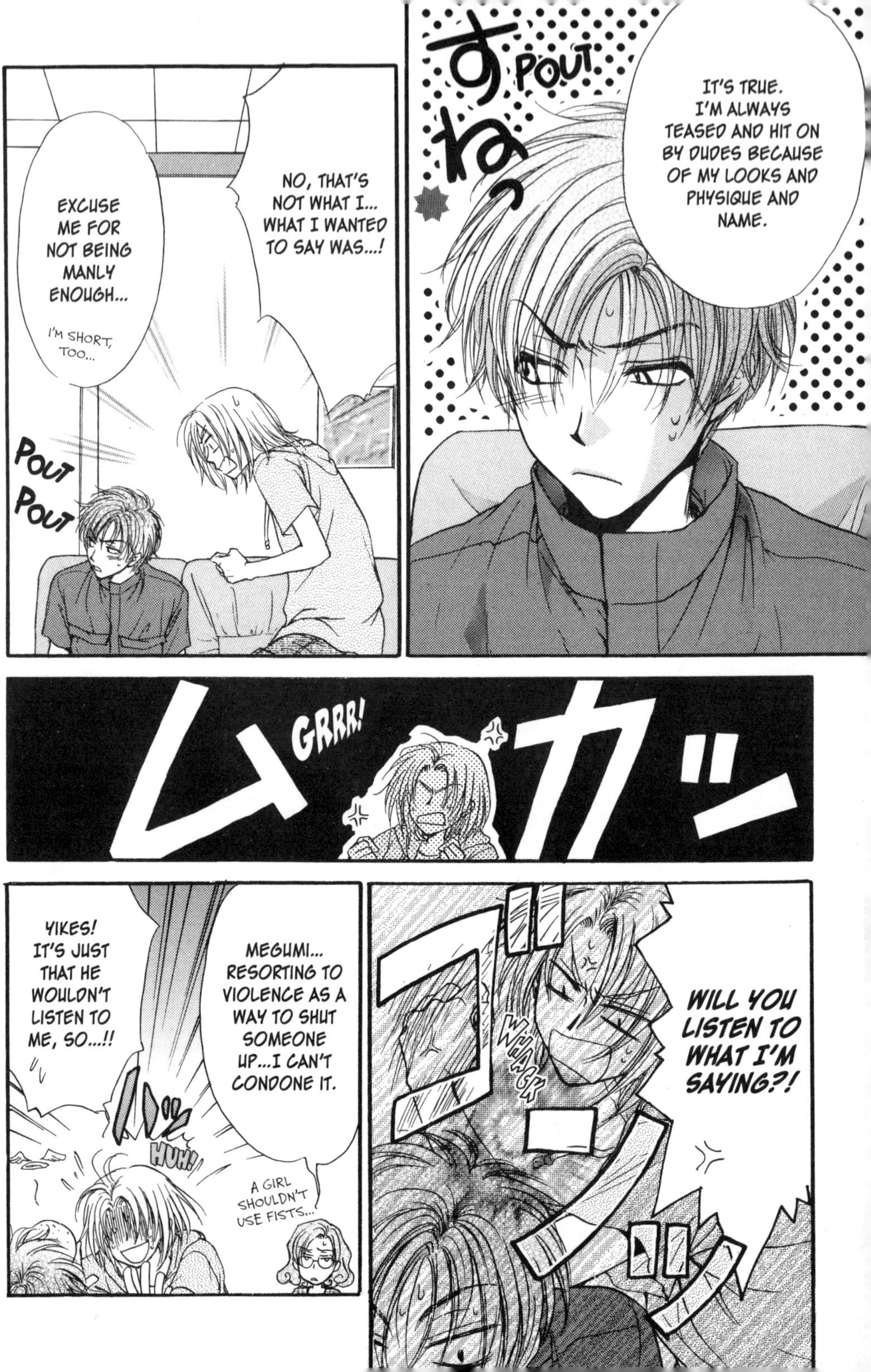
すねっ
POUT
IT'S TRUE. I'M ALWAYS TEASED AND HIT ON BY DUDES BECAUSE OF MY LOOKS AND PHYSIQUE AND NAME.
NO, THAT'S NOT WHAT I... WHAT I WANTED TO SAY WAS...!
EXCUSE ME FOR NOT BEING MANLY ENOUGH...
I'M SHORT, TOO...
POUT POUT
ムカッ
GRRR!
ゴッ
WHACK
WILL YOU LISTEN TO WHAT I'M SAYING?!
MEGUMI... RESORTING TO VIOLENCE AS A WAY TO SHUT SOMEONE UP...I CAN'T CONDONE IT.
A GIRL SHOULDN'T USE FISTS...
YIKES! IT'S JUST THAT HE WOULDN'T LISTEN TO ME, SO...!!
HUH!

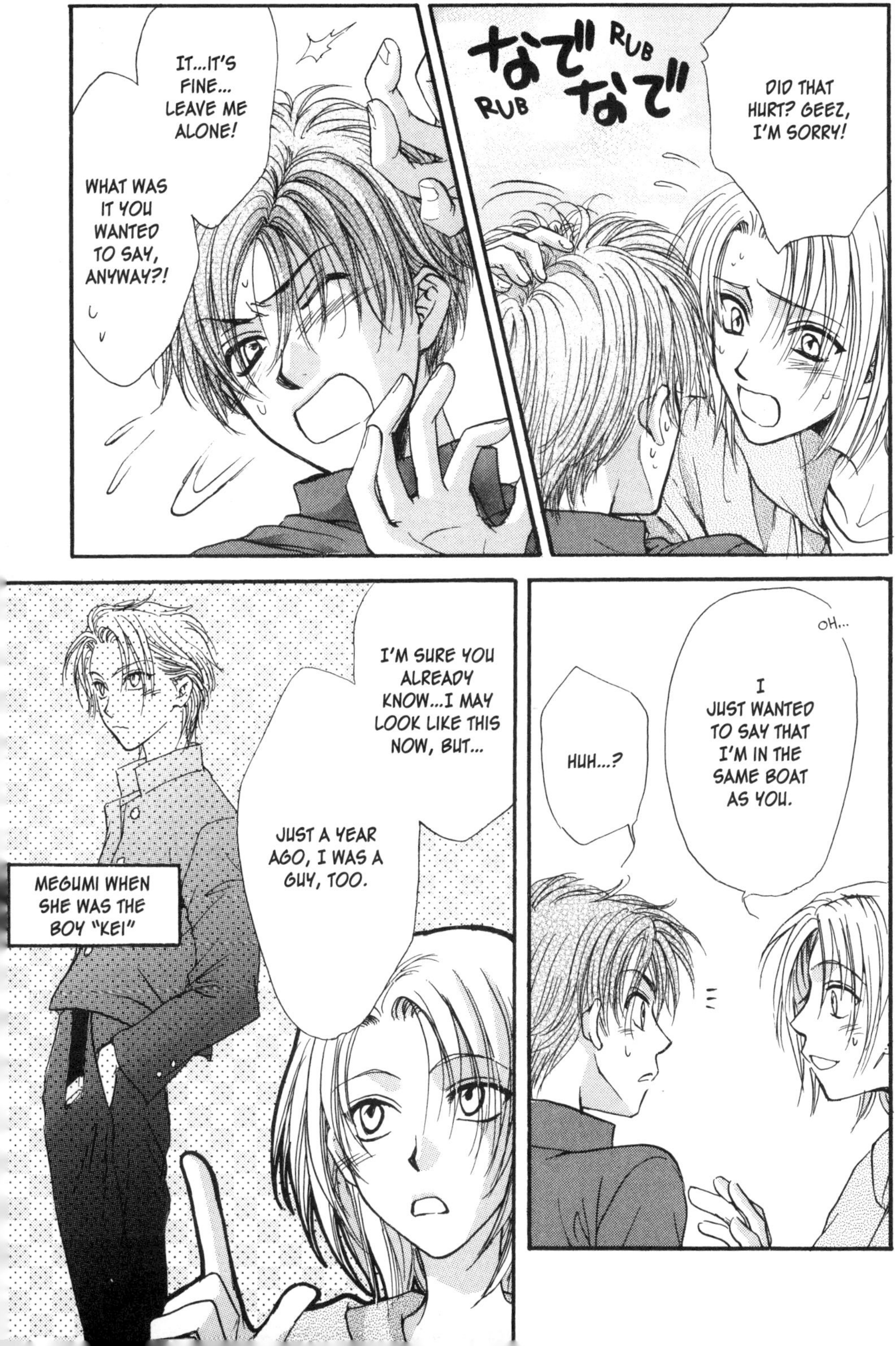
なでなで
RUB RUB
DID THAT HURT? GEEZ, I'M SORRY!
IT...IT'S FINE... LEAVE ME ALONE!
WHAT WAS IT YOU WANTED TO SAY, ANYWAY?!
OH...
I JUST WANTED TO SAY THAT I'M IN THE SAME BOAT AS YOU.
HUH...?
I'M SURE YOU ALREADY KNOW...I MAY LOOK LIKE THIS NOW, BUT...
JUST A YEAR AGO, I WAS A GUY, TOO.
MEGUMI WHEN SHE WAS THE BOY "KEI"

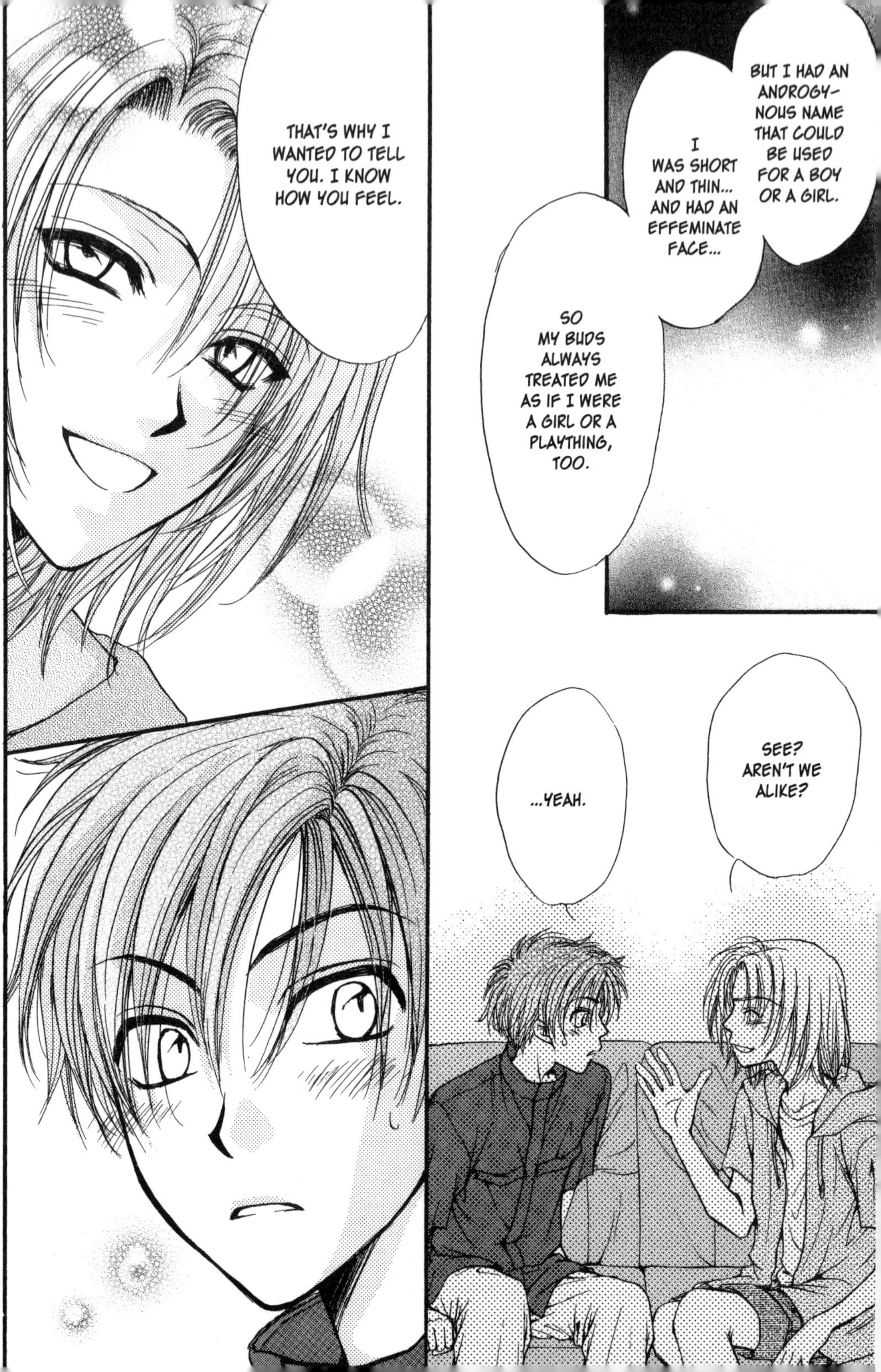
BUT I HAD AN ANDROGY-NOUS NAME THAT COULD BE USED FOR A BOY OR A GIRL.
I WAS SHORT AND THIN... AND HAD AN EFFEMINATE FACE...
SO MY BUDS ALWAYS TREATED ME AS IF I WERE A GIRL OR A PLAYTHING, TOO.
THAT'S WHY I WANTED TO TELL YOU. I KNOW HOW YOU FEEL.
SEE? AREN'T WE ALIKE?
...YEAH.

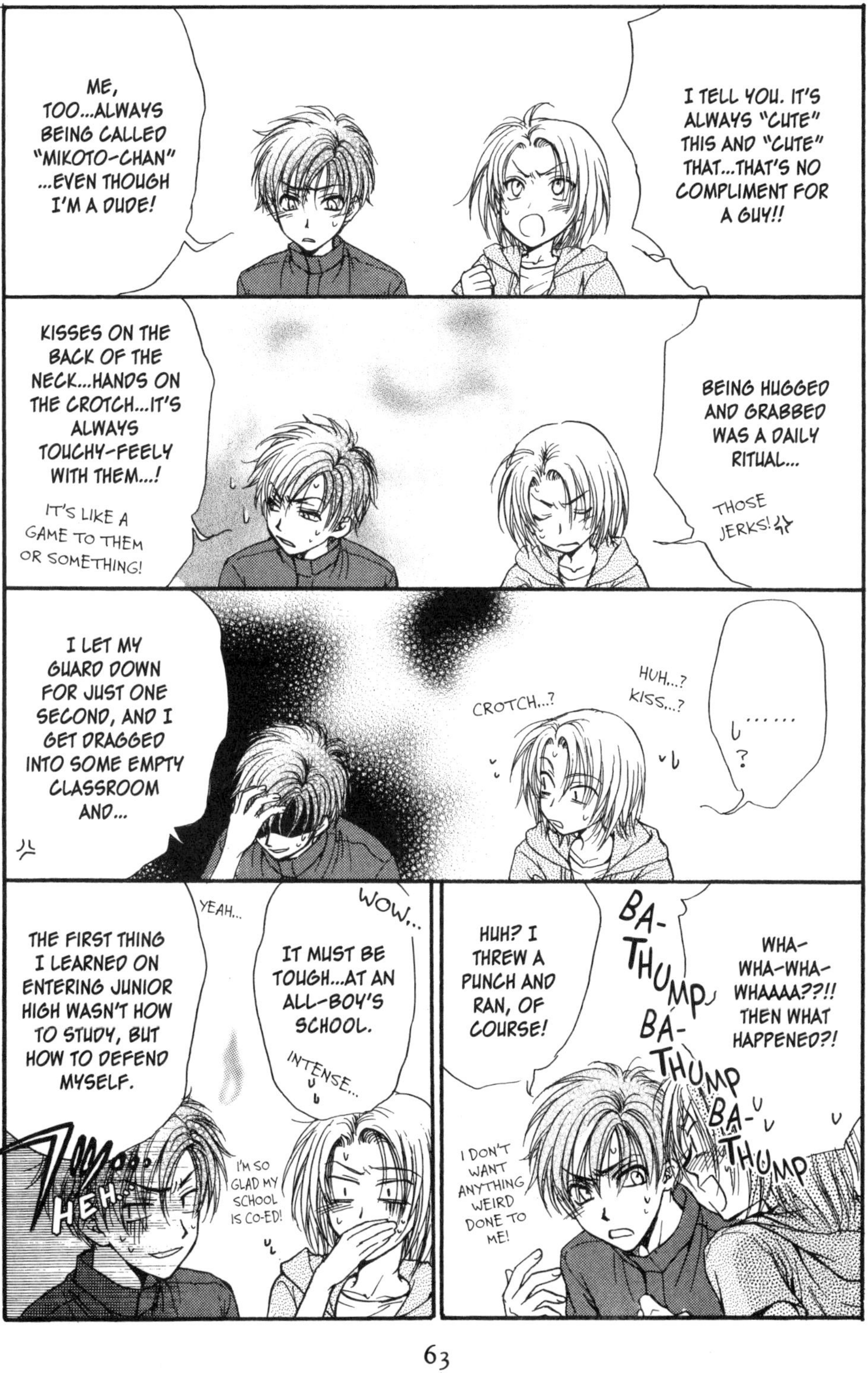

I TELL YOU. IT'S ALWAYS "CUTE" THIS AND "CUTE" THAT...THAT'S NO COMPLIMENT FOR A GUY!!
ME, TOO...ALWAYS BEING CALLED "MIKOTO-CHAN" ...EVEN THOUGH I'M A DUDE!
BEING HUGGED AND GRABBED WAS A DAILY RITUAL...
THOSE JERKS!
KISSES ON THE BACK OF THE NECK...HANDS ON THE CROTCH...IT'S ALWAYS TOUCHY-FEELY WITH THEM...!
IT'S LIKE A GAME TO THEM OR SOMETHING!
......?
HUH...? KISS...?
CROTCH...?
I LET MY GUARD DOWN FOR JUST ONE SECOND, AND I GET DRAGGED INTO SOME EMPTY CLASSROOM AND...
WHA-WHA-WHA-WHAAAA??!! THEN WHAT HAPPENED?!
BA-THUMP BA-THUMP BA-THUMP
HUH? I THREW A PUNCH AND RAN, OF COURSE!
I DON'T WANT ANYTHING WEIRD DONE TO ME!
WOW...
IT MUST BE TOUGH...AT AN ALL-BOY'S SCHOOL.
INTENSE...
YEAH...
THE FIRST THING I LEARNED ON ENTERING JUNIOR HIGH WASN'T HOW TO STUDY, BUT HOW TO DEFEND MYSELF.
HEH...
I'M SO GLAD MY SCHOOL IS CO-ED!

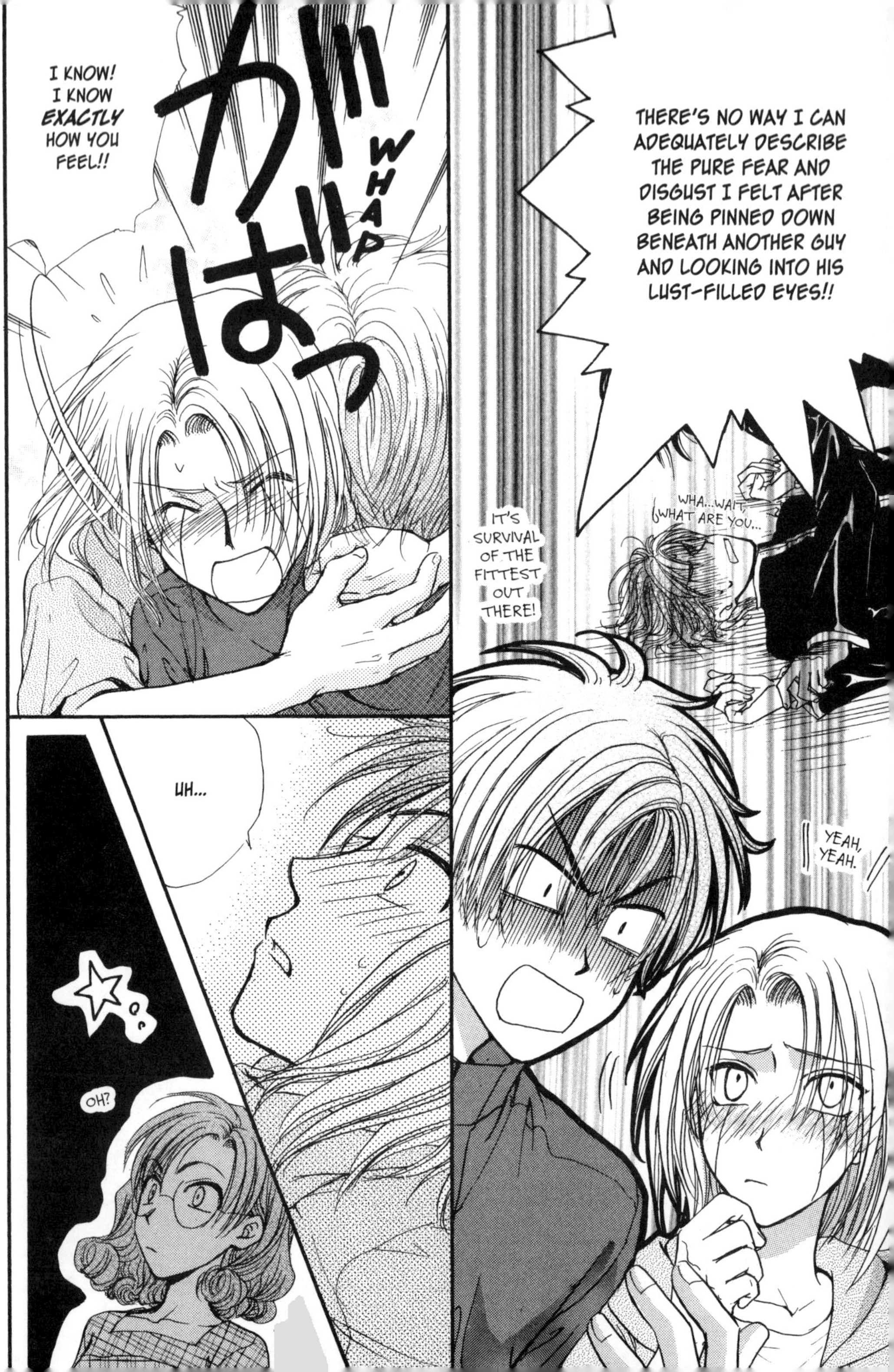
THERE'S NO WAY I CAN ADEQUATELY DESCRIBE THE PURE FEAR AND DISGUST I FELT AFTER BEING PINNED DOWN BENEATH ANOTHER GUY AND LOOKING INTO HIS LUST-FILLED EYES!!
WHA...WAIT, WHAT ARE YOU...
IT'S SURVIVAL OF THE FITTEST OUT THERE!
YEAH, YEAH.
I KNOW! I KNOW *EXACTLY* HOW YOU FEEL!!
がばっ
WHAP
UH...
OH?

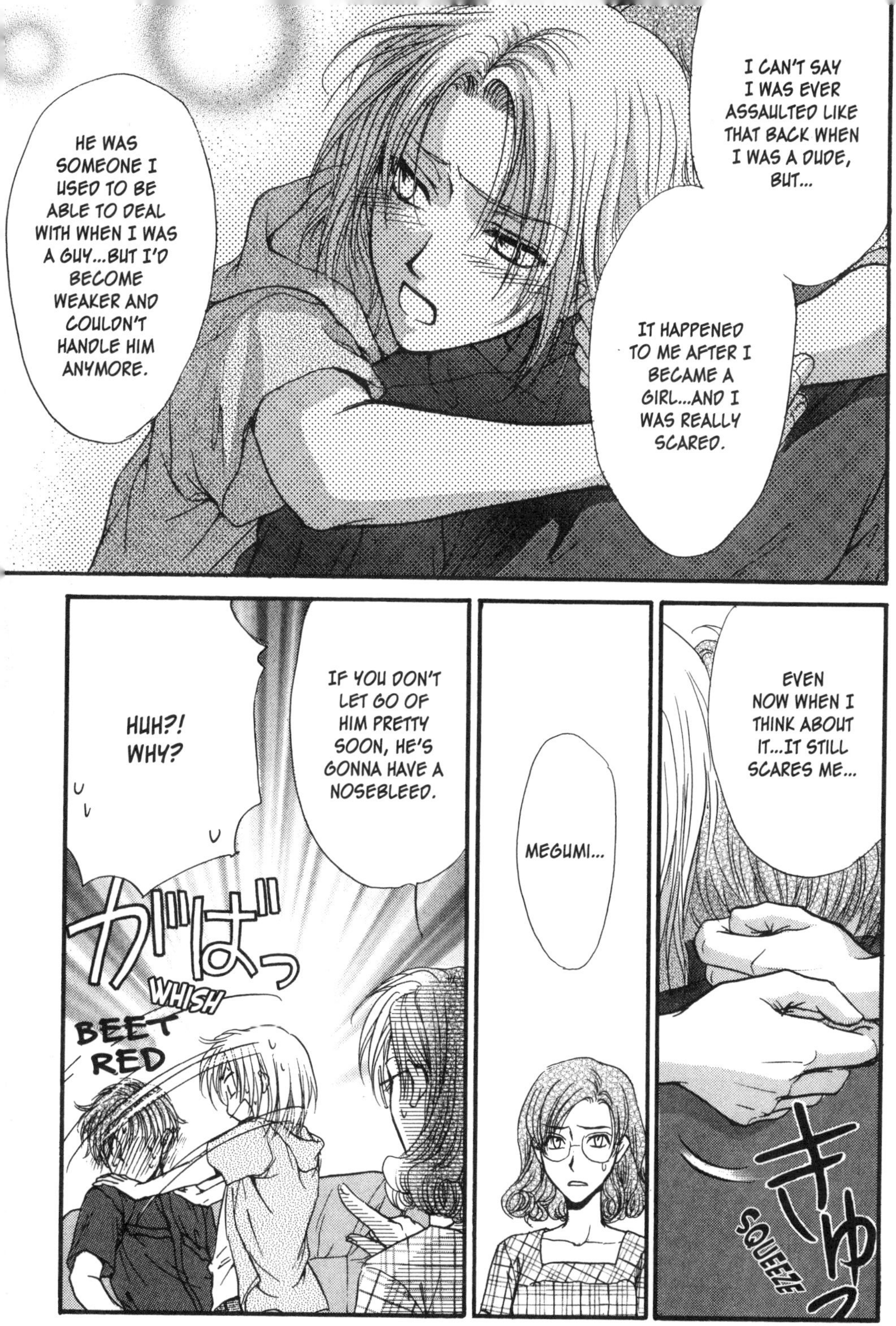
I CAN'T SAY I WAS EVER ASSAULTED LIKE THAT BACK WHEN I WAS A DUDE, BUT...
IT HAPPENED TO ME AFTER I BECAME A GIRL...AND I WAS REALLY SCARED.
HE WAS SOMEONE I USED TO BE ABLE TO DEAL WITH WHEN I WAS A GUY...BUT I'D BECOME WEAKER AND COULDN'T HANDLE HIM ANYMORE.
EVEN NOW WHEN I THINK ABOUT IT...IT STILL SCARES ME...
きゅっ
SQUEEZE
MEGUMI...
IF YOU DON'T LET GO OF HIM PRETTY SOON, HE'S GONNA HAVE A NOSEBLEED.
HUH?! WHY?
がばっ
WHISH
BEET RED

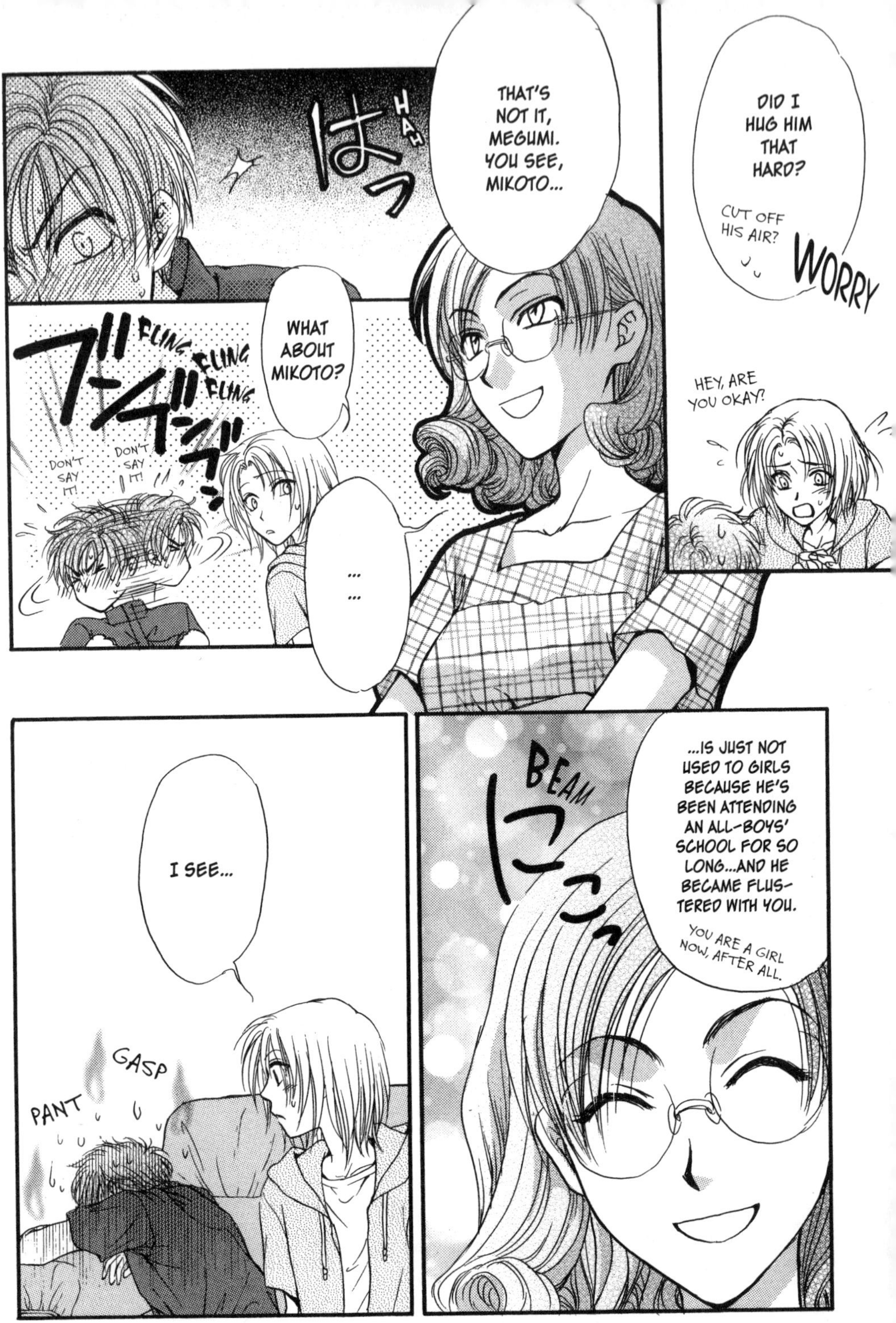
DID I HUG HIM THAT HARD?
CUT OFF HIS AIR?
WORRY
HEY, ARE YOU OKAY?
THAT'S NOT IT, MEGUMI. YOU SEE, MIKOTO...
HAH
WHAT ABOUT MIKOTO?
FLING FLING FLING
DON'T SAY IT!
DON'T SAY IT!
... ...
...IS JUST NOT USED TO GIRLS BECAUSE HE'S BEEN ATTENDING AN ALL-BOYS' SCHOOL FOR SO LONG...AND HE BECAME FLUSTERED WITH YOU.
YOU ARE A GIRL NOW, AFTER ALL.
BEAM
I SEE...
GASP
PANT

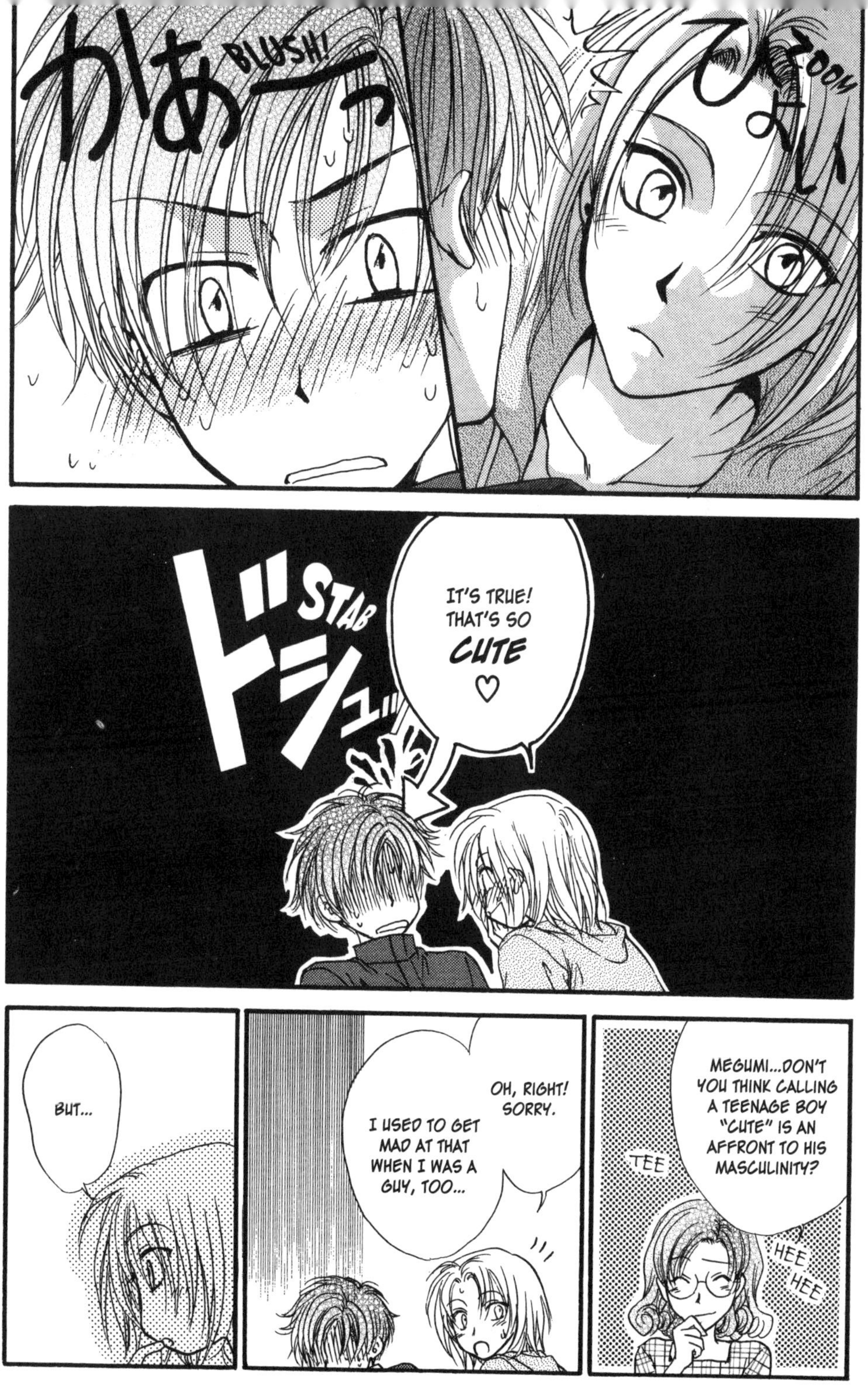
ZOOM
かぁーっ
BLUSH!
IT'S TRUE! THAT'S SO CUTE ♡
STAB
MEGUMI...DON'T YOU THINK CALLING A TEENAGE BOY "CUTE" IS AN AFFRONT TO HIS MASCULINITY?
TEE
HEE, HEE
OH, RIGHT! SORRY.
I USED TO GET MAD AT THAT WHEN I WAS A GUY, TOO...
BUT...

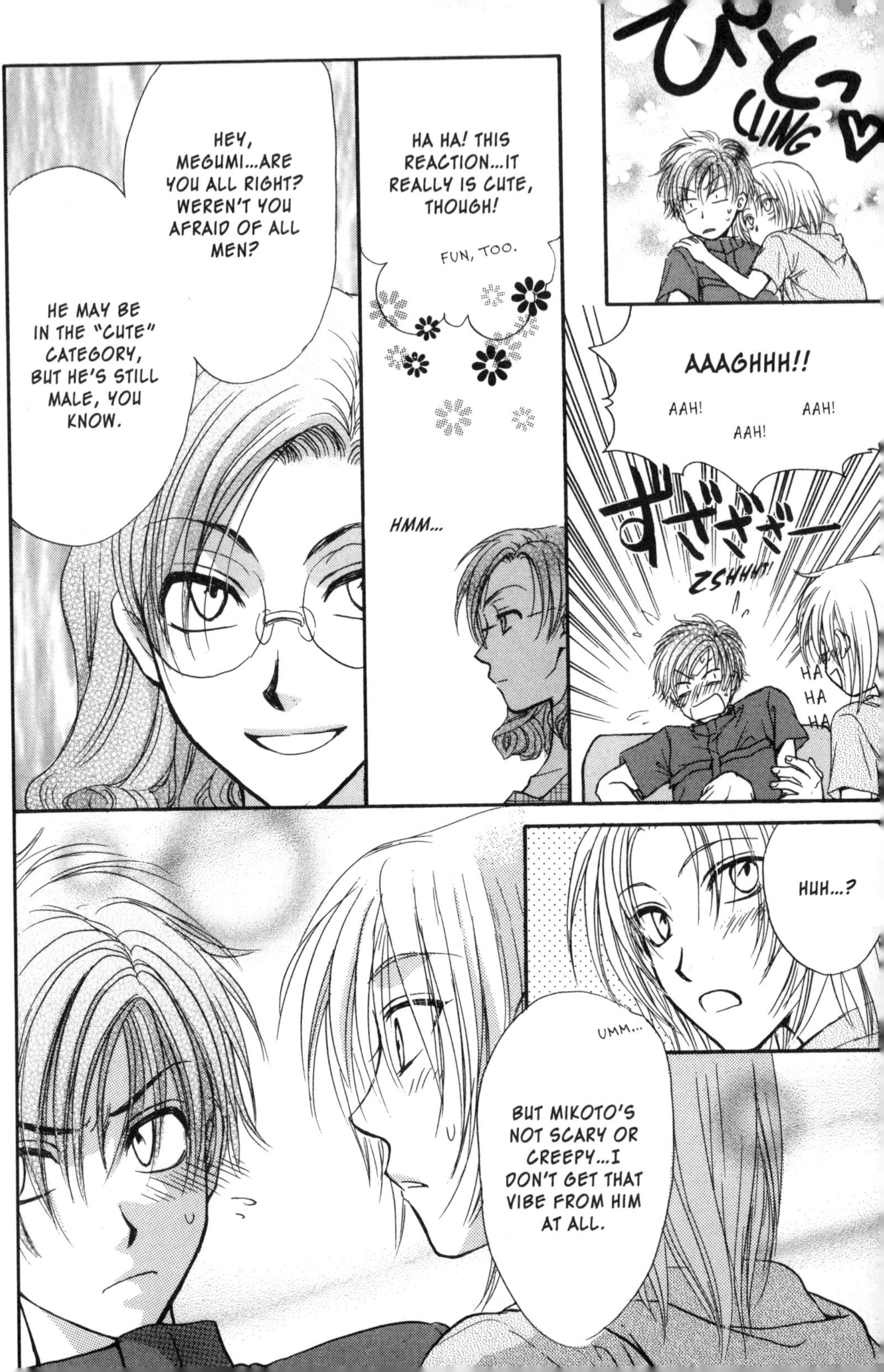
ぴとっ
CLING
AAAGHHH!!
AAH!
AAH!
AAH!
ずざざー
ZSHHH!
HA HA HA
HA HA! THIS REACTION...IT REALLY IS CUTE, THOUGH!
FUN, TOO.
HMM...
HEY, MEGUMI...ARE YOU ALL RIGHT? WEREN'T YOU AFRAID OF ALL MEN?
HE MAY BE IN THE "CUTE" CATEGORY, BUT HE'S STILL MALE, YOU KNOW.
HUH...?
UMM...
BUT MIKOTO'S NOT SCARY OR CREEPY...I DON'T GET THAT VIBE FROM HIM AT ALL.

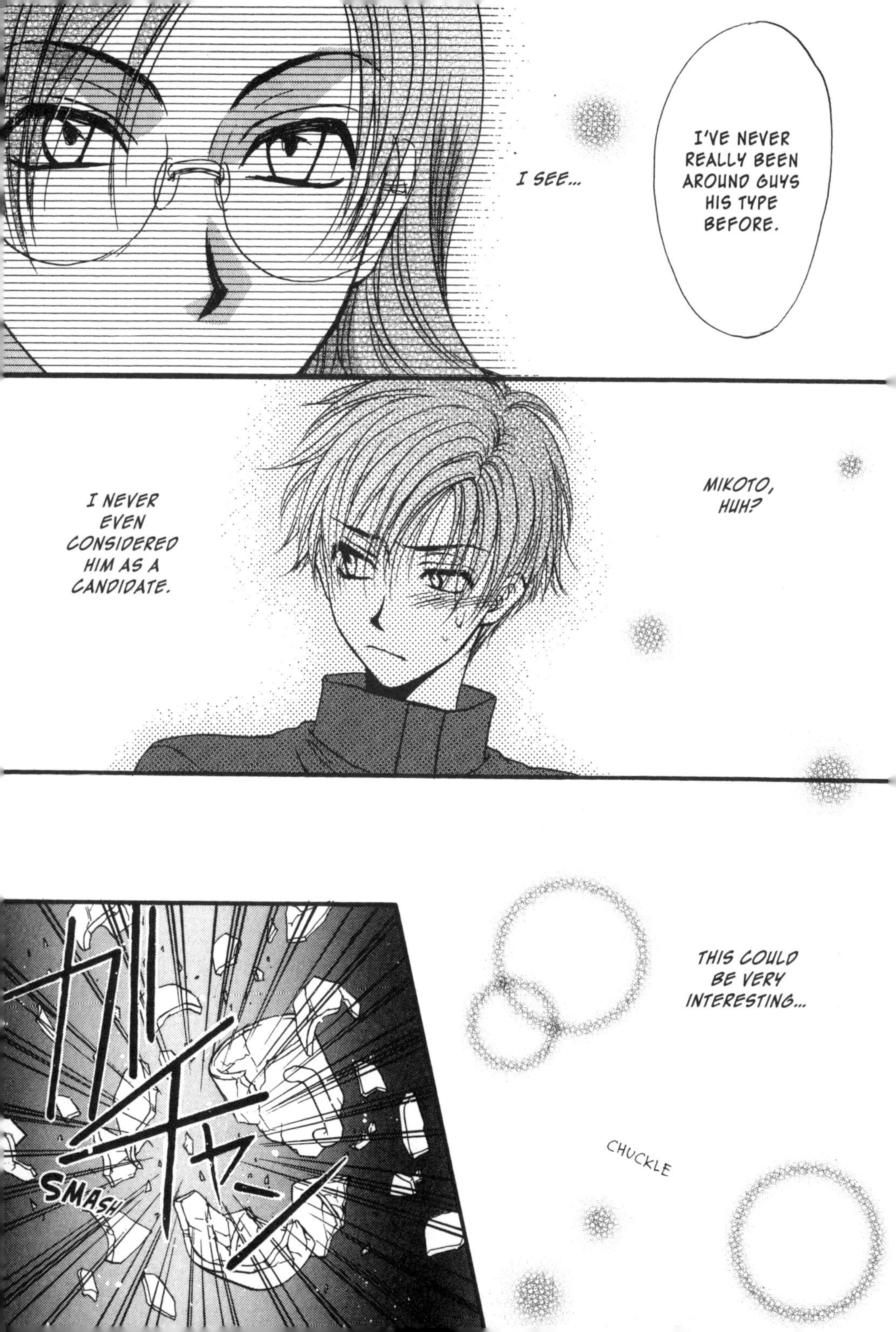
I'VE NEVER REALLY BEEN AROUND GUYS HIS TYPE BEFORE.
I SEE...
MIKOTO, HUH?
I NEVER EVEN CONSIDERED HIM AS A CANDIDATE.
THIS COULD BE VERY INTERESTING...
CHUCKLE
SMASH

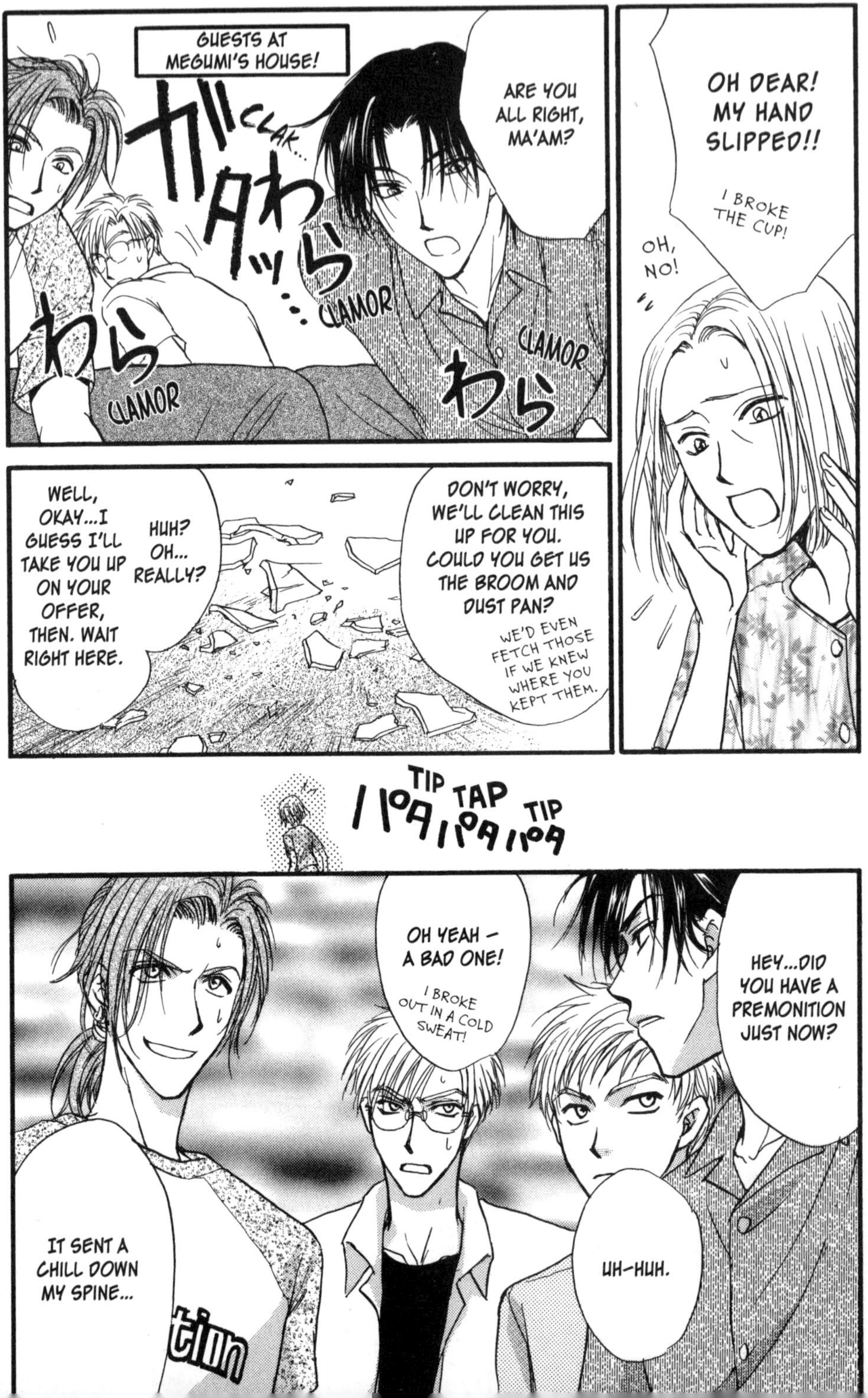

OH DEAR! MY HAND SLIPPED!!
I BROKE THE CUP!
OH, NO!
GUESTS AT MEGUMI'S HOUSE!
ARE YOU ALL RIGHT, MA'AM?
ガタッ
CLAK...
わらわら
CLAMOR
CLAMOR
わら
CLAMOR
わら
CLAMOR
DON'T WORRY, WE'LL CLEAN THIS UP FOR YOU. COULD YOU GET US THE BROOM AND DUST PAN?
WE'D EVEN FETCH THOSE IF WE KNEW WHERE YOU KEPT THEM.
HUH? OH... REALLY?
WELL, OKAY...I GUESS I'LL TAKE YOU UP ON YOUR OFFER, THEN. WAIT RIGHT HERE.
パタパタパタ
TIP TAP TIP
HEY...DID YOU HAVE A PREMONITION JUST NOW?
UH-HUH.
OH YEAH – A BAD ONE!
I BROKE OUT IN A COLD SWEAT!
IT SENT A CHILL DOWN MY SPINE...
tion

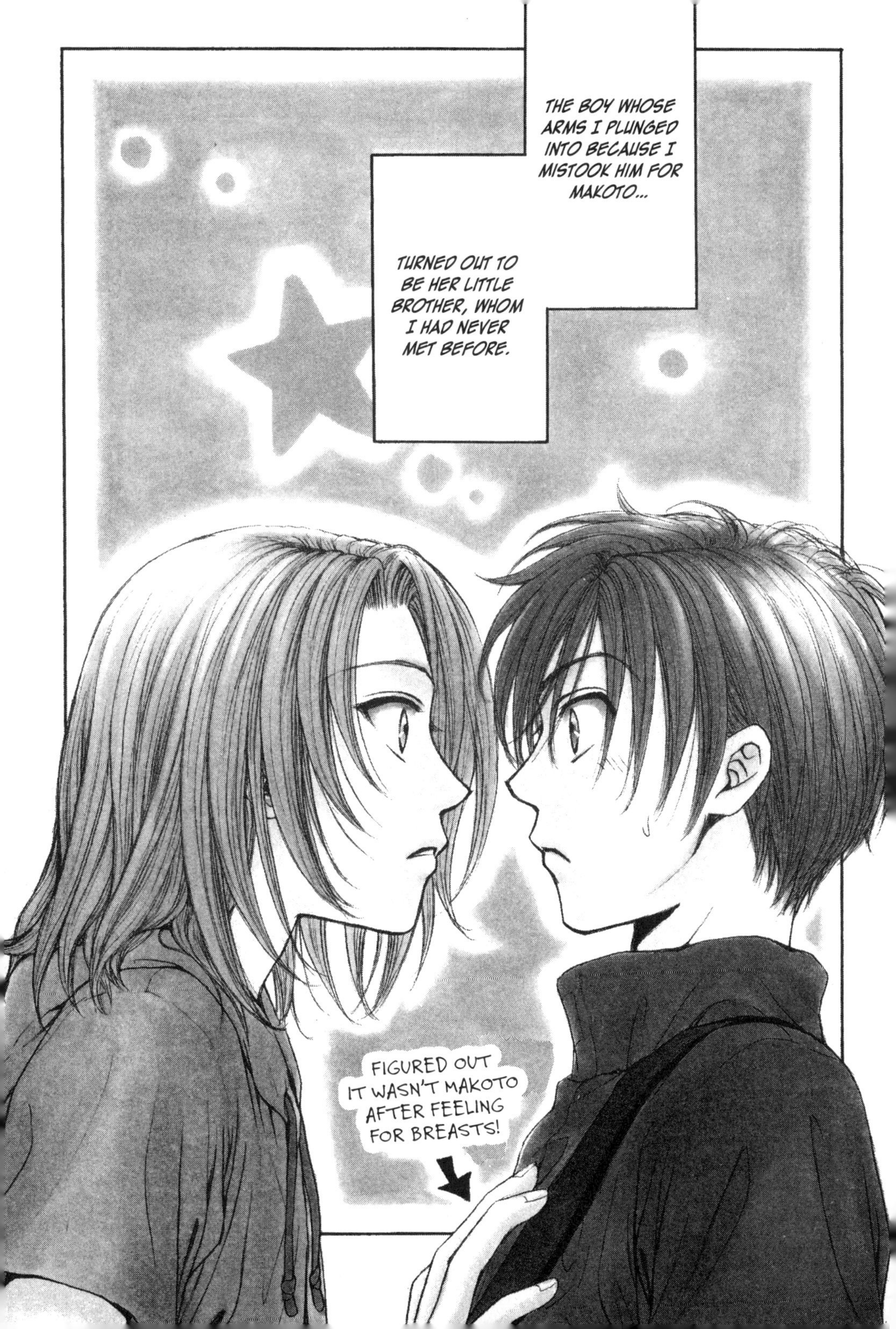
THE BOY WHOSE ARMS I PLUNGED INTO BECAUSE I MISTOOK HIM FOR MAKOTO...
TURNED OUT TO BE HER LITTLE BROTHER, WHOM I HAD NEVER MET BEFORE.
FIGURED OUT IT WASN'T MAKOTO AFTER FEELING FOR BREASTS!

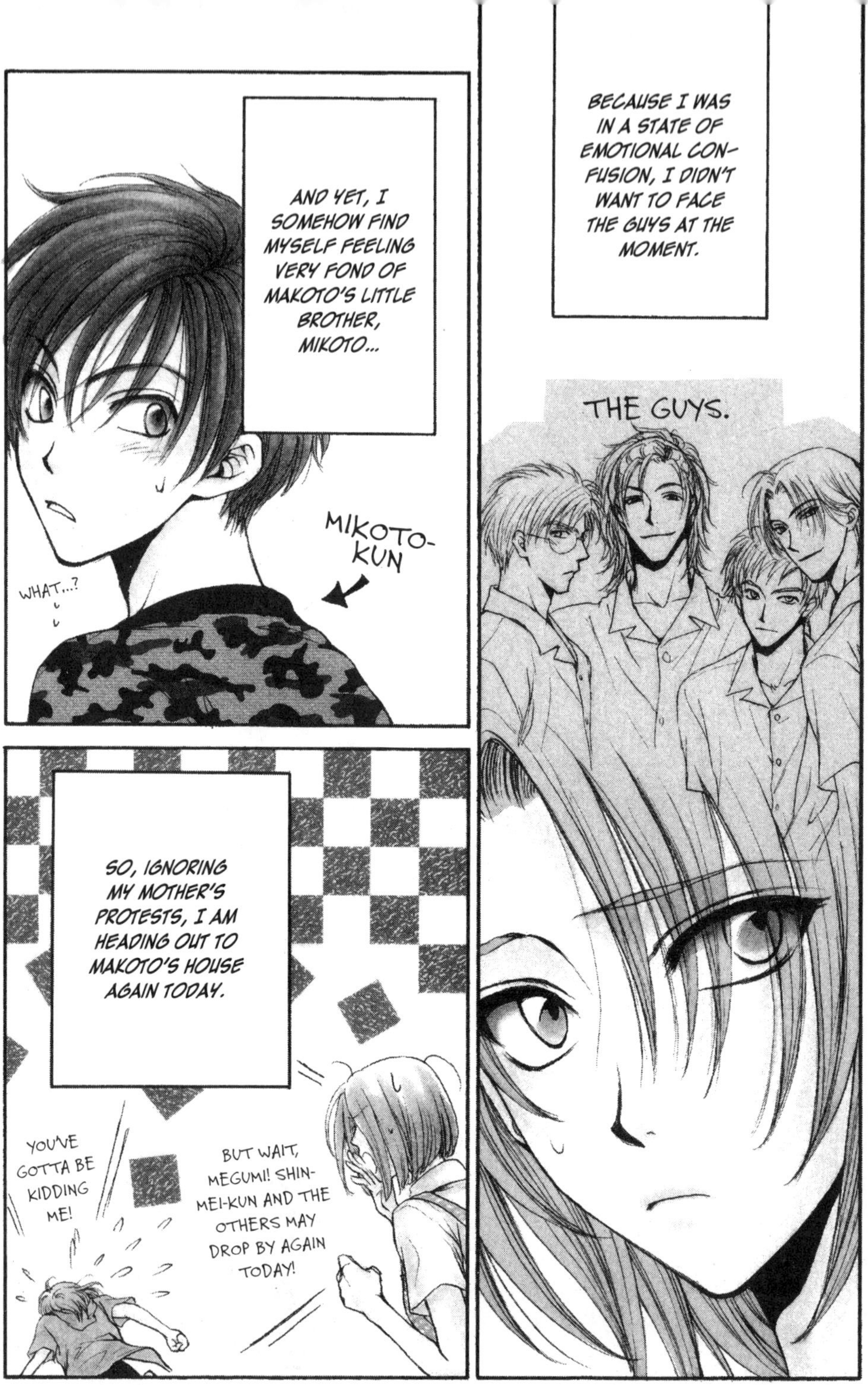
BECAUSE I WAS IN A STATE OF EMOTIONAL CON-FUSION, I DIDN'T WANT TO FACE THE GUYS AT THE MOMENT.
THE GUYS.
AND YET, I SOMEHOW FIND MYSELF FEELING VERY FOND OF MAKOTO'S LITTLE BROTHER, MIKOTO...
MIKOTO-KUN
WHAT...?
SO, IGNORING MY MOTHER'S PROTESTS, I AM HEADING OUT TO MAKOTO'S HOUSE AGAIN TODAY.
BUT WAIT, MEGUMI! SHIN-MEI-KUN AND THE OTHERS MAY DROP BY AGAIN TODAY!
YOU'VE GOTTA BE KIDDING ME!

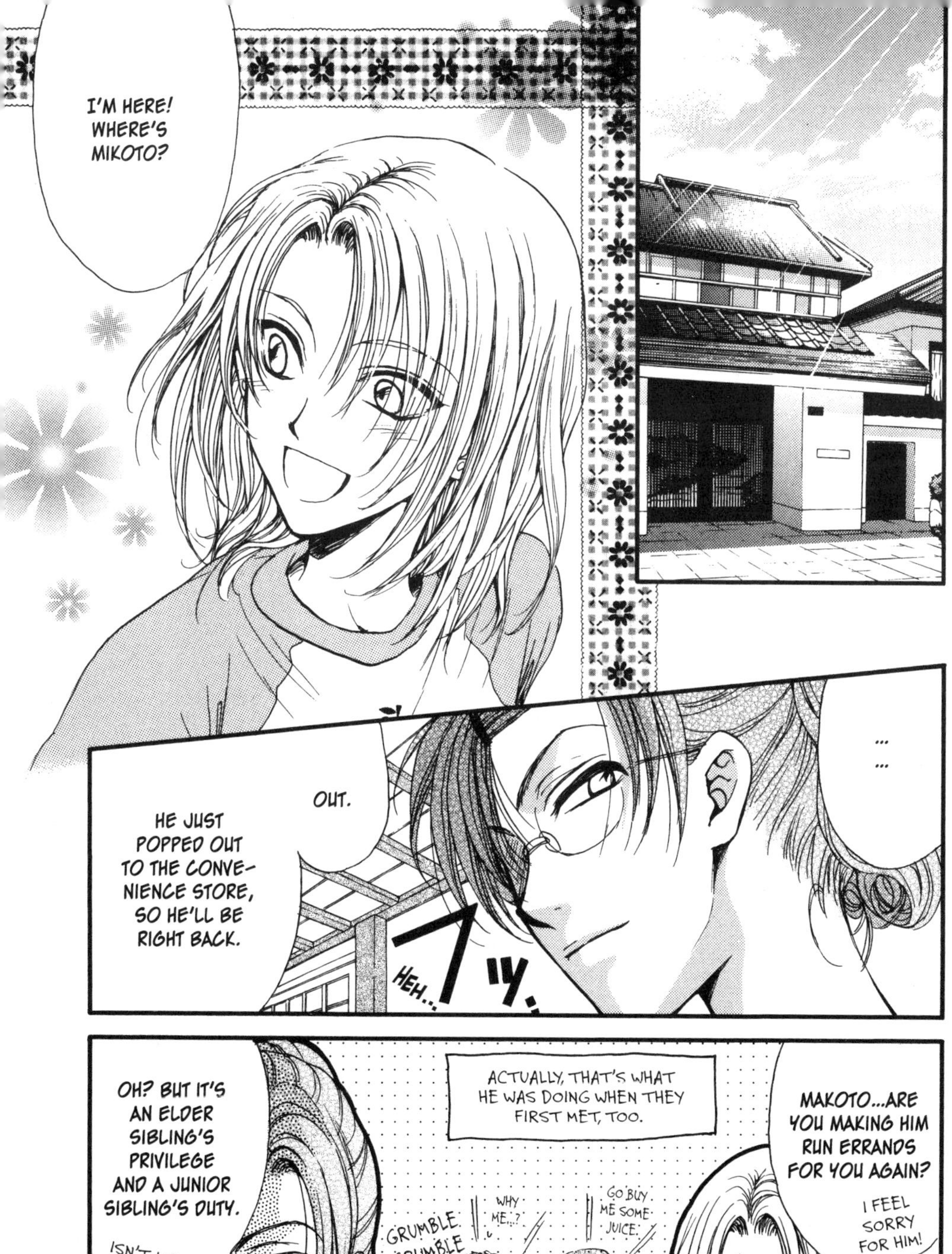
I'M HERE! WHERE'S MIKOTO?
...
...
OUT.
HE JUST POPPED OUT TO THE CONVE-NIENCE STORE, SO HE'LL BE RIGHT BACK.
HEH...
MAKOTO...ARE YOU MAKING HIM RUN ERRANDS FOR YOU AGAIN?
I FEEL SORRY FOR HIM!
ACTUALLY, THAT'S WHAT HE WAS DOING WHEN THEY FIRST MET, TOO.
GO BUY ME SOME JUICE.
WHY ME..?
GRUMBLE GRUMBLE
OH? BUT IT'S AN ELDER SIBLING'S PRIVILEGE AND A JUNIOR SIBLING'S DUTY.
ISN'T IT?

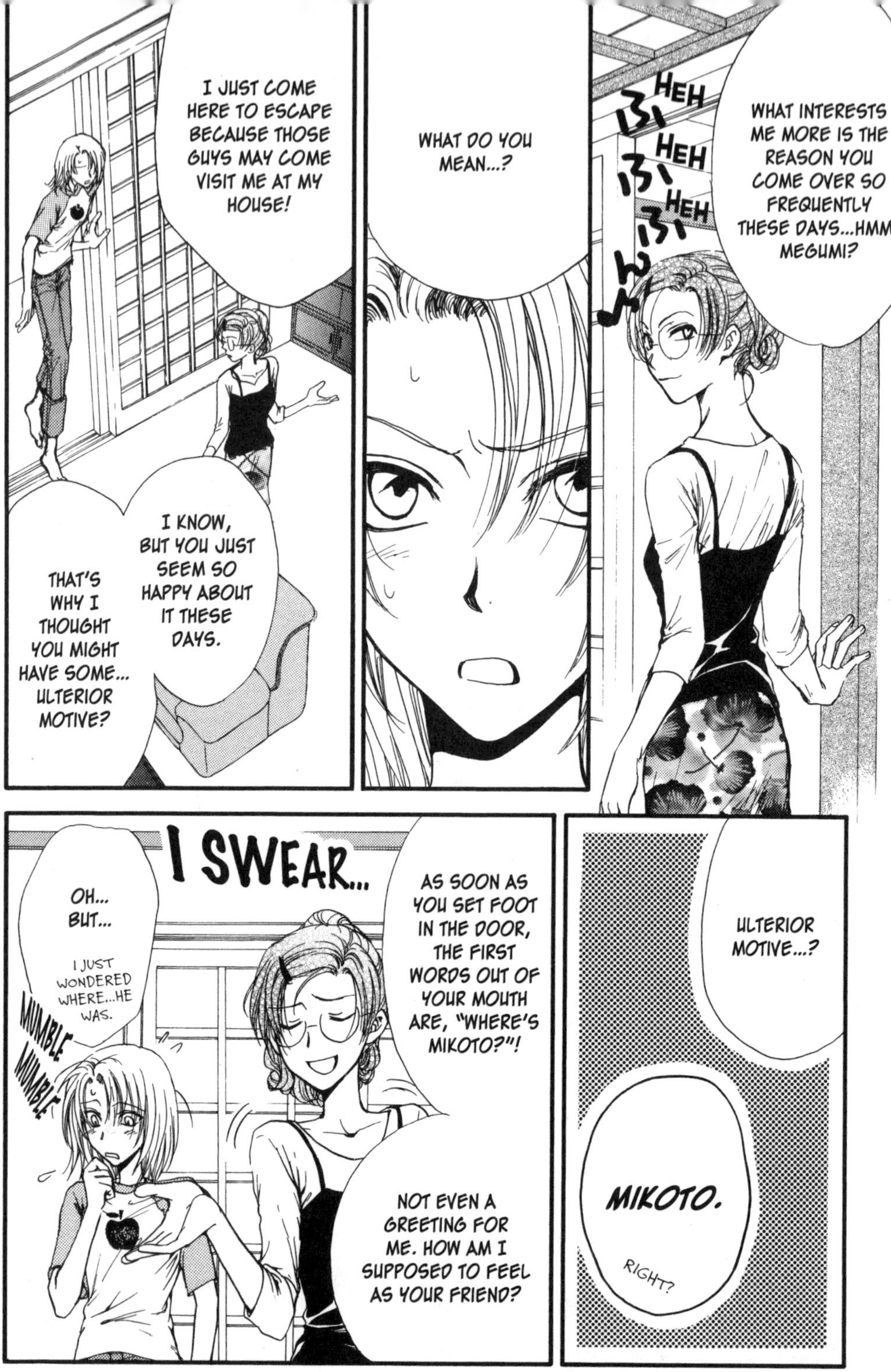
HEH HEH HEH
WHAT INTERESTS ME MORE IS THE REASON YOU COME OVER SO FREQUENTLY THESE DAYS...HMM, MEGUMI?
WHAT DO YOU MEAN...?
I JUST COME HERE TO ESCAPE BECAUSE THOSE GUYS MAY COME VISIT ME AT MY HOUSE!
I KNOW, BUT YOU JUST SEEM SO HAPPY ABOUT IT THESE DAYS.
THAT'S WHY I THOUGHT YOU MIGHT HAVE SOME... ULTERIOR MOTIVE?
ULTERIOR MOTIVE...?
MIKOTO.
RIGHT?
I SWEAR...
AS SOON AS YOU SET FOOT IN THE DOOR, THE FIRST WORDS OUT OF YOUR MOUTH ARE, "WHERE'S MIKOTO?"!
NOT EVEN A GREETING FOR ME. HOW AM I SUPPOSED TO FEEL AS YOUR FRIEND?
OH... BUT...
I JUST WONDERED WHERE...HE WAS.
MUMBLE MUMBLE

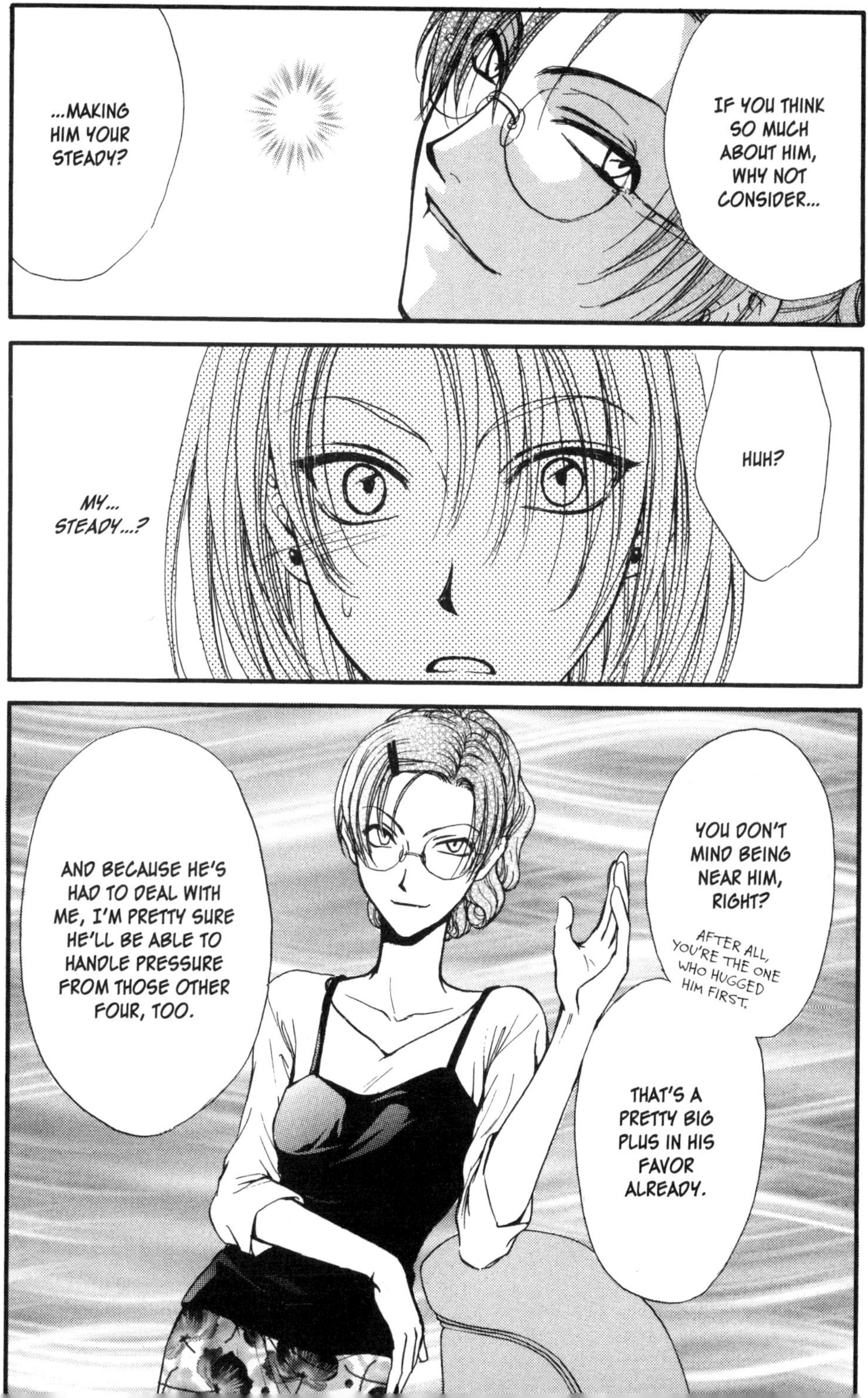
IF YOU THINK SO MUCH ABOUT HIM, WHY NOT CONSIDER...
...MAKING HIM YOUR STEADY?
HUH?
MY... STEADY...?
YOU DON'T MIND BEING NEAR HIM, RIGHT?
AFTER ALL, YOU'RE THE ONE WHO HUGGED HIM FIRST.
THAT'S A PRETTY BIG PLUS IN HIS FAVOR ALREADY.
AND BECAUSE HE'S HAD TO DEAL WITH ME, I'M PRETTY SURE HE'LL BE ABLE TO HANDLE PRESSURE FROM THOSE OTHER FOUR, TOO.

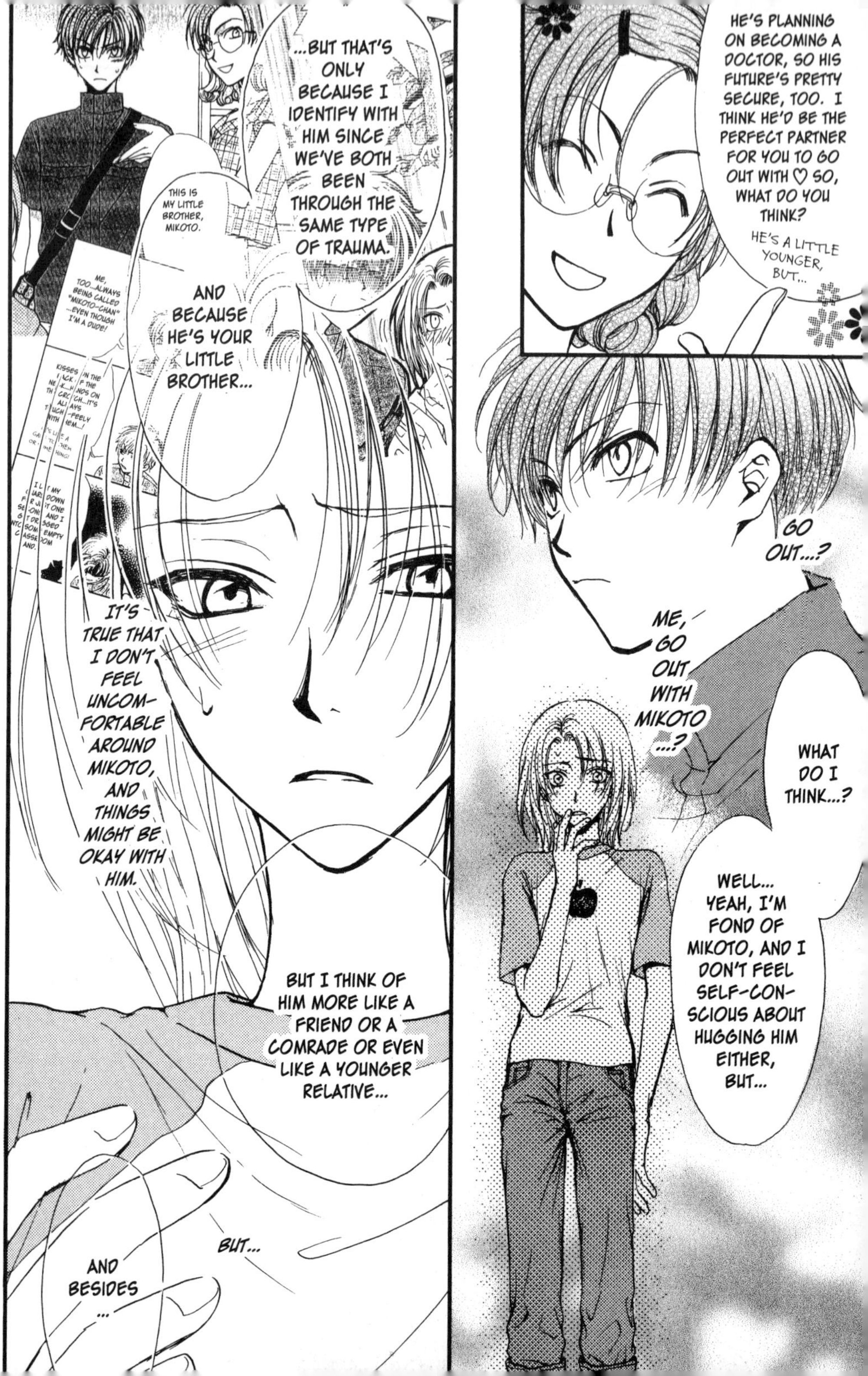
HE'S PLANNING ON BECOMING A DOCTOR, SO HIS FUTURE'S PRETTY SECURE, TOO. I THINK HE'D BE THE PERFECT PARTNER FOR YOU TO GO OUT WITH ♡ SO, WHAT DO YOU THINK?
HE'S A LITTLE YOUNGER, BUT...
GO OUT...?
ME, GO OUT WITH MIKOTO...?
WHAT DO I THINK...?
WELL... YEAH, I'M FOND OF MIKOTO, AND I DON'T FEEL SELF-CON-SCIOUS ABOUT HUGGING HIM EITHER, BUT...
...BUT THAT'S ONLY BECAUSE I IDENTIFY WITH HIM SINCE WE'VE BOTH BEEN THROUGH THE SAME TYPE OF TRAUMA.
THIS IS MY LITTLE BROTHER, MIKOTO.
ME, TOO...ALWAYS BEING CALLED "MIKOTO-CHAN" ...EVEN THOUGH I'M A DUDE!
AND BECAUSE HE'S YOUR LITTLE BROTHER...
IT'S TRUE THAT I DON'T FEEL UNCOM-FORTABLE AROUND MIKOTO, AND THINGS MIGHT BE OKAY WITH HIM.
BUT I THINK OF HIM MORE LIKE A FRIEND OR A COMRADE OR EVEN LIKE A YOUNGER RELATIVE...
BUT...
AND BESIDES ...

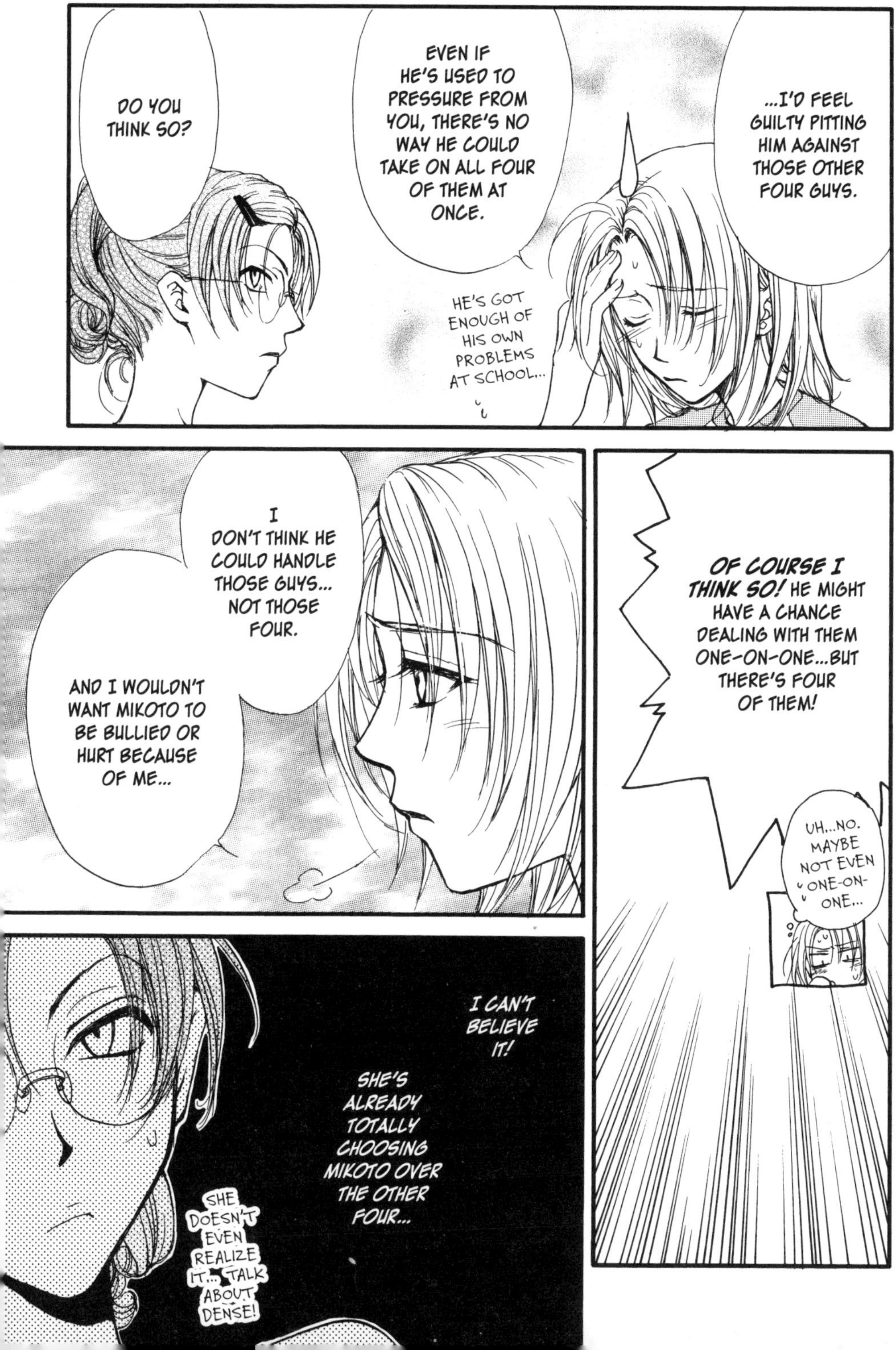
...I'D FEEL GUILTY PITTING HIM AGAINST THOSE OTHER FOUR GUYS.
EVEN IF HE'S USED TO PRESSURE FROM YOU, THERE'S NO WAY HE COULD TAKE ON ALL FOUR OF THEM AT ONCE.
HE'S GOT ENOUGH OF HIS OWN PROBLEMS AT SCHOOL...
DO YOU THINK SO?
OF COURSE I THINK SO! HE MIGHT HAVE A CHANCE DEALING WITH THEM ONE-ON-ONE...BUT THERE'S FOUR OF THEM!
UH...NO. MAYBE NOT EVEN ONE-ON-ONE...
I DON'T THINK HE COULD HANDLE THOSE GUYS... NOT THOSE FOUR.
AND I WOULDN'T WANT MIKOTO TO BE BULLIED OR HURT BECAUSE OF ME...
I CAN'T BELIEVE IT!
SHE'S ALREADY TOTALLY CHOOSING MIKOTO OVER THE OTHER FOUR...
SHE DOESN'T EVEN REALIZE IT... TALK ABOUT DENSE!

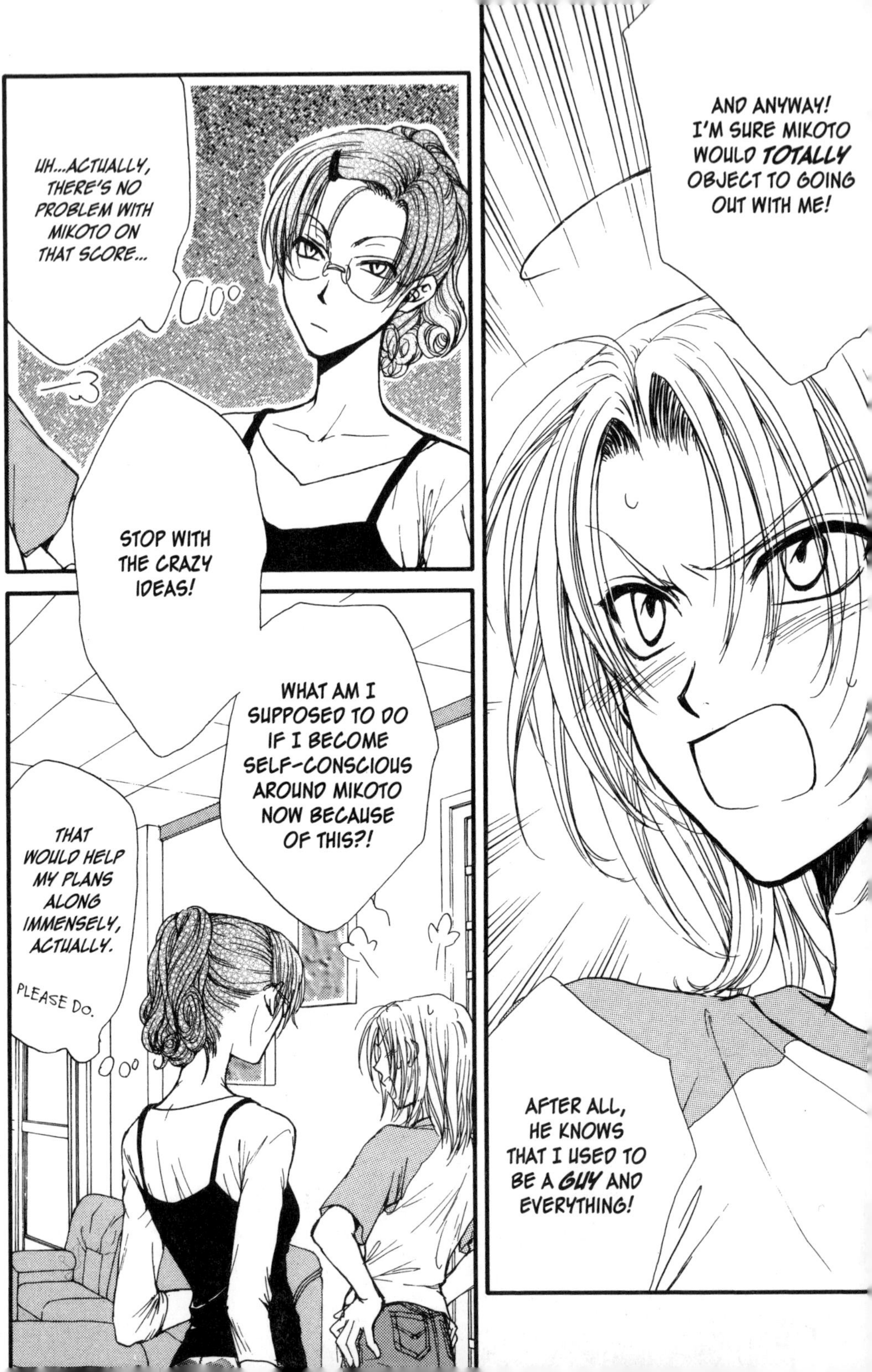
AND ANYWAY! I'M SURE MIKOTO WOULD TOTALLY OBJECT TO GOING OUT WITH ME!
AFTER ALL, HE KNOWS THAT I USED TO BE A GUY AND EVERYTHING!
STOP WITH THE CRAZY IDEAS!
UH...ACTUALLY, THERE'S NO PROBLEM WITH MIKOTO ON THAT SCORE...
WHAT AM I SUPPOSED TO DO IF I BECOME SELF-CONSCIOUS AROUND MIKOTO NOW BECAUSE OF THIS?!
THAT WOULD HELP MY PLANS ALONG IMMENSELY, ACTUALLY.
PLEASE DO.

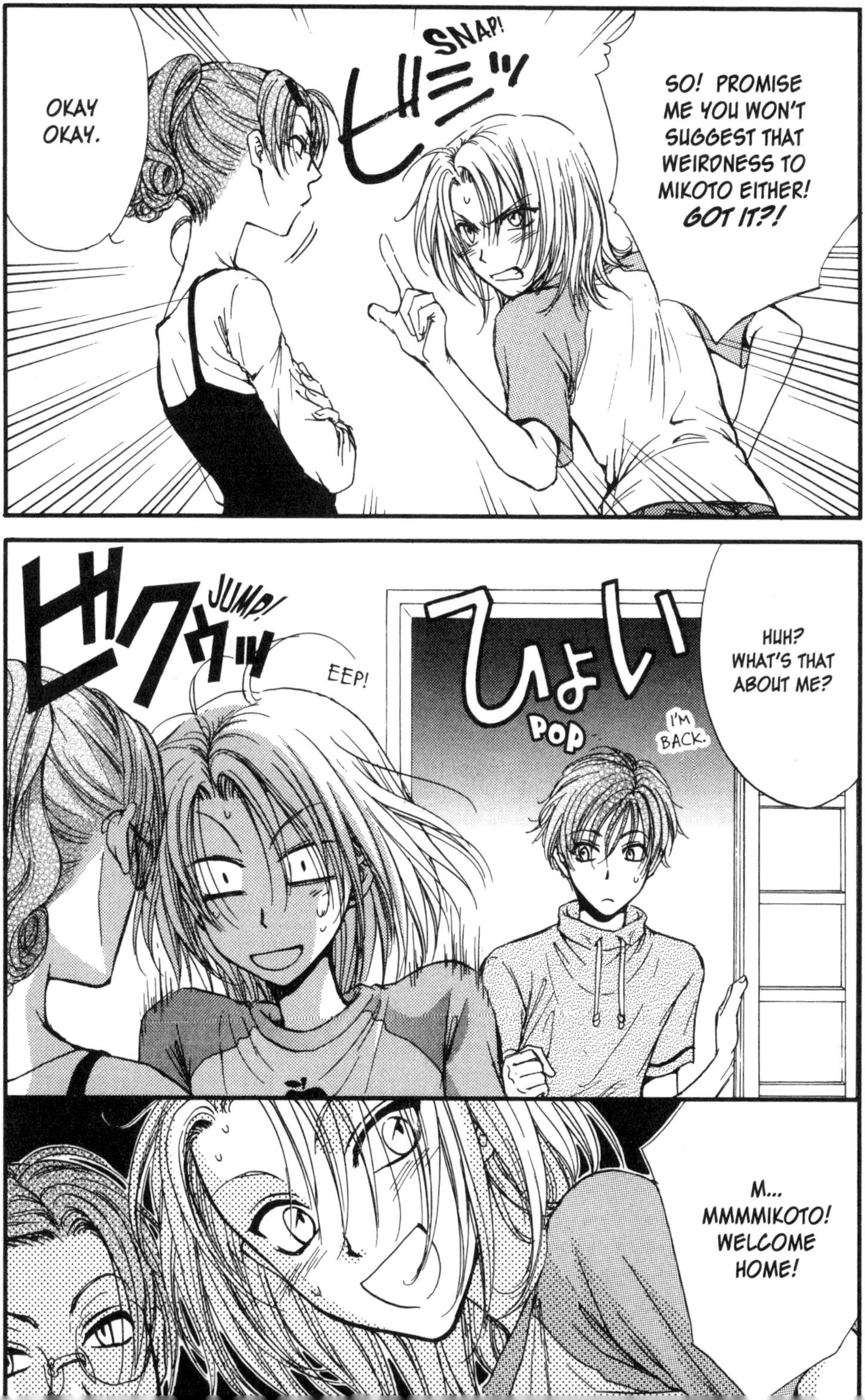
SO! PROMISE ME YOU WON'T SUGGEST THAT WEIRDNESS TO MIKOTO EITHER! GOT IT?!
ビシッ
SNAP!
OKAY OKAY.
HUH? WHAT'S THAT ABOUT ME?
I'M BACK.
ひょい
POP
EEP!
ビクゥッ
JUMP!
M... MMMMIKOTO! WELCOME HOME!

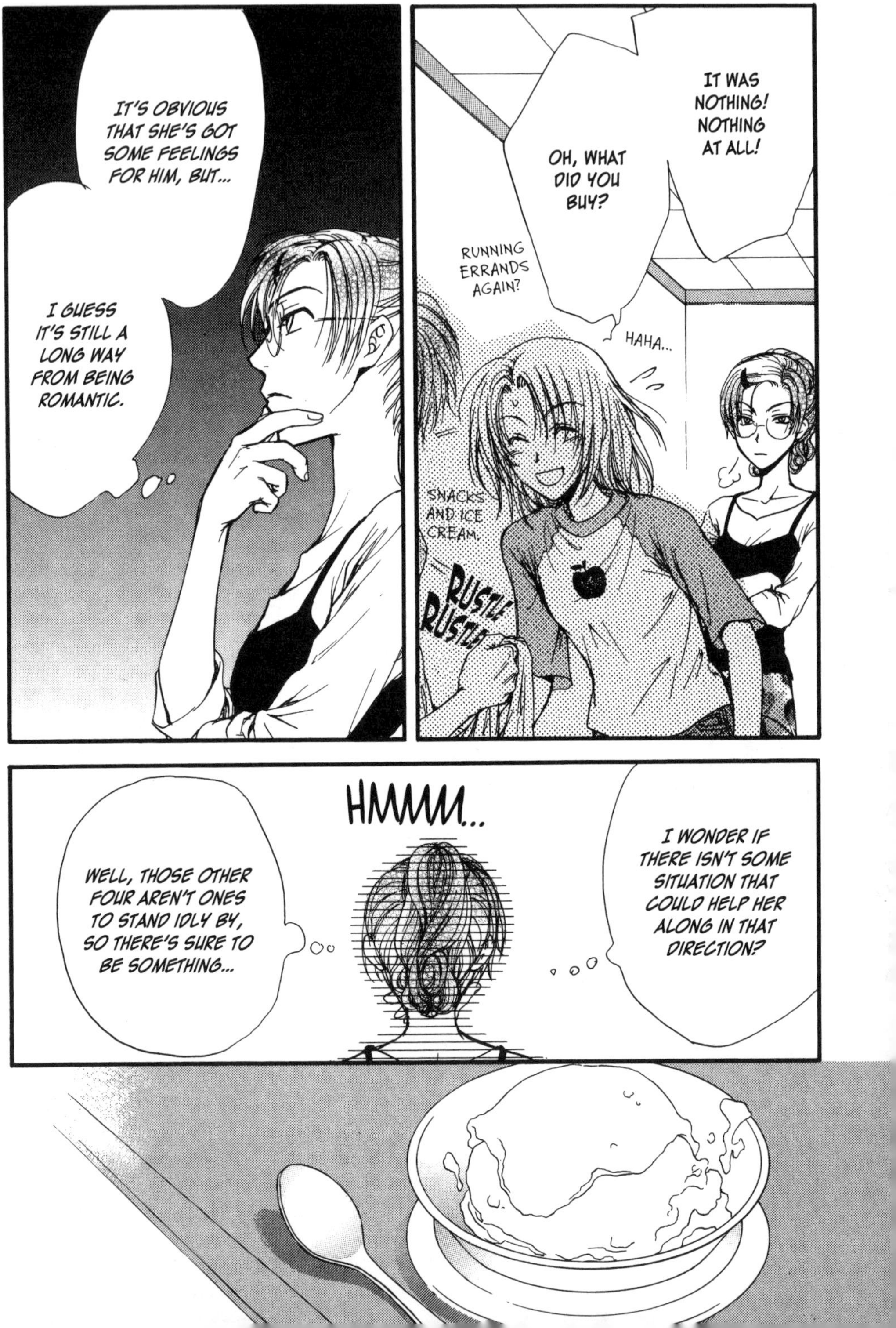
IT WAS NOTHING! NOTHING AT ALL!
OH, WHAT DID YOU BUY?
RUNNING ERRANDS AGAIN?
HAHA...
SNACKS AND ICE CREAM.
RUSTLE RUSTLE
IT'S OBVIOUS THAT SHE'S GOT SOME FEELINGS FOR HIM, BUT...
I GUESS IT'S STILL A LONG WAY FROM BEING ROMANTIC.
HMMMM...
I WONDER IF THERE ISN'T SOME SITUATION THAT COULD HELP HER ALONG IN THAT DIRECTION?
WELL, THOSE OTHER FOUR AREN'T ONES TO STAND IDLY BY, SO THERE'S SURE TO BE SOMETHING...

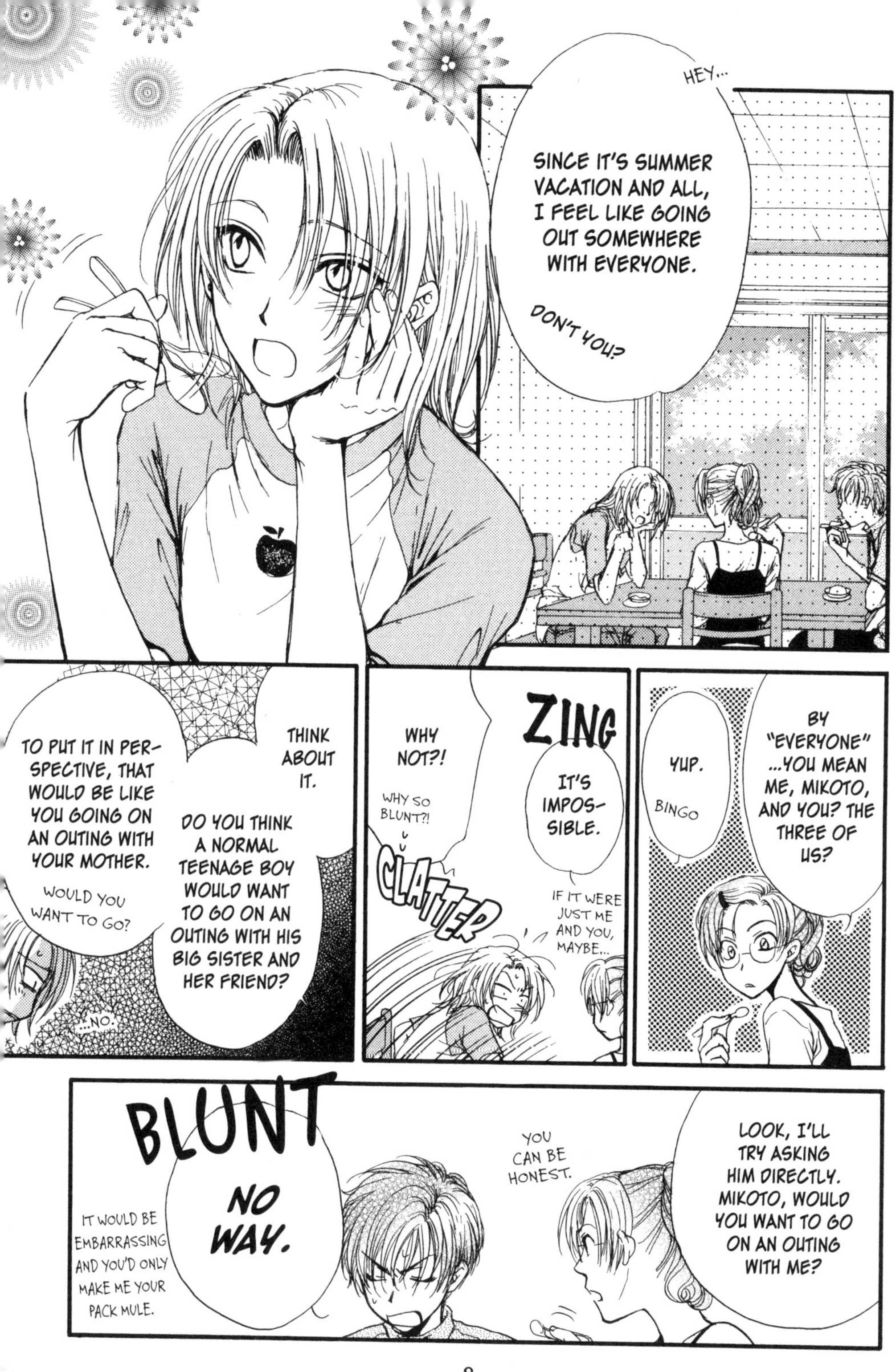
HEY...
SINCE IT'S SUMMER VACATION AND ALL, I FEEL LIKE GOING OUT SOMEWHERE WITH EVERYONE.
DON'T YOU?
BY "EVERYONE" ...YOU MEAN ME, MIKOTO, AND YOU? THE THREE OF US?
YUP.
BINGO
ZING
IT'S IMPOS-SIBLE.
IF IT WERE JUST ME AND YOU, MAYBE...
WHY NOT?!
WHY SO BLUNT?!
CLATTER
THINK ABOUT IT.
DO YOU THINK A NORMAL TEENAGE BOY WOULD WANT TO GO ON AN OUTING WITH HIS BIG SISTER AND HER FRIEND?
TO PUT IT IN PER-SPECTIVE, THAT WOULD BE LIKE YOU GOING ON AN OUTING WITH YOUR MOTHER.
WOULD YOU WANT TO GO?
...NO.
LOOK, I'LL TRY ASKING HIM DIRECTLY. MIKOTO, WOULD YOU WANT TO GO ON AN OUTING WITH ME?
YOU CAN BE HONEST.
BLUNT
NO WAY.
IT WOULD BE EMBARRASSING AND YOU'D ONLY MAKE ME YOUR PACK MULE.

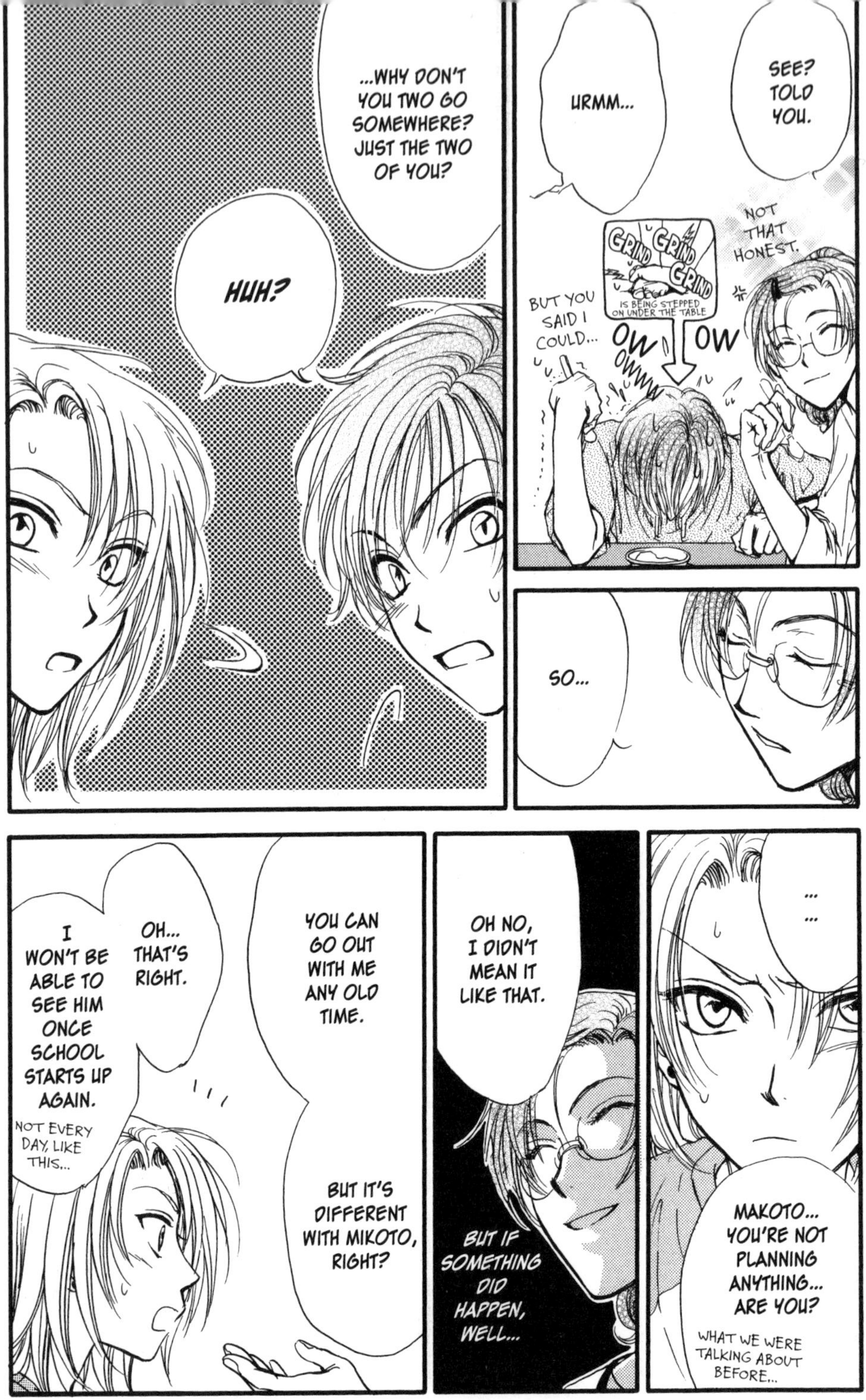
SEE? TOLD YOU.
NOT THAT HONEST.
URMM...
GRIND GRIND GRIND
IS BEING STEPPED ON UNDER THE TABLE
OW
OW OWWW
BUT YOU SAID I COULD...
SO...
...WHY DON'T YOU TWO GO SOMEWHERE? JUST THE TWO OF YOU?
HUH?
... ...
MAKOTO... YOU'RE NOT PLANNING ANYTHING... ARE YOU?
WHAT WE WERE TALKING ABOUT BEFORE...
OH NO, I DIDN'T MEAN IT LIKE THAT.
BUT IF SOMETHING DID HAPPEN, WELL...
YOU CAN GO OUT WITH ME ANY OLD TIME.
BUT IT'S DIFFERENT WITH MIKOTO, RIGHT?
OH... THAT'S RIGHT.
I WON'T BE ABLE TO SEE HIM ONCE SCHOOL STARTS UP AGAIN.
NOT EVERY DAY, LIKE THIS...

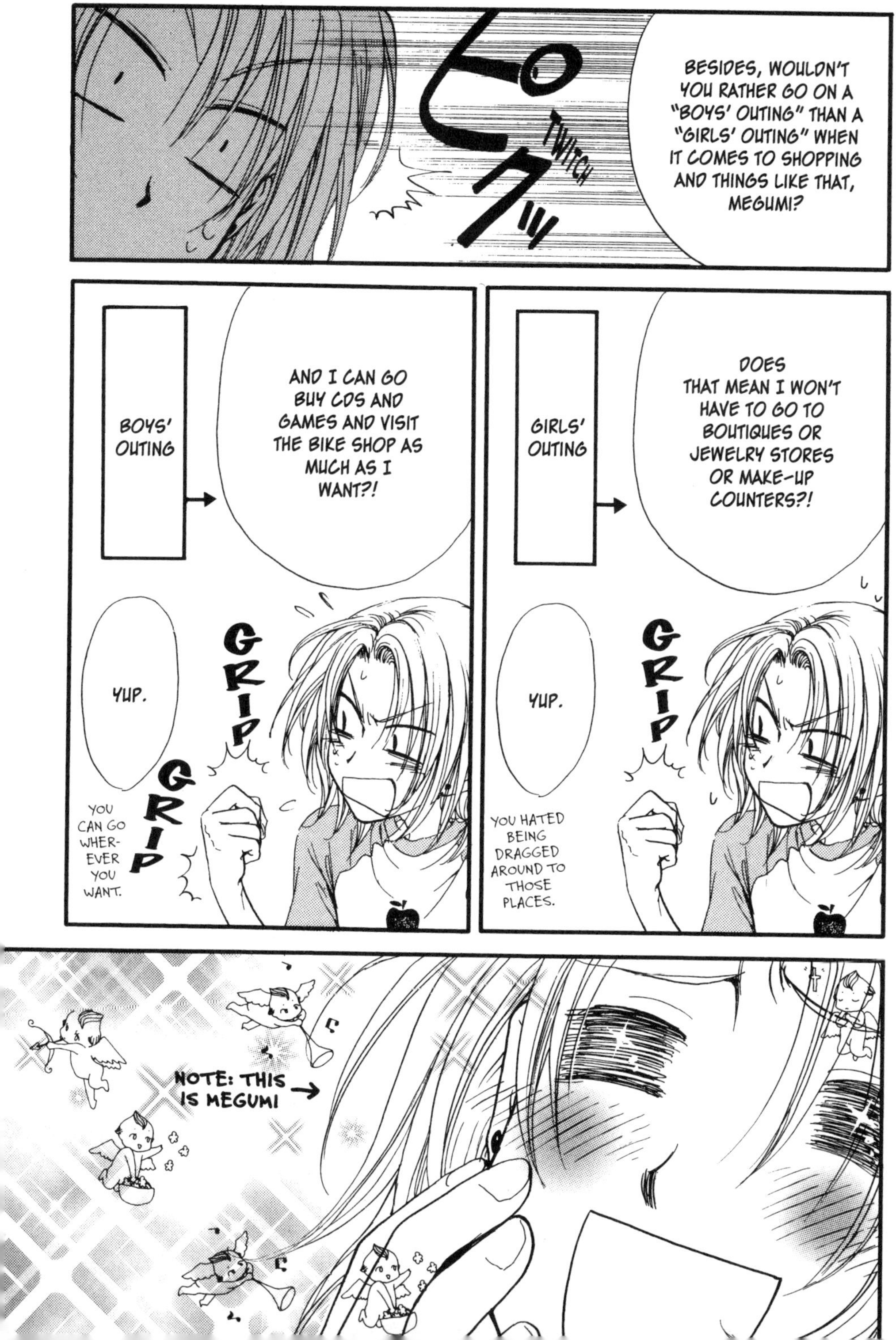
BESIDES, WOULDN'T YOU RATHER GO ON A "BOYS' OUTING" THAN A "GIRLS' OUTING" WHEN IT COMES TO SHOPPING AND THINGS LIKE THAT, MEGUMI?
TWITCH
DOES THAT MEAN I WON'T HAVE TO GO TO BOUTIQUES OR JEWELRY STORES OR MAKE-UP COUNTERS?!
GIRLS' OUTING
GRIP
YUP.
YOU HATED BEING DRAGGED AROUND TO THOSE PLACES.
AND I CAN GO BUY CDS AND GAMES AND VISIT THE BIKE SHOP AS MUCH AS I WANT?!
BOYS' OUTING
GRIP
YUP.
GRIP
YOU CAN GO WHER-EVER YOU WANT.
NOTE: THIS IS MEGUMI

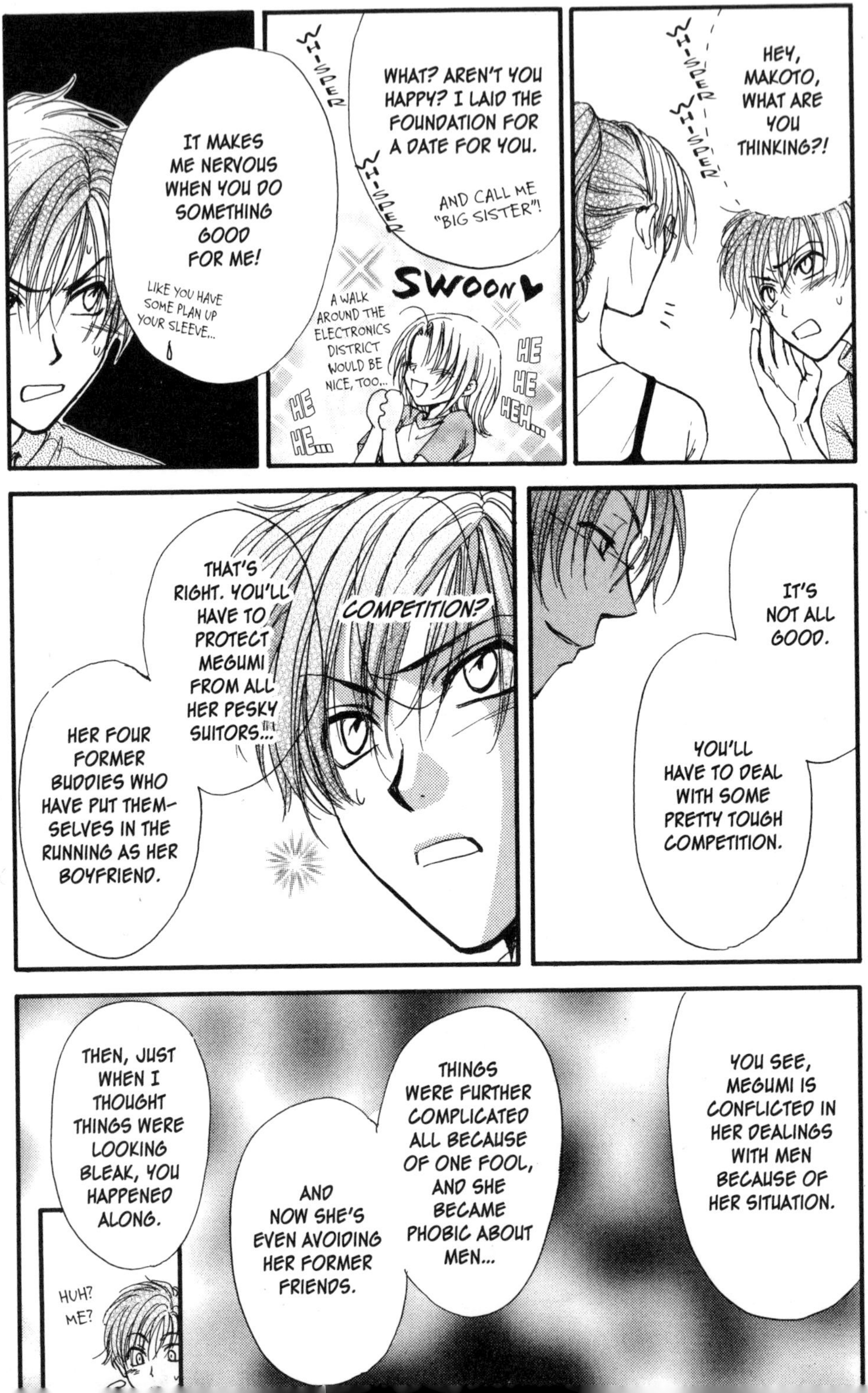
WHISPER
WHISPER
HEY, MAKOTO, WHAT ARE YOU THINKING?!
WHISPER
WHAT? AREN'T YOU HAPPY? I LAID THE FOUNDATION FOR A DATE FOR YOU.
WHISPER
AND CALL ME "BIG SISTER"!
SWOON
HE HE HEH...
A WALK AROUND THE ELECTRONICS DISTRICT WOULD BE NICE, TOO...
HE HE...
IT MAKES ME NERVOUS WHEN YOU DO SOMETHING GOOD FOR ME!
LIKE YOU HAVE SOME PLAN UP YOUR SLEEVE...
IT'S NOT ALL GOOD.
YOU'LL HAVE TO DEAL WITH SOME PRETTY TOUGH COMPETITION.
COMPETITION?
THAT'S RIGHT. YOU'LL HAVE TO PROTECT MEGUMI FROM ALL HER PESKY SUITORS...
HER FOUR FORMER BUDDIES WHO HAVE PUT THEMSELVES IN THE RUNNING AS HER BOYFRIEND.
YOU SEE, MEGUMI IS CONFLICTED IN HER DEALINGS WITH MEN BECAUSE OF HER SITUATION.
THINGS WERE FURTHER COMPLICATED ALL BECAUSE OF ONE FOOL, AND SHE BECAME PHOBIC ABOUT MEN...
AND NOW SHE'S EVEN AVOIDING HER FORMER FRIENDS.
THEN, JUST WHEN I THOUGHT THINGS WERE LOOKING BLEAK, YOU HAPPENED ALONG.
HUH? ME?

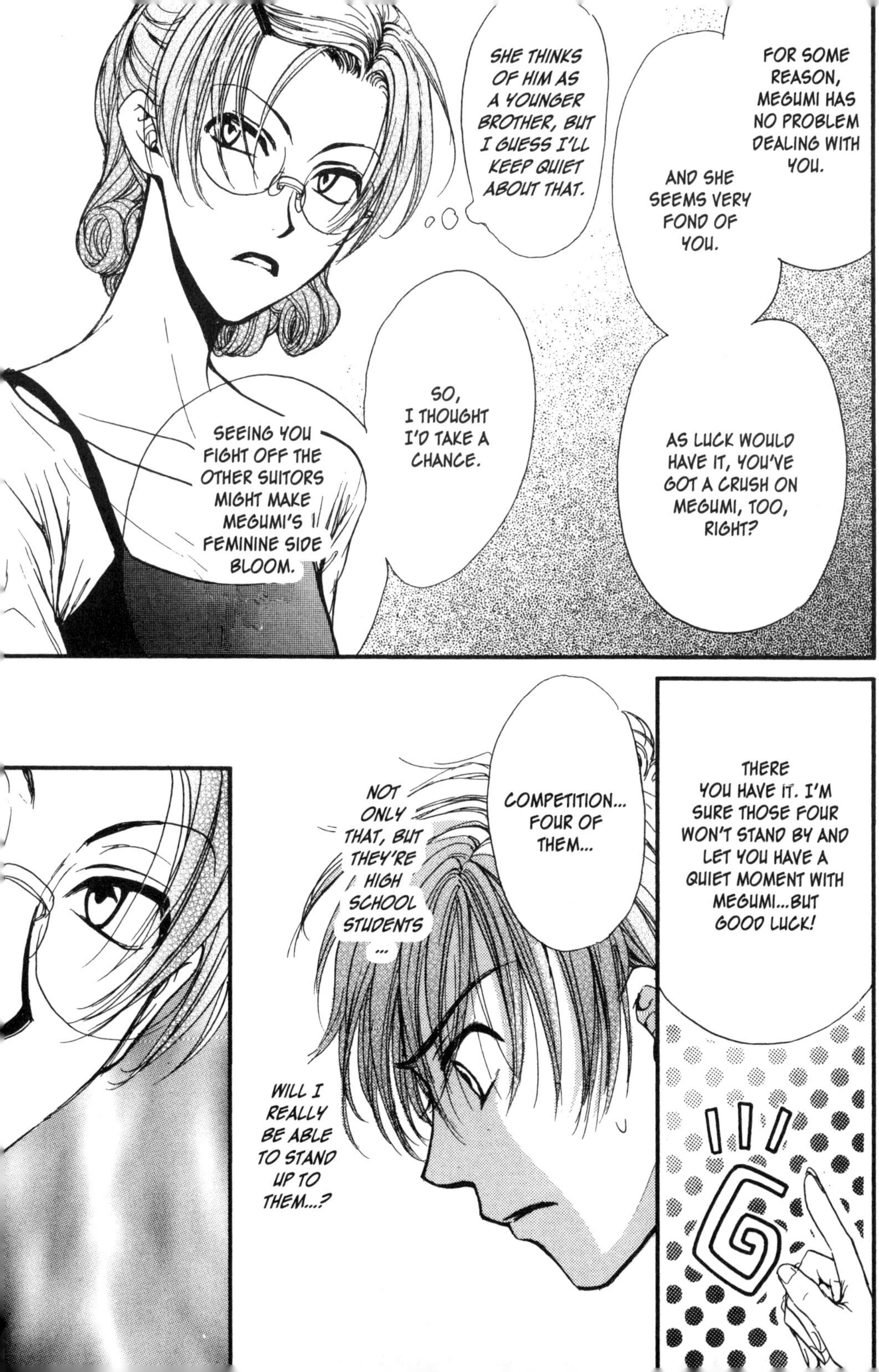
FOR SOME REASON, MEGUMI HAS NO PROBLEM DEALING WITH YOU.
AND SHE SEEMS VERY FOND OF YOU.
SHE THINKS OF HIM AS A YOUNGER BROTHER, BUT I GUESS I'LL KEEP QUIET ABOUT THAT.
AS LUCK WOULD HAVE IT, YOU'VE GOT A CRUSH ON MEGUMI, TOO, RIGHT?
SO, I THOUGHT I'D TAKE A CHANCE.
SEEING YOU FIGHT OFF THE OTHER SUITORS MIGHT MAKE MEGUMI'S FEMININE SIDE BLOOM.
THERE YOU HAVE IT. I'M SURE THOSE FOUR WON'T STAND BY AND LET YOU HAVE A QUIET MOMENT WITH MEGUMI...BUT GOOD LUCK!
COMPETITION... FOUR OF THEM...
NOT ONLY THAT, BUT THEY'RE HIGH SCHOOL STUDENTS...
WILL I REALLY BE ABLE TO STAND UP TO THEM...?

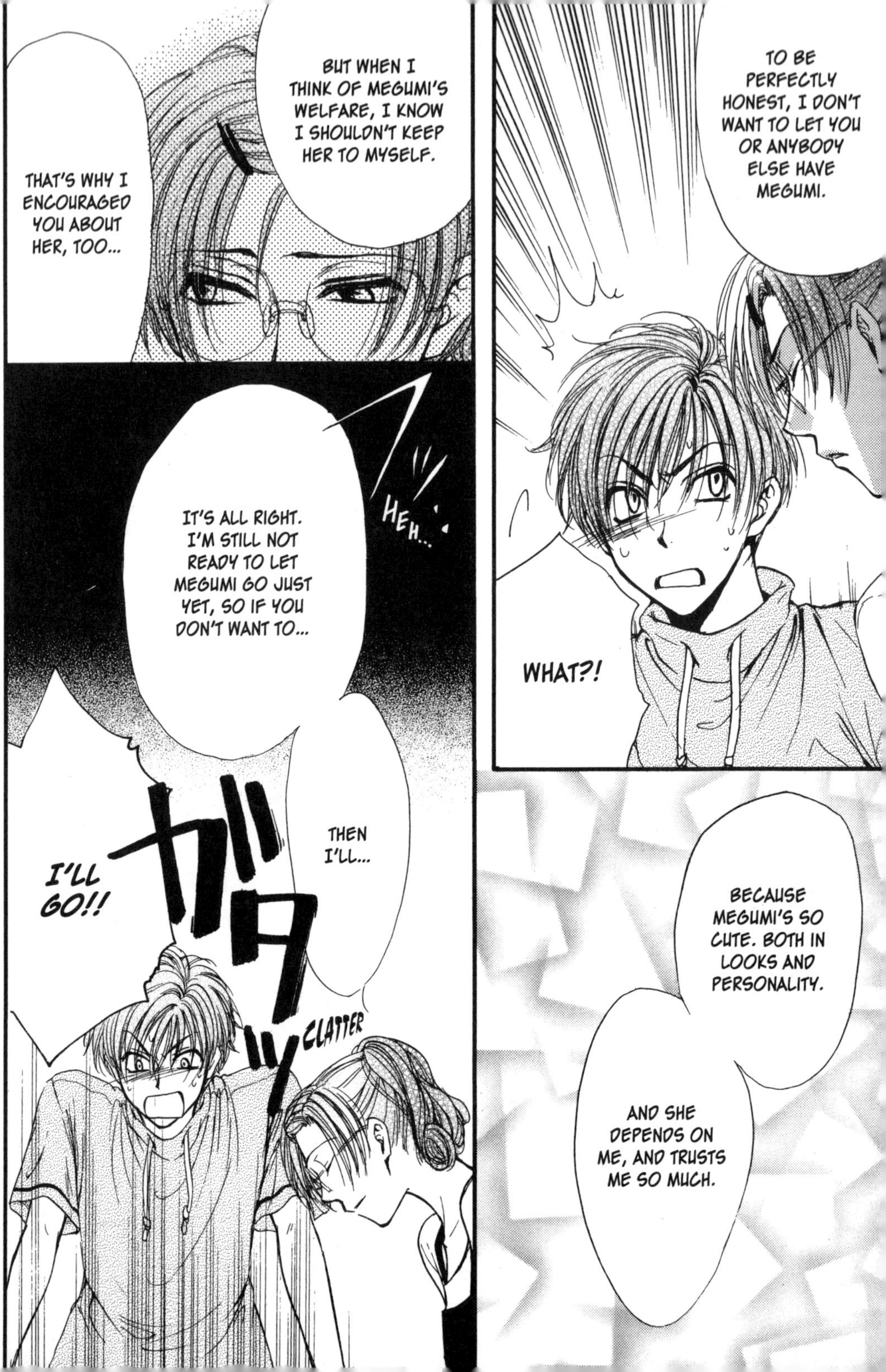

TO BE PERFECTLY HONEST, I DON'T WANT TO LET YOU OR ANYBODY ELSE HAVE MEGUMI.
WHAT?!
BECAUSE MEGUMI'S SO CUTE. BOTH IN LOOKS AND PERSONALITY.
AND SHE DEPENDS ON ME, AND TRUSTS ME SO MUCH.
BUT WHEN I THINK OF MEGUMI'S WELFARE, I KNOW I SHOULDN'T KEEP HER TO MYSELF.
THAT'S WHY I ENCOURAGED YOU ABOUT HER, TOO...
HEH...
IT'S ALL RIGHT. I'M STILL NOT READY TO LET MEGUMI GO JUST YET, SO IF YOU DON'T WANT TO...
THEN I'LL...
ガタッ
CLATTER
I'LL GO!!

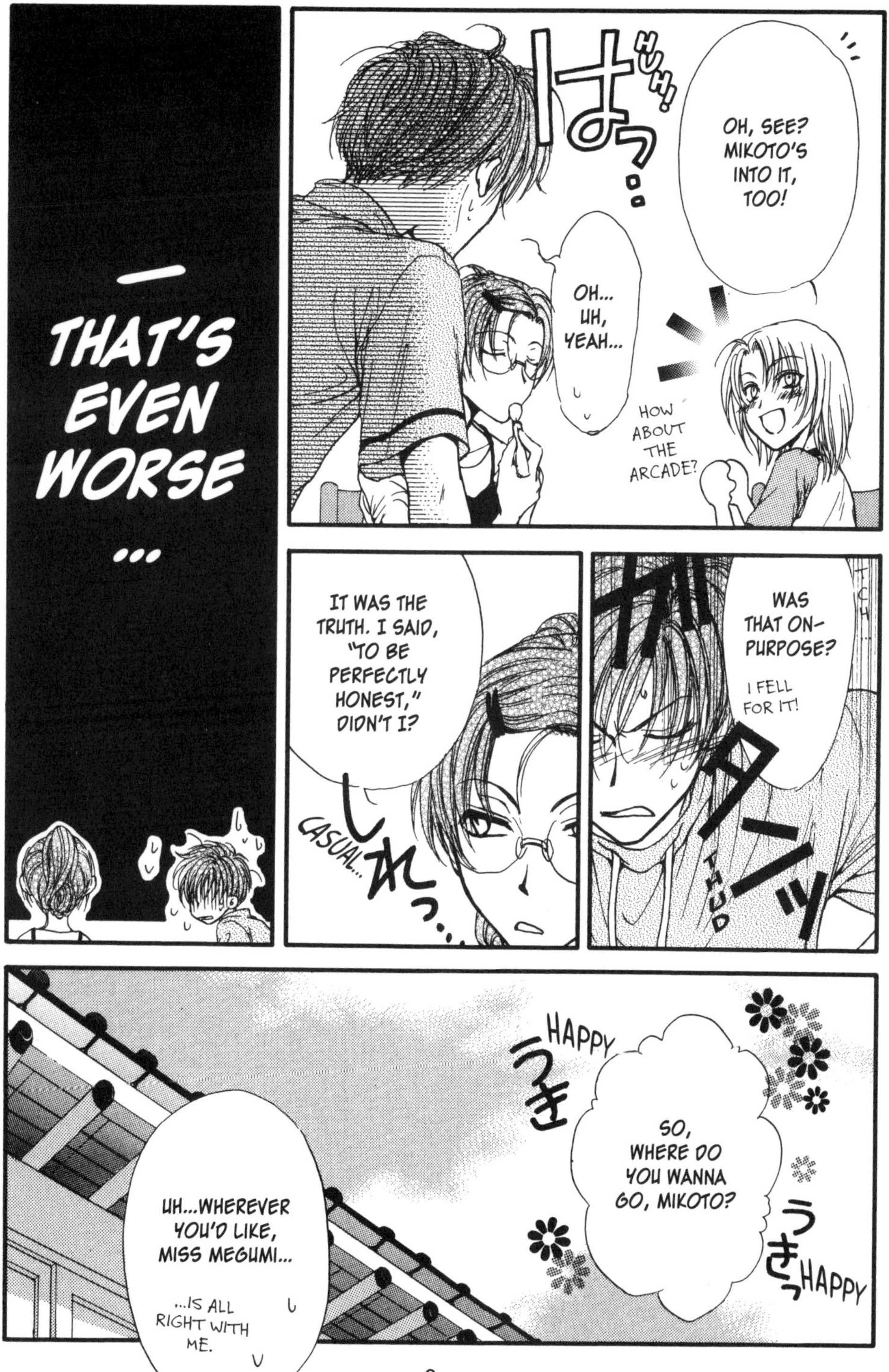
OH, SEE? MIKOTO'S INTO IT, TOO!
HUH!
はっ
OH... UH, YEAH...
HOW ABOUT THE ARCADE?
WAS THAT ON-PURPOSE?
I FELL FOR IT!
TCH...
タンッ
THUD
IT WAS THE TRUTH. I SAID, "TO BE PERFECTLY HONEST," DIDN'T I?
しれっ
CASUAL...
— THAT'S EVEN WORSE ...
うき
HAPPY
SO, WHERE DO YOU WANNA GO, MIKOTO?
うきっ
HAPPY
UH...WHEREVER YOU'D LIKE, MISS MEGUMI...
...IS ALL RIGHT WITH ME.

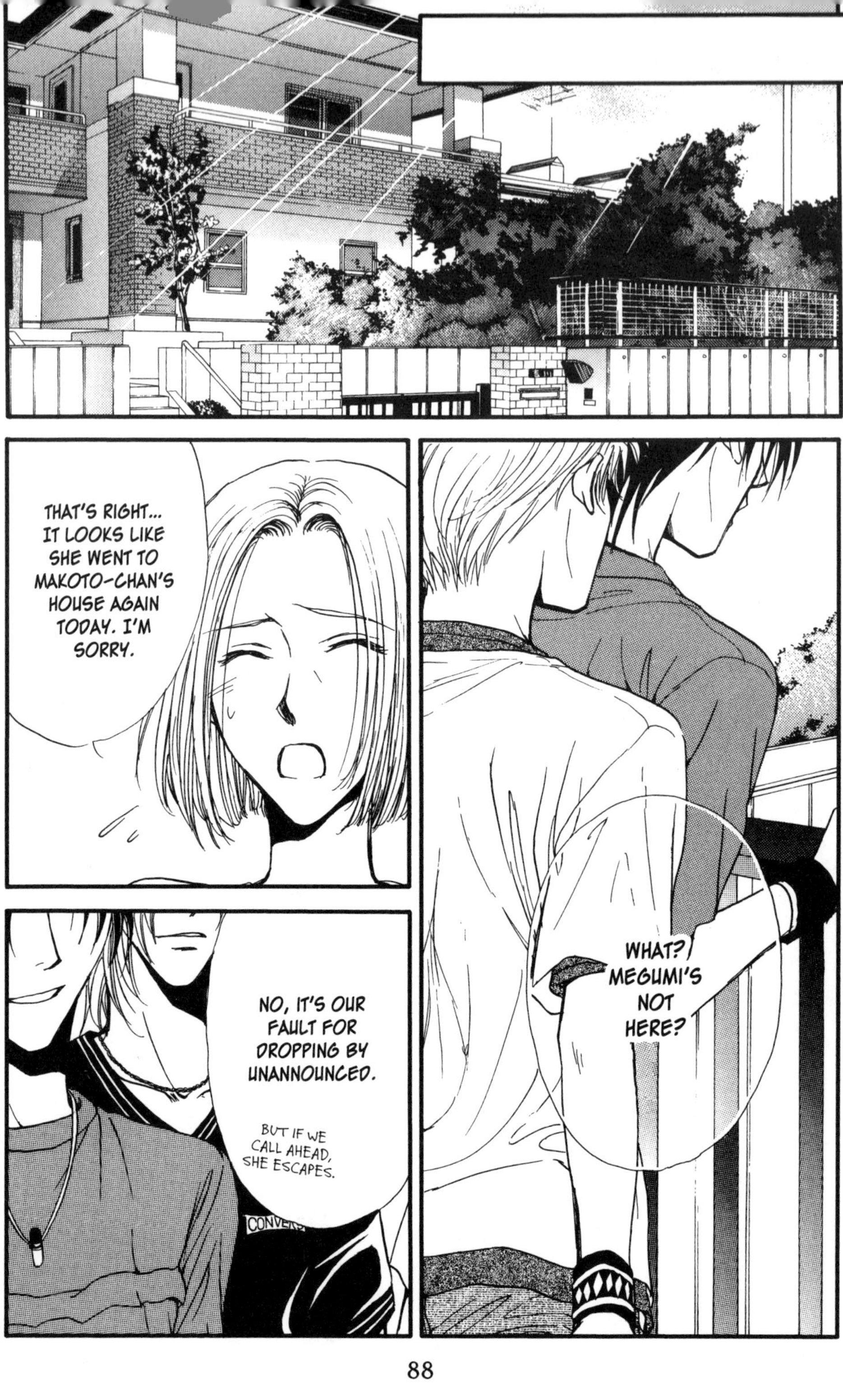
WHAT? MEGUMI'S NOT HERE?
THAT'S RIGHT... IT LOOKS LIKE SHE WENT TO MAKOTO-CHAN'S HOUSE AGAIN TODAY. I'M SORRY.
NO, IT'S OUR FAULT FOR DROPPING BY UNANNOUNCED.
BUT IF WE CALL AHEAD, SHE ESCAPES.

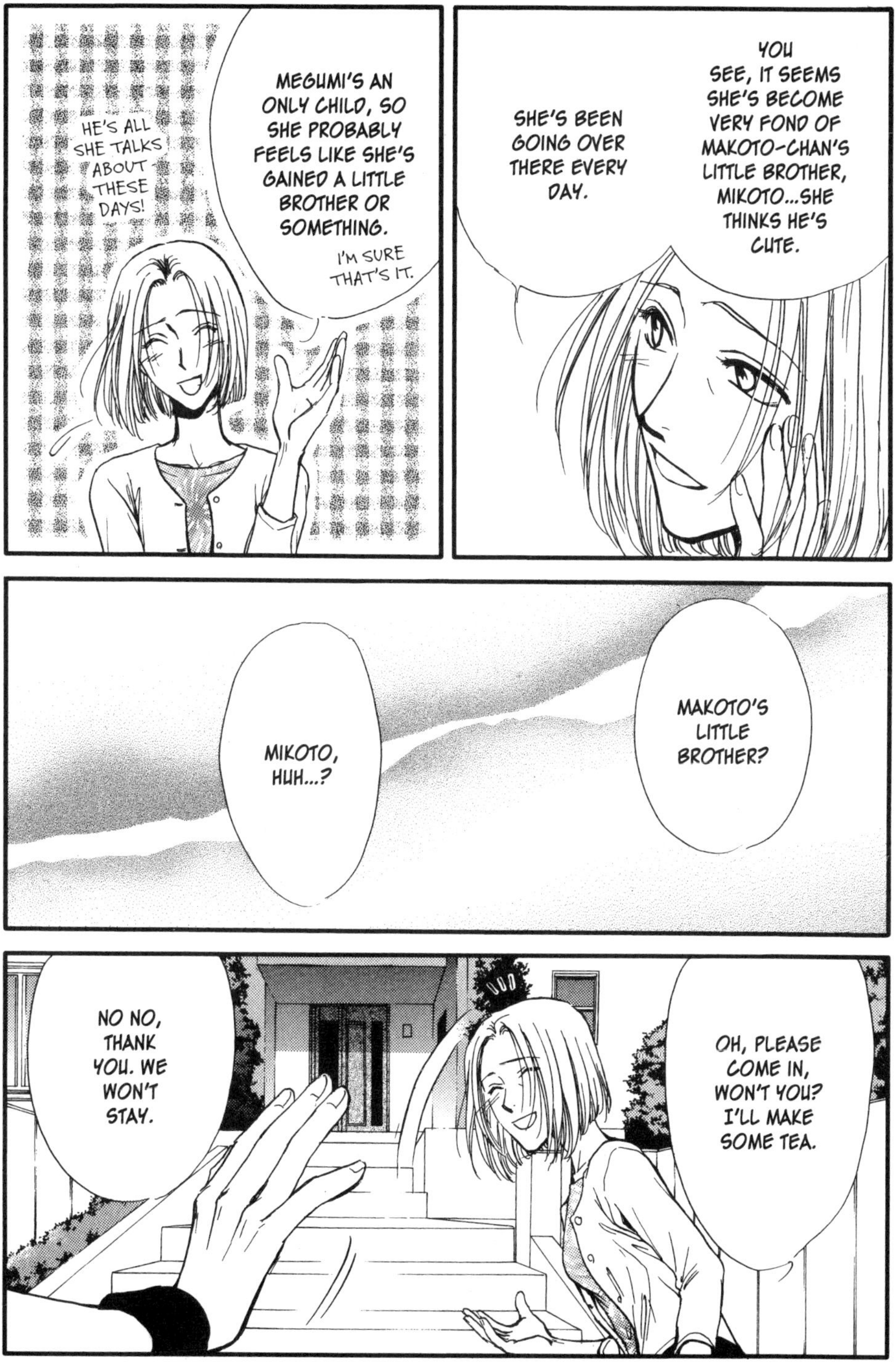
YOU SEE, IT SEEMS SHE'S BECOME VERY FOND OF MAKOTO-CHAN'S LITTLE BROTHER, MIKOTO...SHE THINKS HE'S CUTE.
SHE'S BEEN GOING OVER THERE EVERY DAY.
MEGUMI'S AN ONLY CHILD, SO SHE PROBABLY FEELS LIKE SHE'S GAINED A LITTLE BROTHER OR SOMETHING.
I'M SURE THAT'S IT.
HE'S ALL SHE TALKS ABOUT THESE DAYS!
MAKOTO'S LITTLE BROTHER?
MIKOTO, HUH...?
OH, PLEASE COME IN, WON'T YOU? I'LL MAKE SOME TEA.
NO NO, THANK YOU. WE WON'T STAY.

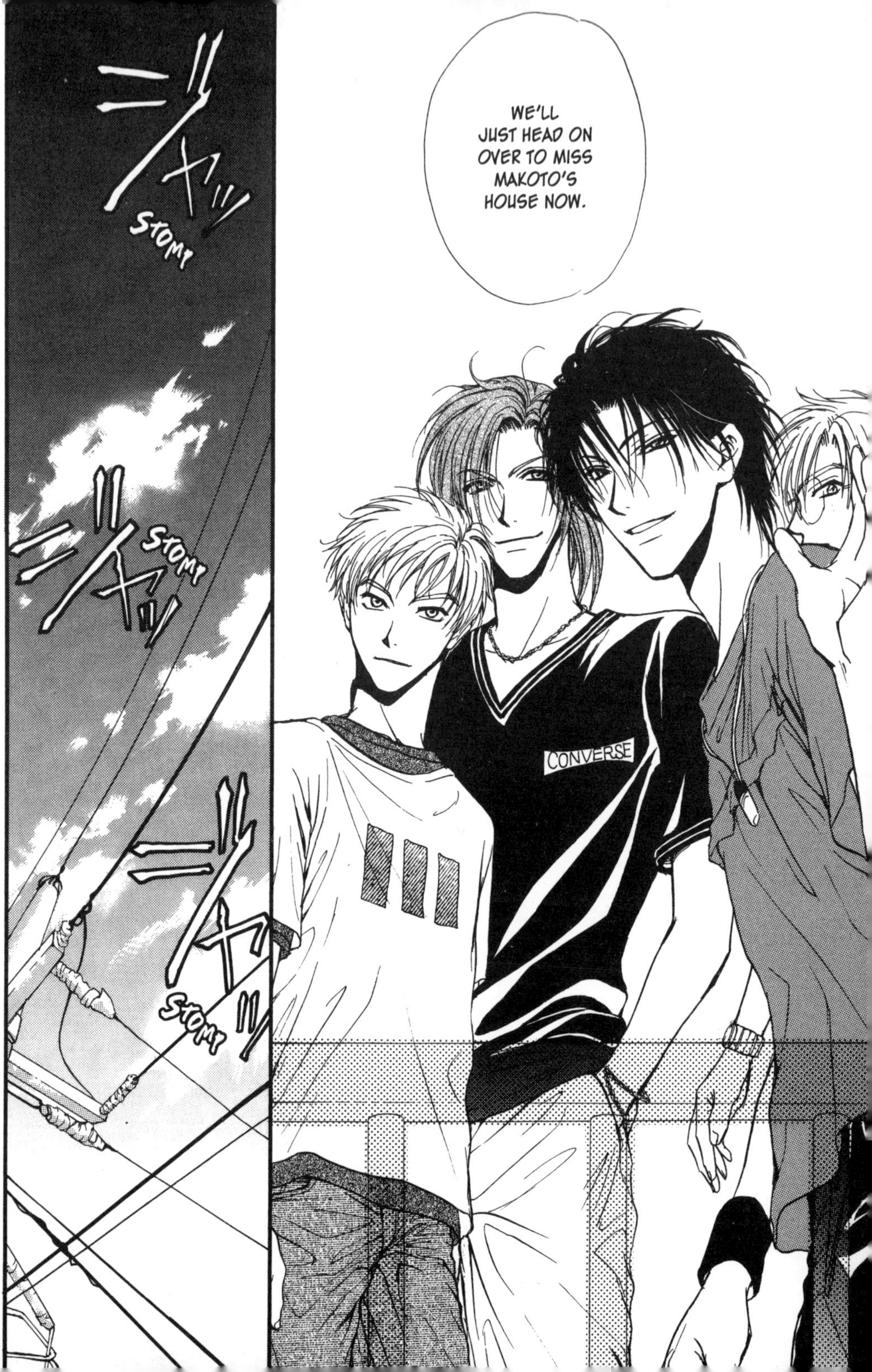
WE'LL JUST HEAD ON OVER TO MISS MAKOTO'S HOUSE NOW.
STOMP
STOMP
STOMP

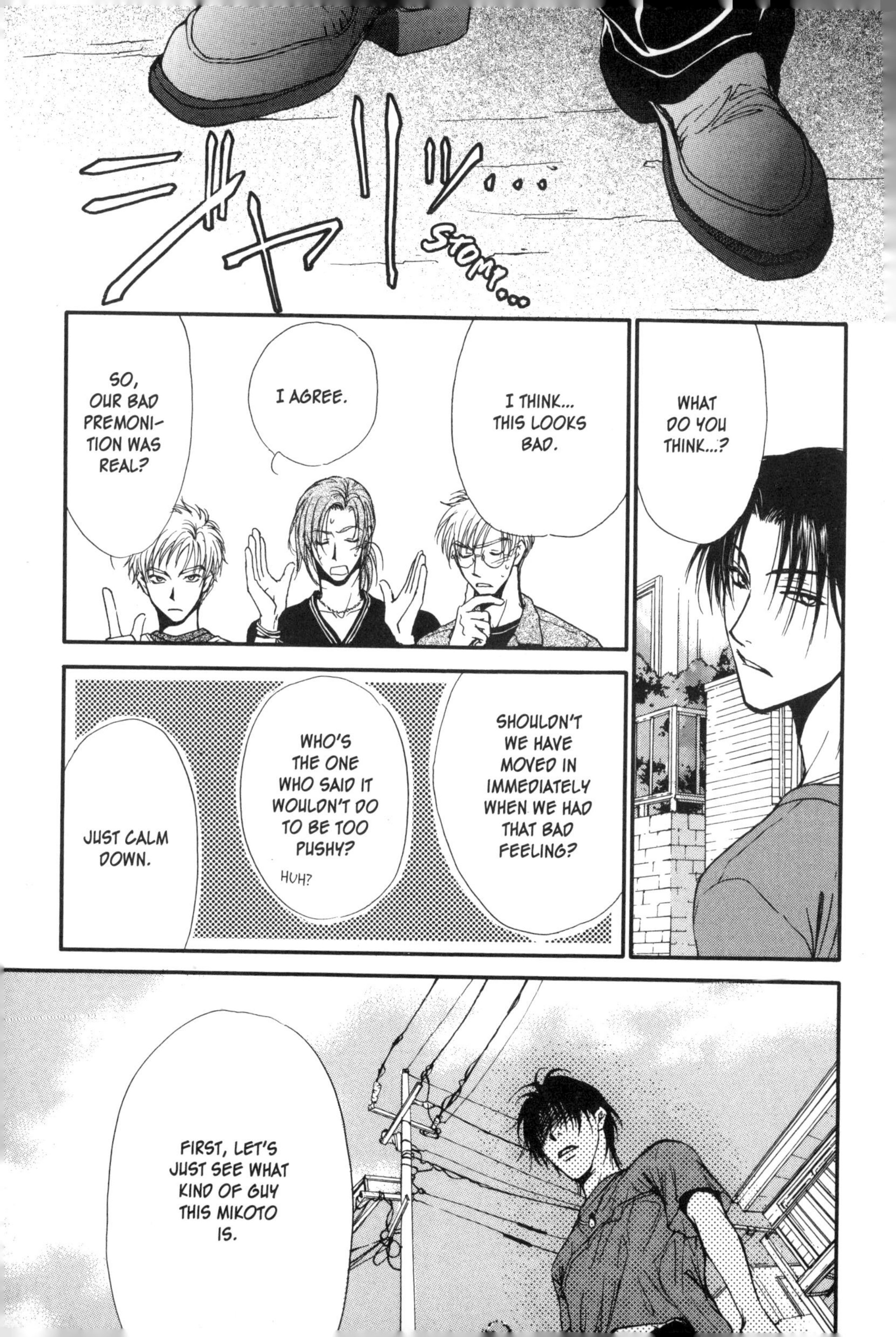
ジャリッ...
STOMP...
WHAT DO YOU THINK...?
I THINK... THIS LOOKS BAD.
I AGREE.
SO, OUR BAD PREMONITION WAS REAL?
SHOULDN'T WE HAVE MOVED IN IMMEDIATELY WHEN WE HAD THAT BAD FEELING?
WHO'S THE ONE WHO SAID IT WOULDN'T DO TO BE TOO PUSHY?
HUH?
JUST CALM DOWN.
FIRST, LET'S JUST SEE WHAT KIND OF GUY THIS MIKOTO IS.

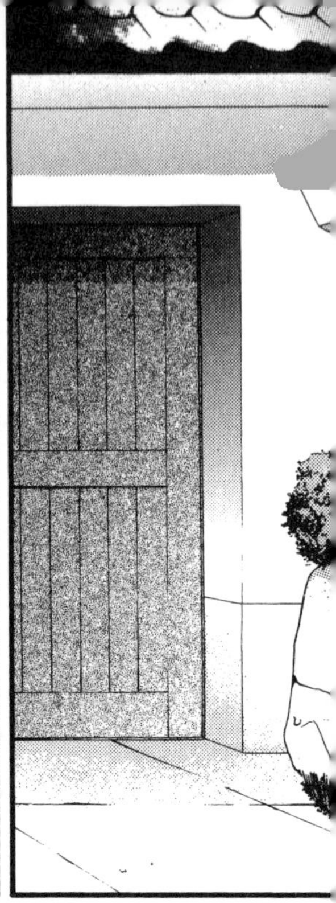

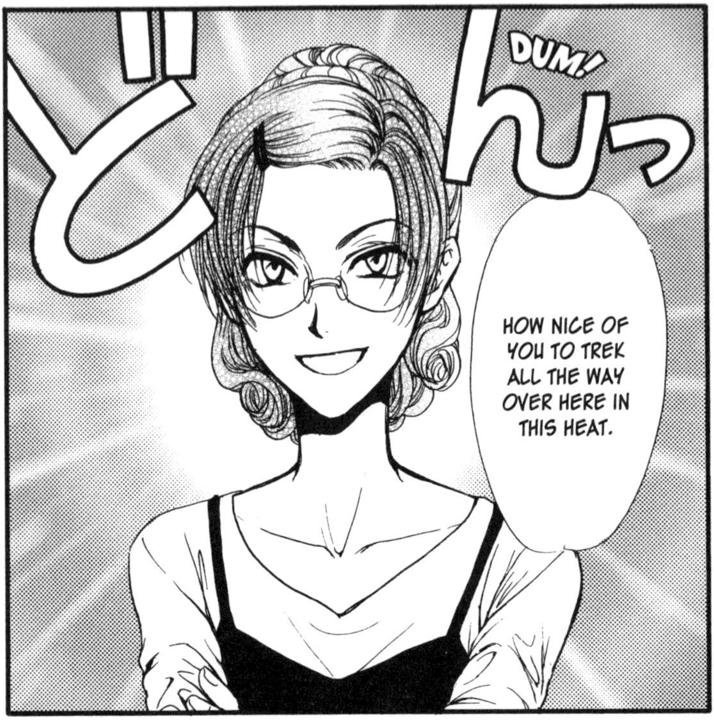
どんっ
DUM!
HOW NICE OF YOU TO TREK ALL THE WAY OVER HERE IN THIS HEAT.

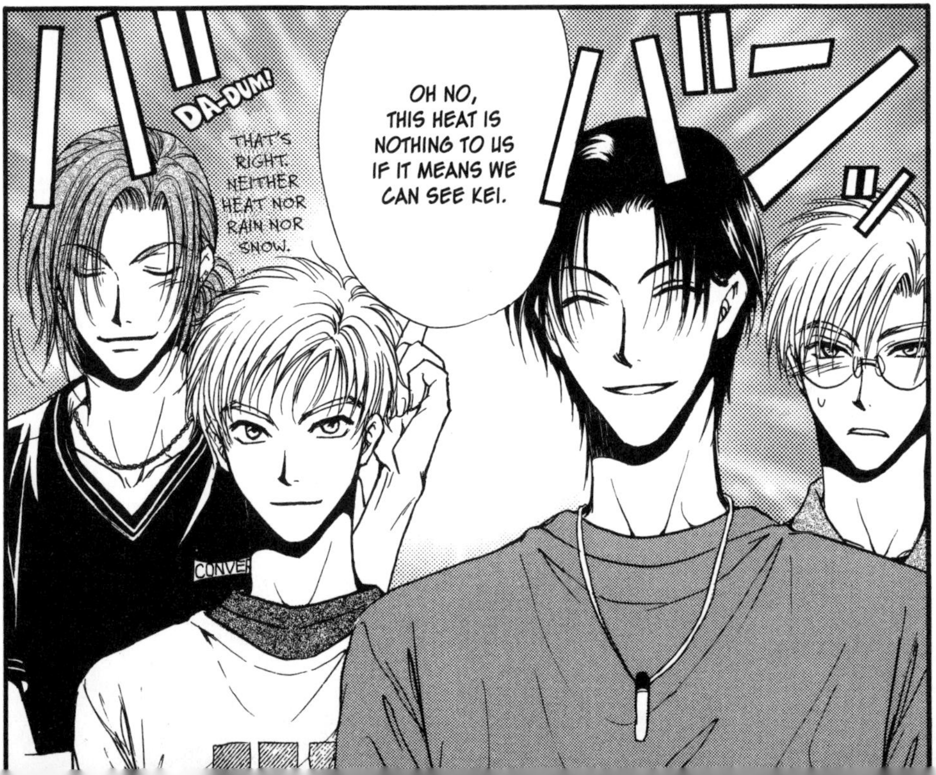
OH NO, THIS HEAT IS NOTHING TO US IF IT MEANS WE CAN SEE KEI.
DA-DUM!
THAT'S RIGHT. NEITHER HEAT NOR RAIN NOR SNOW.
CONVEI

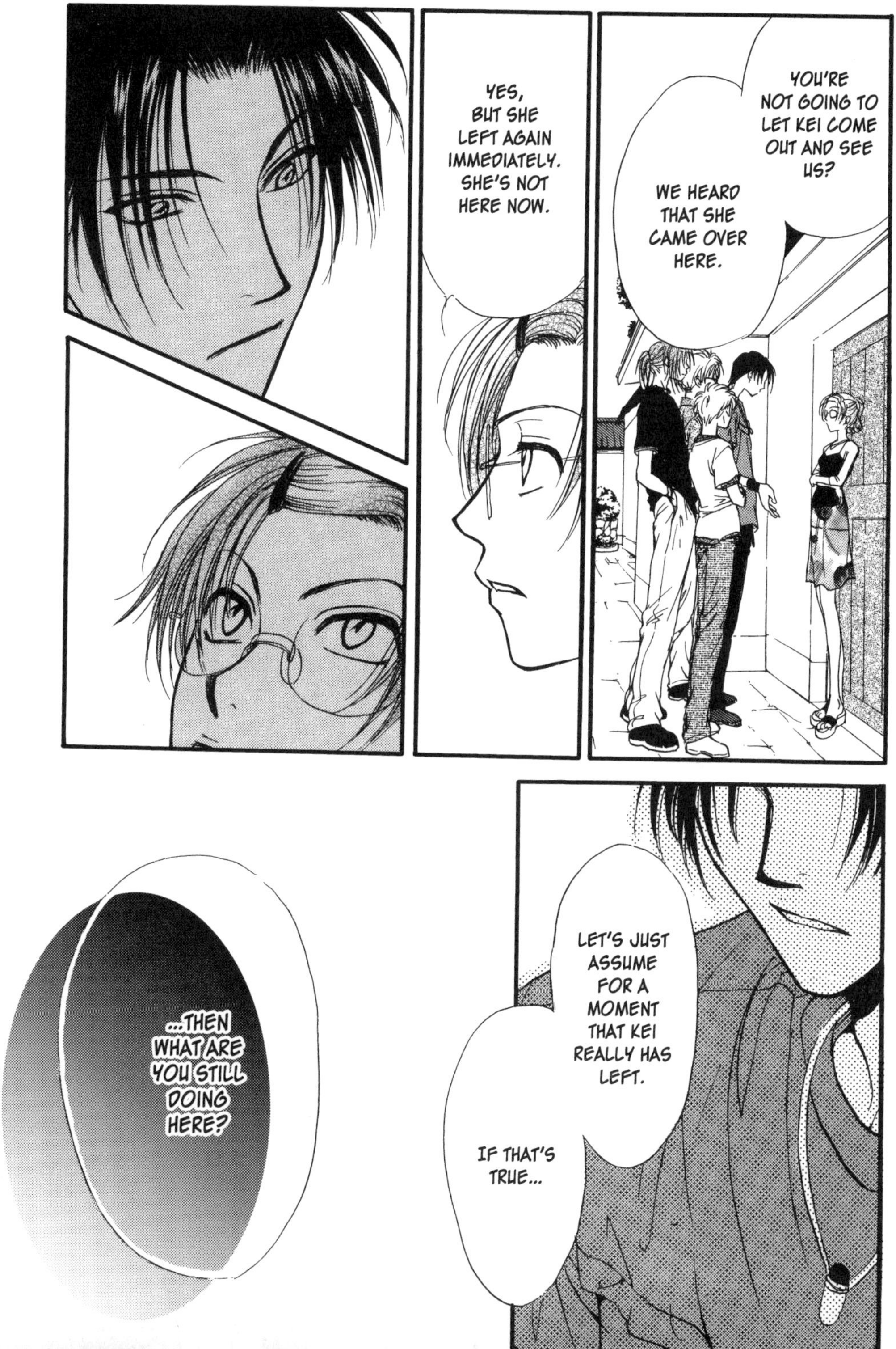
YOU'RE NOT GOING TO LET KEI COME OUT AND SEE US?
WE HEARD THAT SHE CAME OVER HERE.
YES, BUT SHE LEFT AGAIN IMMEDIATELY. SHE'S NOT HERE NOW.
LET'S JUST ASSUME FOR A MOMENT THAT KEI REALLY HAS LEFT.
IF THAT'S TRUE...
...THEN WHAT ARE YOU STILL DOING HERE?

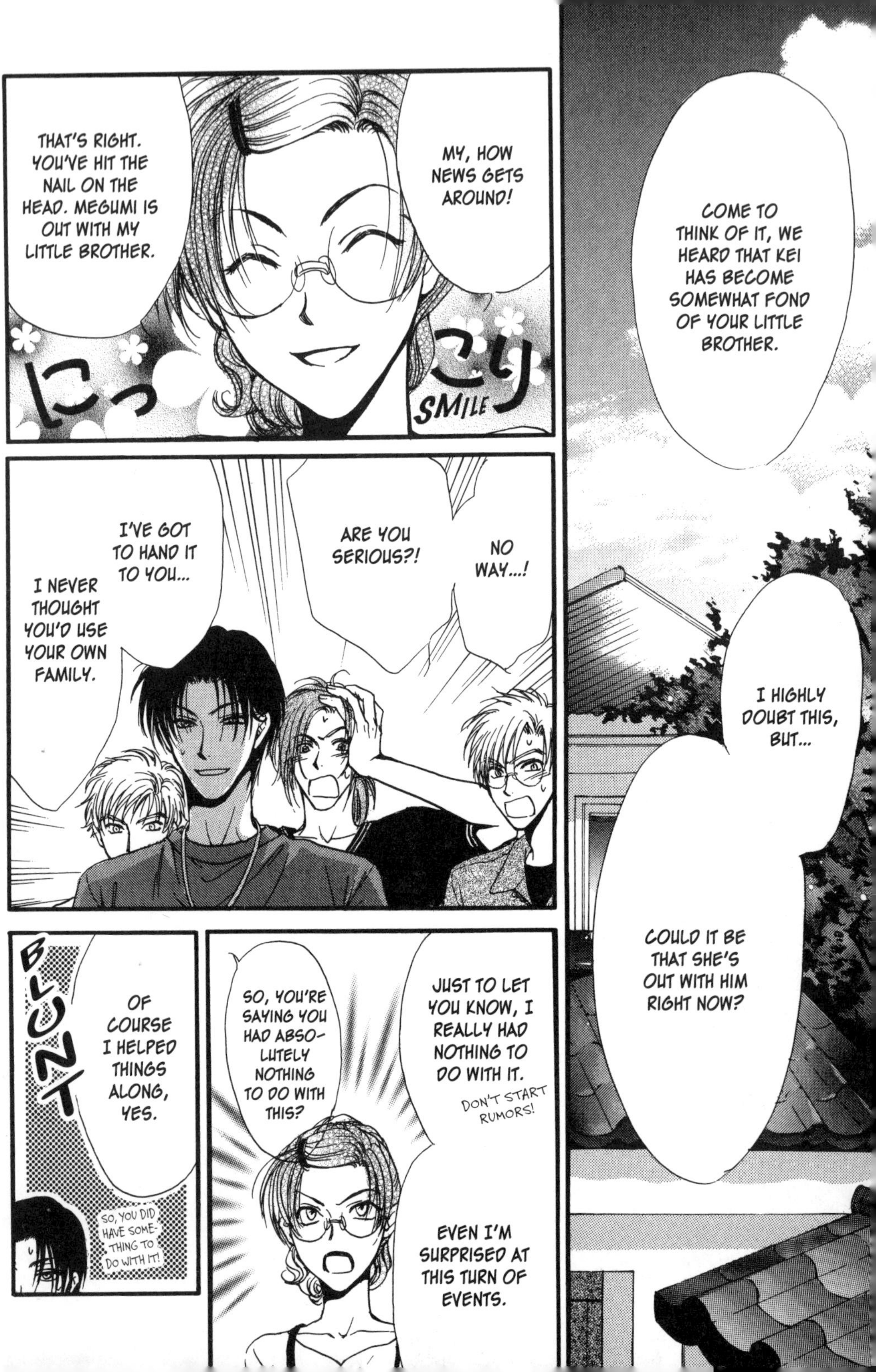
COME TO THINK OF IT, WE HEARD THAT KEI HAS BECOME SOMEWHAT FOND OF YOUR LITTLE BROTHER.
I HIGHLY DOUBT THIS, BUT...
COULD IT BE THAT SHE'S OUT WITH HIM RIGHT NOW?
MY, HOW NEWS GETS AROUND!
THAT'S RIGHT. YOU'VE HIT THE NAIL ON THE HEAD. MEGUMI IS OUT WITH MY LITTLE BROTHER.
にっこり
SMILE
NO WAY...!
ARE YOU SERIOUS?!
I'VE GOT TO HAND IT TO YOU...
I NEVER THOUGHT YOU'D USE YOUR OWN FAMILY.
JUST TO LET YOU KNOW, I REALLY HAD NOTHING TO DO WITH IT.
SO, YOU'RE SAYING YOU HAD ABSOLUTELY NOTHING TO DO WITH THIS?
DON'T START RUMORS!
EVEN I'M SURPRISED AT THIS TURN OF EVENTS.
BLUNT
OF COURSE I HELPED THINGS ALONG, YES.
SO, YOU DID HAVE SOMETHING TO DO WITH IT!

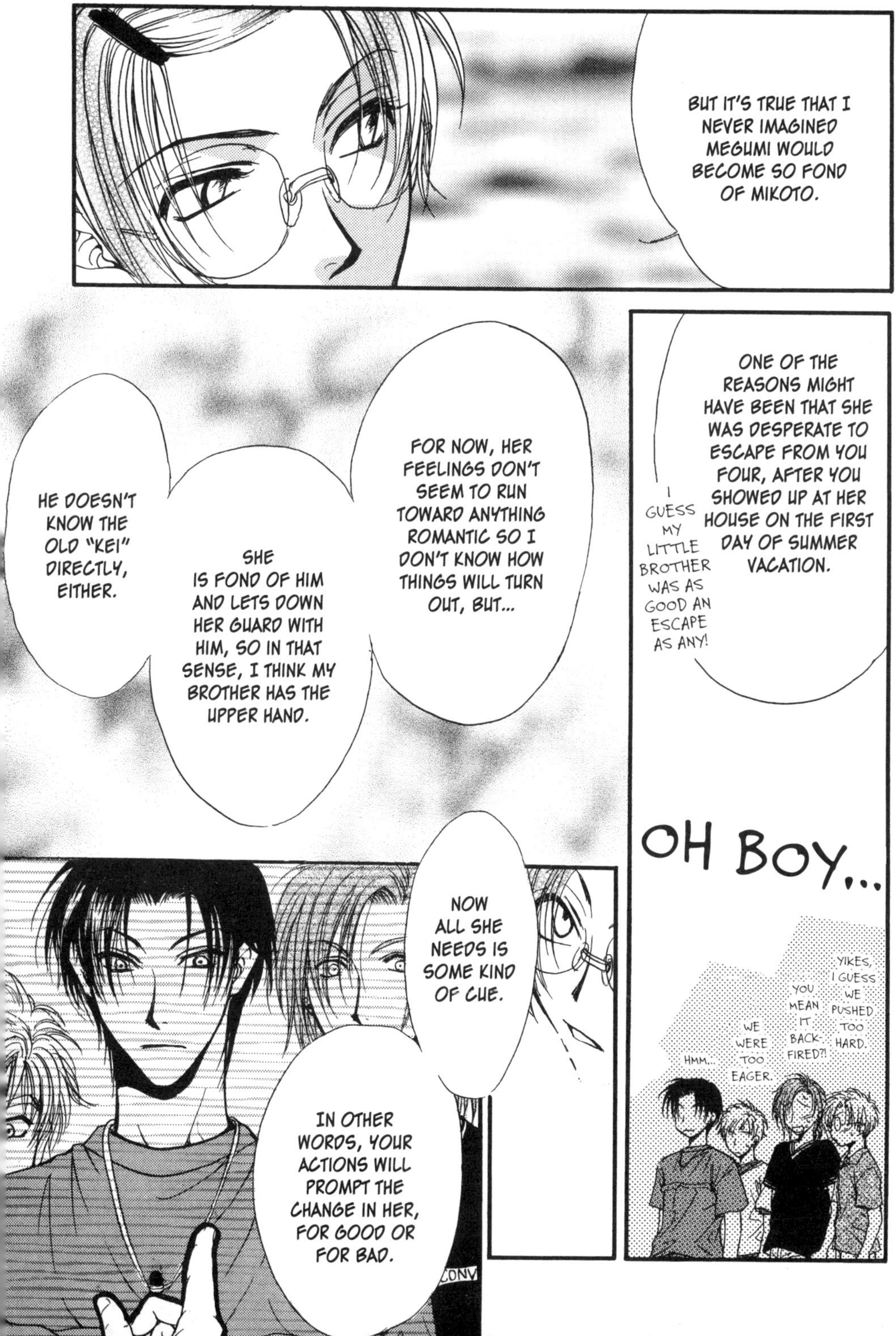
BUT IT'S TRUE THAT I NEVER IMAGINED MEGUMI WOULD BECOME SO FOND OF MIKOTO.
ONE OF THE REASONS MIGHT HAVE BEEN THAT SHE WAS DESPERATE TO ESCAPE FROM YOU FOUR, AFTER YOU SHOWED UP AT HER HOUSE ON THE FIRST DAY OF SUMMER VACATION.
I GUESS MY LITTLE BROTHER WAS AS GOOD AN ESCAPE AS ANY!
FOR NOW, HER FEELINGS DON'T SEEM TO RUN TOWARD ANYTHING ROMANTIC SO I DON'T KNOW HOW THINGS WILL TURN OUT, BUT...
SHE IS FOND OF HIM AND LETS DOWN HER GUARD WITH HIM, SO IN THAT SENSE, I THINK MY BROTHER HAS THE UPPER HAND.
HE DOESN'T KNOW THE OLD "KEI" DIRECTLY, EITHER.
NOW ALL SHE NEEDS IS SOME KIND OF CUE.
IN OTHER WORDS, YOUR ACTIONS WILL PROMPT THE CHANGE IN HER, FOR GOOD OR FOR BAD.
CONV
OH BOY...
YIKES, I GUESS WE PUSHED TOO HARD.
YOU MEAN IT BACKFIRED?!
WE WERE TOO EAGER.
HMM...

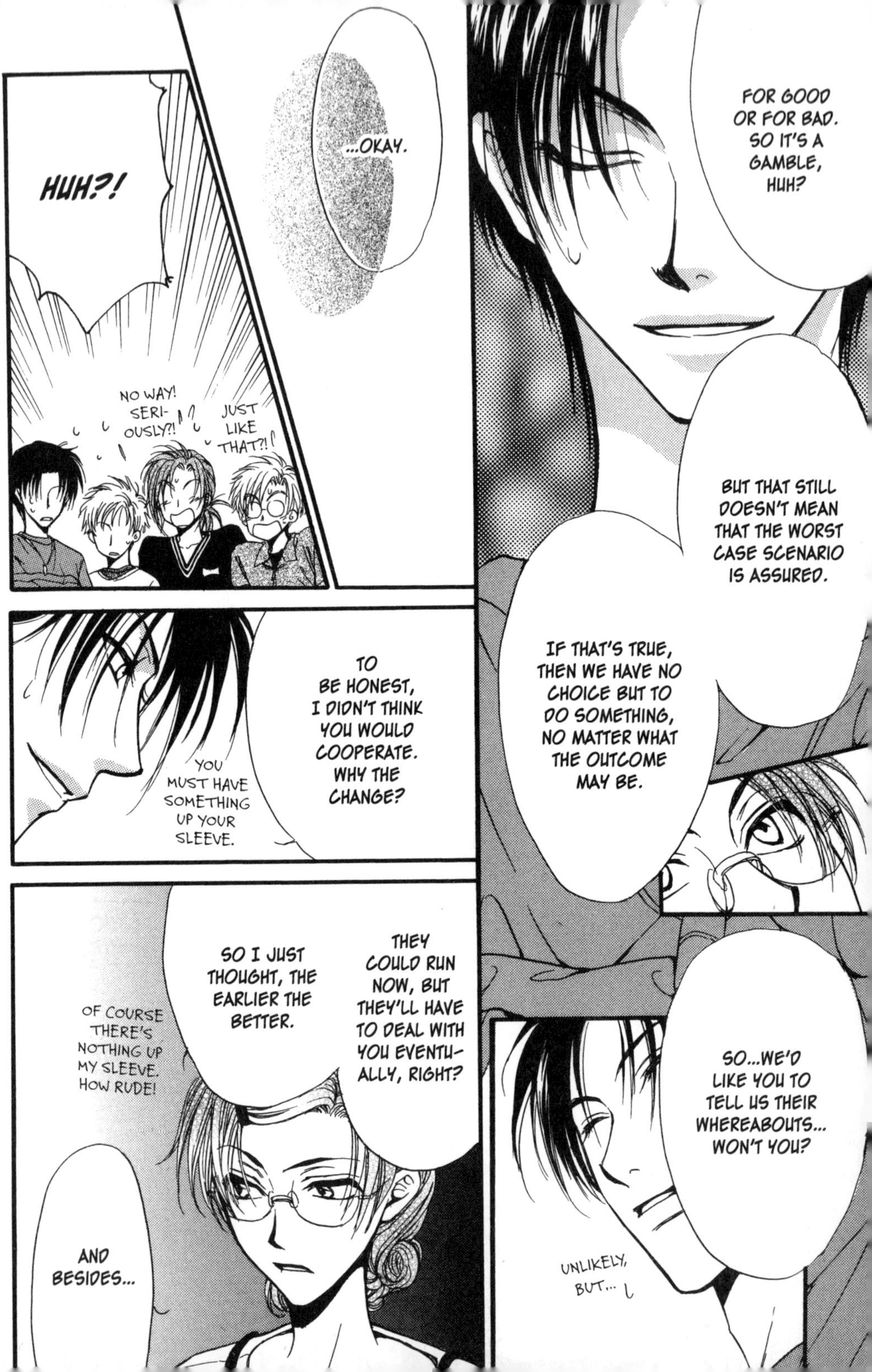

FOR GOOD OR FOR BAD. SO IT'S A GAMBLE, HUH?
BUT THAT STILL DOESN'T MEAN THAT THE WORST CASE SCENARIO IS ASSURED.
IF THAT'S TRUE, THEN WE HAVE NO CHOICE BUT TO DO SOMETHING, NO MATTER WHAT THE OUTCOME MAY BE.
SO...WE'D LIKE YOU TO TELL US THEIR WHEREABOUTS... WON'T YOU?
UNLIKELY, BUT...
...OKAY.
HUH?!
JUST LIKE THAT?!
NO WAY! SERIOUSLY?!
TO BE HONEST, I DIDN'T THINK YOU WOULD COOPERATE. WHY THE CHANGE?
YOU MUST HAVE SOMETHING UP YOUR SLEEVE.
THEY COULD RUN NOW, BUT THEY'LL HAVE TO DEAL WITH YOU EVENTUALLY, RIGHT?
SO I JUST THOUGHT, THE EARLIER THE BETTER.
OF COURSE THERE'S NOTHING UP MY SLEEVE. HOW RUDE!
AND BESIDES...

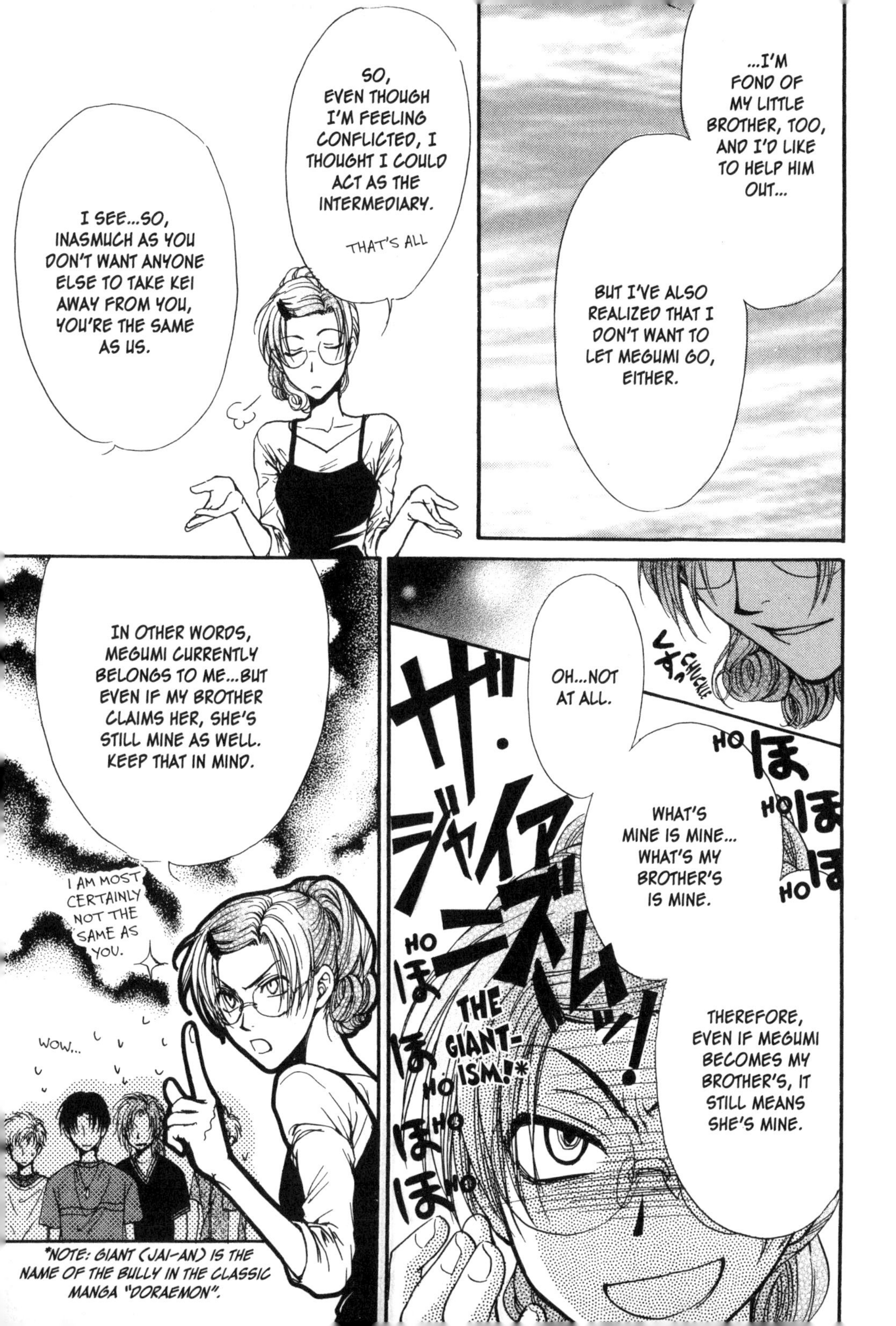
...I'M FOND OF MY LITTLE BROTHER, TOO, AND I'D LIKE TO HELP HIM OUT...
BUT I'VE ALSO REALIZED THAT I DON'T WANT TO LET MEGUMI GO, EITHER.
SO, EVEN THOUGH I'M FEELING CONFLICTED, I THOUGHT I COULD ACT AS THE INTERMEDIARY.
THAT'S ALL
I SEE...SO, INASMUCH AS YOU DON'T WANT ANYONE ELSE TO TAKE KEI AWAY FROM YOU, YOU'RE THE SAME AS US.
くすっ CHUCKLE
OH...NOT AT ALL.
HO ほ HO ほ HO ほ
WHAT'S MINE IS MINE... WHAT'S MY BROTHER'S IS MINE.
ザ・ジャイアニズムッ! THE GIANT-ISM!*
HO ほ HO ほ HO ほ HO ほ
THEREFORE, EVEN IF MEGUMI BECOMES MY BROTHER'S, IT STILL MEANS SHE'S MINE.
IN OTHER WORDS, MEGUMI CURRENTLY BELONGS TO ME...BUT EVEN IF MY BROTHER CLAIMS HER, SHE'S STILL MINE AS WELL. KEEP THAT IN MIND.
I AM MOST CERTAINLY NOT THE SAME AS YOU.
WOW...
*NOTE: GIANT (JAI-AN) IS THE NAME OF THE BULLY IN THE CLASSIC MANGA "DORAEMON".

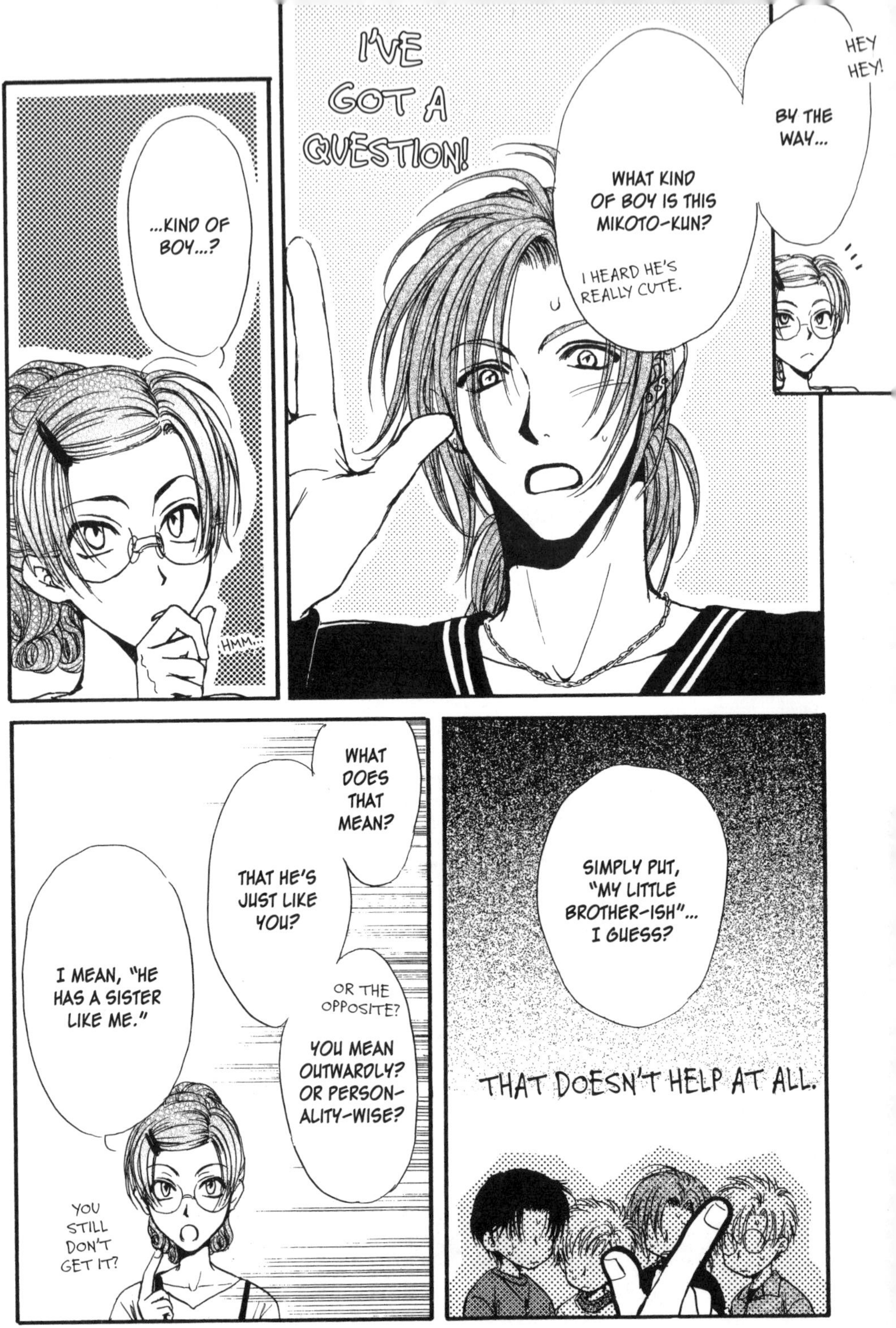
HEY HEY!
BY THE WAY...
I'VE GOT A QUESTION!
WHAT KIND OF BOY IS THIS MIKOTO-KUN?
I HEARD HE'S REALLY CUTE.
...KIND OF BOY...?
HMM...
SIMPLY PUT, "MY LITTLE BROTHER-ISH"... I GUESS?
THAT DOESN'T HELP AT ALL.
WHAT DOES THAT MEAN?
THAT HE'S JUST LIKE YOU?
OR THE OPPOSITE?
YOU MEAN OUTWARDLY? OR PERSON-ALITY-WISE?
I MEAN, "HE HAS A SISTER LIKE ME."
YOU STILL DON'T GET IT?

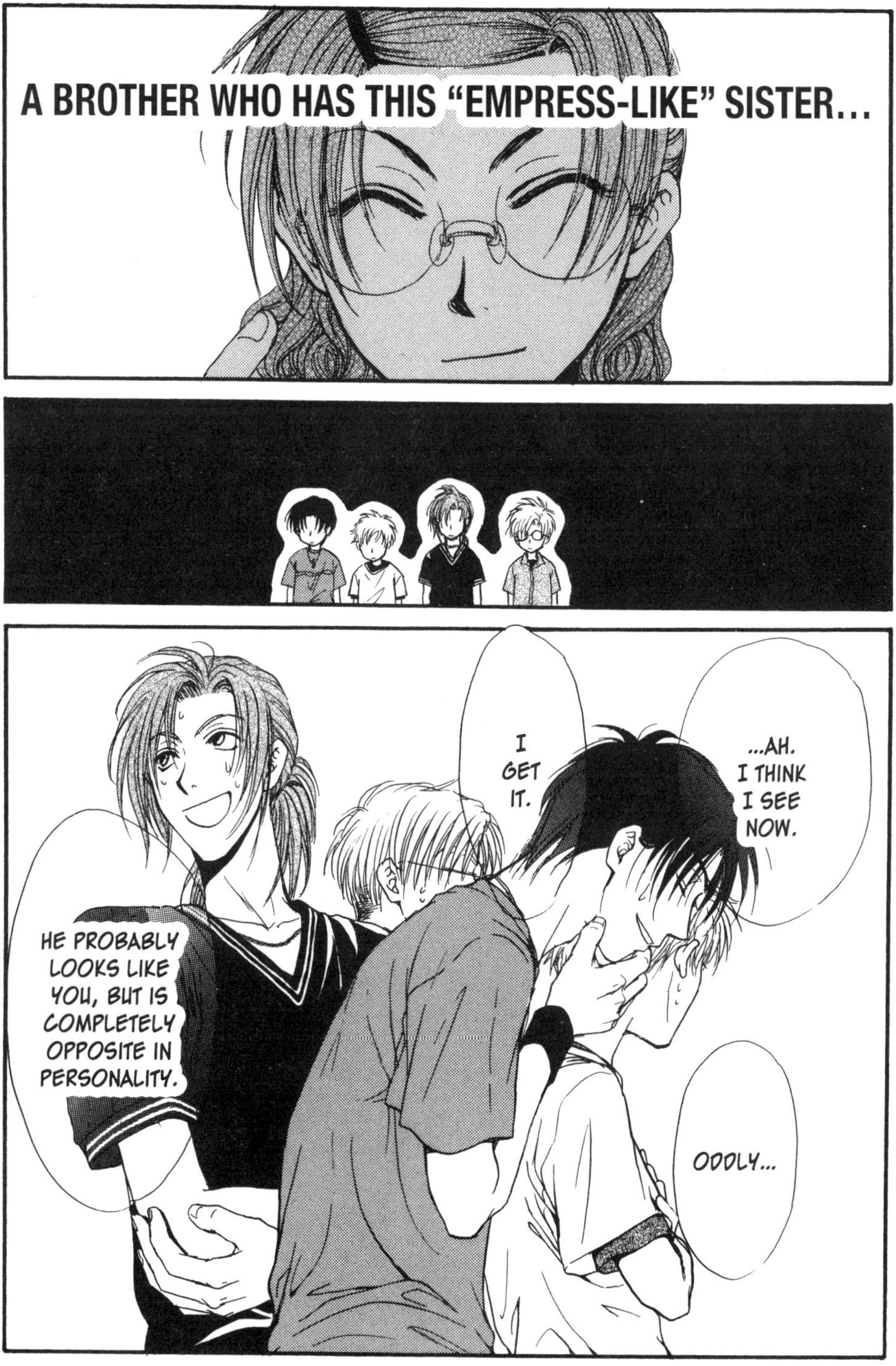
A BROTHER WHO HAS THIS "EMPRESS-LIKE" SISTER…
...AH. I THINK I SEE NOW.
I GET IT.
ODDLY...
HE PROBABLY LOOKS LIKE YOU, BUT IS COMPLETELY OPPOSITE IN PERSONALITY.

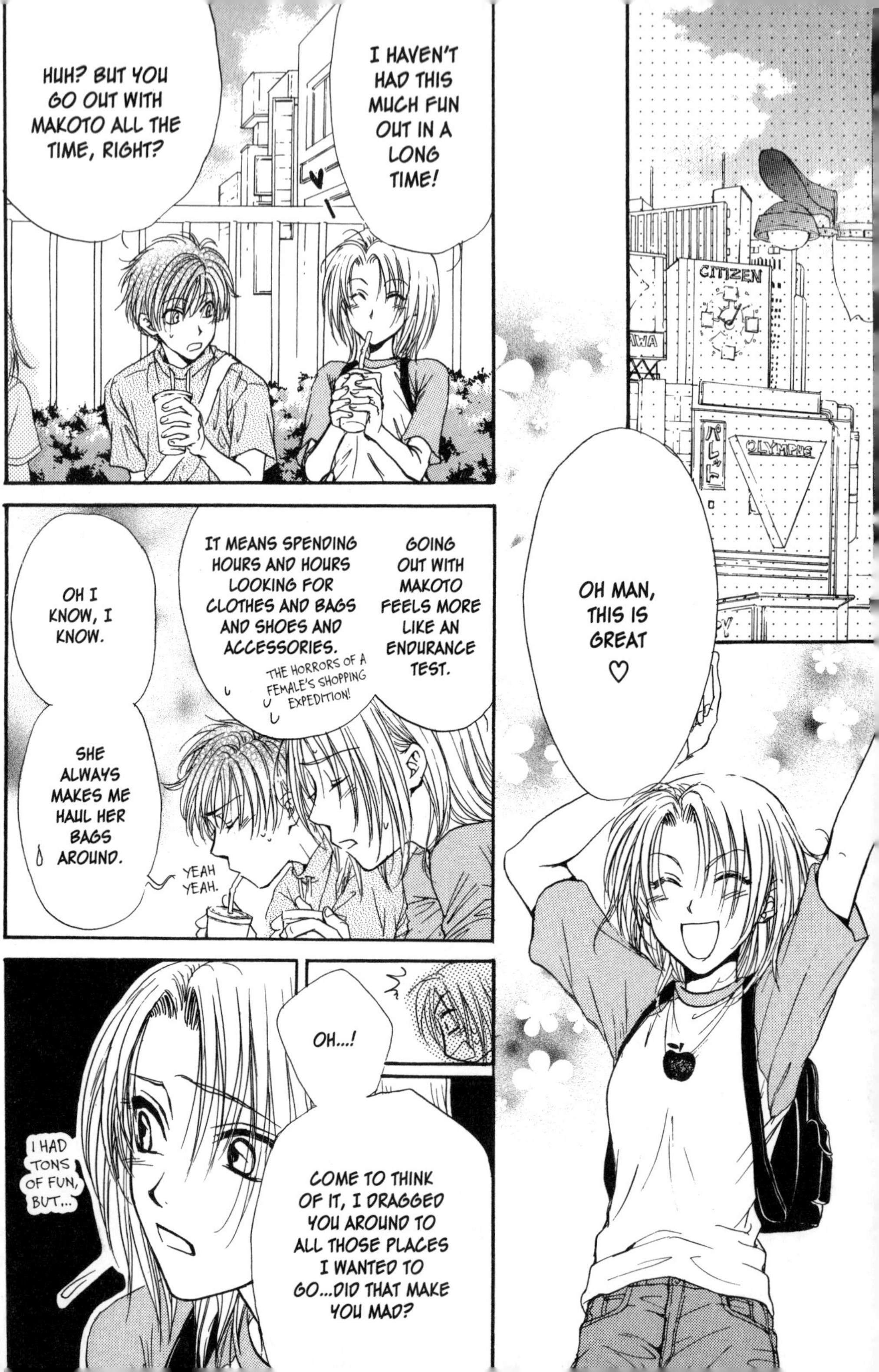
OH MAN, THIS IS GREAT ♡
CITIZEN
OLYMPUS
パレット
I HAVEN'T HAD THIS MUCH FUN OUT IN A LONG TIME! ♥
HUH? BUT YOU GO OUT WITH MAKOTO ALL THE TIME, RIGHT?
GOING OUT WITH MAKOTO FEELS MORE LIKE AN ENDURANCE TEST.
IT MEANS SPENDING HOURS AND HOURS LOOKING FOR CLOTHES AND BAGS AND SHOES AND ACCESSORIES.
THE HORRORS OF A FEMALE'S SHOPPING EXPEDITION!
OH I KNOW, I KNOW.
SHE ALWAYS MAKES ME HAUL HER BAGS AROUND.
YEAH YEAH.
OH...!
I HAD TONS OF FUN, BUT...
COME TO THINK OF IT, I DRAGGED YOU AROUND TO ALL THOSE PLACES I WANTED TO GO...DID THAT MAKE YOU MAD?

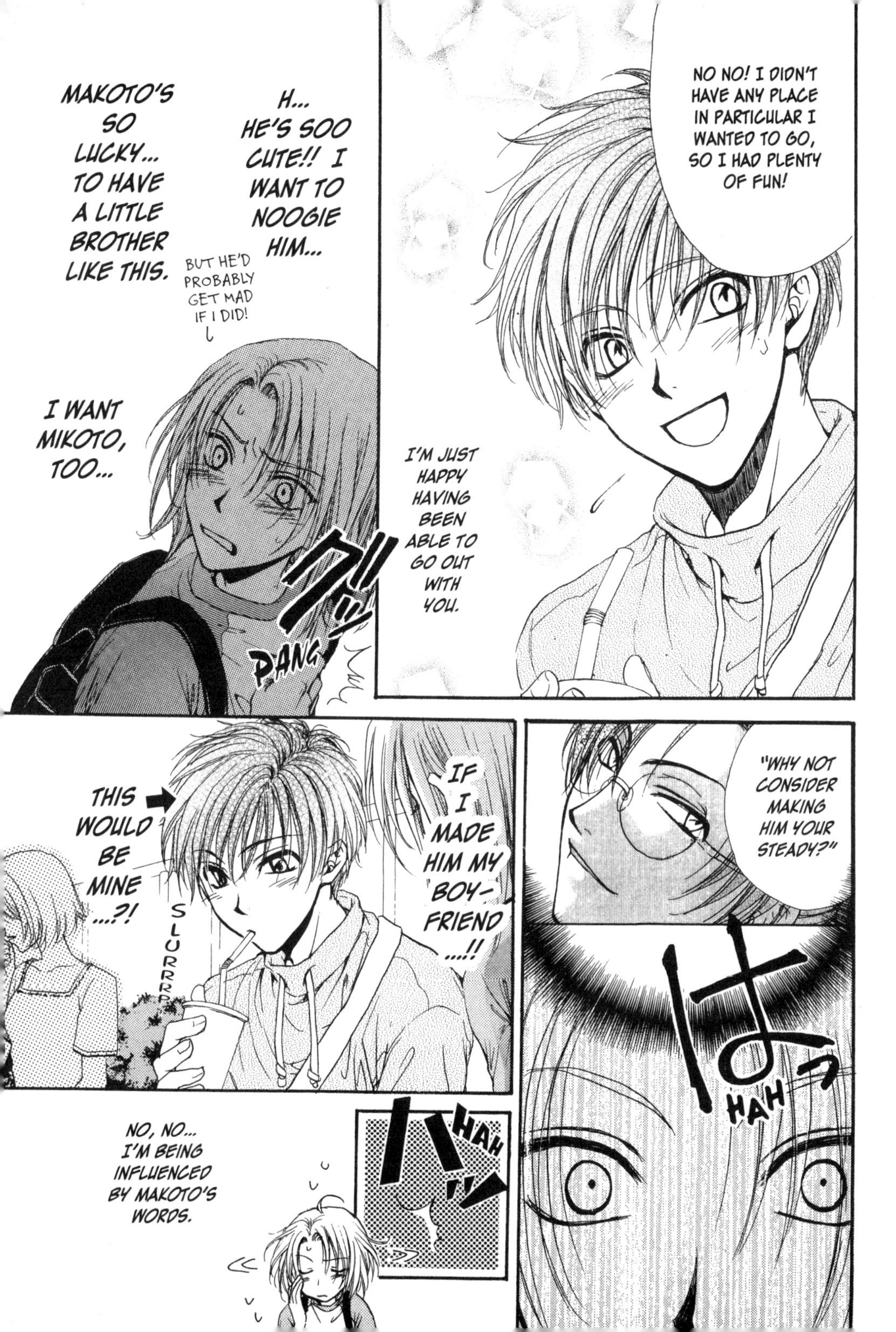
NO NO! I DIDN'T HAVE ANY PLACE IN PARTICULAR I WANTED TO GO, SO I HAD PLENTY OF FUN!
I'M JUST HAPPY HAVING BEEN ABLE TO GO OUT WITH YOU.
H... HE'S SOO CUTE!! I WANT TO NOOGIE HIM...
MAKOTO'S SO LUCKY... TO HAVE A LITTLE BROTHER LIKE THIS.
BUT HE'D PROBABLY GET MAD IF I DID!
I WANT MIKOTO, TOO...
PANG
"WHY NOT CONSIDER MAKING HIM YOUR STEADY?"
IF I MADE HIM MY BOY-FRIEND ...!!
THIS WOULD BE MINE ...?!
SLURRRP
HAH
HAH
NO, NO... I'M BEING INFLUENCED BY MAKOTO'S WORDS.

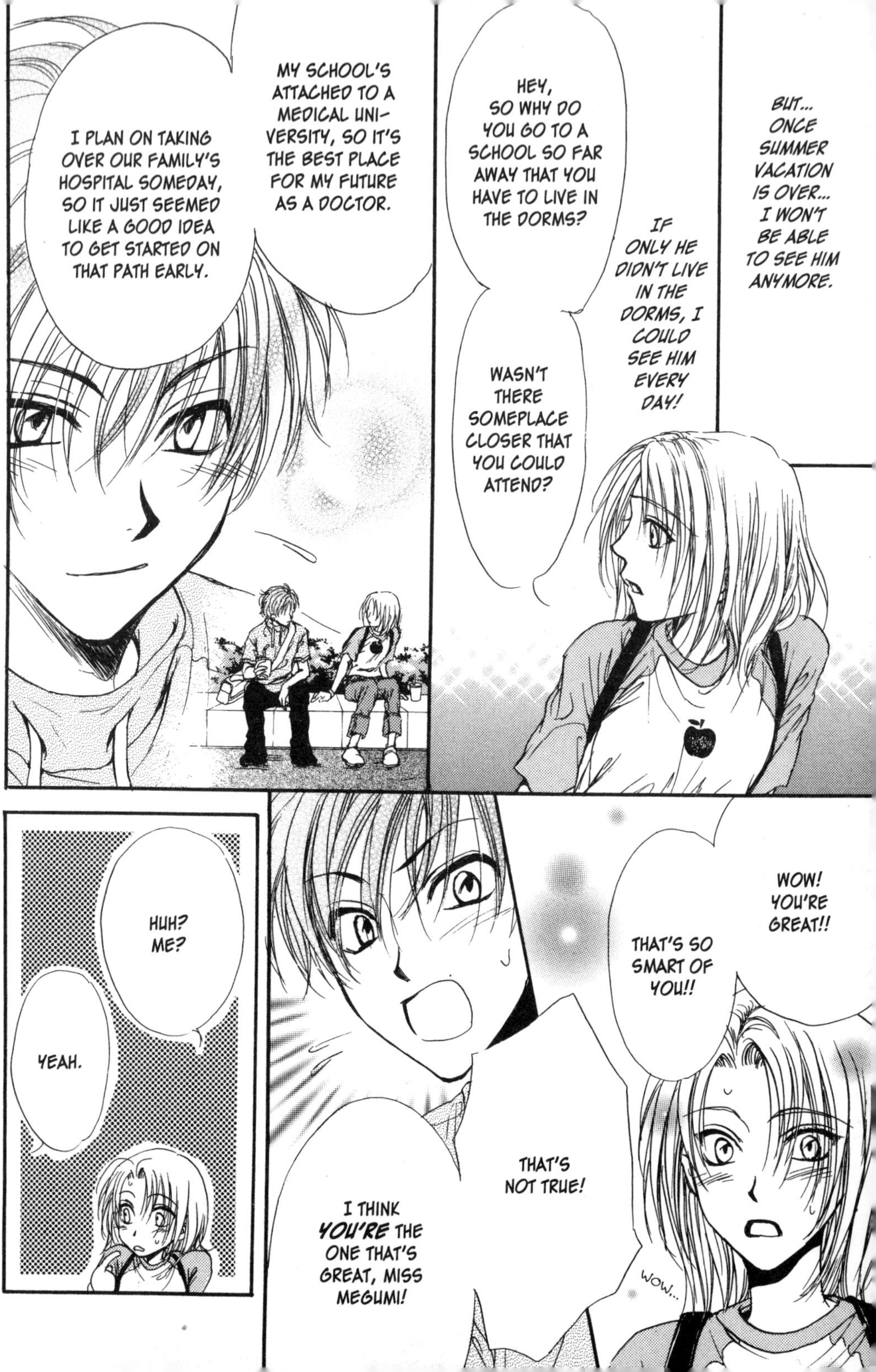
BUT... ONCE SUMMER VACATION IS OVER... I WON'T BE ABLE TO SEE HIM ANYMORE.
IF ONLY HE DIDN'T LIVE IN THE DORMS, I COULD SEE HIM EVERY DAY!
HEY, SO WHY DO YOU GO TO A SCHOOL SO FAR AWAY THAT YOU HAVE TO LIVE IN THE DORMS?
WASN'T THERE SOMEPLACE CLOSER THAT YOU COULD ATTEND?
MY SCHOOL'S ATTACHED TO A MEDICAL UNI-VERSITY, SO IT'S THE BEST PLACE FOR MY FUTURE AS A DOCTOR.
I PLAN ON TAKING OVER OUR FAMILY'S HOSPITAL SOMEDAY, SO IT JUST SEEMED LIKE A GOOD IDEA TO GET STARTED ON THAT PATH EARLY.
WOW! YOU'RE GREAT!!
THAT'S SO SMART OF YOU!!
WOW...
THAT'S NOT TRUE!
I THINK ***YOU'RE*** THE ONE THAT'S GREAT, MISS MEGUMI!
HUH? ME?
YEAH.

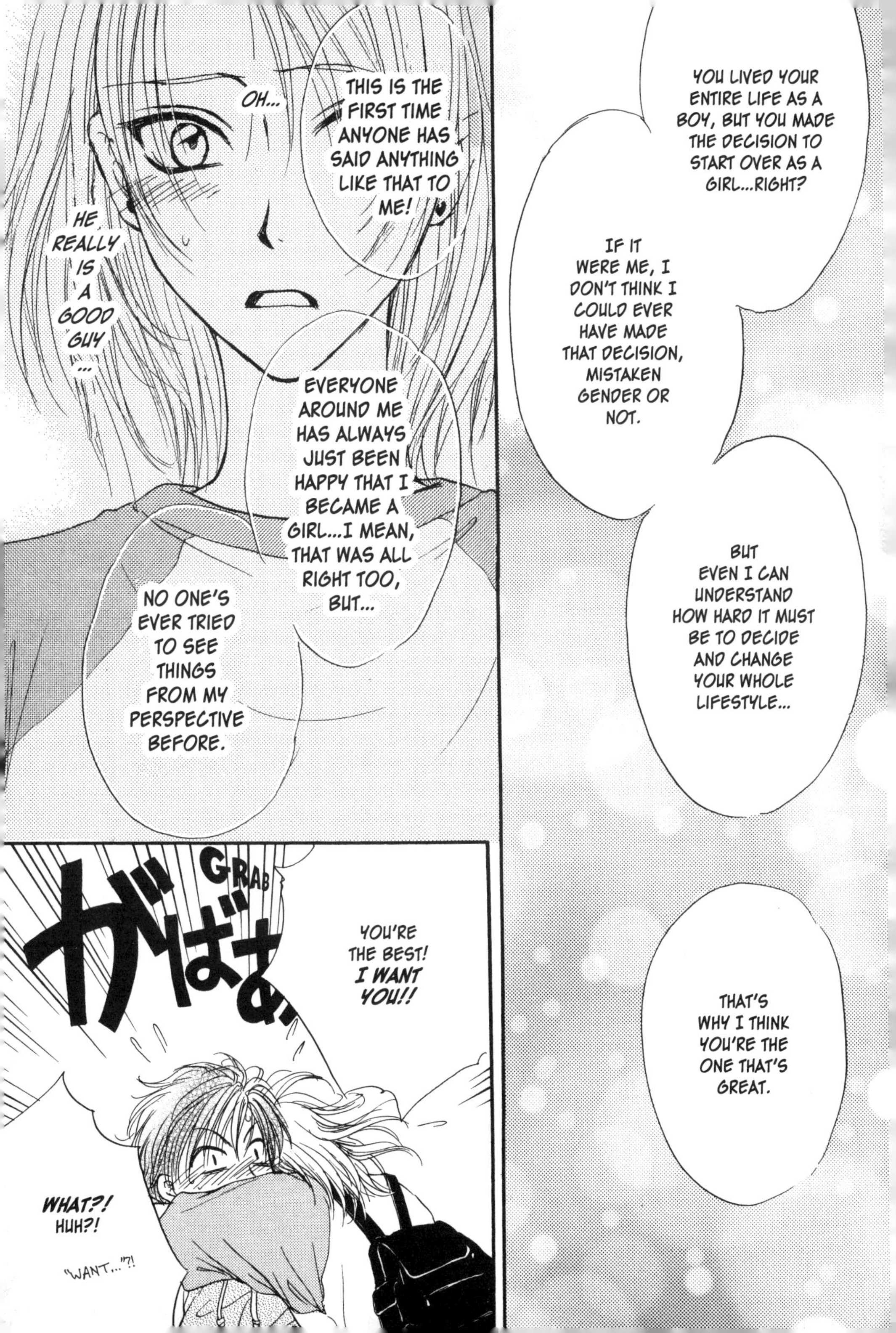
YOU LIVED YOUR ENTIRE LIFE AS A BOY, BUT YOU MADE THE DECISION TO START OVER AS A GIRL...RIGHT?
IF IT WERE ME, I DON'T THINK I COULD EVER HAVE MADE THAT DECISION, MISTAKEN GENDER OR NOT.
BUT EVEN I CAN UNDERSTAND HOW HARD IT MUST BE TO DECIDE AND CHANGE YOUR WHOLE LIFESTYLE...
THAT'S WHY I THINK YOU'RE THE ONE THAT'S GREAT.
OH...
THIS IS THE FIRST TIME ANYONE HAS SAID ANYTHING LIKE THAT TO ME!
HE REALLY IS A GOOD GUY...
EVERYONE AROUND ME HAS ALWAYS JUST BEEN HAPPY THAT I BECAME A GIRL...I MEAN, THAT WAS ALL RIGHT TOO, BUT...
NO ONE'S EVER TRIED TO SEE THINGS FROM MY PERSPECTIVE BEFORE.
GRAB
YOU'RE THE BEST! I WANT YOU!!
WHAT?! HUH?!
"WANT..."?!

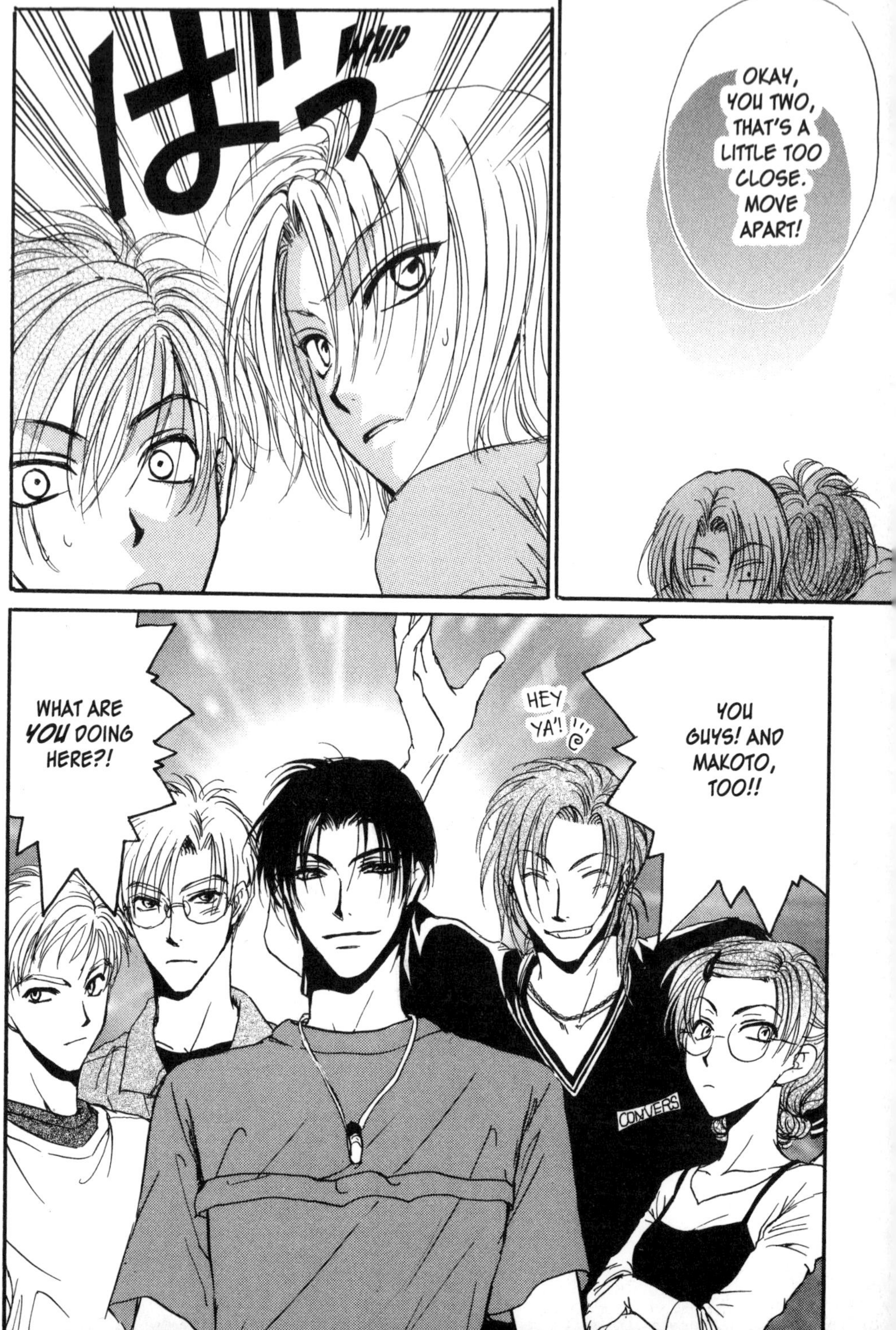
OKAY, YOU TWO, THAT'S A LITTLE TOO CLOSE. MOVE APART!
ばっ
WHIP
YOU GUYS! AND MAKOTO, TOO!!
HEY YA'!
WHAT ARE *YOU* DOING HERE?!
CONVERS

A TALE OF STRANGE COINCIDENCE — ONE READER'S LETTER —

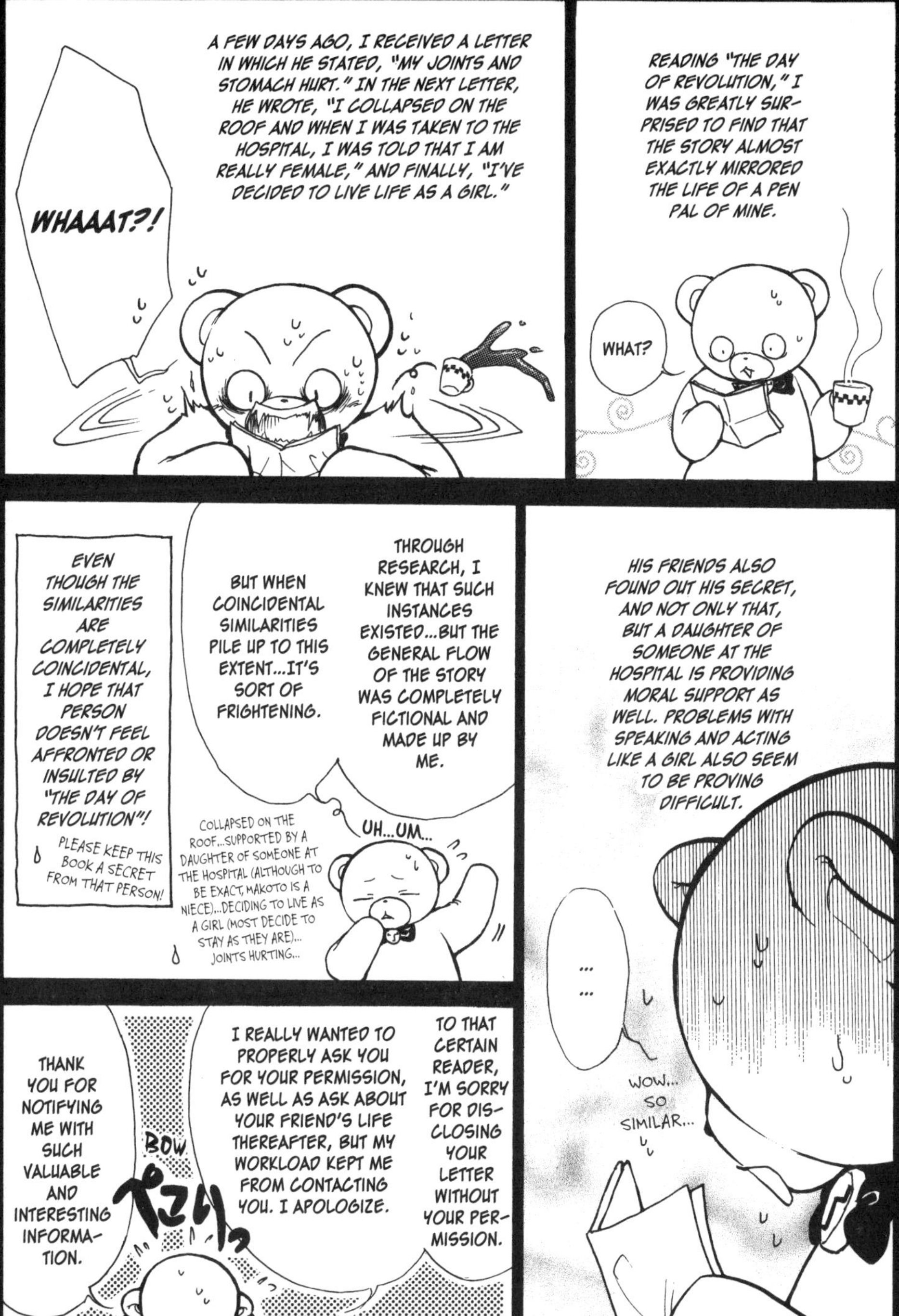

READING "THE DAY OF REVOLUTION," I WAS GREATLY SURPRISED TO FIND THAT THE STORY ALMOST EXACTLY MIRRORED THE LIFE OF A PEN PAL OF MINE.
WHAT?
A FEW DAYS AGO, I RECEIVED A LETTER IN WHICH HE STATED, "MY JOINTS AND STOMACH HURT." IN THE NEXT LETTER, HE WROTE, "I COLLAPSED ON THE ROOF AND WHEN I WAS TAKEN TO THE HOSPITAL, I WAS TOLD THAT I AM REALLY FEMALE," AND FINALLY, "I'VE DECIDED TO LIVE LIFE AS A GIRL."
WHAAAT?!
HIS FRIENDS ALSO FOUND OUT HIS SECRET, AND NOT ONLY THAT, BUT A DAUGHTER OF SOMEONE AT THE HOSPITAL IS PROVIDING MORAL SUPPORT AS WELL. PROBLEMS WITH SPEAKING AND ACTING LIKE A GIRL ALSO SEEM TO BE PROVING DIFFICULT.
...
...
WOW... SO SIMILAR...
THROUGH RESEARCH, I KNEW THAT SUCH INSTANCES EXISTED...BUT THE GENERAL FLOW OF THE STORY WAS COMPLETELY FICTIONAL AND MADE UP BY ME.
BUT WHEN COINCIDENTAL SIMILARITIES PILE UP TO THIS EXTENT...IT'S SORT OF FRIGHTENING.
EVEN THOUGH THE SIMILARITIES ARE COMPLETELY COINCIDENTAL, I HOPE THAT PERSON DOESN'T FEEL AFFRONTED OR INSULTED BY "THE DAY OF REVOLUTION"!
PLEASE KEEP THIS BOOK A SECRET FROM THAT PERSON!
UH...UM...
COLLAPSED ON THE ROOF...SUPPORTED BY A DAUGHTER OF SOMEONE AT THE HOSPITAL (ALTHOUGH TO BE EXACT, MAKOTO IS A NIECE)...DECIDING TO LIVE AS A GIRL (MOST DECIDE TO STAY AS THEY ARE)... JOINTS HURTING...
TO THAT CERTAIN READER, I'M SORRY FOR DISCLOSING YOUR LETTER WITHOUT YOUR PERMISSION.
I REALLY WANTED TO PROPERLY ASK YOU FOR YOUR PERMISSION, AS WELL AS ASK ABOUT YOUR FRIEND'S LIFE THEREAFTER, BUT MY WORKLOAD KEPT ME FROM CONTACTING YOU. I APOLOGIZE.
THANK YOU FOR NOTIFYING ME WITH SUCH VALUABLE AND INTERESTING INFORMATION.
BOW

A TALE OF STRANGE COINCIDENCE ✹ END

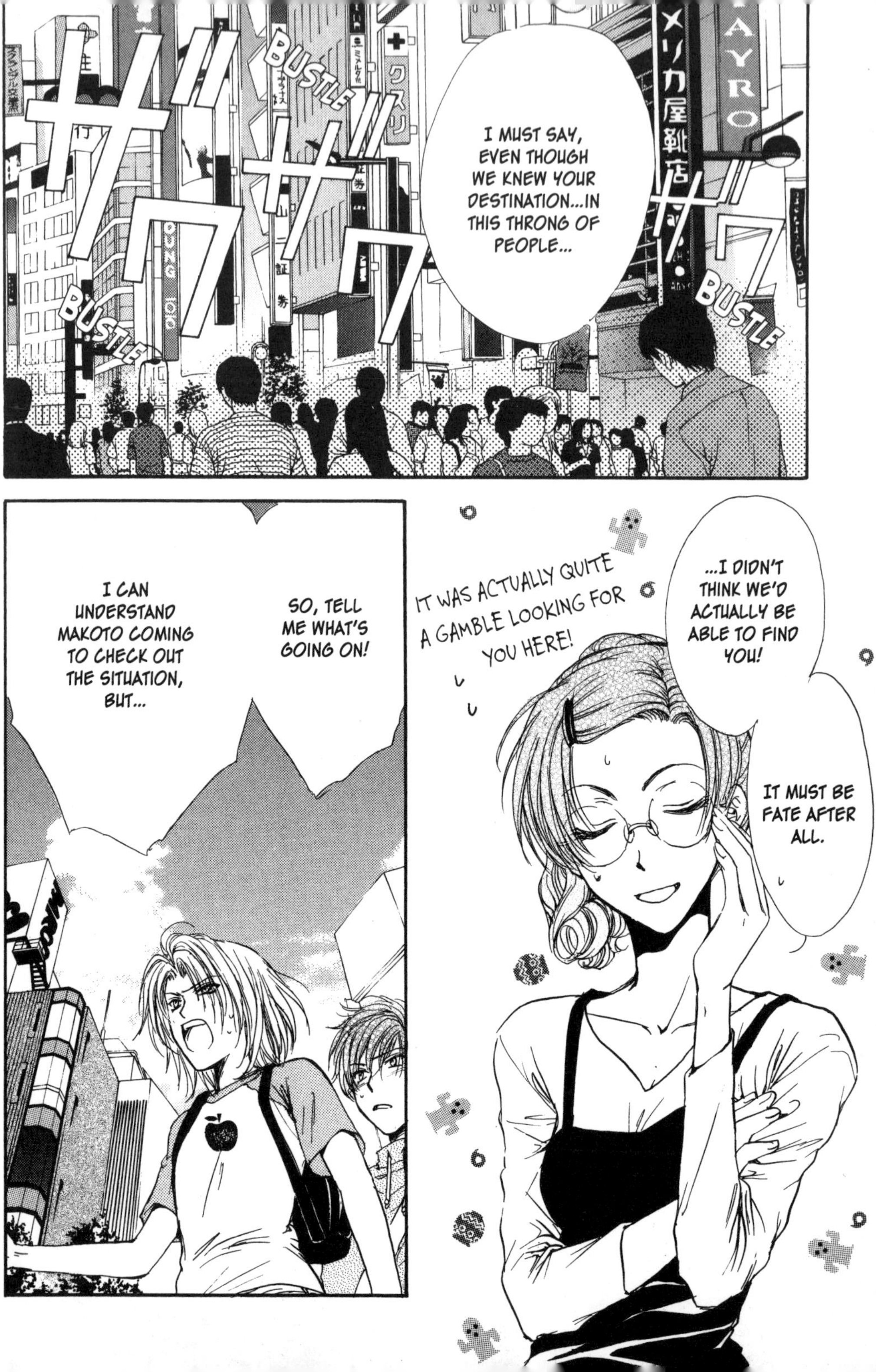
BUSTLE
I MUST SAY, EVEN THOUGH WE KNEW YOUR DESTINATION...IN THIS THRONG OF PEOPLE...
BUSTLE
BUSTLE
...I DIDN'T THINK WE'D ACTUALLY BE ABLE TO FIND YOU!
IT WAS ACTUALLY QUITE A GAMBLE LOOKING FOR YOU HERE!
IT MUST BE FATE AFTER ALL.
SO, TELL ME WHAT'S GOING ON!
I CAN UNDERSTAND MAKOTO COMING TO CHECK OUT THE SITUATION, BUT...

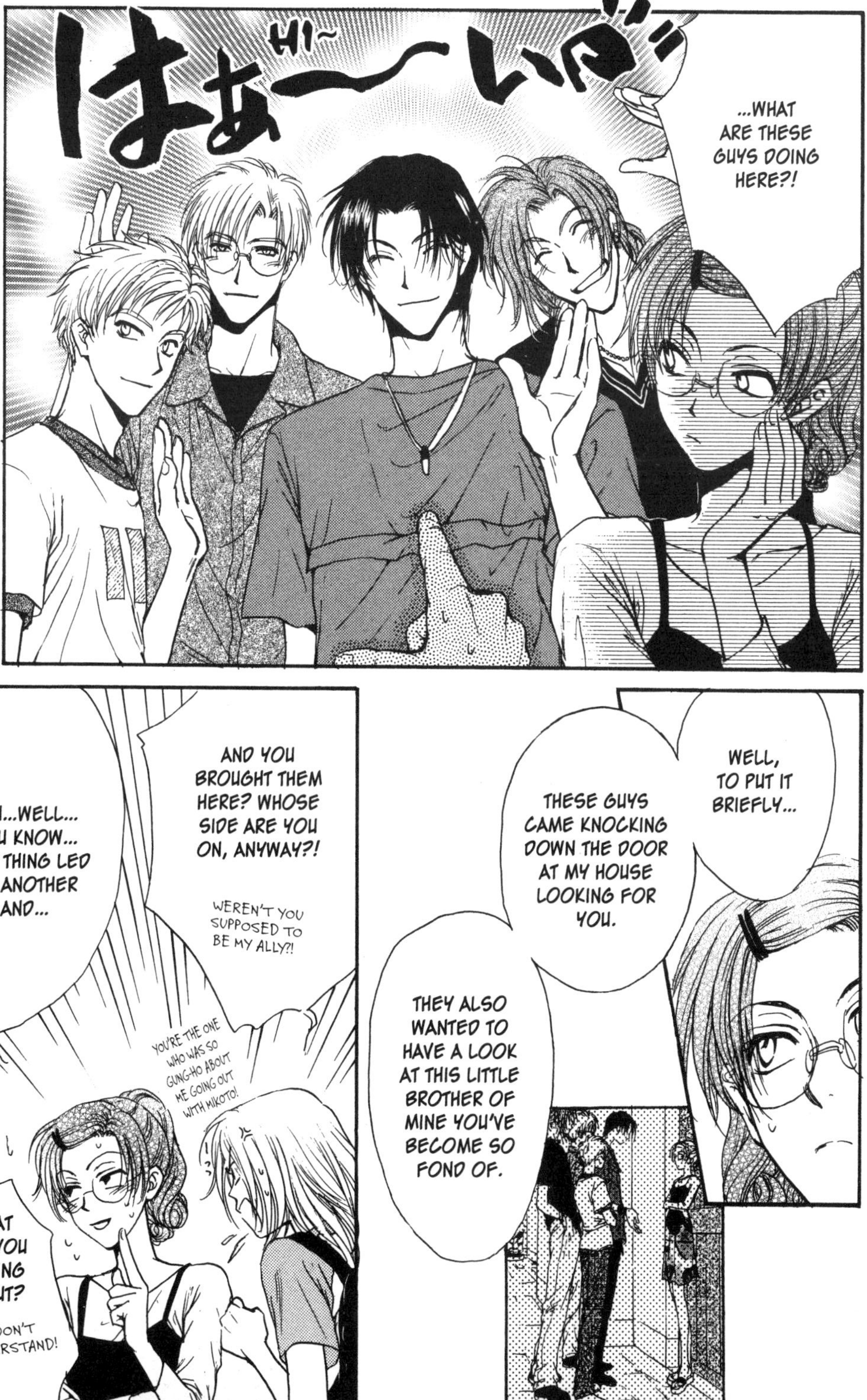

はぁ～い
HI~
...WHAT ARE THESE GUYS DOING HERE?!
WELL, TO PUT IT BRIEFLY...
THESE GUYS CAME KNOCKING DOWN THE DOOR AT MY HOUSE LOOKING FOR YOU.
THEY ALSO WANTED TO HAVE A LOOK AT THIS LITTLE BROTHER OF MINE YOU'VE BECOME SO FOND OF.
AND YOU BROUGHT THEM HERE? WHOSE SIDE ARE YOU ON, ANYWAY?!
WEREN'T YOU SUPPOSED TO BE MY ALLY?!
UHH...WELL... YOU KNOW... ONE THING LED TO ANOTHER AND...
YOU'RE THE ONE WHO WAS SO GUNG-HO ABOUT ME GOING OUT WITH MIKOTO!
WHAT ARE YOU TALKING ABOUT?
I DON'T UNDERSTAND!

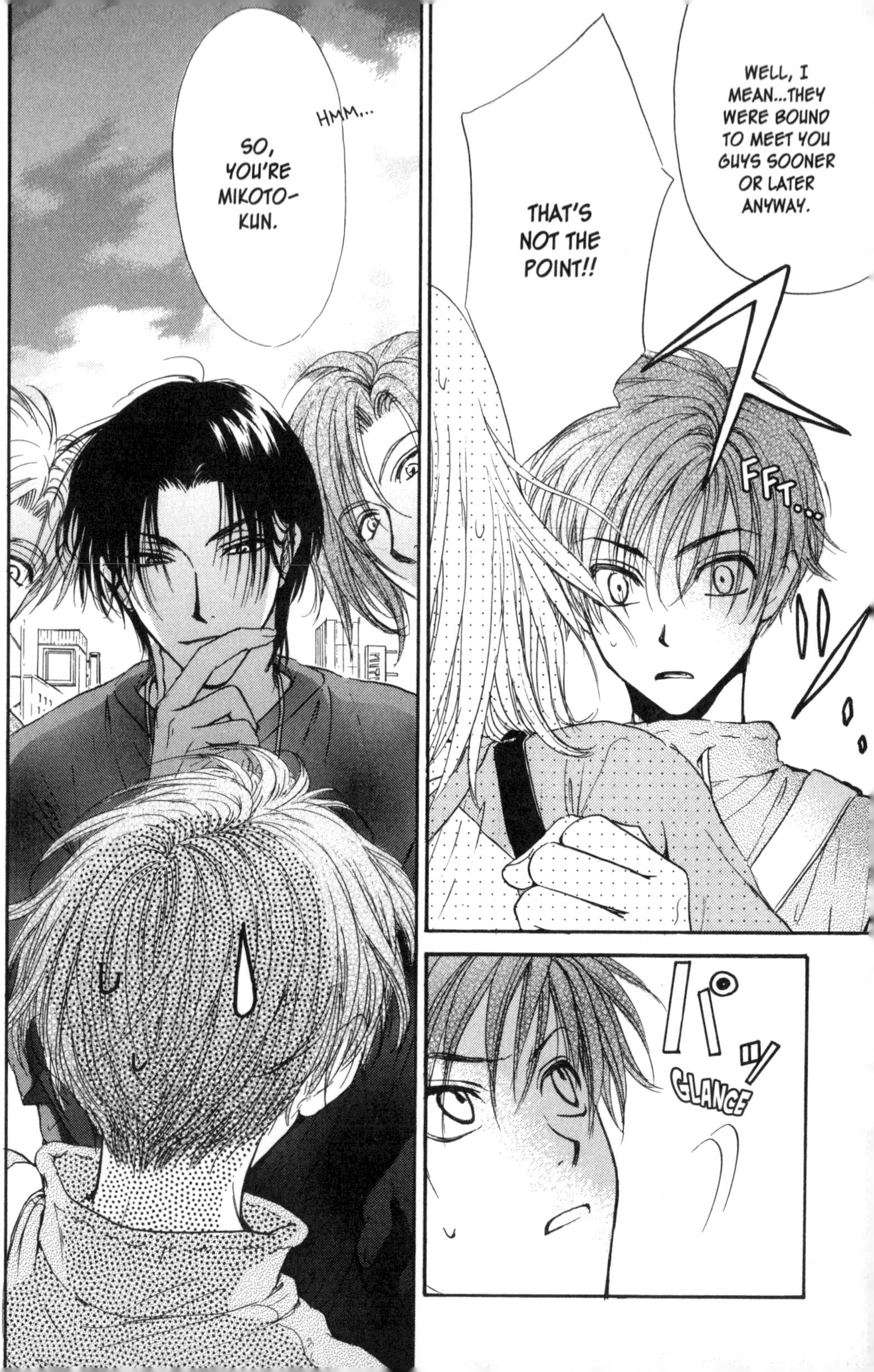
WELL, I MEAN...THEY WERE BOUND TO MEET YOU GUYS SOONER OR LATER ANYWAY.
THAT'S NOT THE POINT!!
FFT...
GLANCE
HMM...
SO, YOU'RE MIKOTO-KUN.

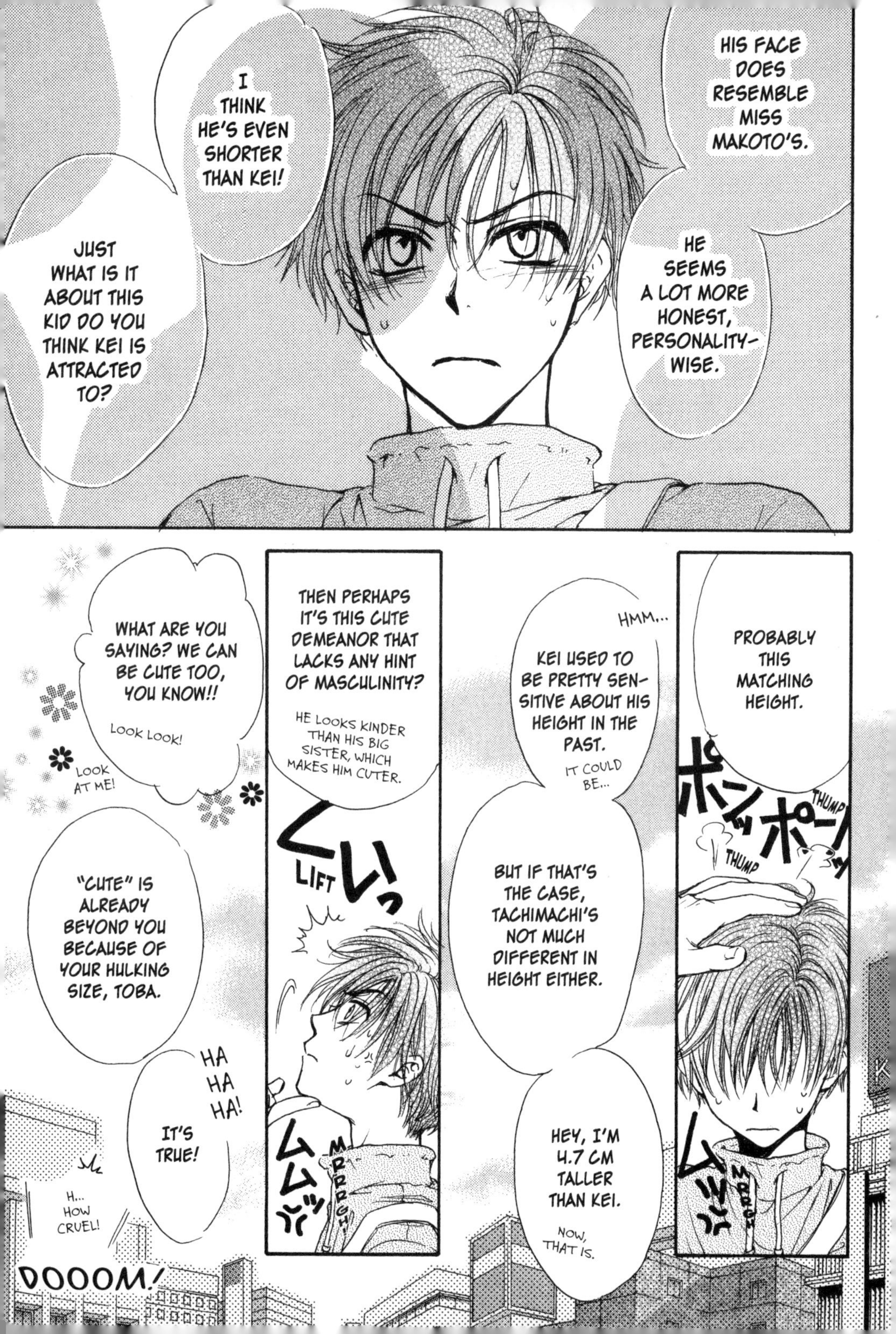
HIS FACE DOES RESEMBLE MISS MAKOTO'S.
HE SEEMS A LOT MORE HONEST, PERSONALITY-WISE.
I THINK HE'S EVEN SHORTER THAN KEI!
JUST WHAT IS IT ABOUT THIS KID DO YOU THINK KEI IS ATTRACTED TO?
PROBABLY THIS MATCHING HEIGHT.
ポンッポーン
THUMP
THUMP
ムッ
MRRGH
HMM...
KEI USED TO BE PRETTY SEN-SITIVE ABOUT HIS HEIGHT IN THE PAST.
IT COULD BE...
BUT IF THAT'S THE CASE, TACHIMACHI'S NOT MUCH DIFFERENT IN HEIGHT EITHER.
HEY, I'M 4.7 CM TALLER THAN KEI.
NOW, THAT IS.
THEN PERHAPS IT'S THIS CUTE DEMEANOR THAT LACKS ANY HINT OF MASCULINITY?
HE LOOKS KINDER THAN HIS BIG SISTER, WHICH MAKES HIM CUTER.
くいっ
LIFT
ムムッ
MRRGH
WHAT ARE YOU SAYING? WE CAN BE CUTE TOO, YOU KNOW!!
LOOK LOOK!
LOOK AT ME!
"CUTE" IS ALREADY BEYOND YOU BECAUSE OF YOUR HULKING SIZE, TOBA.
HA HA HA!
IT'S TRUE!
H... HOW CRUEL!
DOOOM!

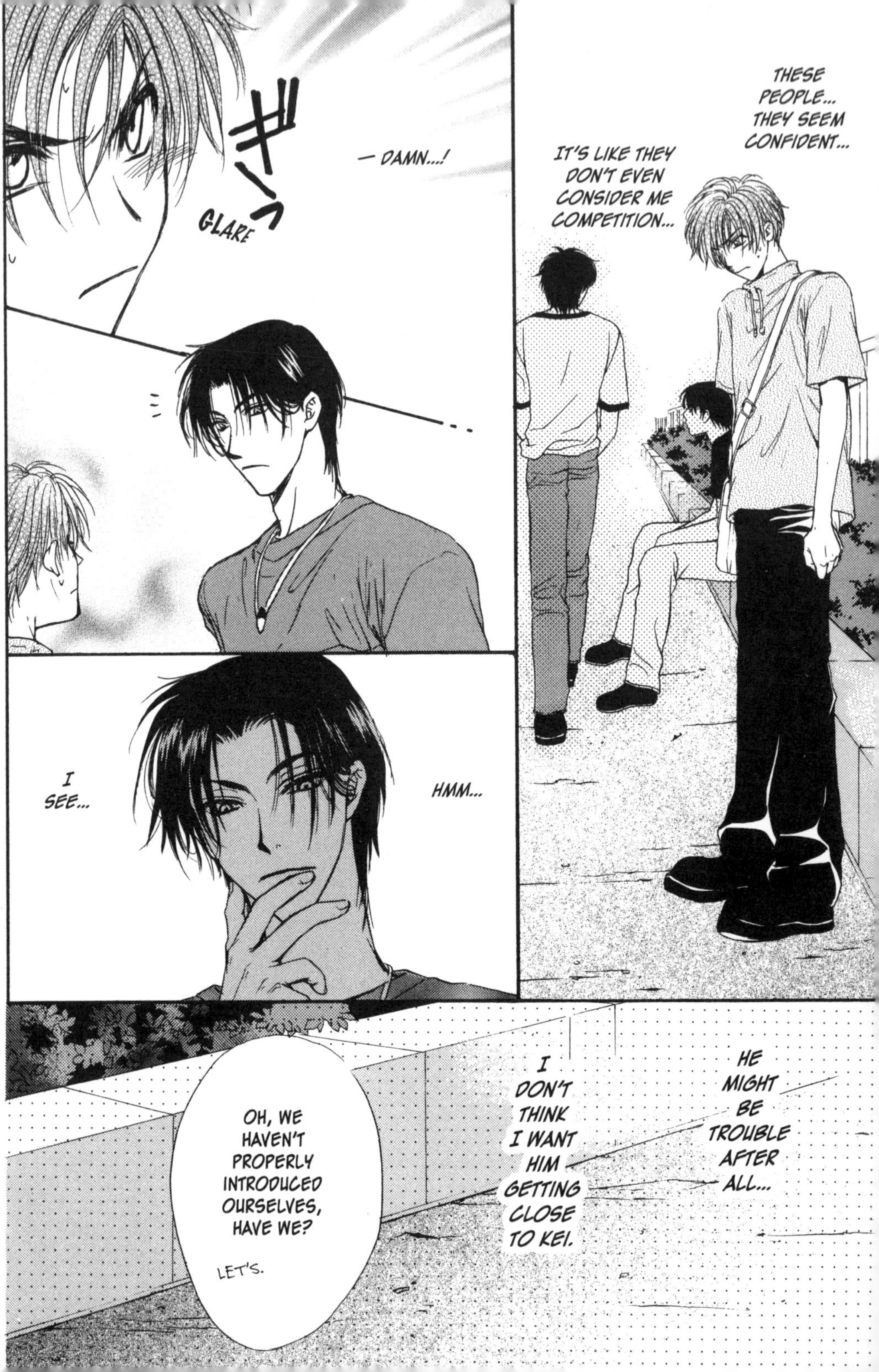
THESE PEOPLE... THEY SEEM CONFIDENT...
IT'S LIKE THEY DON'T EVEN CONSIDER ME COMPETITION...
GLARE
— DAMN...!
HMM...
I SEE...
HE MIGHT BE TROUBLE AFTER ALL...
I DON'T THINK I WANT HIM GETTING CLOSE TO KEI.
OH, WE HAVEN'T PROPERLY INTRODUCED OURSELVES, HAVE WE?
LET'S.

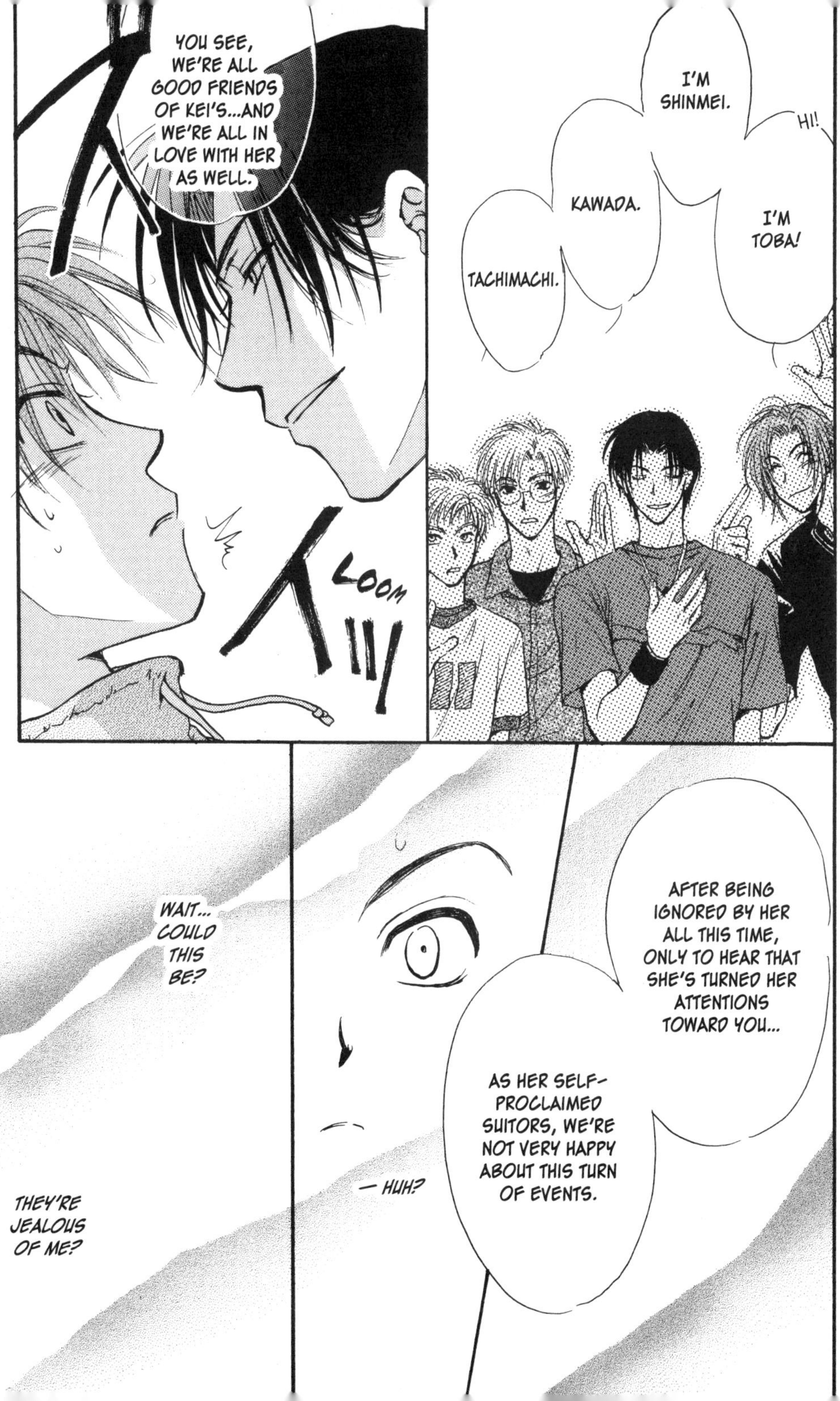
HI!
I'M SHINMEI.
I'M TOBA!
KAWADA.
TACHIMACHI.
YOU SEE, WE'RE ALL GOOD FRIENDS OF KEI'S...AND WE'RE ALL IN LOVE WITH HER AS WELL.
LOOM
AFTER BEING IGNORED BY HER ALL THIS TIME, ONLY TO HEAR THAT SHE'S TURNED HER ATTENTIONS TOWARD YOU...
AS HER SELF-PROCLAIMED SUITORS, WE'RE NOT VERY HAPPY ABOUT THIS TURN OF EVENTS.
— HUH?
WAIT... COULD THIS BE?
THEY'RE JEALOUS OF ME?

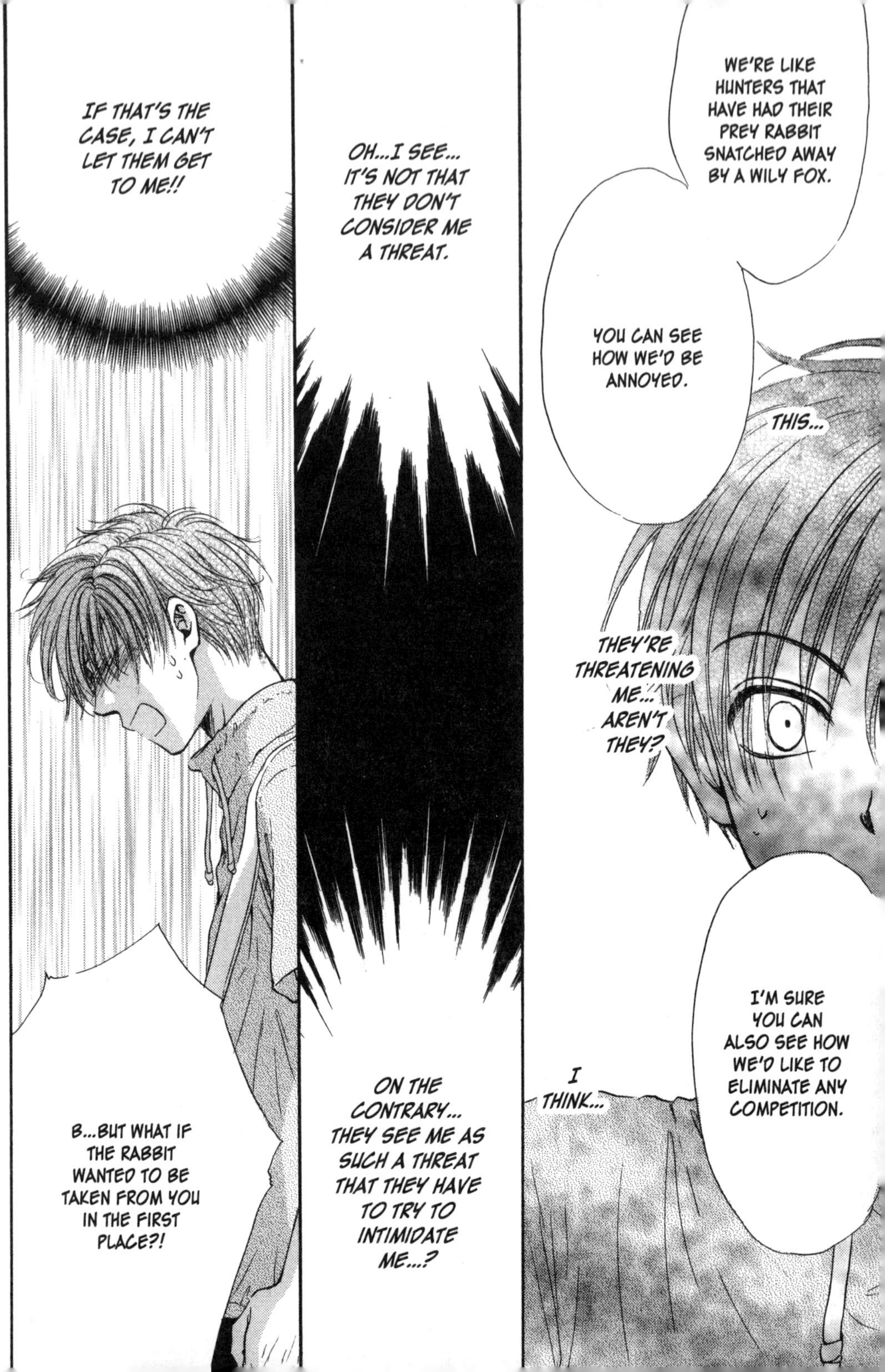
WE'RE LIKE HUNTERS THAT HAVE HAD THEIR PREY RABBIT SNATCHED AWAY BY A WILY FOX.
YOU CAN SEE HOW WE'D BE ANNOYED.
THIS...
THEY'RE THREATENING ME... AREN'T THEY?
I'M SURE YOU CAN ALSO SEE HOW WE'D LIKE TO ELIMINATE ANY COMPETITION.
I THINK...
OH...I SEE... IT'S NOT THAT THEY DON'T CONSIDER ME A THREAT.
ON THE CONTRARY... THEY SEE ME AS SUCH A THREAT THAT THEY HAVE TO TRY TO INTIMIDATE ME...?
IF THAT'S THE CASE, I CAN'T LET THEM GET TO ME!!
B...BUT WHAT IF THE RABBIT WANTED TO BE TAKEN FROM YOU IN THE FIRST PLACE?!

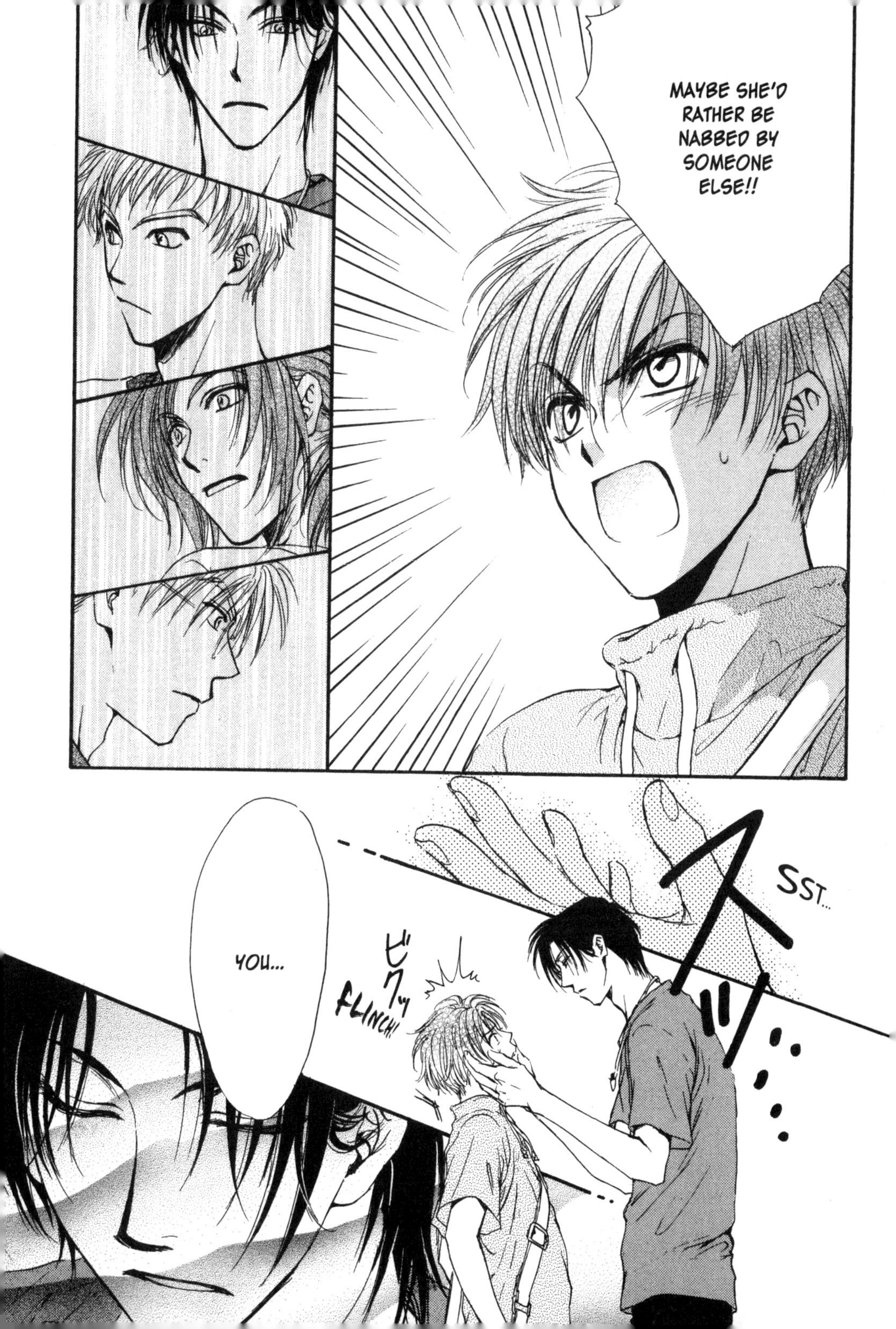
MAYBE SHE'D RATHER BE NABBED BY SOMEONE ELSE!!
SST...
ビクッ
FLINCH!
YOU...

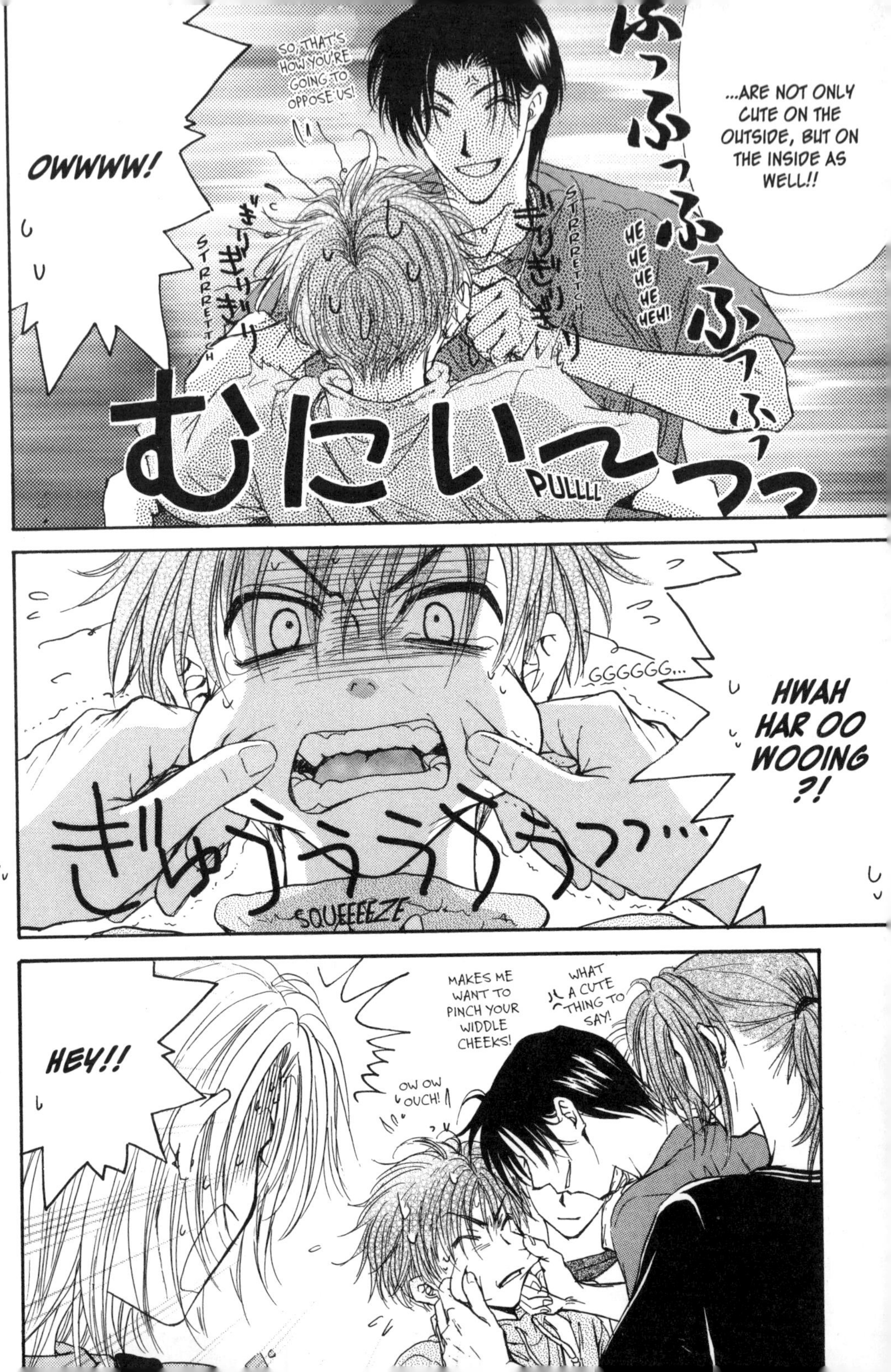
...ARE NOT ONLY CUTE ON THE OUTSIDE, BUT ON THE INSIDE AS WELL!!
ふっふっふっふっ
HE HE HE HE HEH!
ぎりぎりぎり
STRRRETTCH
SO, THAT'S HOW YOU'RE GOING TO OPPOSE US!
ぎりぎりぎり
STRRRETTCH
OWWWW!
むにいいっっ
PULLLL
HWAH HAR OO WOOING?!
GGGGGG...
SQUEEEEZE
WHAT A CUTE THING TO SAY!
MAKES ME WANT TO PINCH YOUR WIDDLE CHEEKS!
OW OW OUCH!
HEY!!

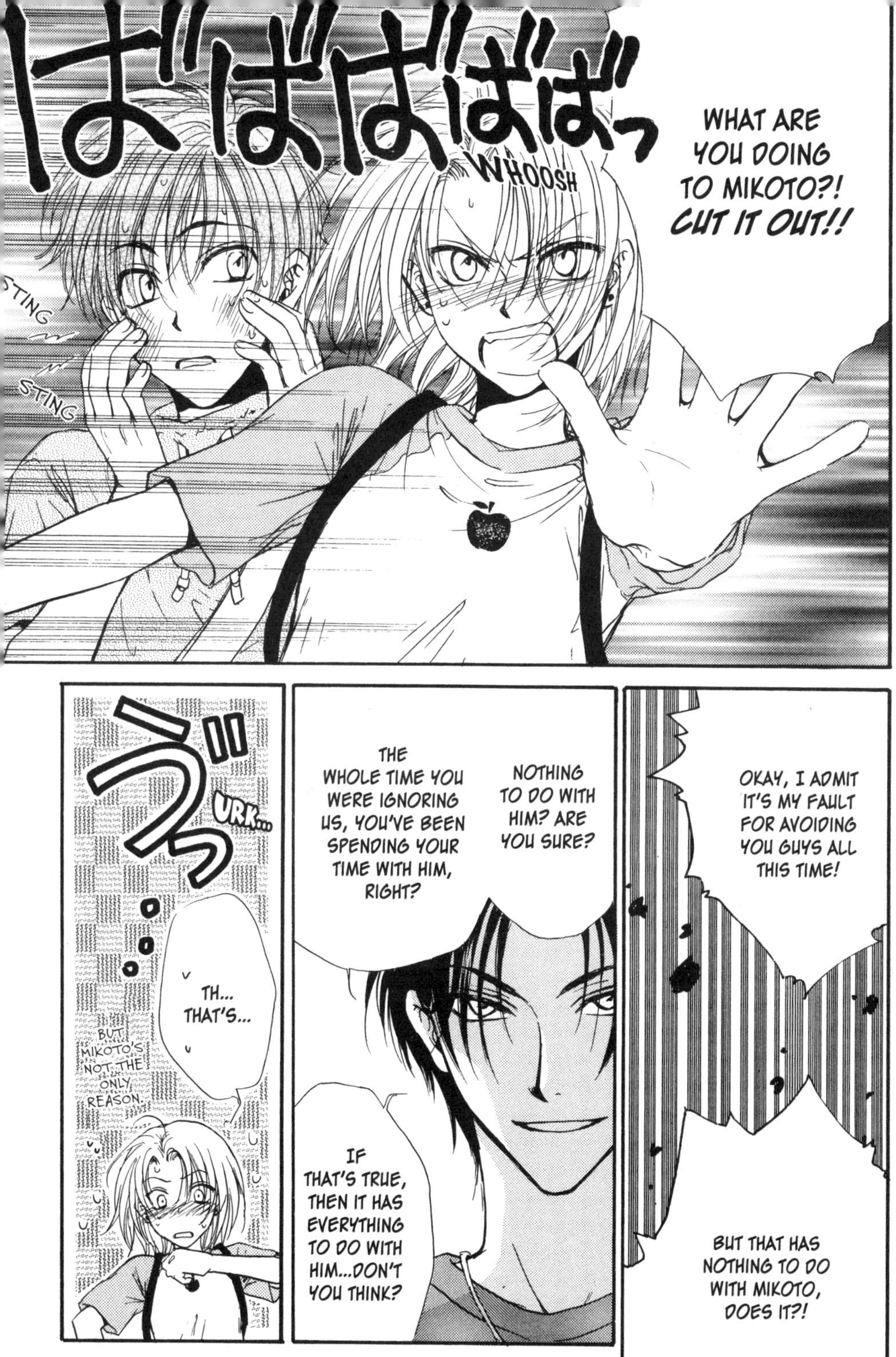
ばばばばばっ
WHOOSH
WHAT ARE YOU DOING TO MIKOTO?! CUT IT OUT!!
STING
STING
OKAY, I ADMIT IT'S MY FAULT FOR AVOIDING YOU GUYS ALL THIS TIME!
BUT THAT HAS NOTHING TO DO WITH MIKOTO, DOES IT?!
NOTHING TO DO WITH HIM? ARE YOU SURE?
THE WHOLE TIME YOU WERE IGNORING US, YOU'VE BEEN SPENDING YOUR TIME WITH HIM, RIGHT?
IF THAT'S TRUE, THEN IT HAS EVERYTHING TO DO WITH HIM...DON'T YOU THINK?
うっ
URK...
...
TH... THAT'S...
BUT MIKOTO'S NOT THE ONLY REASON.

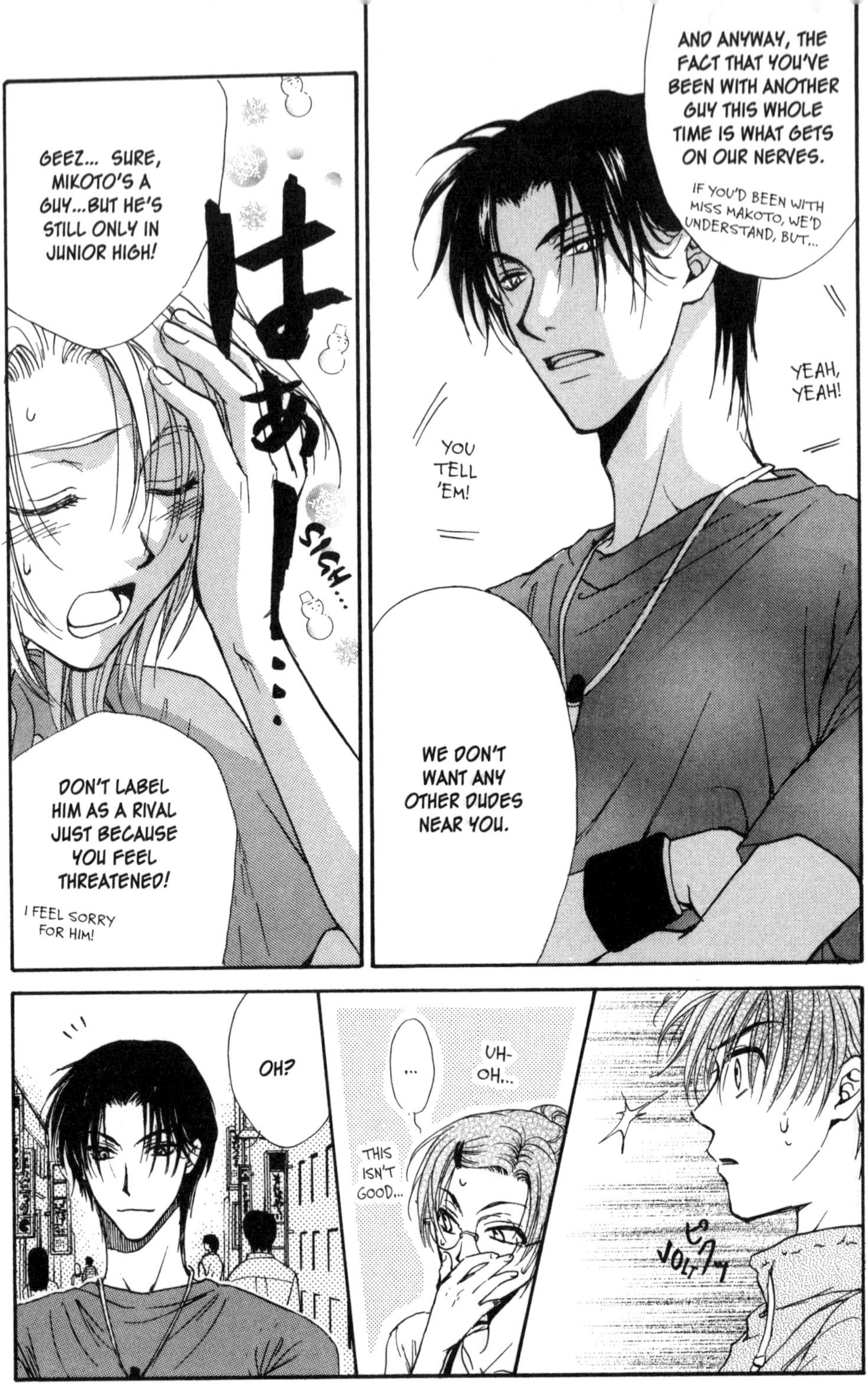
AND ANYWAY, THE FACT THAT YOU'VE BEEN WITH ANOTHER GUY THIS WHOLE TIME IS WHAT GETS ON OUR NERVES.
IF YOU'D BEEN WITH MISS MAKOTO, WE'D UNDERSTAND, BUT...
YEAH, YEAH!
YOU TELL 'EM!
WE DON'T WANT ANY OTHER DUDES NEAR YOU.
GEEZ... SURE, MIKOTO'S A GUY...BUT HE'S STILL ONLY IN JUNIOR HIGH!
はぁ…
SIGH...
DON'T LABEL HIM AS A RIVAL JUST BECAUSE YOU FEEL THREATENED!
I FEEL SORRY FOR HIM!
ピクッ
JOLT
UH-OH...
...
THIS ISN'T GOOD...
OH?

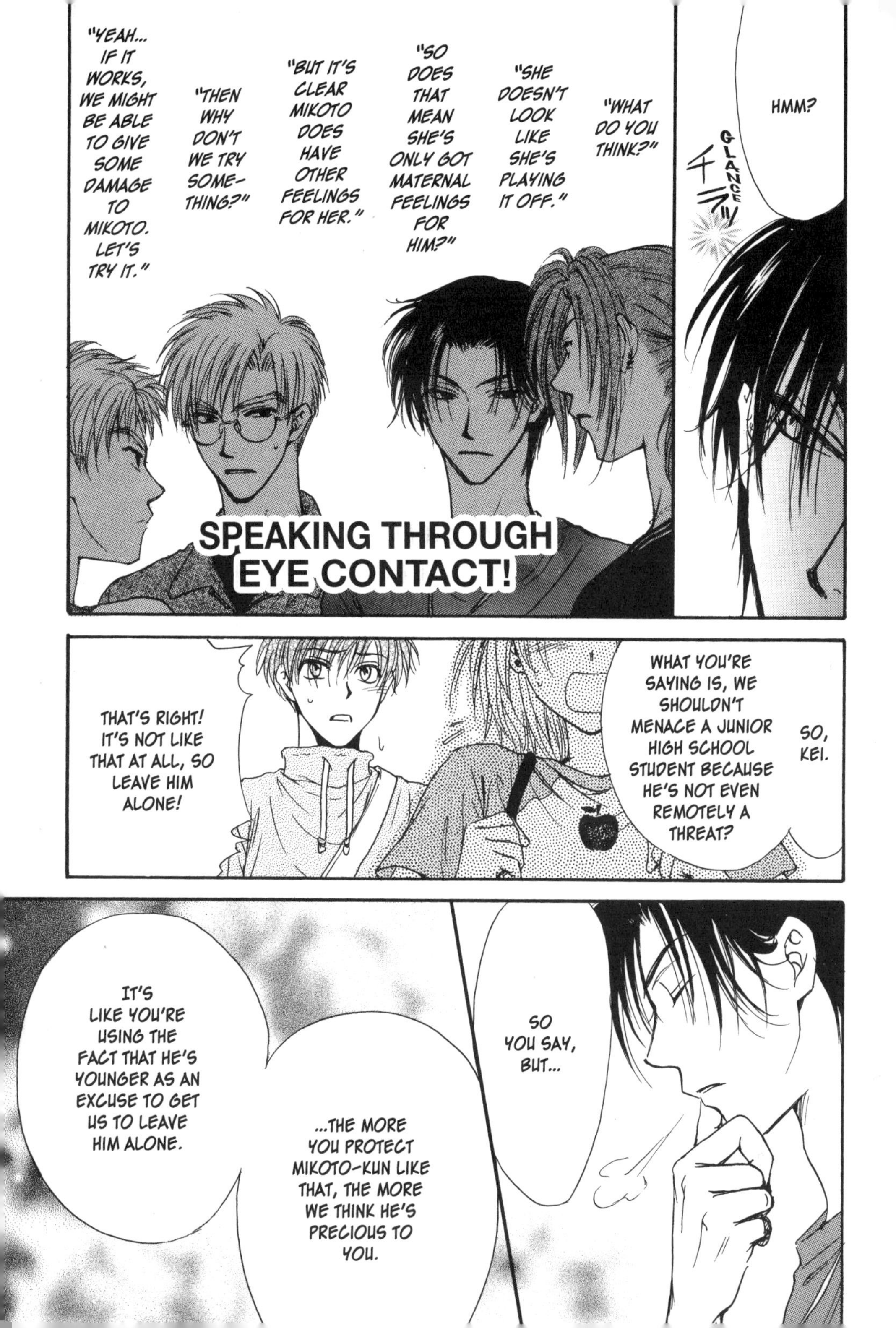
HMM?
GLANCE
チラッ
"WHAT DO YOU THINK?"
"SHE DOESN'T LOOK LIKE SHE'S PLAYING IT OFF."
"SO DOES THAT MEAN SHE'S ONLY GOT MATERNAL FEELINGS FOR HIM?"
"BUT IT'S CLEAR MIKOTO DOES HAVE OTHER FEELINGS FOR HER."
"THEN WHY DON'T WE TRY SOME-THING?"
"YEAH... IF IT WORKS, WE MIGHT BE ABLE TO GIVE SOME DAMAGE TO MIKOTO. LET'S TRY IT."
SPEAKING THROUGH EYE CONTACT!
SO, KEI.
WHAT YOU'RE SAYING IS, WE SHOULDN'T MENACE A JUNIOR HIGH SCHOOL STUDENT BECAUSE HE'S NOT EVEN REMOTELY A THREAT?
THAT'S RIGHT! IT'S NOT LIKE THAT AT ALL, SO LEAVE HIM ALONE!
SO YOU SAY, BUT...
...THE MORE YOU PROTECT MIKOTO-KUN LIKE THAT, THE MORE WE THINK HE'S PRECIOUS TO YOU.
IT'S LIKE YOU'RE USING THE FACT THAT HE'S YOUNGER AS AN EXCUSE TO GET US TO LEAVE HIM ALONE.

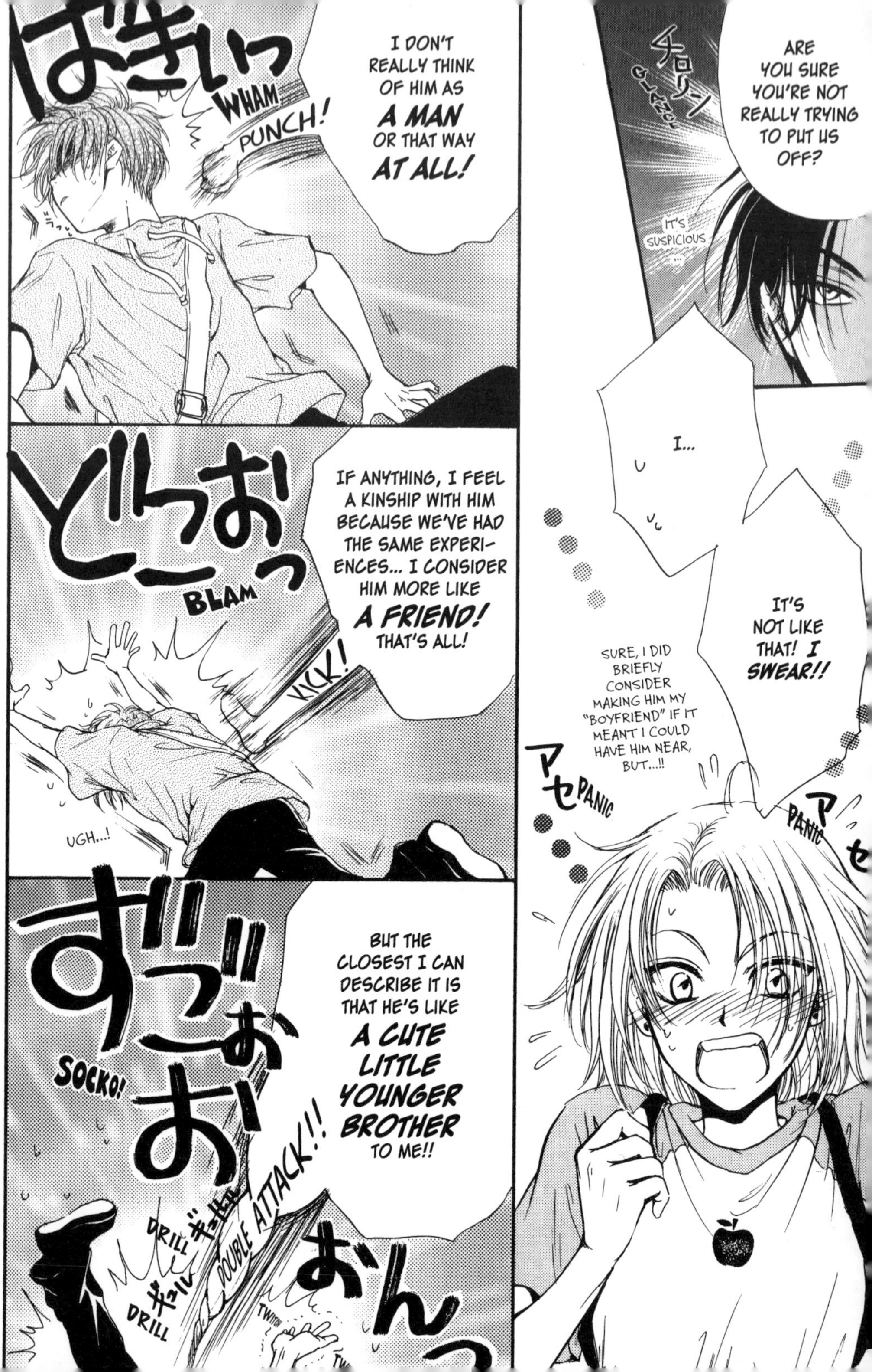

ARE YOU SURE YOU'RE NOT REALLY TRYING TO PUT US OFF?
GLANCE
IT'S SUSPICIOUS...
I...
IT'S NOT LIKE THAT! I SWEAR!!
SURE, I DID BRIEFLY CONSIDER MAKING HIM MY "BOYFRIEND" IF IT MEANT I COULD HAVE HIM NEAR, BUT...!!
アセ PANIC
アセ PANIC
I DON'T REALLY THINK OF HIM AS A MAN OR THAT WAY AT ALL!
WHAM
PUNCH!
IF ANYTHING, I FEEL A KINSHIP WITH HIM BECAUSE WE'VE HAD THE SAME EXPERIENCES... I CONSIDER HIM MORE LIKE A FRIEND! THAT'S ALL!
BLAM
KICK!
UGH...!
BUT THE CLOSEST I CAN DESCRIBE IT IS THAT HE'S LIKE A CUTE LITTLE YOUNGER BROTHER TO ME!!
SOCKO!
DOUBLE ATTACK!!
DRILL
DRILL
TWITCH

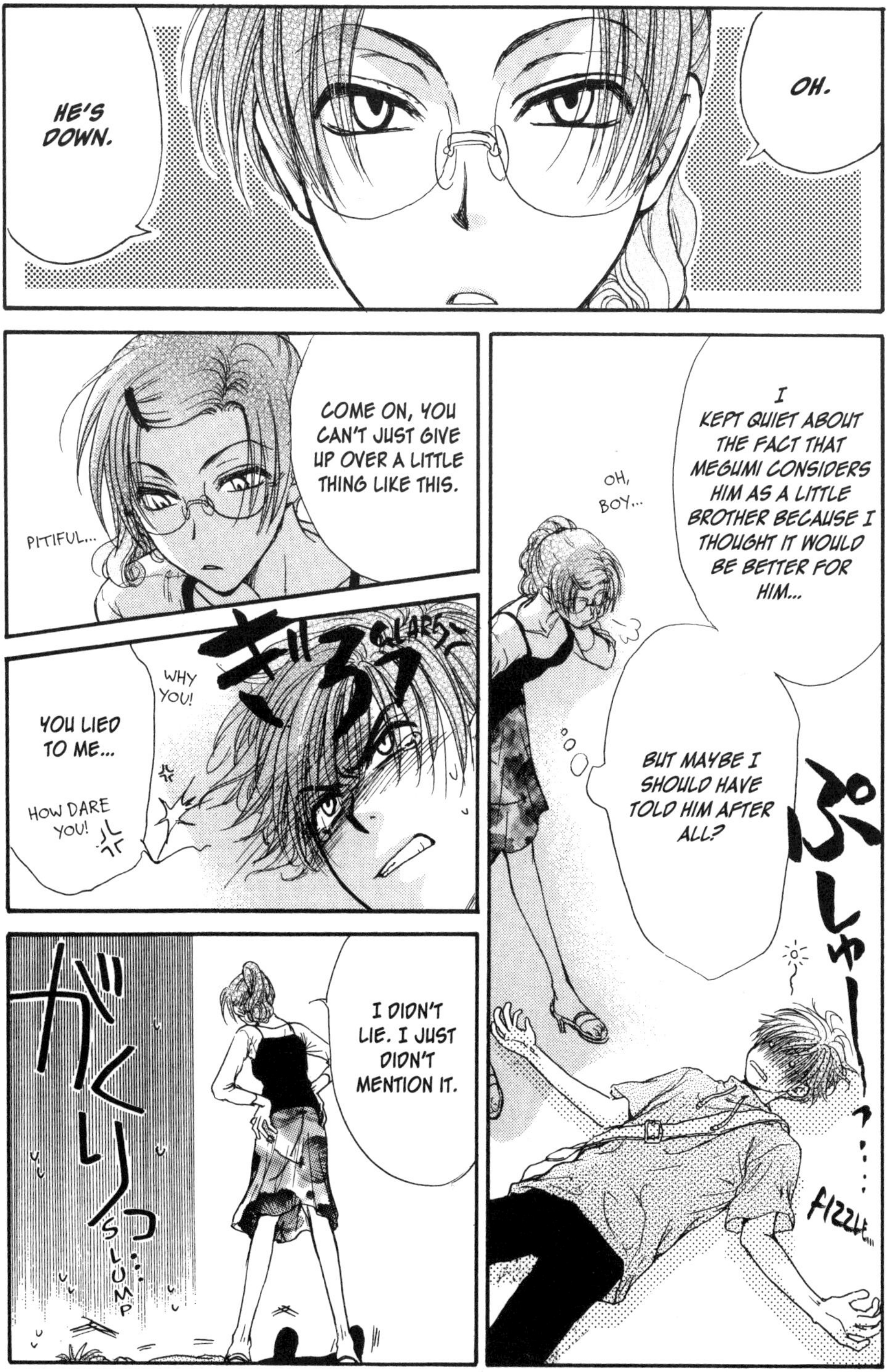
OH.
HE'S DOWN.
I KEPT QUIET ABOUT THE FACT THAT MEGUMI CONSIDERS HIM AS A LITTLE BROTHER BECAUSE I THOUGHT IT WOULD BE BETTER FOR HIM...
OH, BOY...
BUT MAYBE I SHOULD HAVE TOLD HIM AFTER ALL?
FIZZLE
COME ON, YOU CAN'T JUST GIVE UP OVER A LITTLE THING LIKE THIS.
PITIFUL...
GLARE
WHY YOU!
YOU LIED TO ME...
HOW DARE YOU!
I DIDN'T LIE. I JUST DIDN'T MENTION IT.
SLUMP

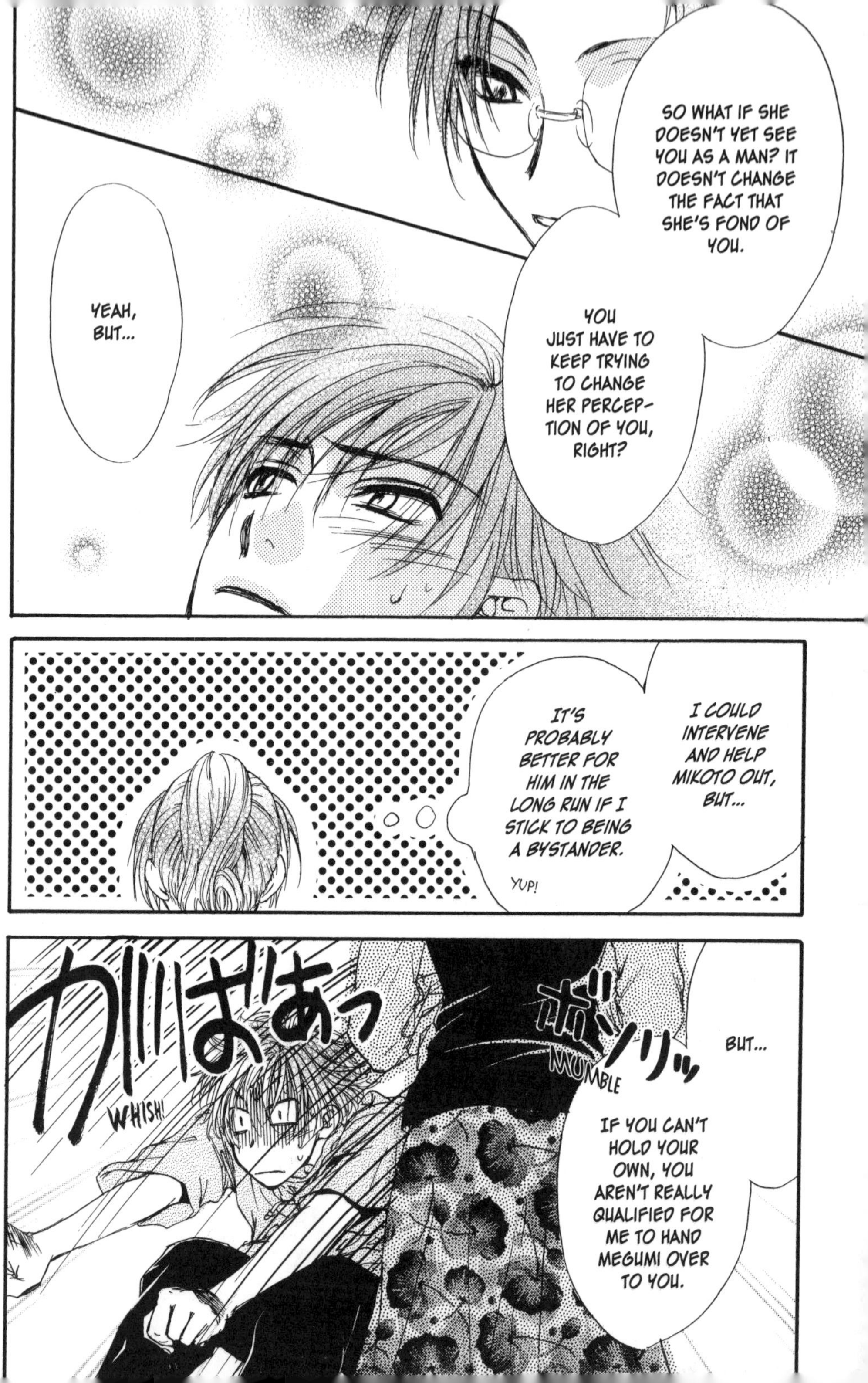
SO WHAT IF SHE DOESN'T YET SEE YOU AS A MAN? IT DOESN'T CHANGE THE FACT THAT SHE'S FOND OF YOU.
YOU JUST HAVE TO KEEP TRYING TO CHANGE HER PERCEPTION OF YOU, RIGHT?
YEAH, BUT...
I COULD INTERVENE AND HELP MIKOTO OUT, BUT...
IT'S PROBABLY BETTER FOR HIM IN THE LONG RUN IF I STICK TO BEING A BYSTANDER.
YUP!
BUT...
MUMBLE
IF YOU CAN'T HOLD YOUR OWN, YOU AREN'T REALLY QUALIFIED FOR ME TO HAND MEGUMI OVER TO YOU.
WHISH!

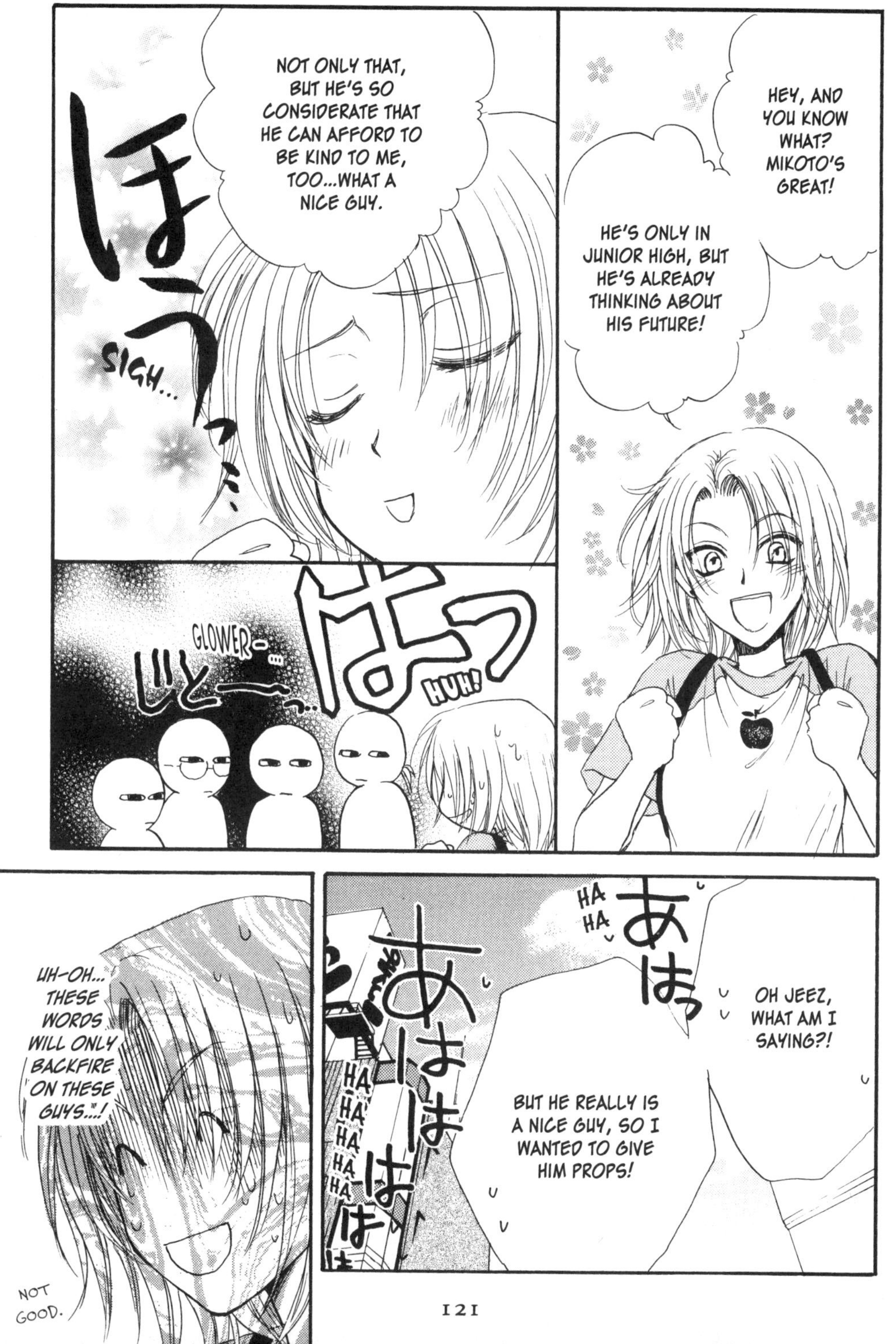
HEY, AND YOU KNOW WHAT? MIKOTO'S GREAT!
HE'S ONLY IN JUNIOR HIGH, BUT HE'S ALREADY THINKING ABOUT HIS FUTURE!
NOT ONLY THAT, BUT HE'S SO CONSIDERATE THAT HE CAN AFFORD TO BE KIND TO ME, TOO...WHAT A NICE GUY.
ほうっ
SIGH...
はっ
HUH!
じとーっ
GLOWER-...
あはっ
HA HA
OH JEEZ, WHAT AM I SAYING?!
BUT HE REALLY IS A NICE GUY, SO I WANTED TO GIVE HIM PROPS!
あははは
HA HA HA HA HA HA
UH-OH... THESE WORDS WILL ONLY BACKFIRE ON THESE GUYS...!
NOT GOOD.

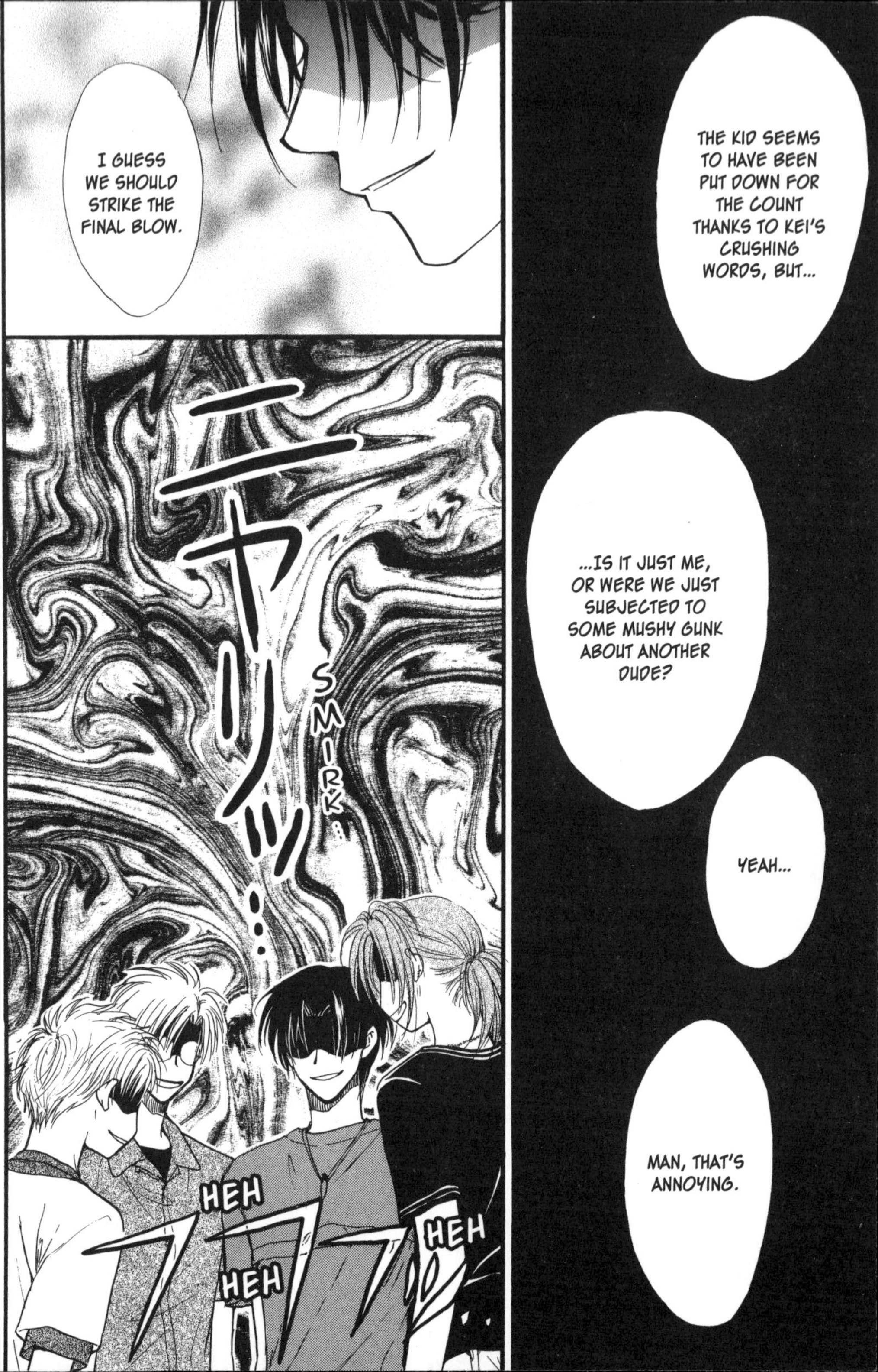
THE KID SEEMS TO HAVE BEEN PUT DOWN FOR THE COUNT THANKS TO KEI'S CRUSHING WORDS, BUT...
...IS IT JUST ME, OR WERE WE JUST SUBJECTED TO SOME MUSHY GUNK ABOUT ANOTHER DUDE?
YEAH...
MAN, THAT'S ANNOYING.
I GUESS WE SHOULD STRIKE THE FINAL BLOW.
SMIRK...
HEH
HEH
HEH

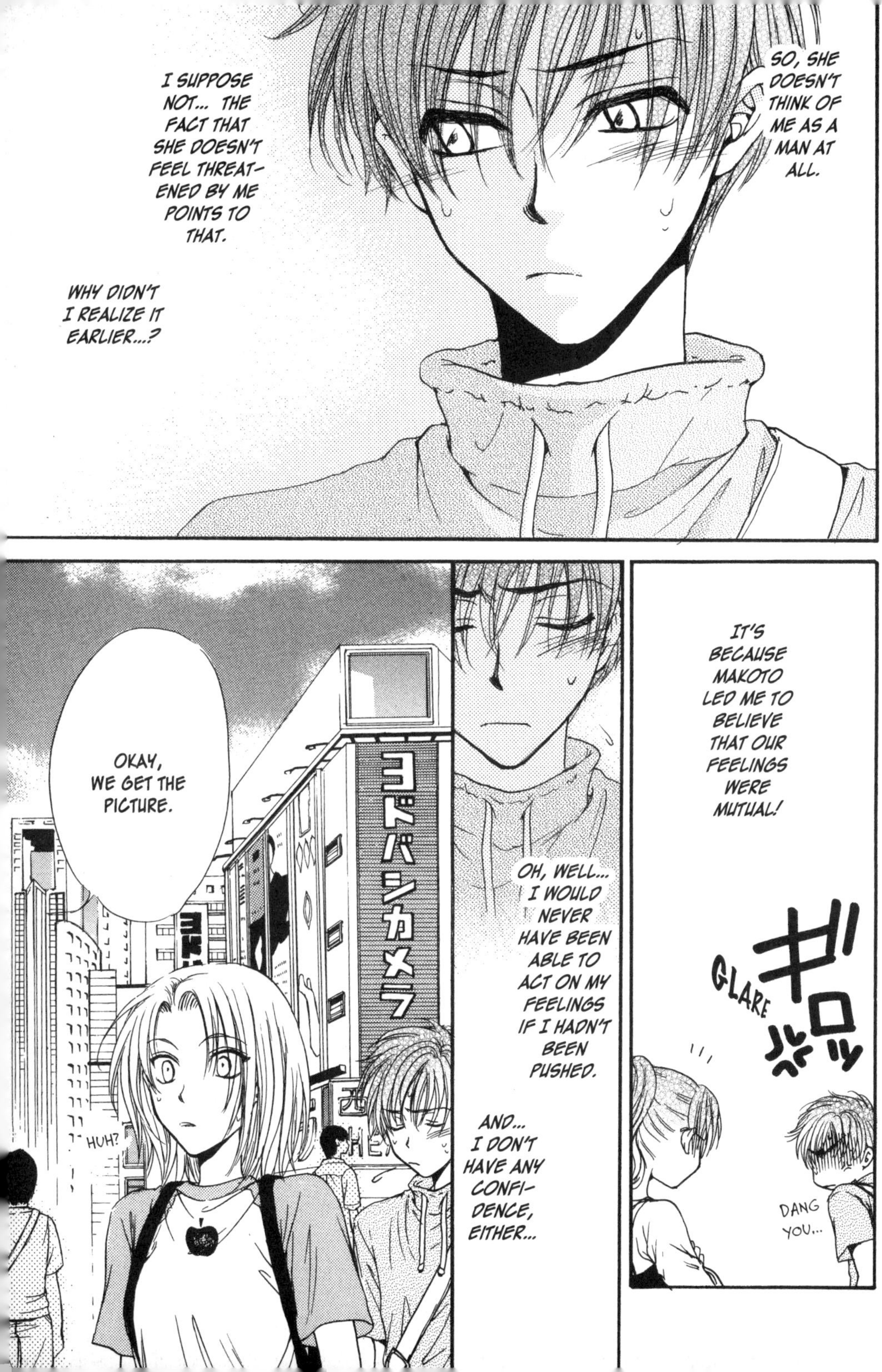
SO, SHE DOESN'T THINK OF ME AS A MAN AT ALL.
I SUPPOSE NOT... THE FACT THAT SHE DOESN'T FEEL THREAT-ENED BY ME POINTS TO THAT.
WHY DIDN'T I REALIZE IT EARLIER...?
IT'S BECAUSE MAKOTO LED ME TO BELIEVE THAT OUR FEELINGS WERE MUTUAL!
ギロッ
GLARE
DANG YOU...
OH, WELL... I WOULD NEVER HAVE BEEN ABLE TO ACT ON MY FEELINGS IF I HADN'T BEEN PUSHED.
AND... I DON'T HAVE ANY CONFI-DENCE, EITHER...
ヨドバシカメラ
OKAY, WE GET THE PICTURE.
HUH?

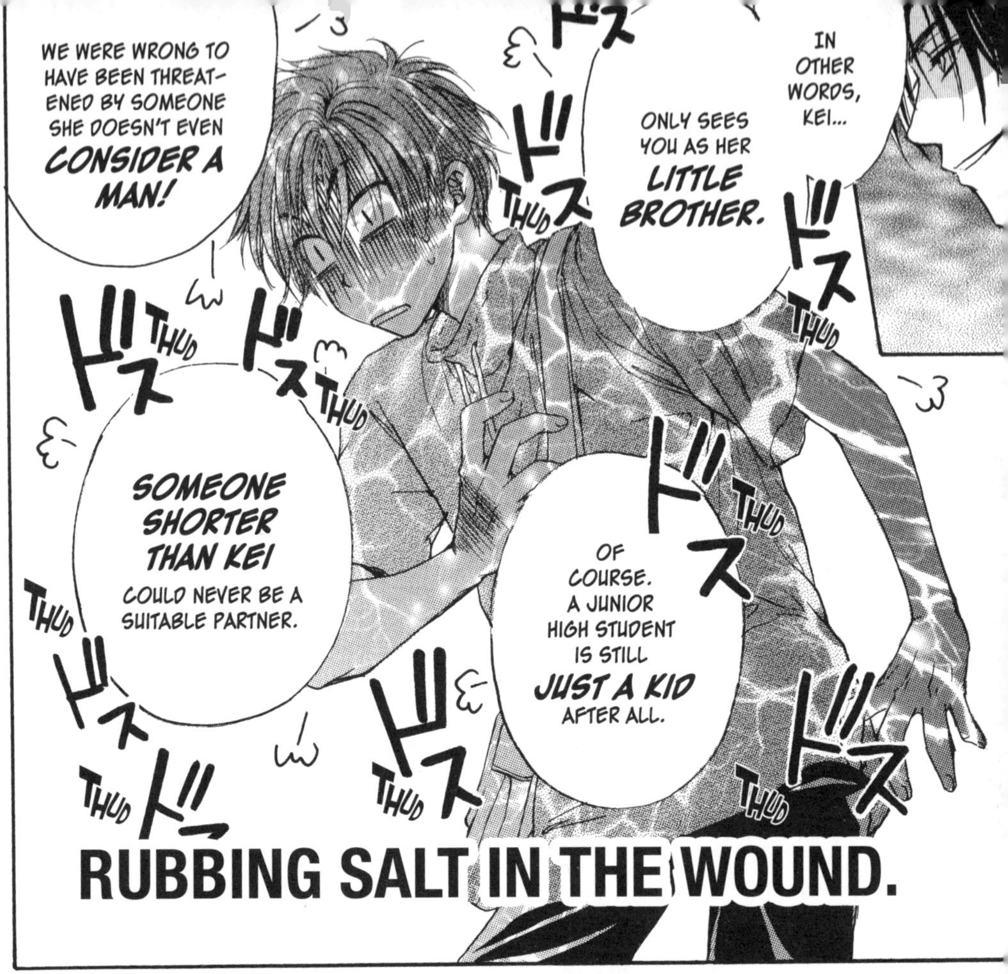
IN OTHER WORDS, KEI...
ONLY SEES YOU AS HER **LITTLE BROTHER.**
WE WERE WRONG TO HAVE BEEN THREATENED BY SOMEONE SHE DOESN'T EVEN **CONSIDER A MAN!**
THUD THUD THUD THUD
OF COURSE. A JUNIOR HIGH STUDENT IS STILL **JUST A KID** AFTER ALL.
SOMEONE SHORTER THAN KEI COULD NEVER BE A SUITABLE PARTNER.
THUD THUD THUD THUD THUD
RUBBING SALT IN THE WOUND.

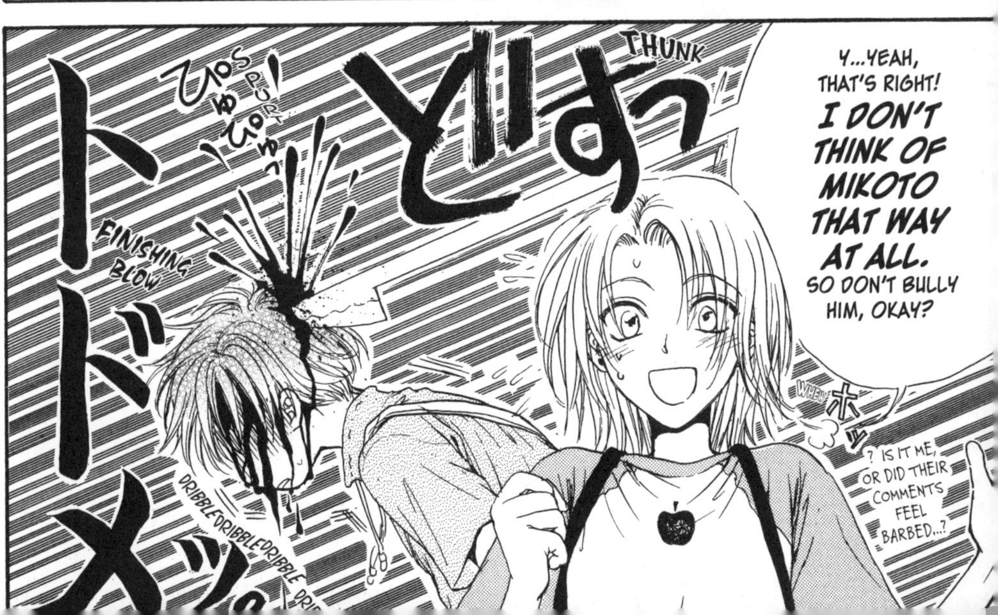
THUNK
Y...YEAH, THAT'S RIGHT! **I DON'T THINK OF MIKOTO THAT WAY AT ALL.** SO DON'T BULLY HIM, OKAY?
WHEW
? IS IT ME, OR DID THEIR COMMENTS FEEL BARBED...?
SPURT
FINISHING BLOW
DRIBBLE DRIBBLE DRIBBLE

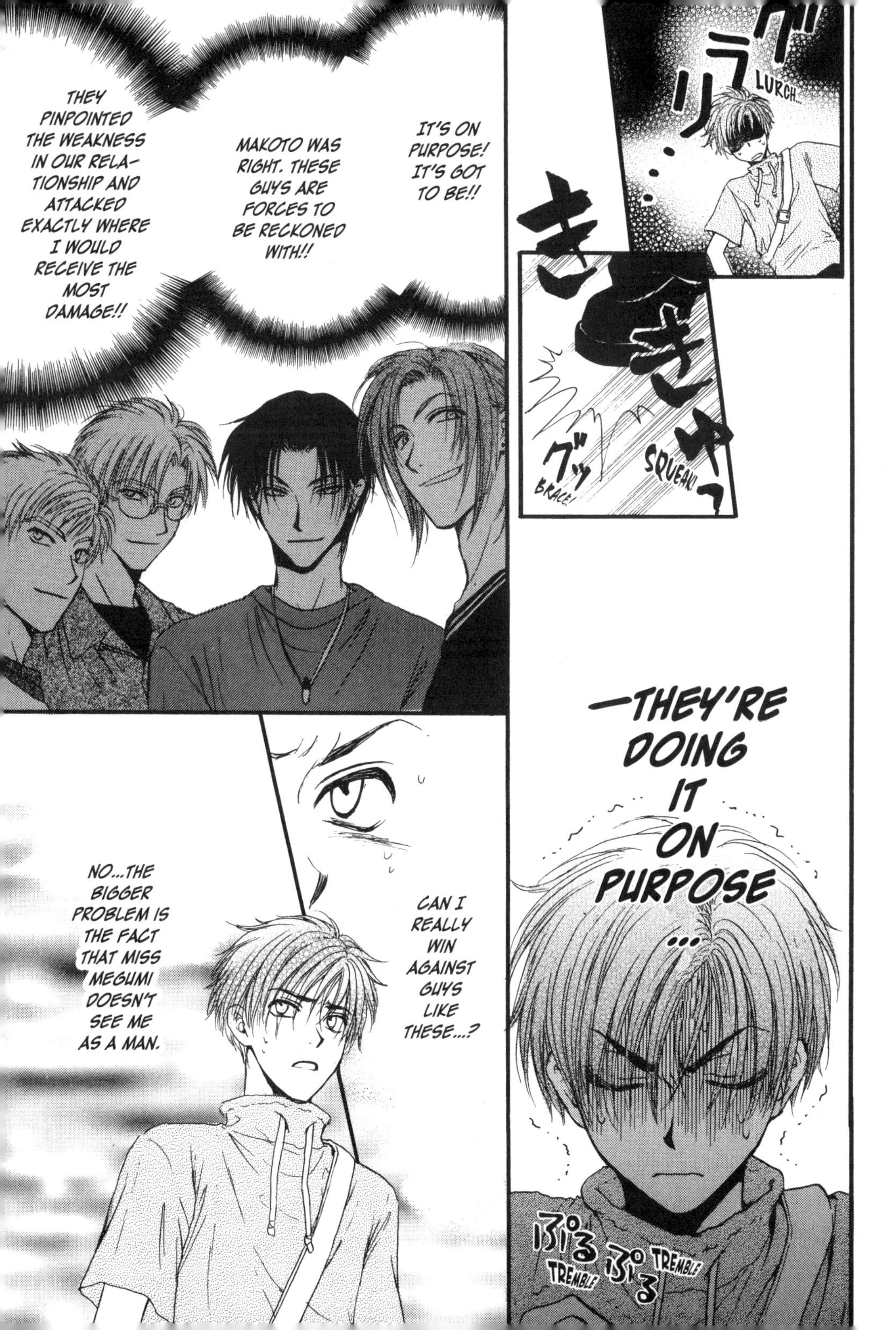

グラリ
LURCH...
...
グッ
BRACE!
SQUEAK!
IT'S ON PURPOSE! IT'S GOT TO BE!!
MAKOTO WAS RIGHT. THESE GUYS ARE FORCES TO BE RECKONED WITH!!
THEY PINPOINTED THE WEAKNESS IN OUR RELA-TIONSHIP AND ATTACKED EXACTLY WHERE I WOULD RECEIVE THE MOST DAMAGE!!
—THEY'RE DOING IT ON PURPOSE...
ぷるぷる
TREMBLE TREMBLE
CAN I REALLY WIN AGAINST GUYS LIKE THESE...?
NO...THE BIGGER PROBLEM IS THE FACT THAT MISS MEGUMI DOESN'T SEE ME AS A MAN.

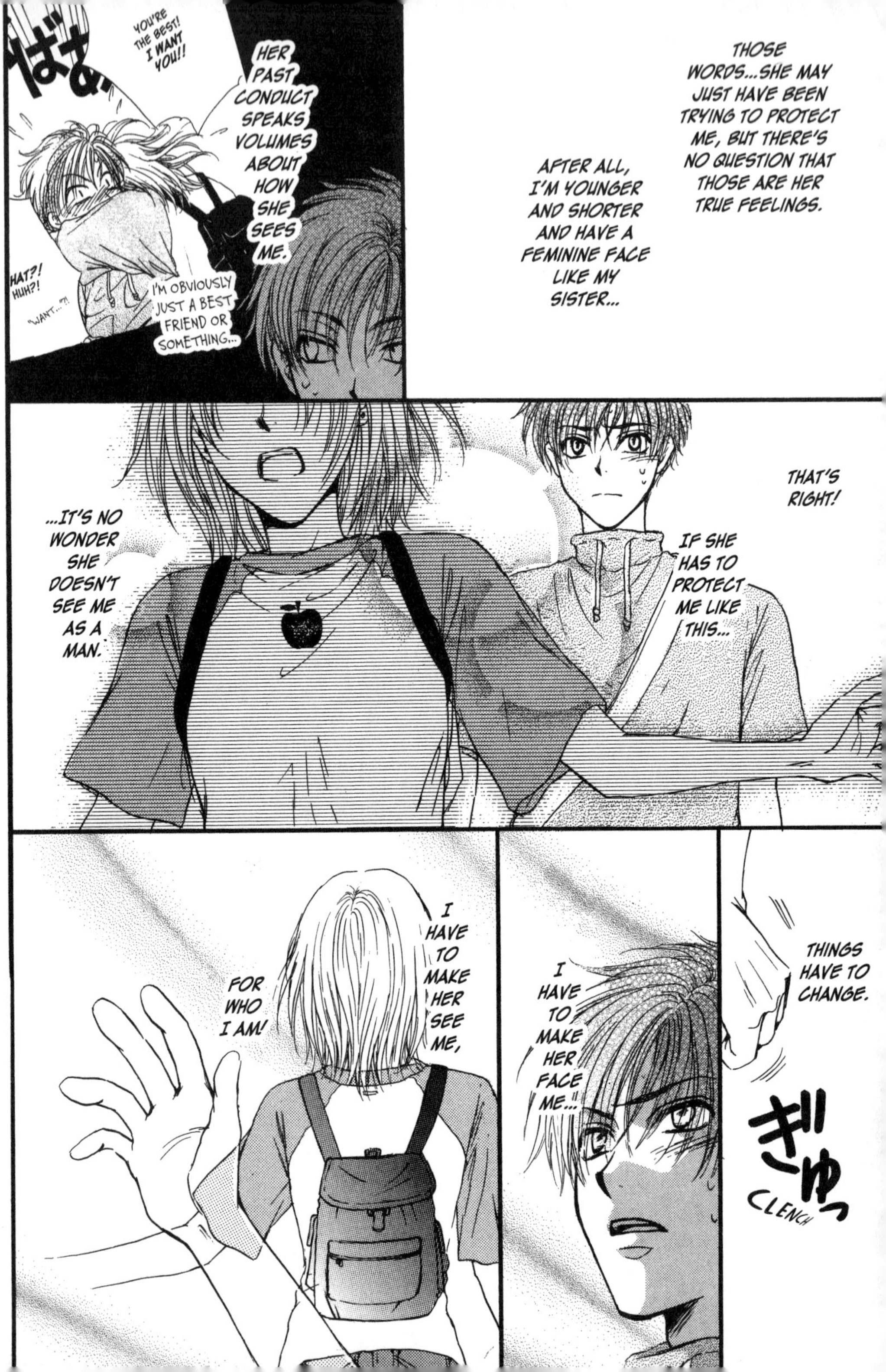
THOSE WORDS...SHE MAY JUST HAVE BEEN TRYING TO PROTECT ME, BUT THERE'S NO QUESTION THAT THOSE ARE HER TRUE FEELINGS.
AFTER ALL, I'M YOUNGER AND SHORTER AND HAVE A FEMININE FACE LIKE MY SISTER...
HER PAST CONDUCT SPEAKS VOLUMES ABOUT HOW SHE SEES ME.
YOU'RE THE BEST! I WANT YOU!!
HAT?! HUH?!
"WANT..."?!
I'M OBVIOUSLY JUST A BEST FRIEND OR SOMETHING...
THAT'S RIGHT!
IF SHE HAS TO PROTECT ME LIKE THIS...
...IT'S NO WONDER SHE DOESN'T SEE ME AS A MAN.
THINGS HAVE TO CHANGE.
ぎゅっ
CLENCH
I HAVE TO MAKE HER FACE ME...
I HAVE TO MAKE HER SEE ME,
FOR WHO I AM!

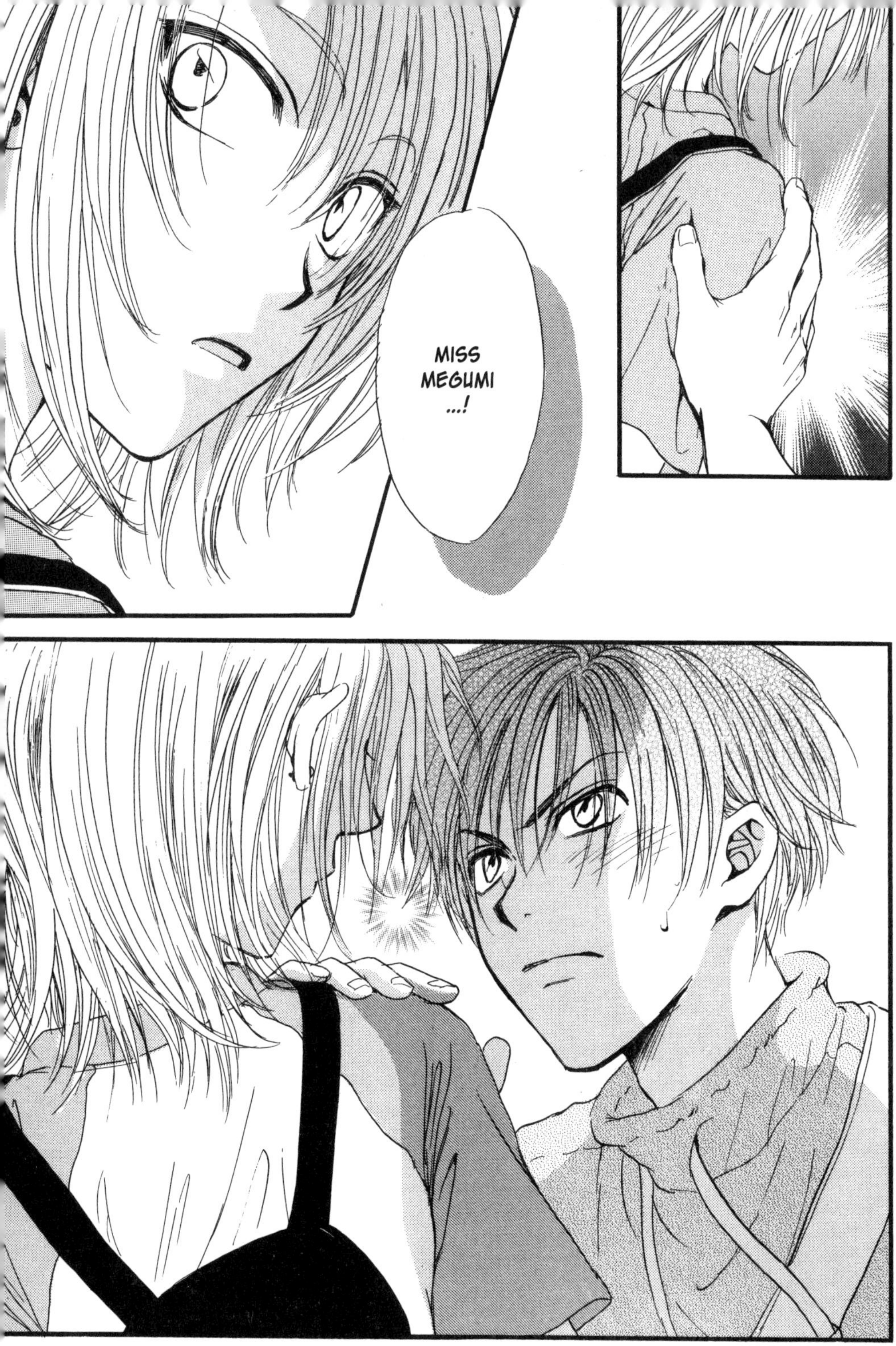
MISS MEGUMI ...!

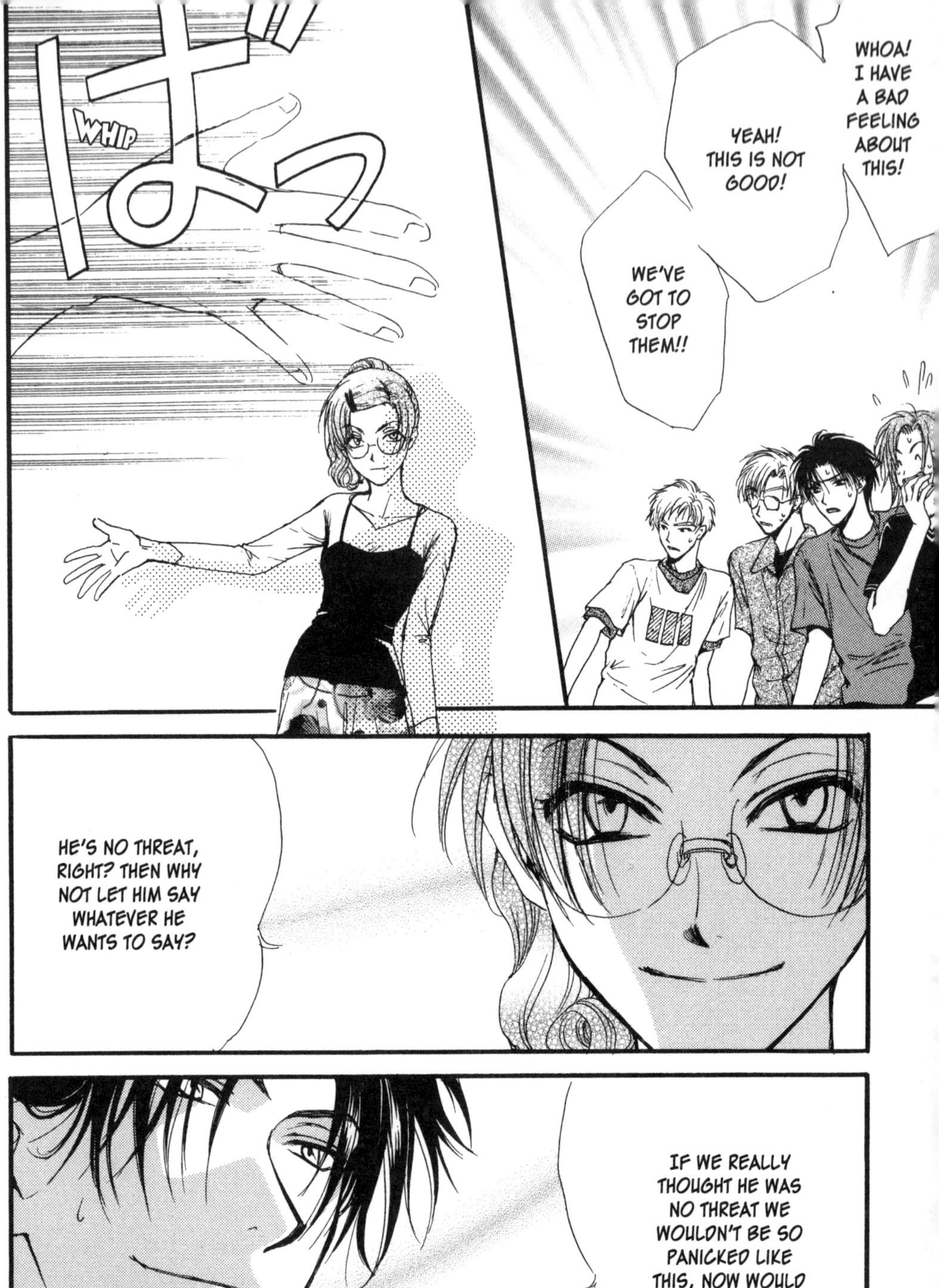
WHOA! I HAVE A BAD FEELING ABOUT THIS!
YEAH! THIS IS NOT GOOD!
WE'VE GOT TO STOP THEM!!
ばっ
WHIP
HE'S NO THREAT, RIGHT? THEN WHY NOT LET HIM SAY WHATEVER HE WANTS TO SAY?
IF WE REALLY THOUGHT HE WAS NO THREAT WE WOULDN'T BE SO PANICKED LIKE THIS, NOW WOULD WE?

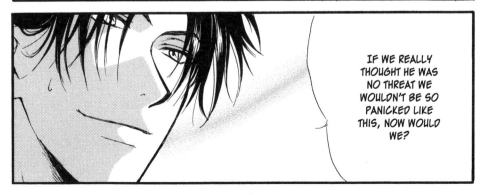

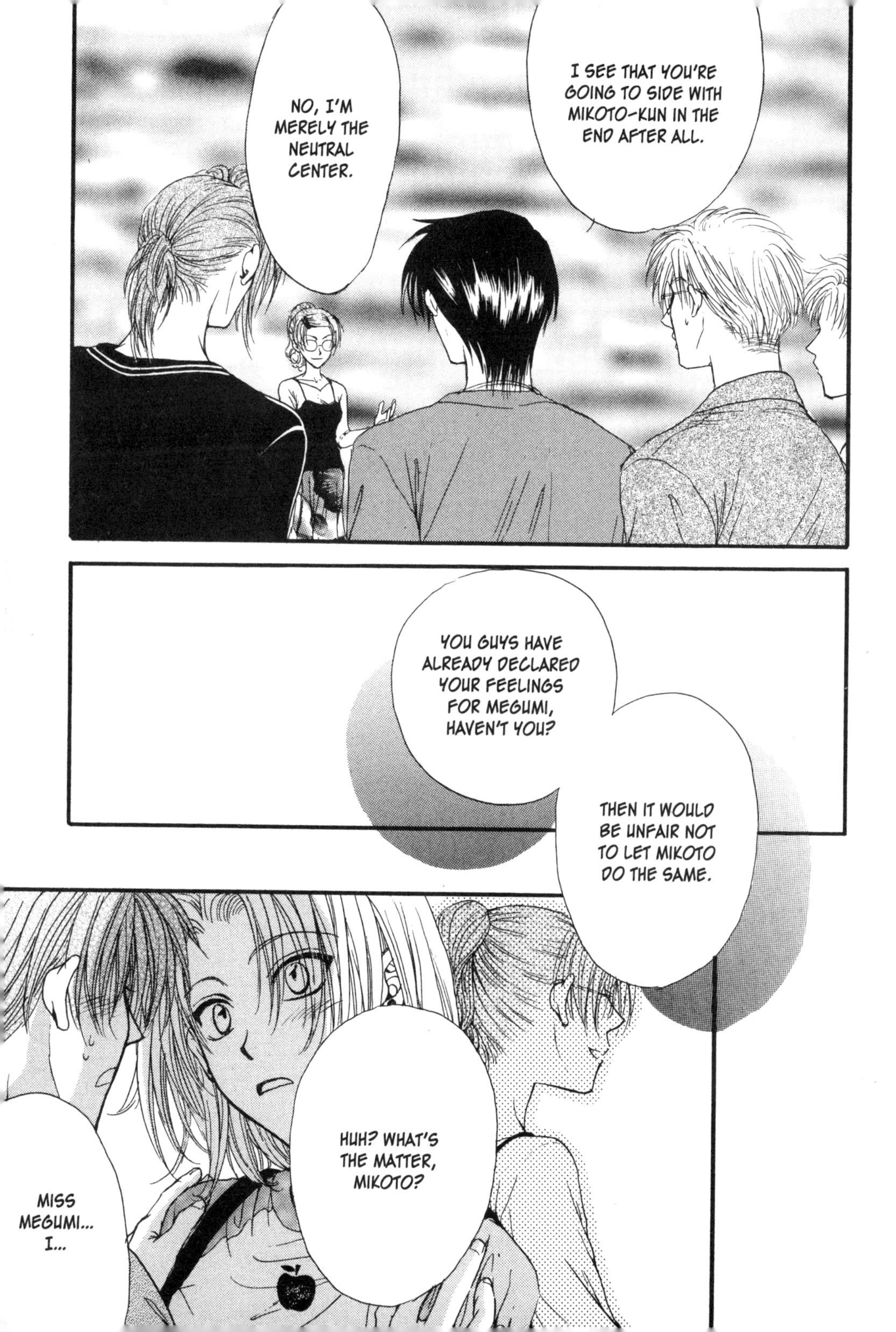
I SEE THAT YOU'RE GOING TO SIDE WITH MIKOTO-KUN IN THE END AFTER ALL.
NO, I'M MERELY THE NEUTRAL CENTER.
YOU GUYS HAVE ALREADY DECLARED YOUR FEELINGS FOR MEGUMI, HAVEN'T YOU?
THEN IT WOULD BE UNFAIR NOT TO LET MIKOTO DO THE SAME.
HUH? WHAT'S THE MATTER, MIKOTO?
MISS MEGUMI... I...

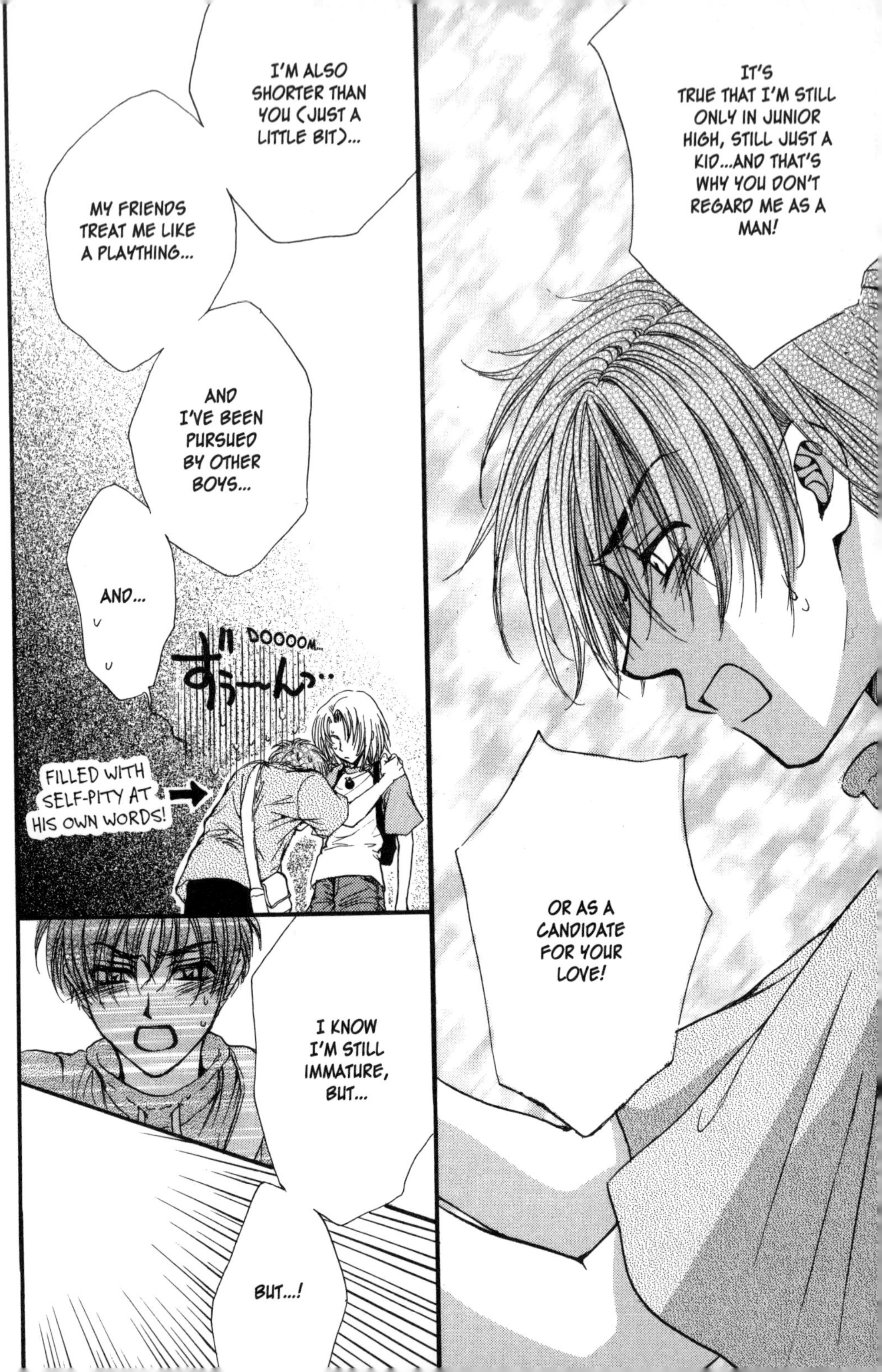
IT'S TRUE THAT I'M STILL ONLY IN JUNIOR HIGH, STILL JUST A KID...AND THAT'S WHY YOU DON'T REGARD ME AS A MAN!
OR AS A CANDIDATE FOR YOUR LOVE!
I'M ALSO SHORTER THAN YOU (JUST A LITTLE BIT)...
MY FRIENDS TREAT ME LIKE A PLAYTHING...
AND I'VE BEEN PURSUED BY OTHER BOYS...
AND...
DOOOOM...
ずぅーんっ…
FILLED WITH SELF-PITY AT HIS OWN WORDS!
I KNOW I'M STILL IMMATURE, BUT...
BUT...!

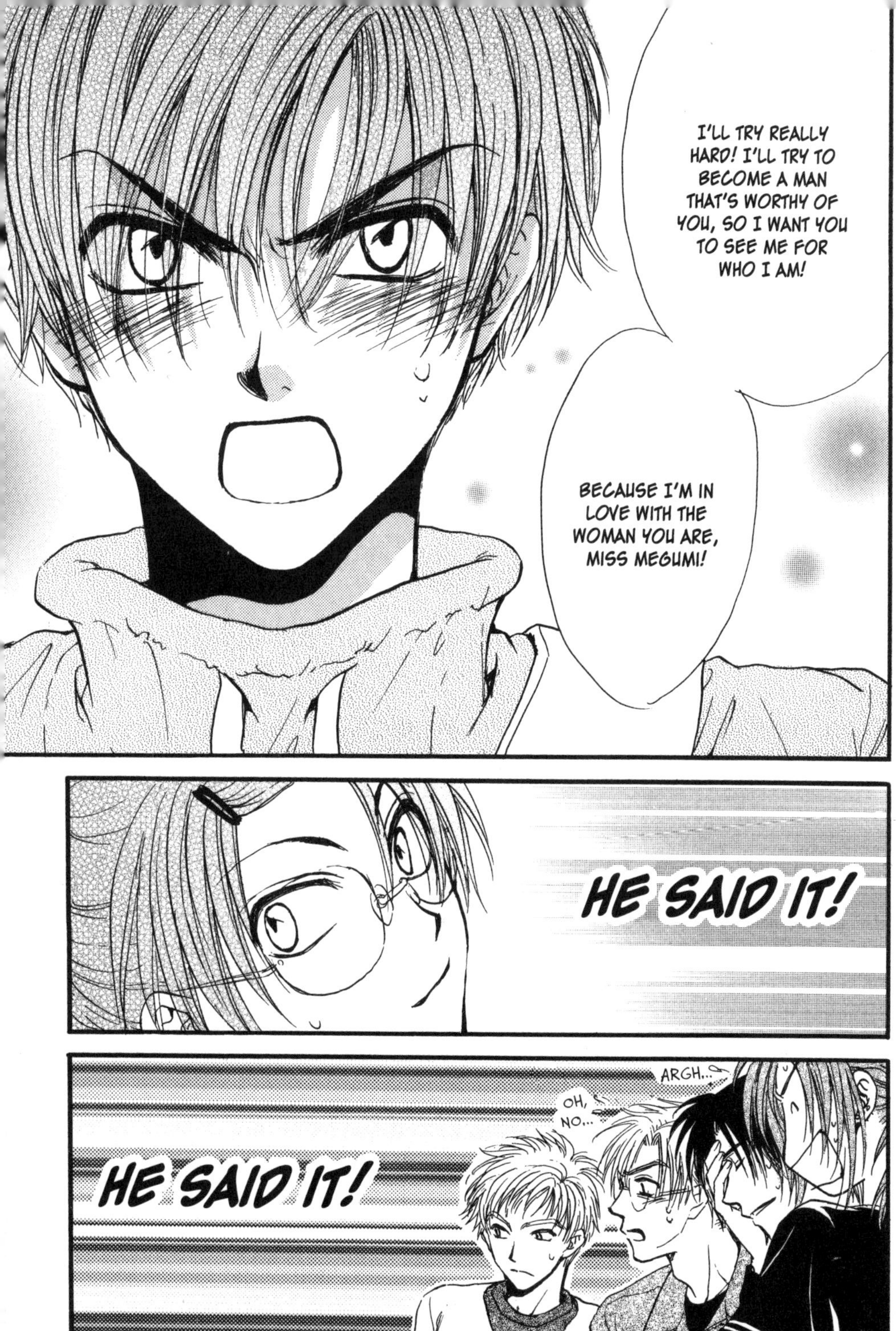
I'LL TRY REALLY HARD! I'LL TRY TO BECOME A MAN THAT'S WORTHY OF YOU, SO I WANT YOU TO SEE ME FOR WHO I AM!
BECAUSE I'M IN LOVE WITH THE WOMAN YOU ARE, MISS MEGUMI!
HE SAID IT!
ARGH...
OH, NO...
HE SAID IT!

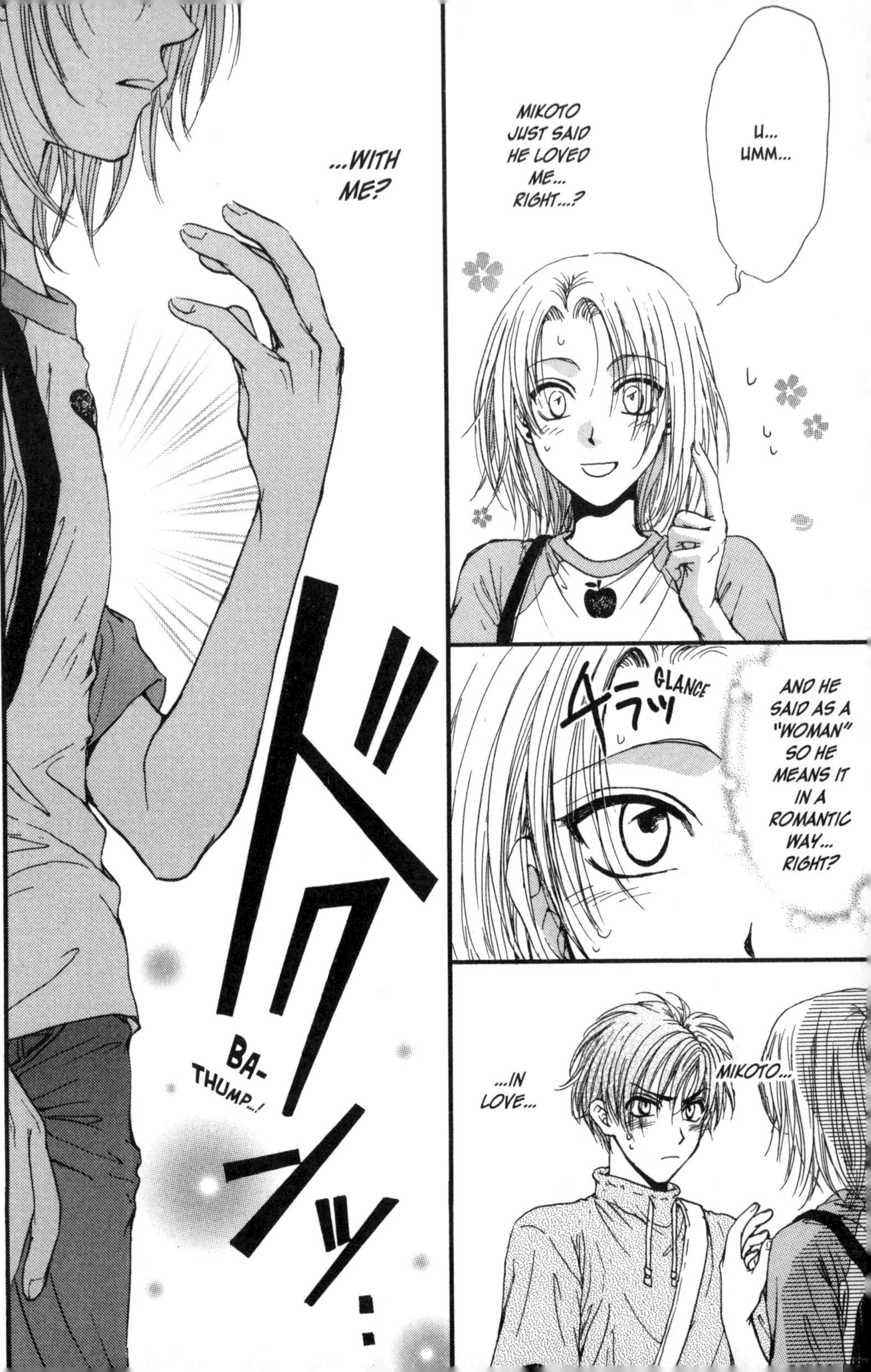
U... UMM...
MIKOTO JUST SAID HE LOVED ME... RIGHT...?
AND HE SAID AS A "WOMAN" SO HE MEANS IT IN A ROMANTIC WAY... RIGHT?
GLANCE
MIKOTO...
...IN LOVE...
...WITH ME?
BA-THUMP...!

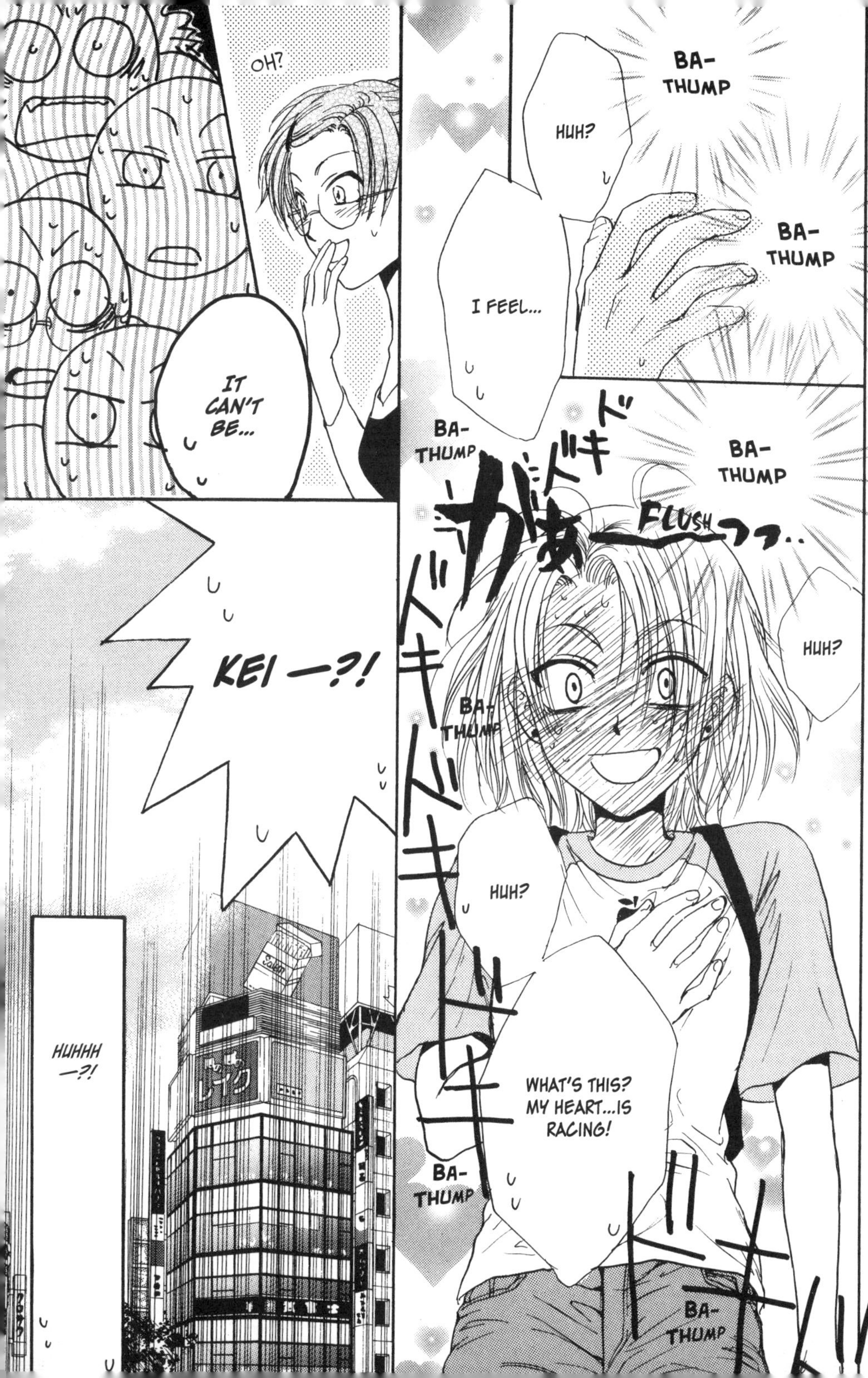
BA-THUMP
HUH?
I FEEL...
BA-THUMP
BA-THUMP
BA-THUMP
FLUSH
HUH?
BA-THUMP
HUH?
WHAT'S THIS? MY HEART...IS RACING!
BA-THUMP
BA-THUMP
OH?
IT CAN'T BE...
KEI —?!
HUHHH —?!

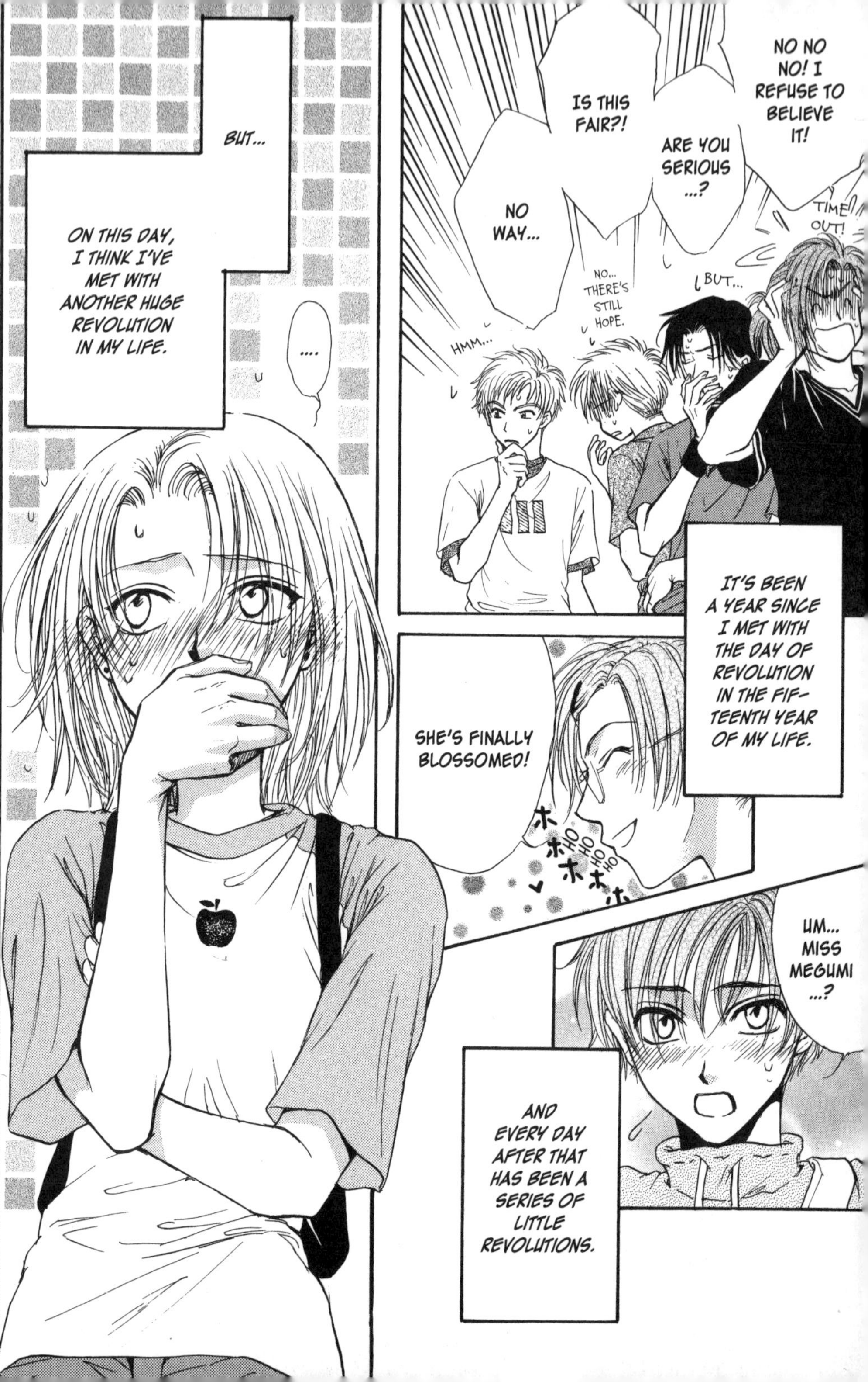
NO NO NO! I REFUSE TO BELIEVE IT!
TIME OUT!
ARE YOU SERIOUS ...?
IS THIS FAIR?!
BUT...
NO... THERE'S STILL HOPE.
NO WAY...
HMM...
IT'S BEEN A YEAR SINCE I MET WITH THE DAY OF REVOLUTION IN THE FIFTEENTH YEAR OF MY LIFE.
SHE'S FINALLY BLOSSOMED!
HOHOHO HOHOHO
UM... MISS MEGUMI ...?
AND EVERY DAY AFTER THAT HAS BEEN A SERIES OF LITTLE REVOLUTIONS.
BUT...
ON THIS DAY, I THINK I'VE MET WITH ANOTHER HUGE REVOLUTION IN MY LIFE.
....

THE DAY OF REVOLUTION 2 END

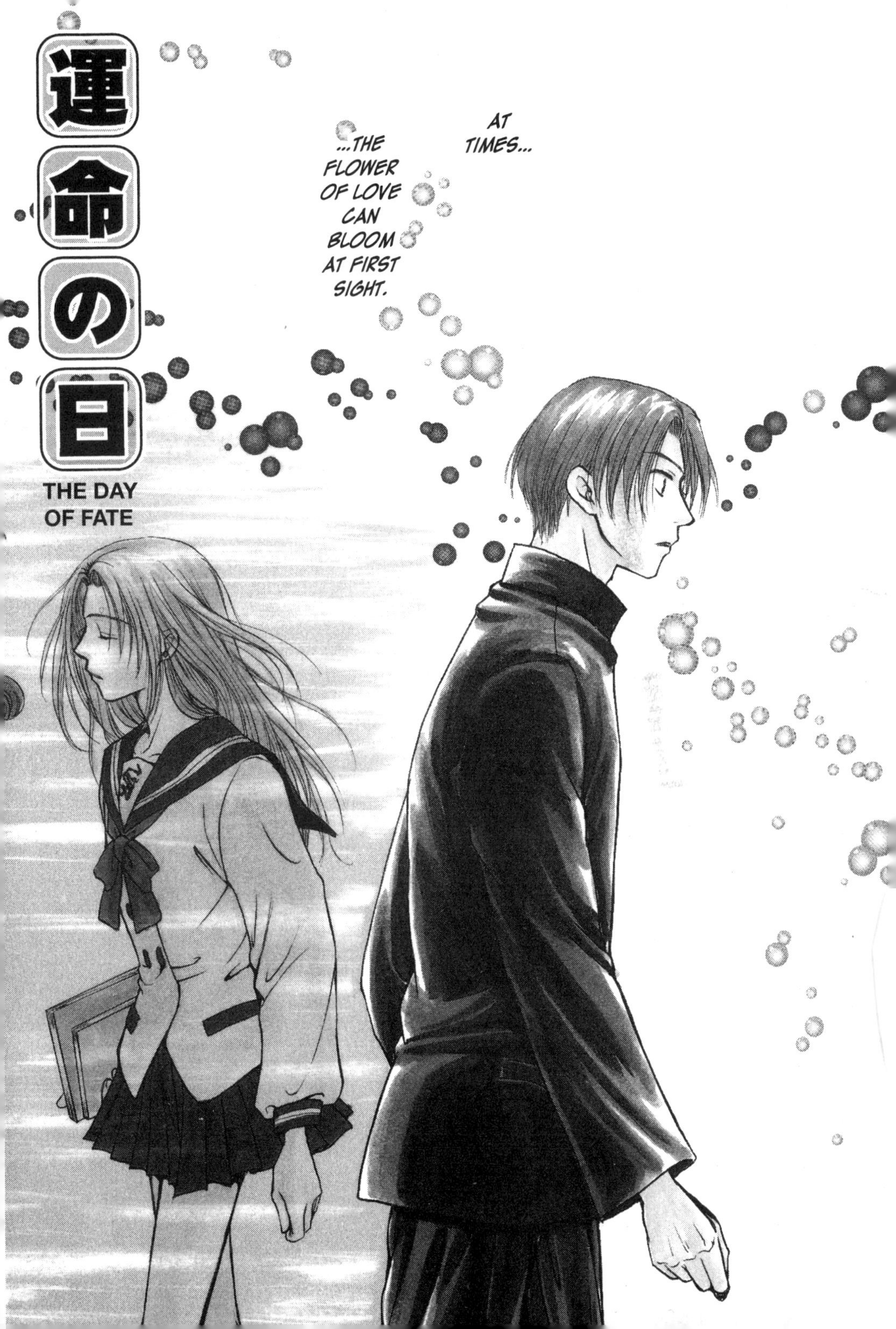
運命の日
THE DAY OF FATE
AT TIMES...
...THE FLOWER OF LOVE CAN BLOOM AT FIRST SIGHT.

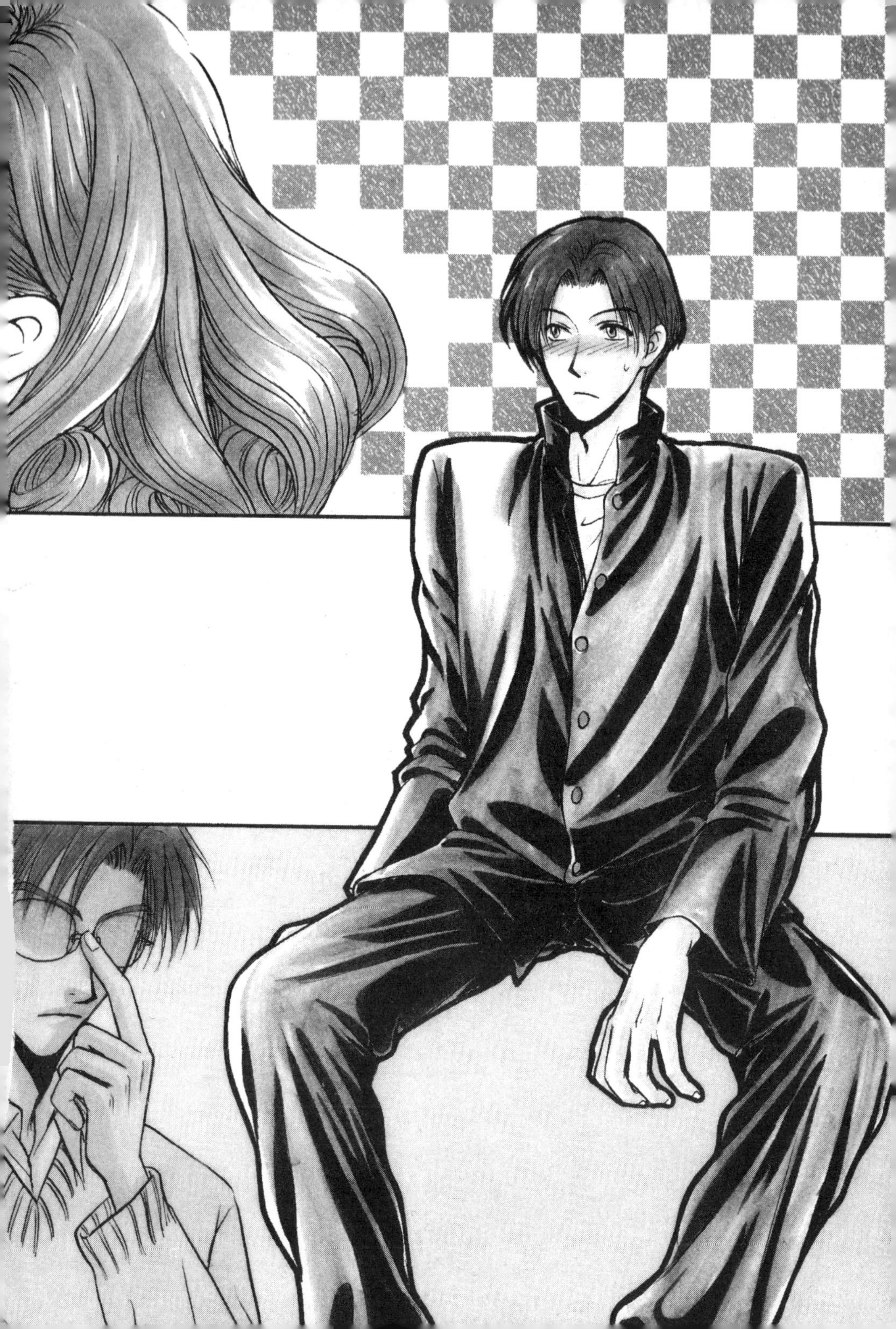

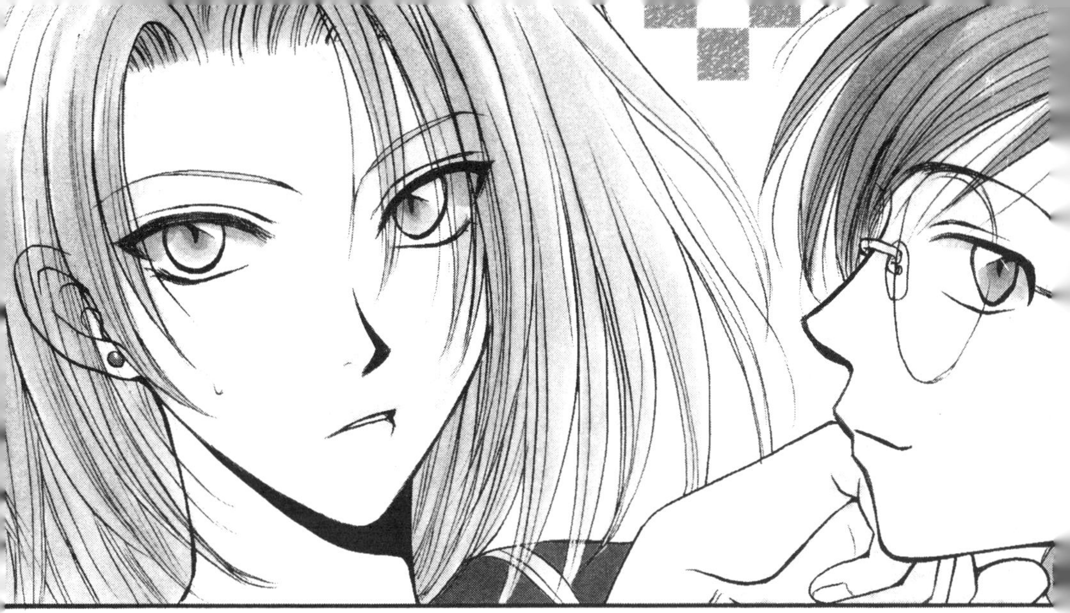

運命の日

THE DAY OF FATE

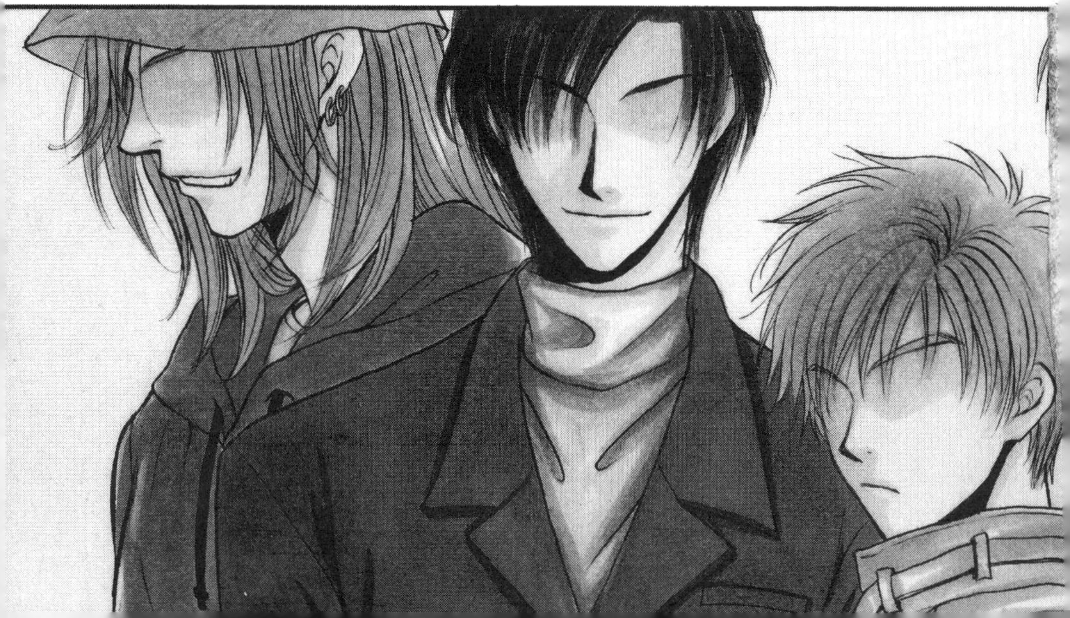

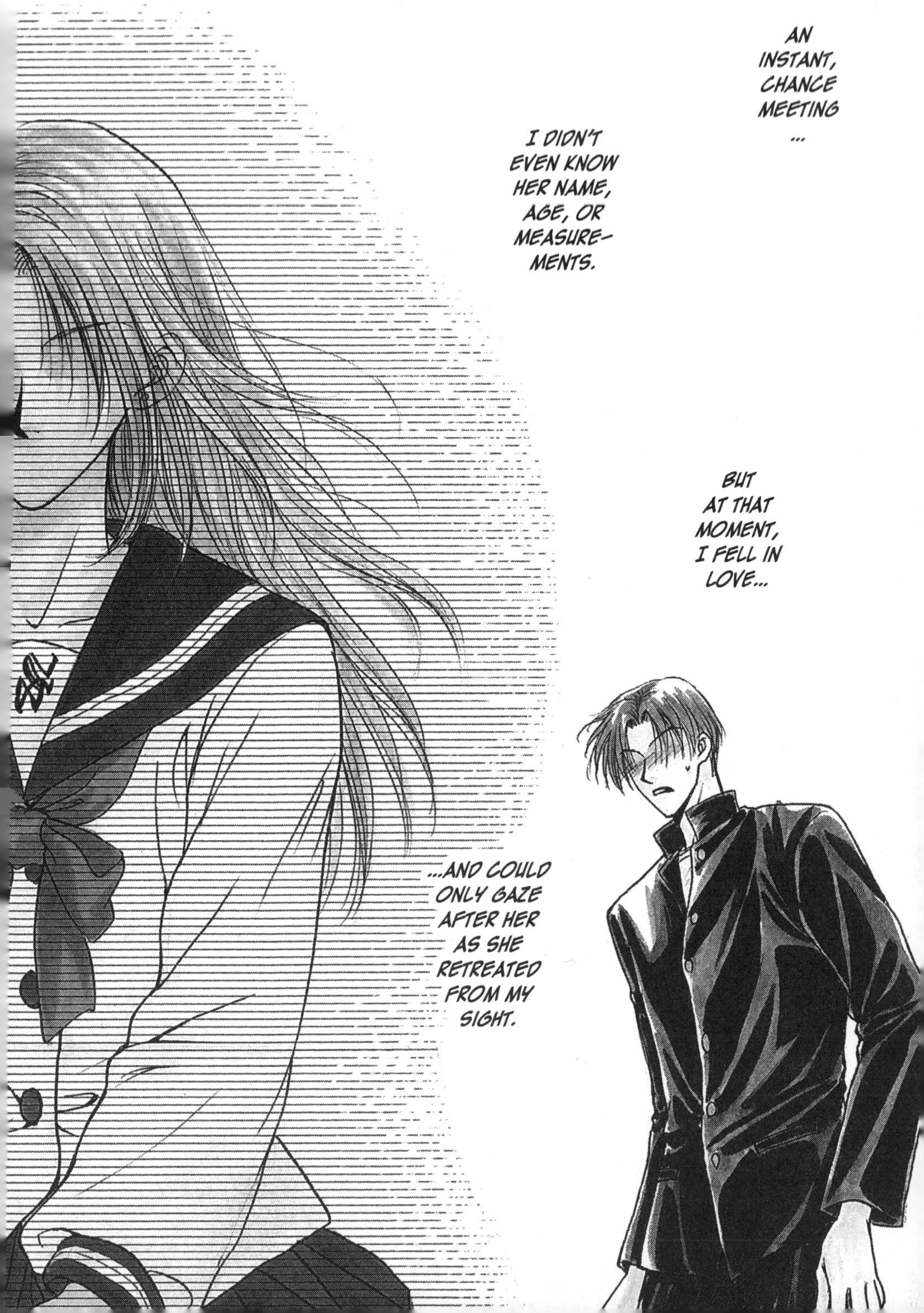
AN INSTANT, CHANCE MEETING...
I DIDN'T EVEN KNOW HER NAME, AGE, OR MEASURE-MENTS.
BUT AT THAT MOMENT, I FELL IN LOVE...
...AND COULD ONLY GAZE AFTER HER AS SHE RETREATED FROM MY SIGHT.

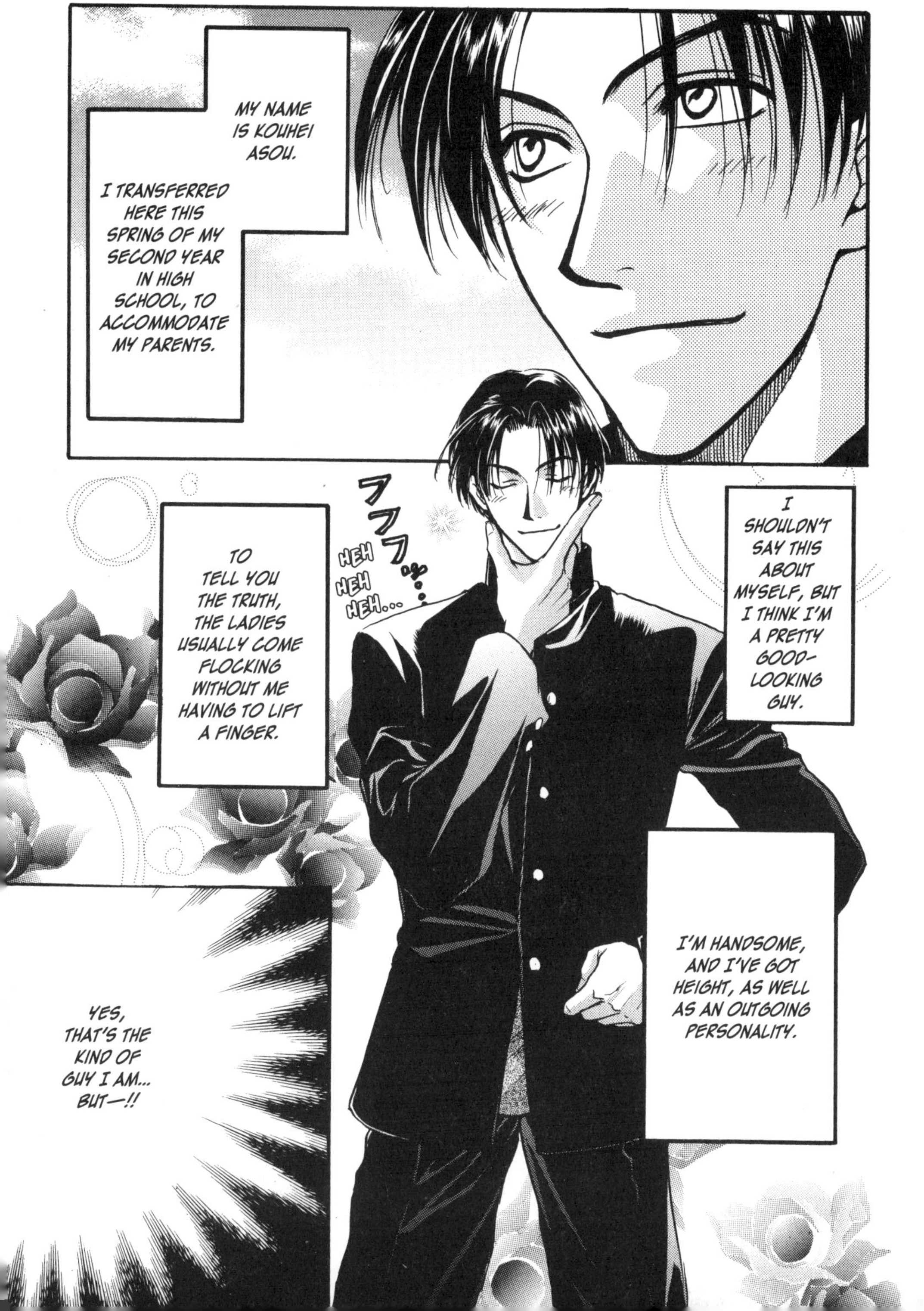
MY NAME IS KOUHEI ASOU.
I TRANSFERRED HERE THIS SPRING OF MY SECOND YEAR IN HIGH SCHOOL, TO ACCOMMODATE MY PARENTS.
I SHOULDN'T SAY THIS ABOUT MYSELF, BUT I THINK I'M A PRETTY GOOD-LOOKING GUY.
フフフ
HEH HEH HEH...
TO TELL YOU THE TRUTH, THE LADIES USUALLY COME FLOCKING WITHOUT ME HAVING TO LIFT A FINGER.
I'M HANDSOME, AND I'VE GOT HEIGHT, AS WELL AS AN OUTGOING PERSONALITY.
YES, THAT'S THE KIND OF GUY I AM... BUT—!!

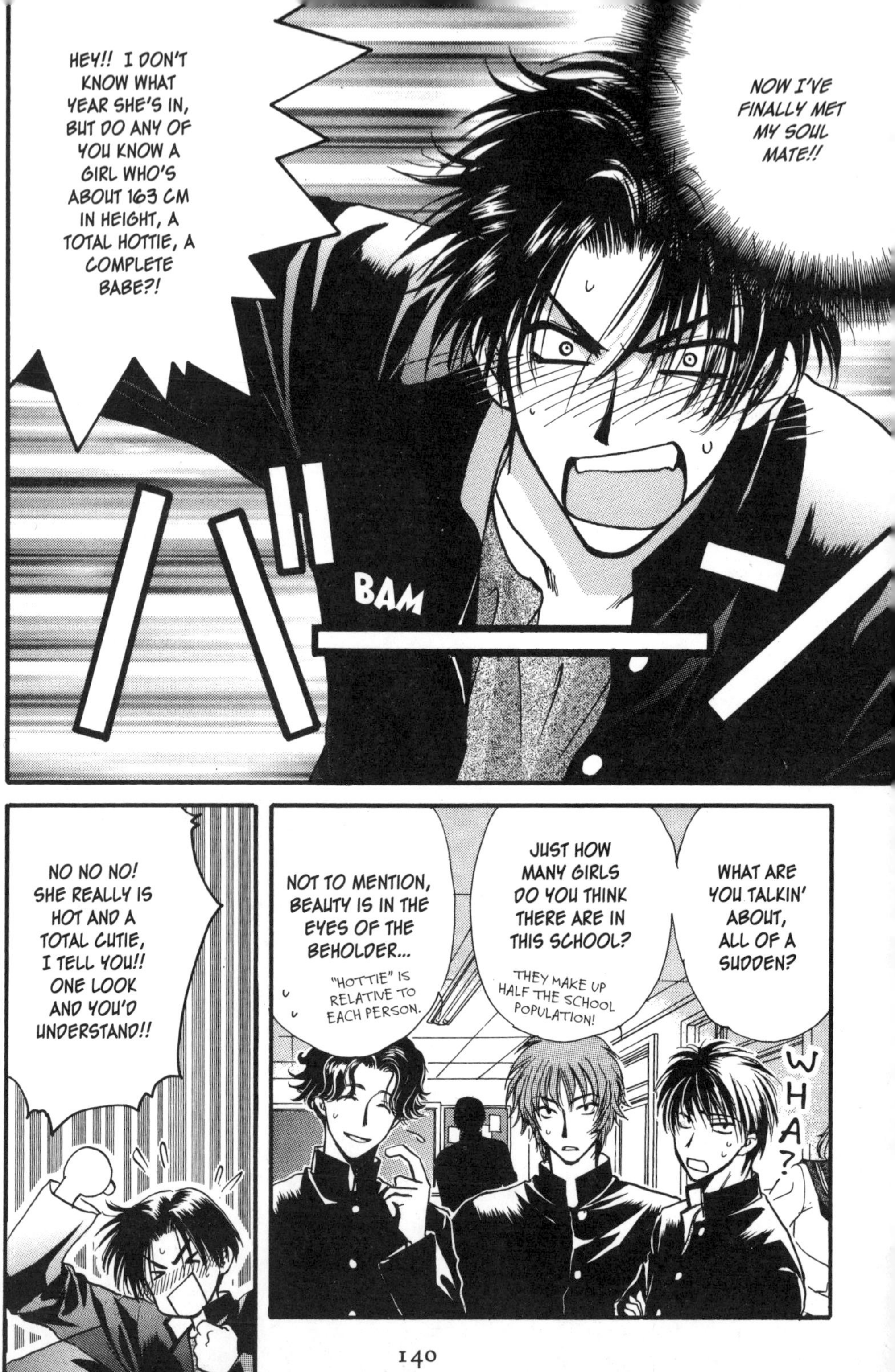
NOW I'VE FINALLY MET MY SOUL MATE!!
HEY!! I DON'T KNOW WHAT YEAR SHE'S IN, BUT DO ANY OF YOU KNOW A GIRL WHO'S ABOUT 163 CM IN HEIGHT, A TOTAL HOTTIE, A COMPLETE BABE?!
BAM
WHAT ARE YOU TALKIN' ABOUT, ALL OF A SUDDEN?
WHA?
JUST HOW MANY GIRLS DO YOU THINK THERE ARE IN THIS SCHOOL?
THEY MAKE UP HALF THE SCHOOL POPULATION!
NOT TO MENTION, BEAUTY IS IN THE EYES OF THE BEHOLDER...
"HOTTIE" IS RELATIVE TO EACH PERSON.
NO NO NO! SHE REALLY IS HOT AND A TOTAL CUTIE, I TELL YOU!! ONE LOOK AND YOU'D UNDERSTAND!!

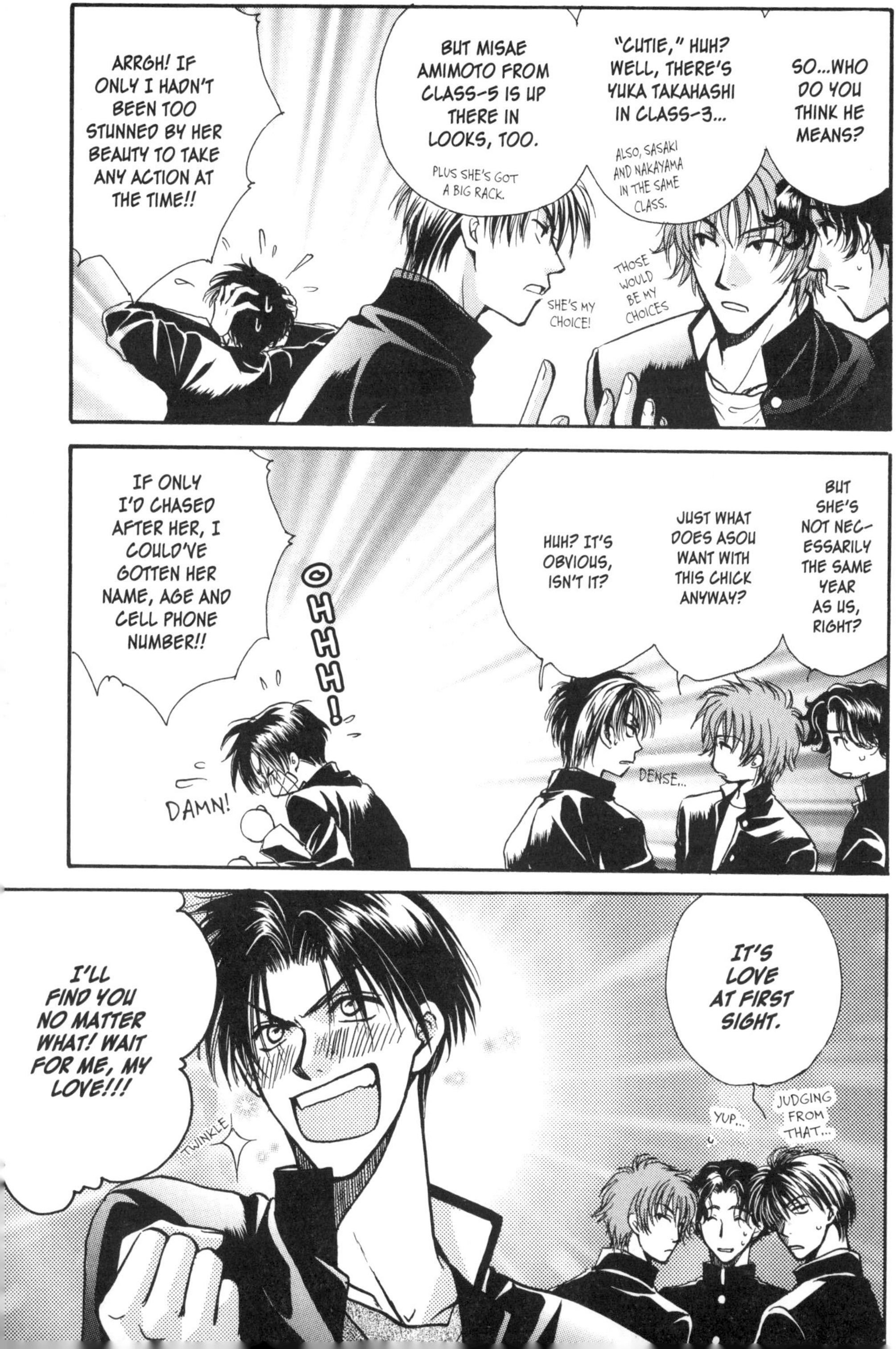
SO...WHO DO YOU THINK HE MEANS?
"CUTIE," HUH? WELL, THERE'S YUKA TAKAHASHI IN CLASS-3...
ALSO, SASAKI AND NAKAYAMA IN THE SAME CLASS.
THOSE WOULD BE MY CHOICES
BUT MISAE AMIMOTO FROM CLASS-5 IS UP THERE IN LOOKS, TOO.
PLUS SHE'S GOT A BIG RACK.
SHE'S MY CHOICE!
ARRGH! IF ONLY I HADN'T BEEN TOO STUNNED BY HER BEAUTY TO TAKE ANY ACTION AT THE TIME!!
BUT SHE'S NOT NEC-ESSARILY THE SAME YEAR AS US, RIGHT?
JUST WHAT DOES ASOU WANT WITH THIS CHICK ANYWAY?
HUH? IT'S OBVIOUS, ISN'T IT?
DENSE...
IF ONLY I'D CHASED AFTER HER, I COULD'VE GOTTEN HER NAME, AGE AND CELL PHONE NUMBER!!
OHHHH!
DAMN!
IT'S LOVE AT FIRST SIGHT.
JUDGING FROM THAT...
YUP...
TWINKLE
I'LL FIND YOU NO MATTER WHAT! WAIT FOR ME, MY LOVE!!!

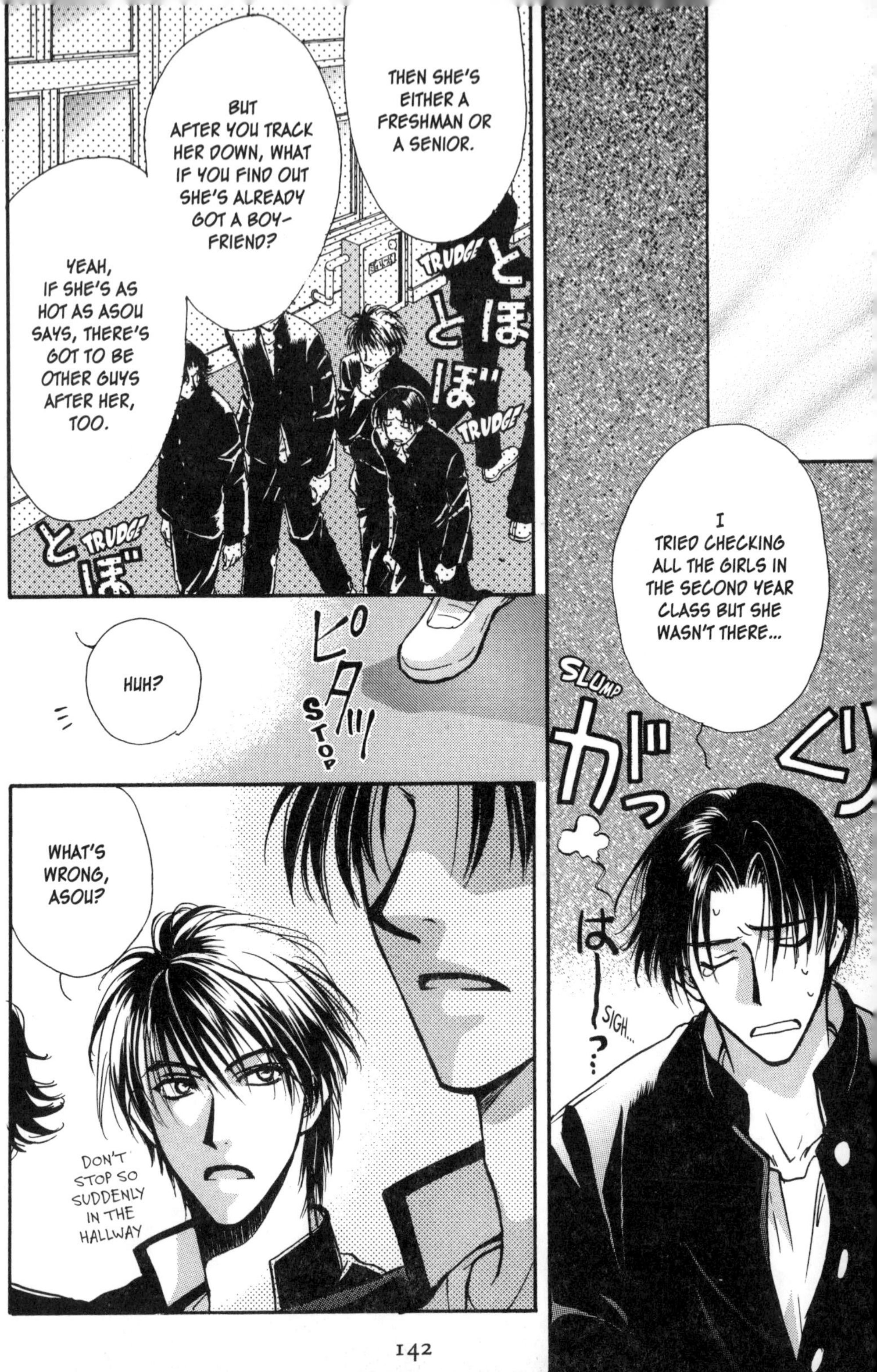
I TRIED CHECKING ALL THE GIRLS IN THE SECOND YEAR CLASS BUT SHE WASN'T THERE...
SLUMP
SIGH...
?...
THEN SHE'S EITHER A FRESHMAN OR A SENIOR.
BUT AFTER YOU TRACK HER DOWN, WHAT IF YOU FIND OUT SHE'S ALREADY GOT A BOY-FRIEND?
TRUDGE
TRUDGE
YEAH, IF SHE'S AS HOT AS ASOU SAYS, THERE'S GOT TO BE OTHER GUYS AFTER HER, TOO.
TRUDGE
STOP
HUH?
WHAT'S WRONG, ASOU?
DON'T STOP SO SUDDENLY IN THE HALLWAY

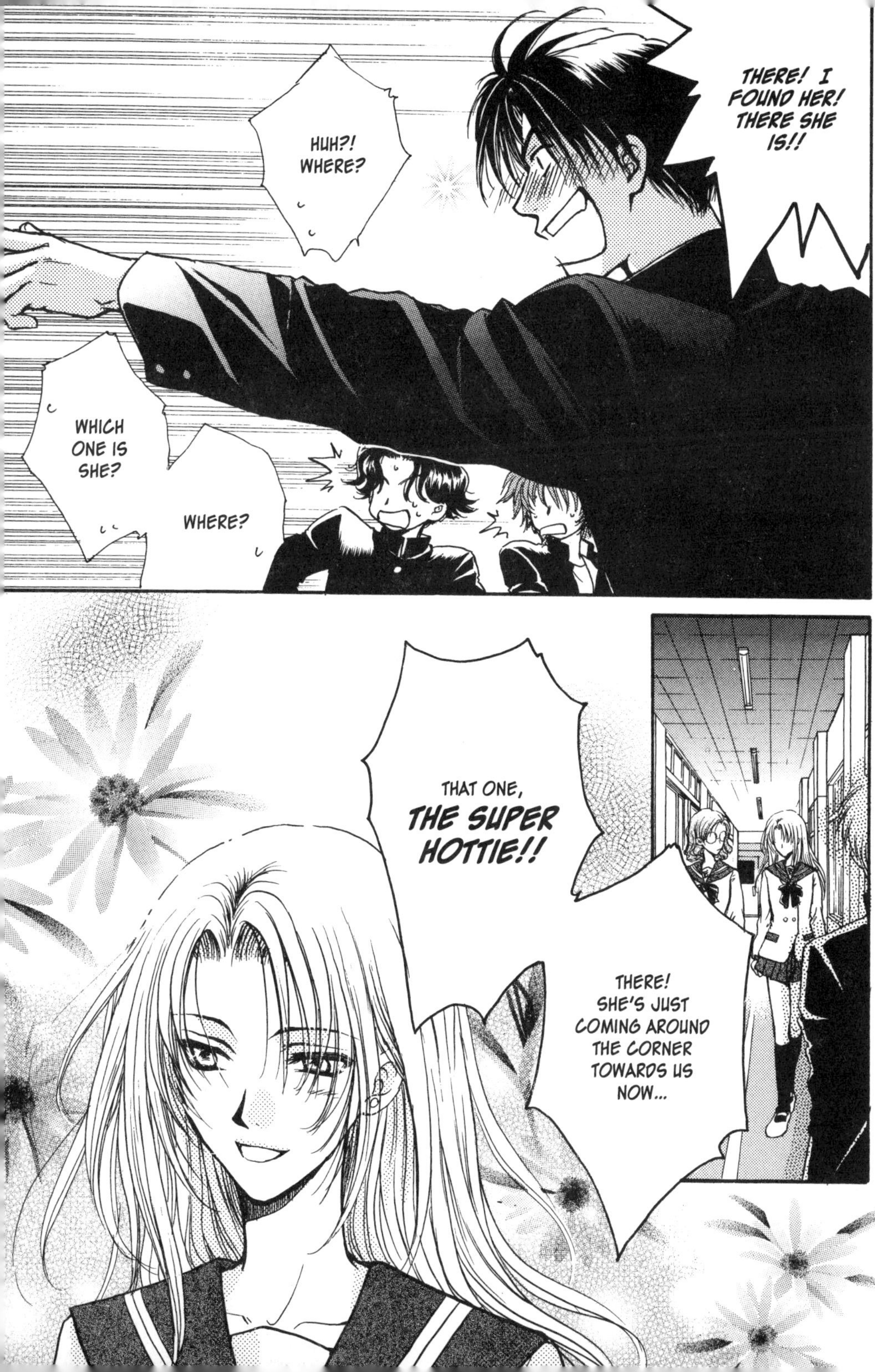
THERE! I FOUND HER! THERE SHE IS!!
HUH?! WHERE?
WHERE?
WHICH ONE IS SHE?
THERE! SHE'S JUST COMING AROUND THE CORNER TOWARDS US NOW...
THAT ONE, THE SUPER HOTTIE!!

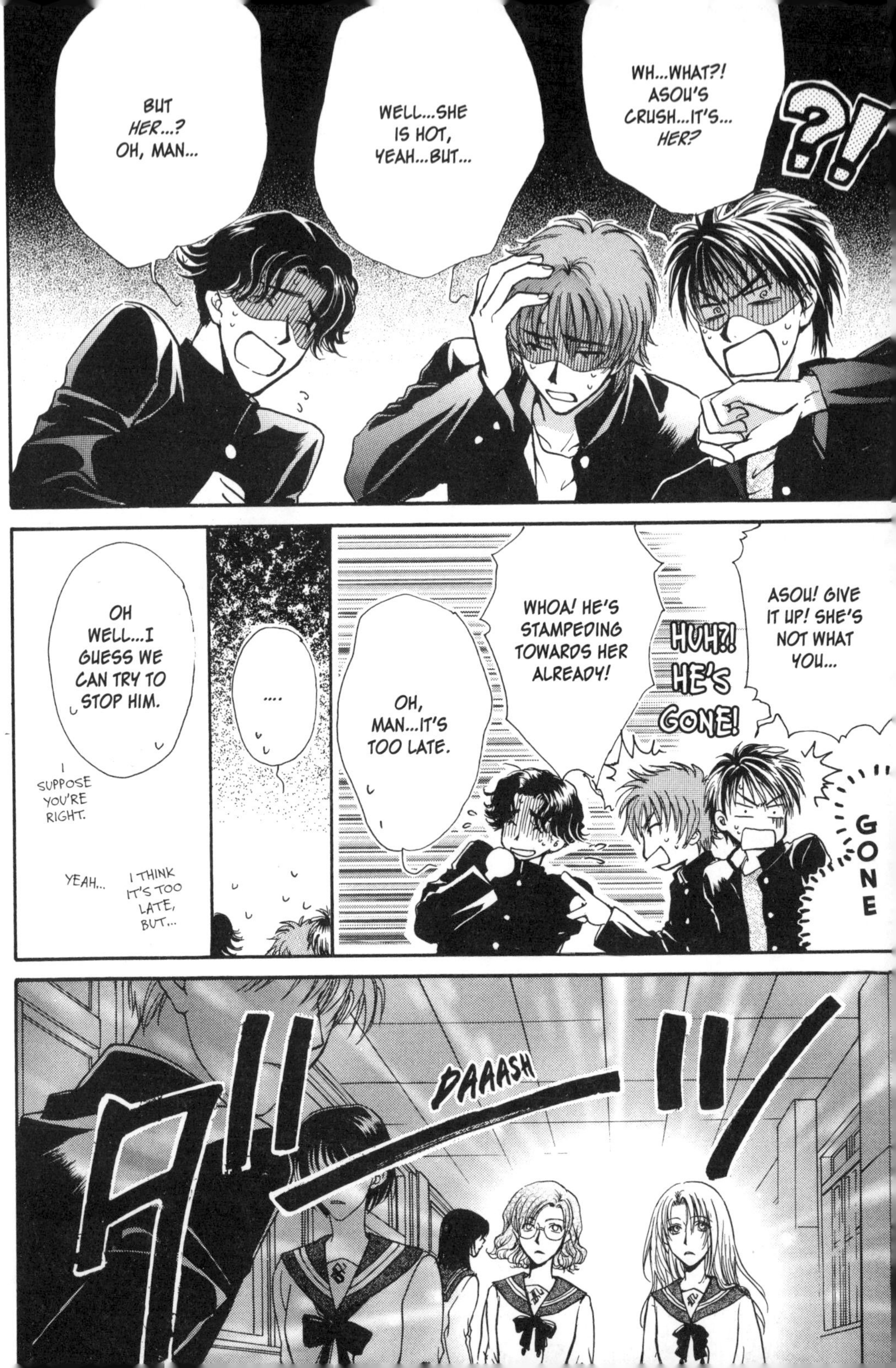
?!
WH...WHAT?! ASOU'S CRUSH...IT'S... HER?
WELL...SHE IS HOT, YEAH...BUT...
BUT HER...? OH, MAN...
ASOU! GIVE IT UP! SHE'S NOT WHAT YOU...
HUH?! HE'S GONE!
WHOA! HE'S STAMPEDING TOWARDS HER ALREADY!
GONE
OH, MAN...IT'S TOO LATE.
....
OH WELL...I GUESS WE CAN TRY TO STOP HIM.
I SUPPOSE YOU'RE RIGHT.
I THINK IT'S TOO LATE, BUT...
YEAH...
DAAASH

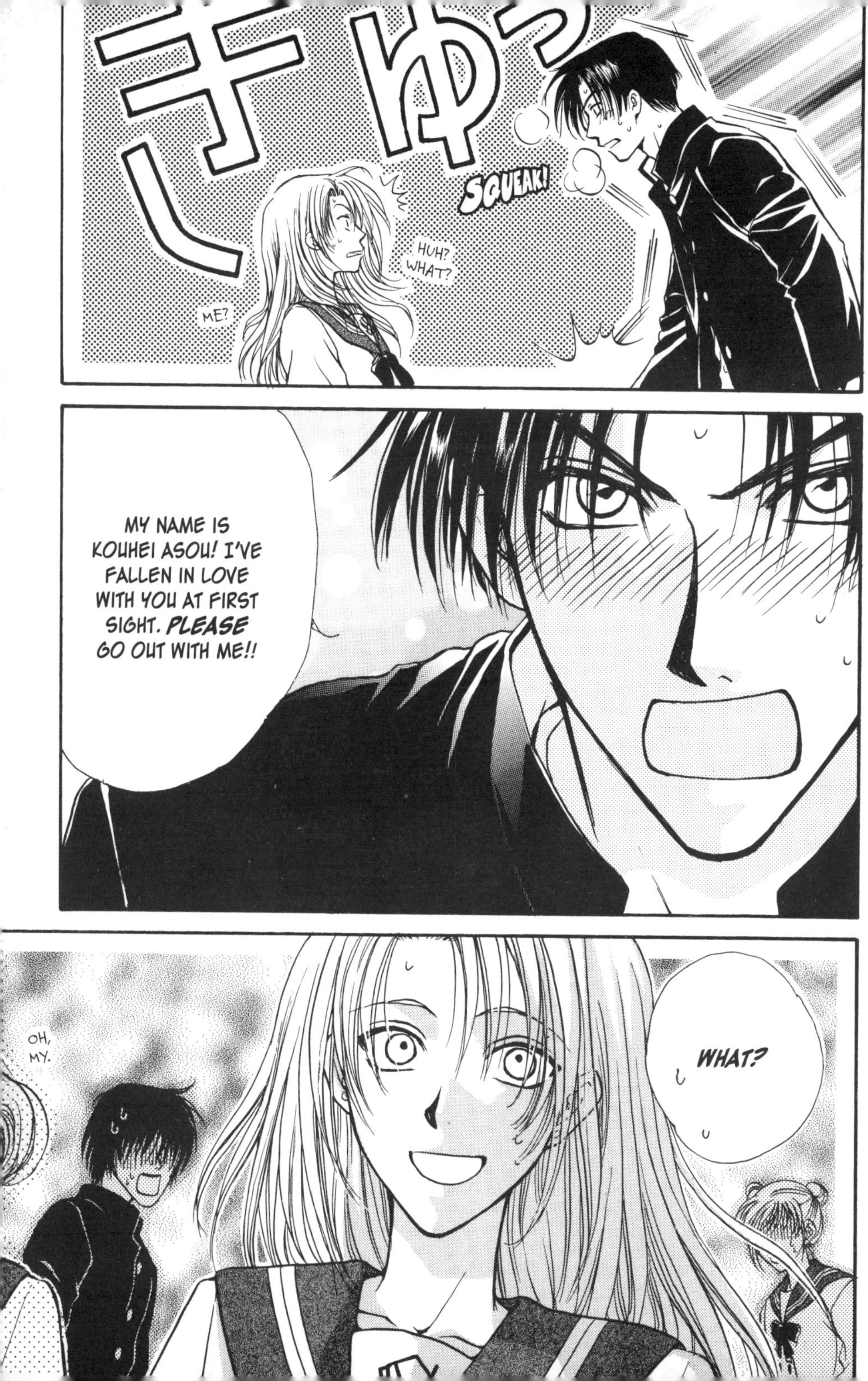
きゅっ
SQUEAK!
HUH? WHAT?
ME?
MY NAME IS KOUHEI ASOU! I'VE FALLEN IN LOVE WITH YOU AT FIRST SIGHT. PLEASE GO OUT WITH ME!!
WHAT?
OH, MY.

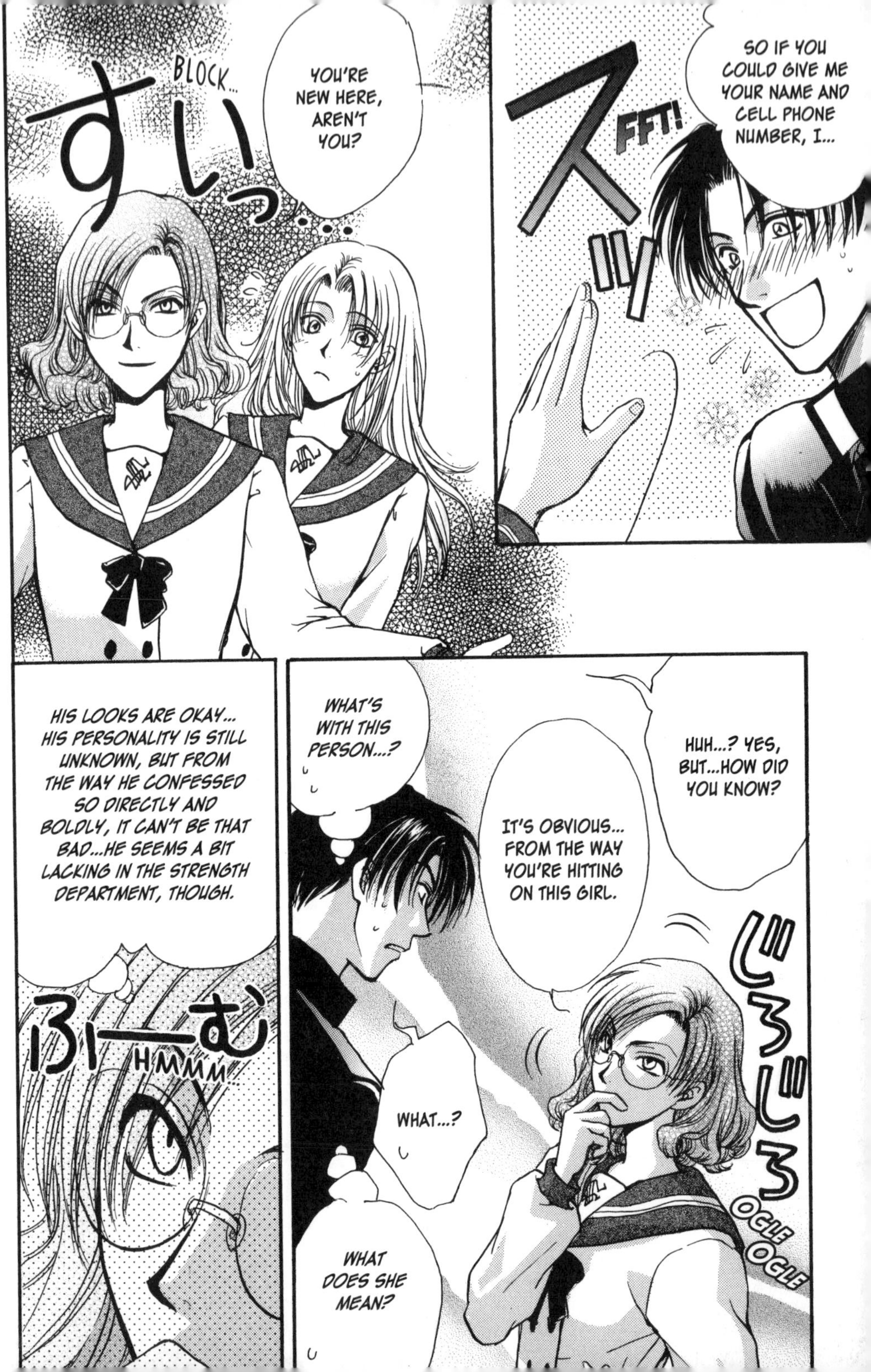
SO IF YOU COULD GIVE ME YOUR NAME AND CELL PHONE NUMBER, I...
ス
FFT!
YOU'RE NEW HERE, AREN'T YOU?
すいっ
BLOCK...
HUH...? YES, BUT...HOW DID YOU KNOW?
IT'S OBVIOUS... FROM THE WAY YOU'RE HITTING ON THIS GIRL.
じろじろ
OGLE OGLE
WHAT'S WITH THIS PERSON...?
WHAT...?
WHAT DOES SHE MEAN?
HIS LOOKS ARE OKAY... HIS PERSONALITY IS STILL UNKNOWN, BUT FROM THE WAY HE CONFESSED SO DIRECTLY AND BOLDLY, IT CAN'T BE THAT BAD...HE SEEMS A BIT LACKING IN THE STRENGTH DEPARTMENT, THOUGH.
ふーむ
HMMM

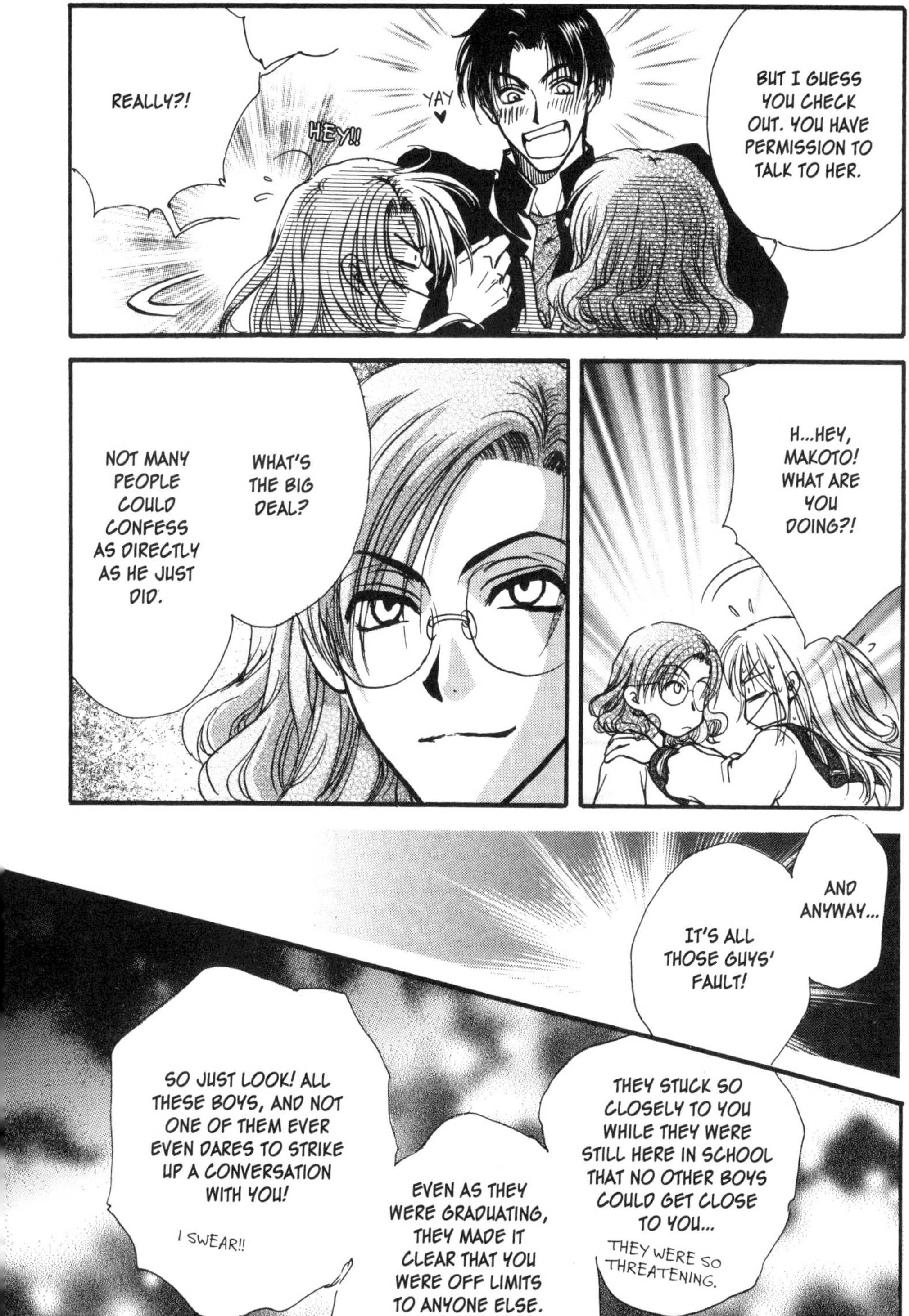
BUT I GUESS YOU CHECK OUT. YOU HAVE PERMISSION TO TALK TO HER.
YAY ♥
REALLY?!
HEY!!
H...HEY, MAKOTO! WHAT ARE YOU DOING?!
WHAT'S THE BIG DEAL?
NOT MANY PEOPLE COULD CONFESS AS DIRECTLY AS HE JUST DID.
AND ANYWAY...
IT'S ALL THOSE GUYS' FAULT!
THEY STUCK SO CLOSELY TO YOU WHILE THEY WERE STILL HERE IN SCHOOL THAT NO OTHER BOYS COULD GET CLOSE TO YOU...
THEY WERE SO THREATENING.
EVEN AS THEY WERE GRADUATING, THEY MADE IT CLEAR THAT YOU WERE OFF LIMITS TO ANYONE ELSE.
SO JUST LOOK! ALL THESE BOYS, AND NOT ONE OF THEM EVER EVEN DARES TO STRIKE UP A CONVERSATION WITH YOU!
I SWEAR!!

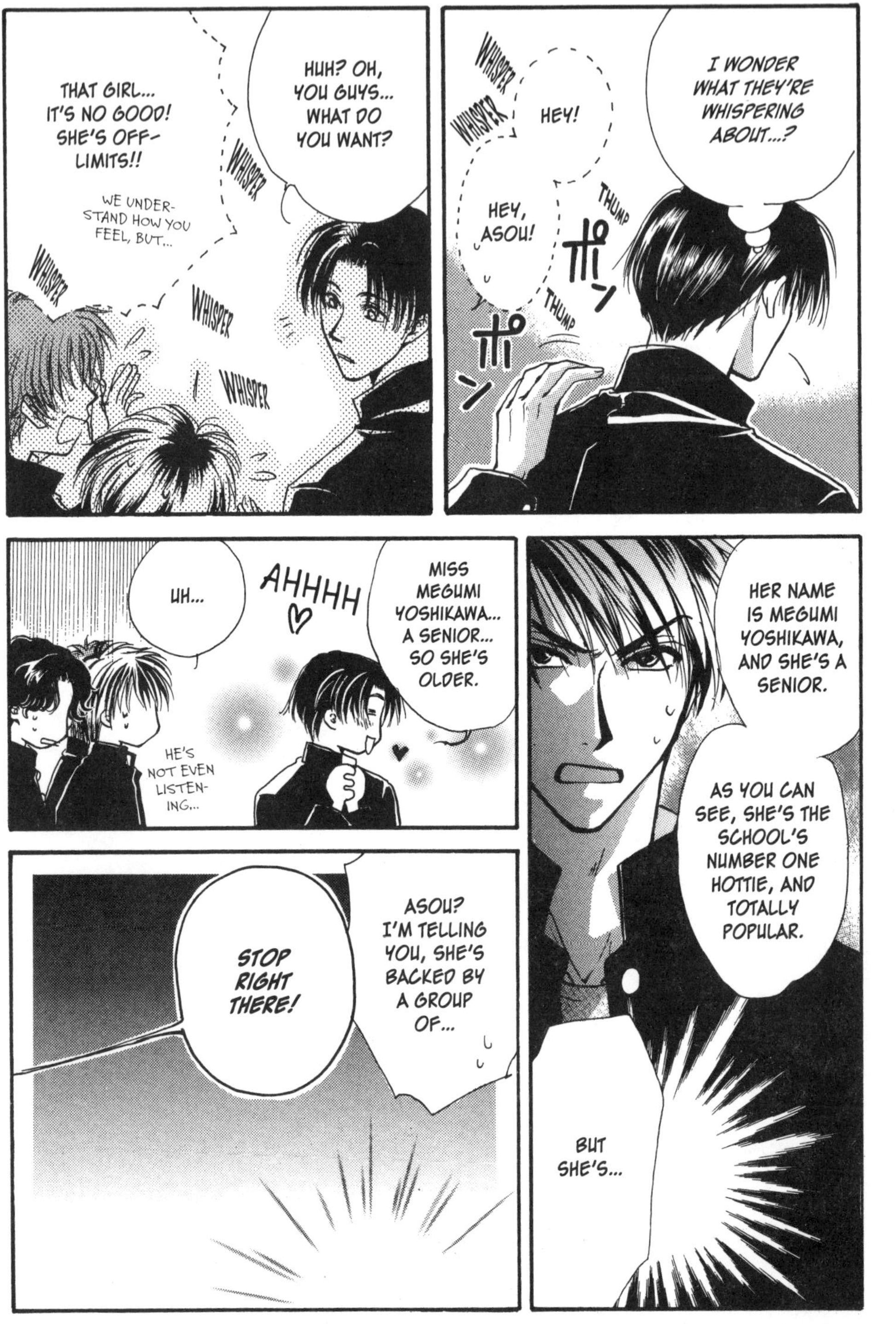
I WONDER WHAT THEY'RE WHISPERING ABOUT...?
WHISPER
WHISPER
HEY!
HEY, ASOU!
THUMP
THUMP
HUH? OH, YOU GUYS... WHAT DO YOU WANT?
THAT GIRL... IT'S NO GOOD! SHE'S OFF-LIMITS!!
WHISPER
WE UNDERSTAND HOW YOU FEEL, BUT...
WHISPER
WHISPER
WHISPER
HER NAME IS MEGUMI YOSHIKAWA, AND SHE'S A SENIOR.
AS YOU CAN SEE, SHE'S THE SCHOOL'S NUMBER ONE HOTTIE, AND TOTALLY POPULAR.
BUT SHE'S...
MISS MEGUMI YOSHIKAWA... A SENIOR... SO SHE'S OLDER.
AHHHH
UH...
HE'S NOT EVEN LISTENING...
ASOU? I'M TELLING YOU, SHE'S BACKED BY A GROUP OF...
STOP RIGHT THERE!

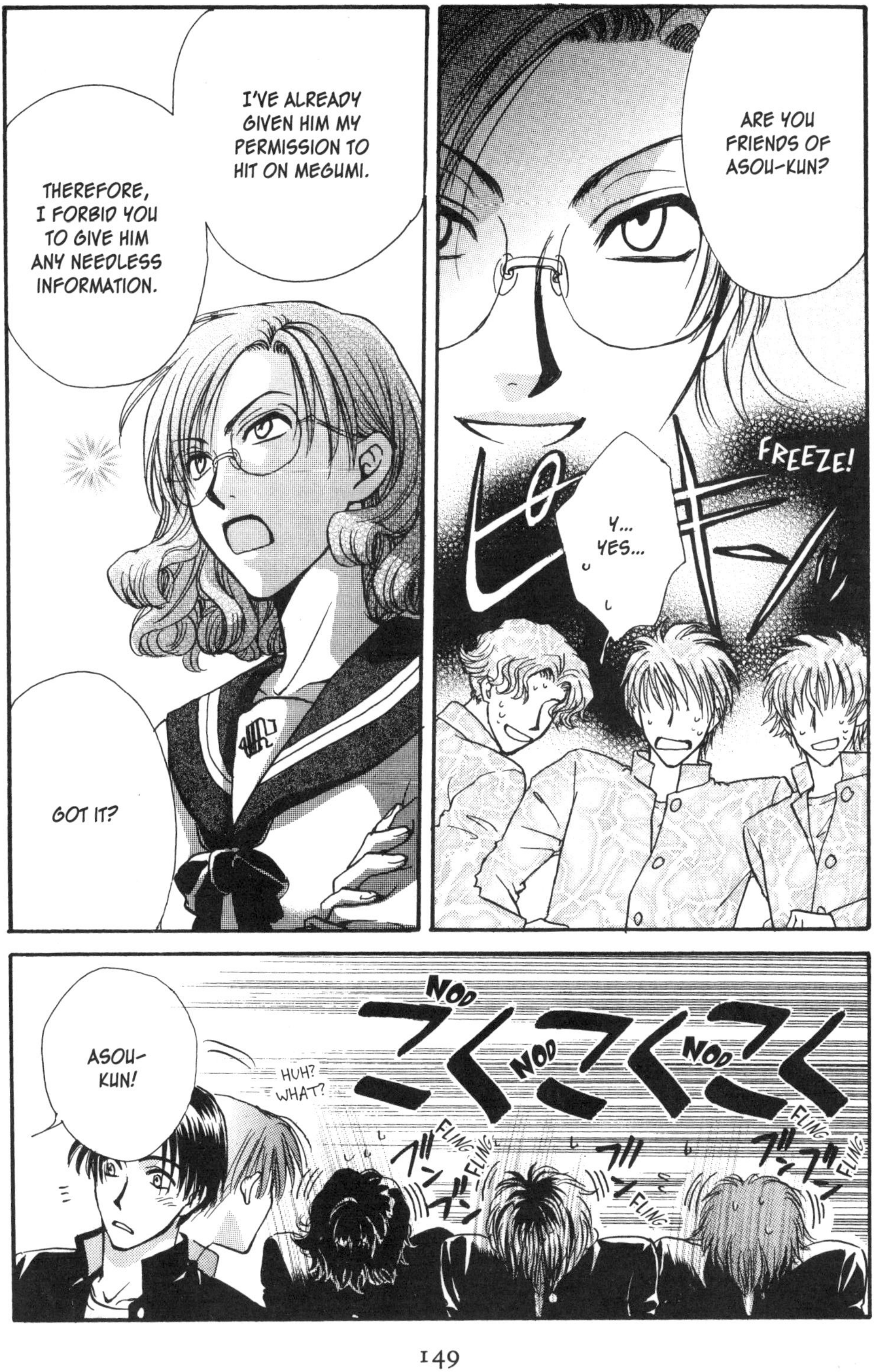

ARE YOU FRIENDS OF ASOU-KUN?
FREEZE!
Y... YES...
I'VE ALREADY GIVEN HIM MY PERMISSION TO HIT ON MEGUMI.
THEREFORE, I FORBID YOU TO GIVE HIM ANY NEEDLESS INFORMATION.
GOT IT?
こくこくこく
NOD
NOD
NOD
FLING
FLING
FLING
FLING
FLING
HUH? WHAT?
ASOU-KUN!

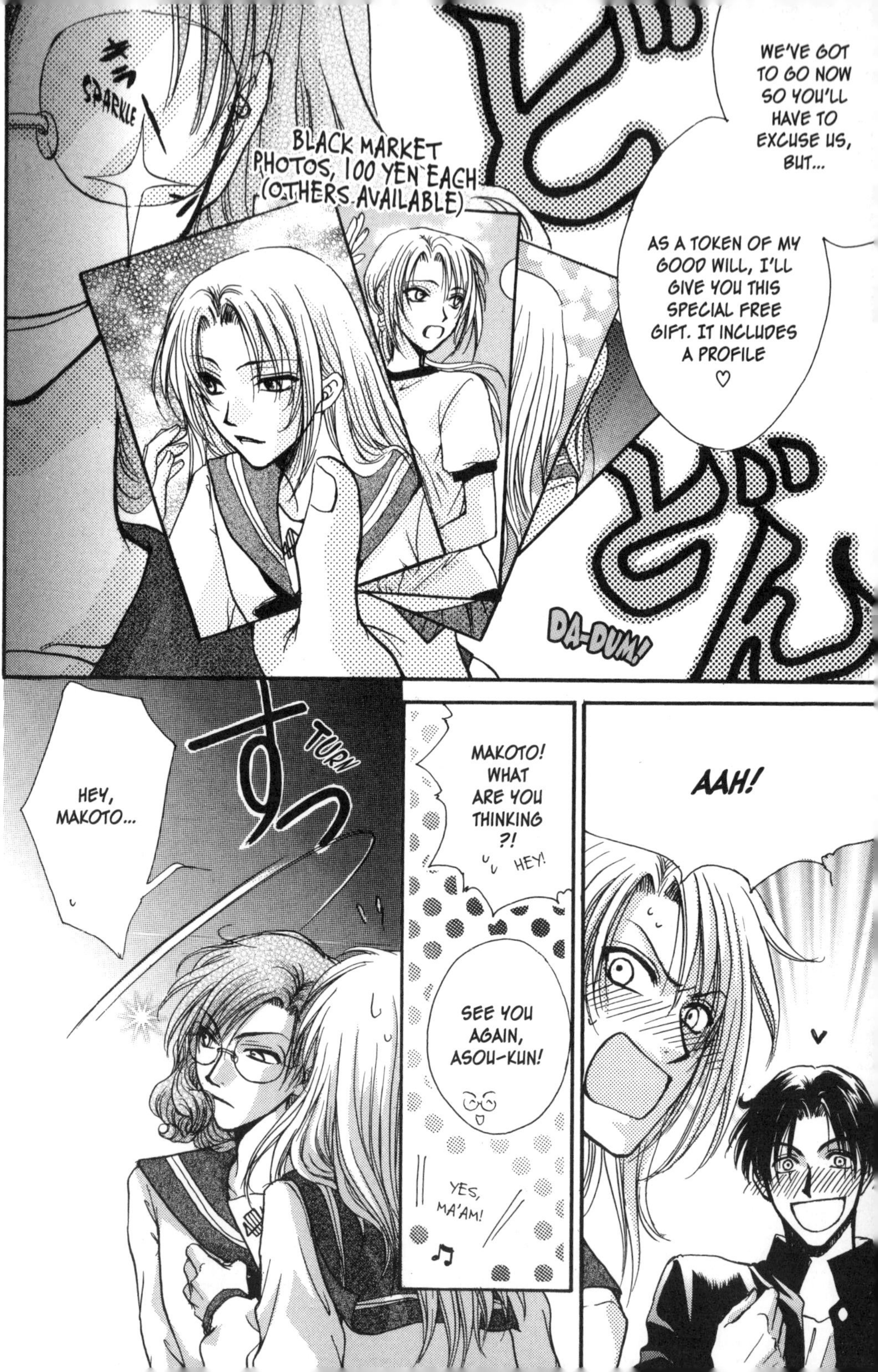
WE'VE GOT TO GO NOW SO YOU'LL HAVE TO EXCUSE US, BUT...
AS A TOKEN OF MY GOOD WILL, I'LL GIVE YOU THIS SPECIAL FREE GIFT. IT INCLUDES A PROFILE ♡
BLACK MARKET PHOTOS, 100 YEN EACH (OTHERS AVAILABLE)
SPARKLE
DA-DUM!
AAH!
MAKOTO! WHAT ARE YOU THINKING ?!
HEY!
SEE YOU AGAIN, ASOU-KUN!
YES, MA'AM!
HEY, MAKOTO...
TURN

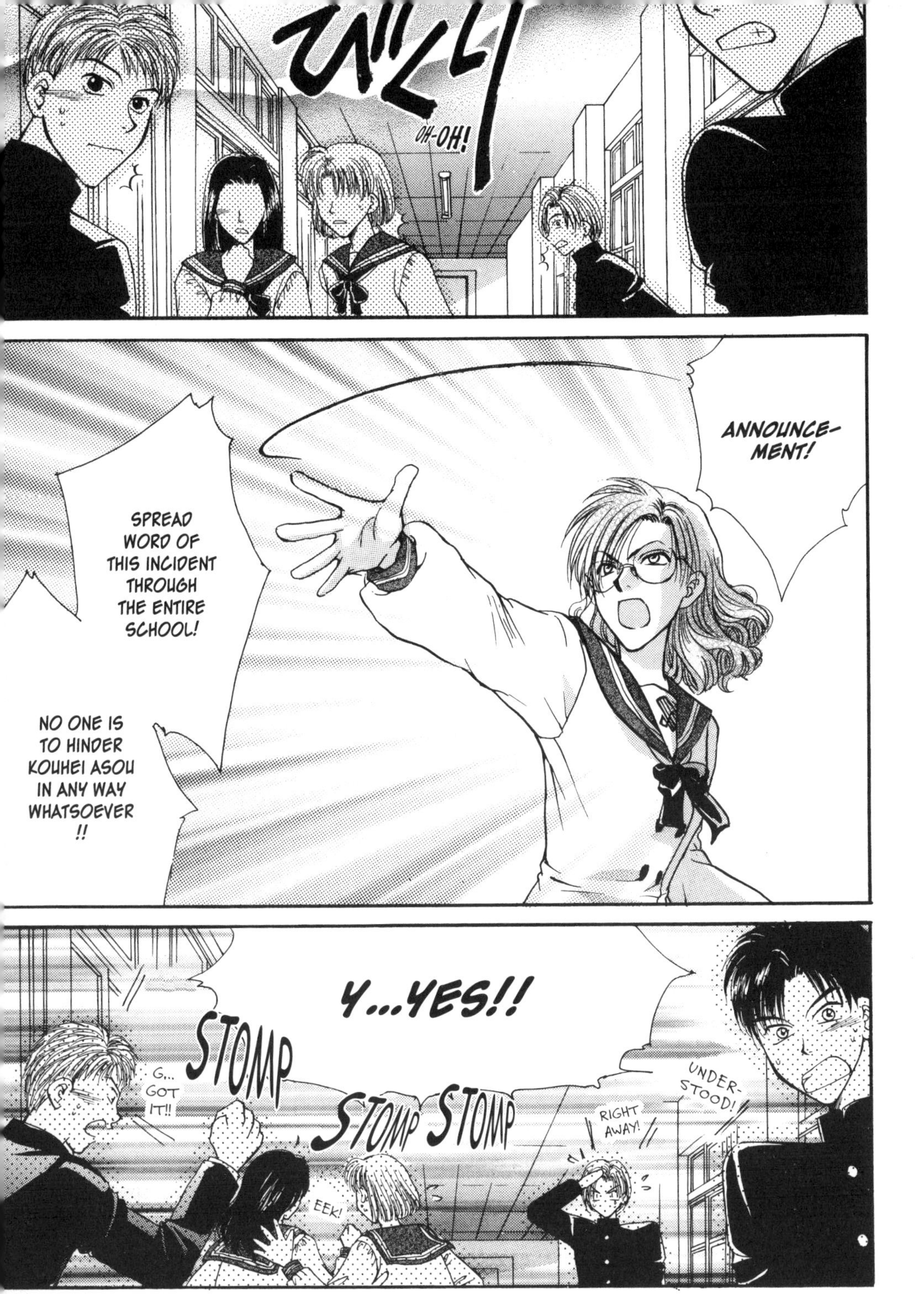
OH-OH!
ANNOUNCE-MENT!
SPREAD WORD OF THIS INCIDENT THROUGH THE ENTIRE SCHOOL!
NO ONE IS TO HINDER KOUHEI ASOU IN ANY WAY WHATSOEVER !!
UNDER-STOOD!
Y...YES!!
RIGHT AWAY!
STOMP
STOMP
STOMP
EEK!
G... GOT IT!!

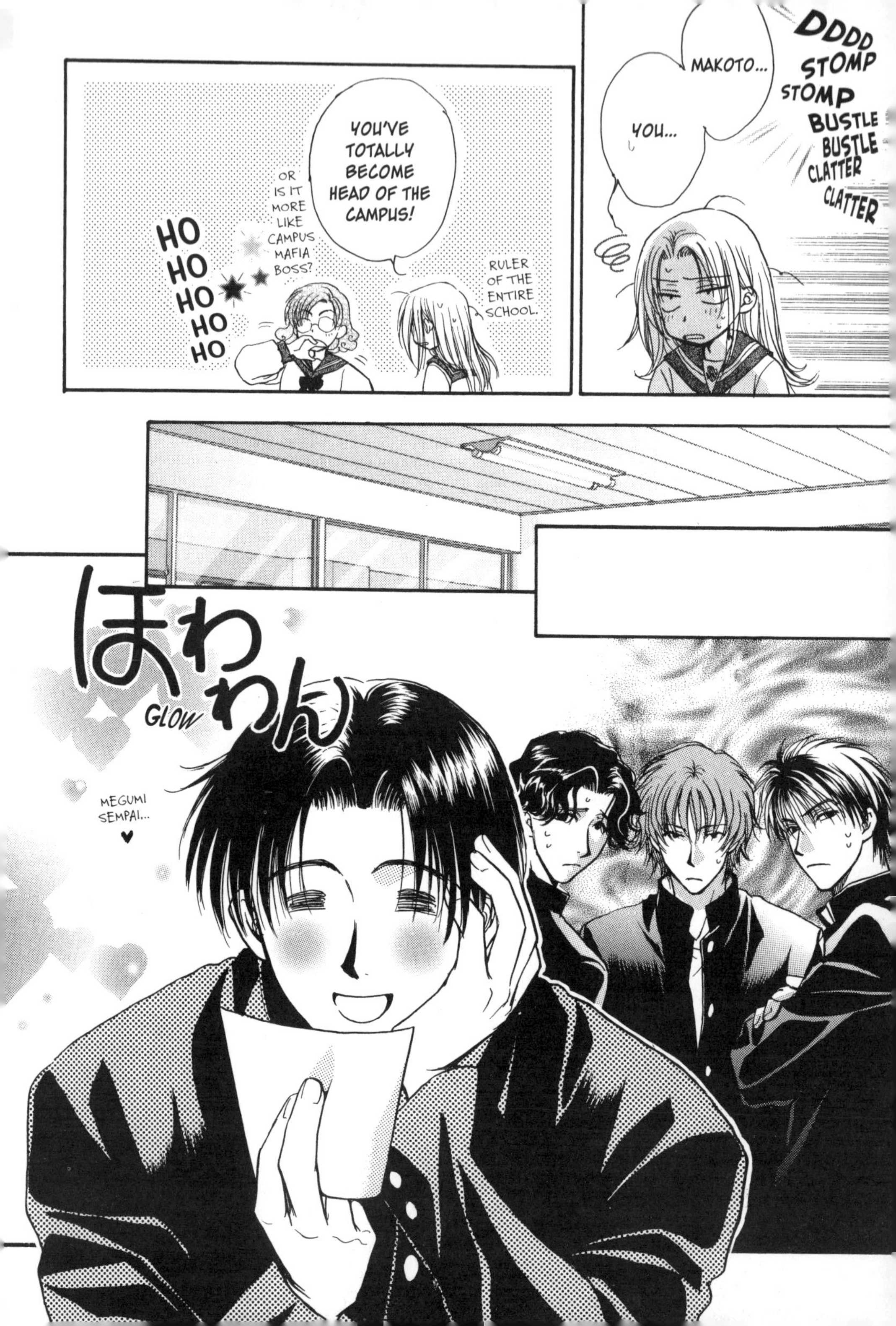
MAKOTO...
YOU...
DDDD STOMP STOMP BUSTLE BUSTLE CLATTER CLATTER
YOU'VE TOTALLY BECOME HEAD OF THE CAMPUS!
RULER OF THE ENTIRE SCHOOL.
OR IS IT MORE LIKE CAMPUS MAFIA BOSS?
HO HO HO HO HO HO
ほわわん
GLOW
MEGUMI SEMPAI... ♥

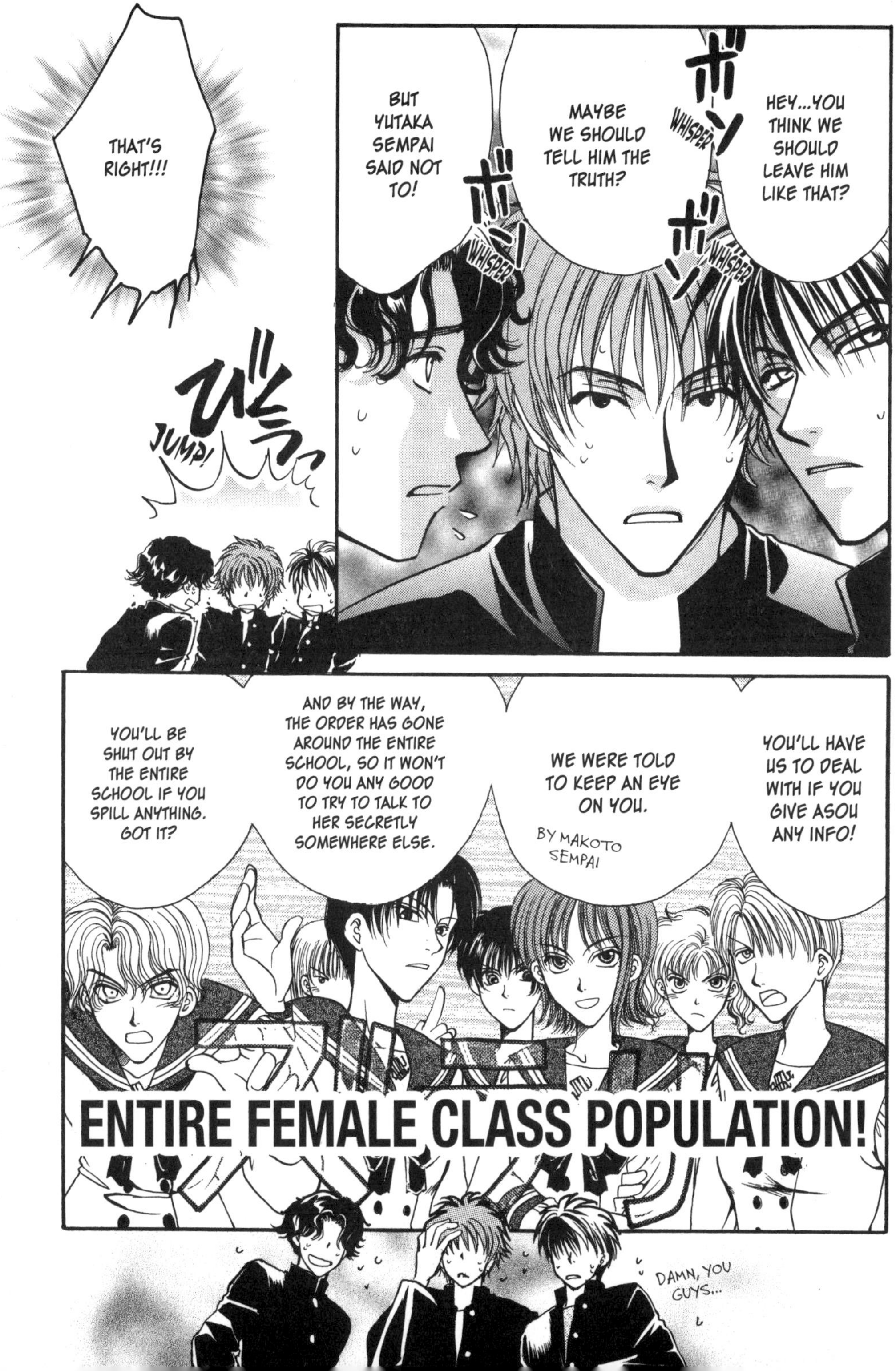
HEY...YOU THINK WE SHOULD LEAVE HIM LIKE THAT?
WHISPER
MAYBE WE SHOULD TELL HIM THE TRUTH?
WHISPER
BUT YUTAKA SEMPAI SAID NOT TO!
WHISPER
THAT'S RIGHT!!!
JUMP!
YOU'LL HAVE US TO DEAL WITH IF YOU GIVE ASOU ANY INFO!
WE WERE TOLD TO KEEP AN EYE ON YOU.
BY MAKOTO SEMPAI
AND BY THE WAY, THE ORDER HAS GONE AROUND THE ENTIRE SCHOOL, SO IT WON'T DO YOU ANY GOOD TO TRY TO TALK TO HER SECRETLY SOMEWHERE ELSE.
YOU'LL BE SHUT OUT BY THE ENTIRE SCHOOL IF YOU SPILL ANYTHING. GOT IT?
ENTIRE FEMALE CLASS POPULATION!
DAMN, YOU GUYS...

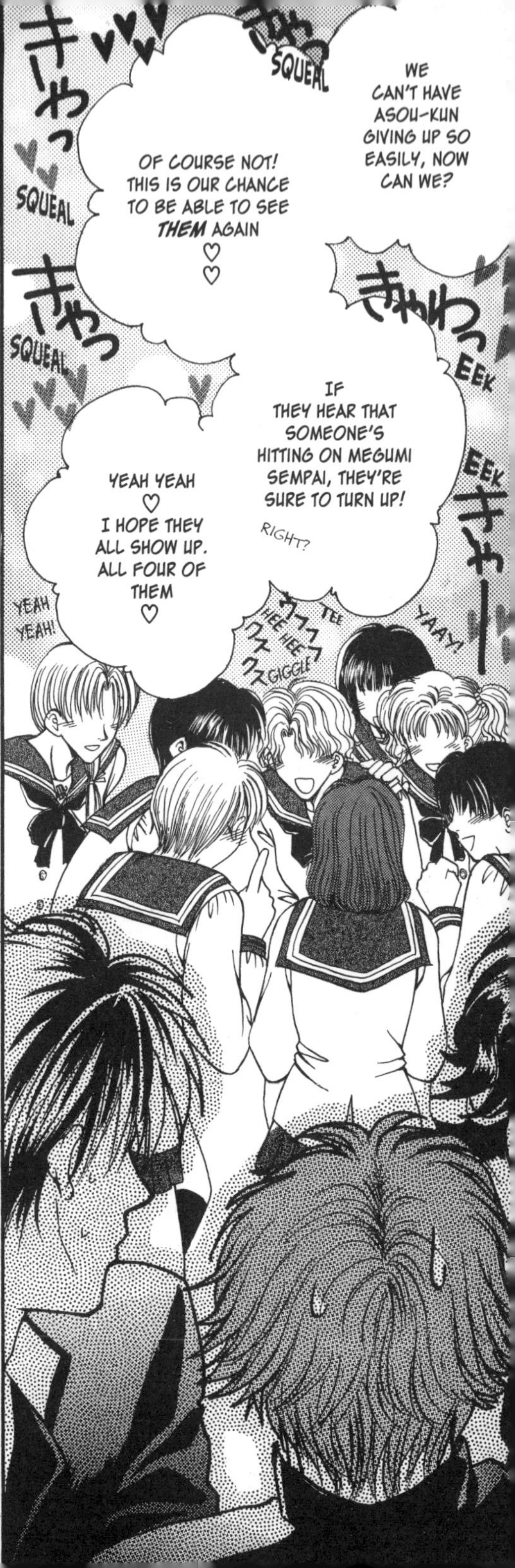
WE CAN'T HAVE ASOU-KUN GIVING UP SO EASILY, NOW CAN WE?
OF COURSE NOT! THIS IS OUR CHANCE TO BE ABLE TO SEE ***THEM*** AGAIN ♡ ♡
SQUEAL
SQUEAL
SQUEAL
EEK
EEK
IF THEY HEAR THAT SOMEONE'S HITTING ON MEGUMI SEMPAI, THEY'RE SURE TO TURN UP!
RIGHT?
YEAH YEAH ♡ I HOPE THEY ALL SHOW UP. ALL FOUR OF THEM ♡
YAAY!
TEE HEE HEE GIGGLE
YEAH YEAH!
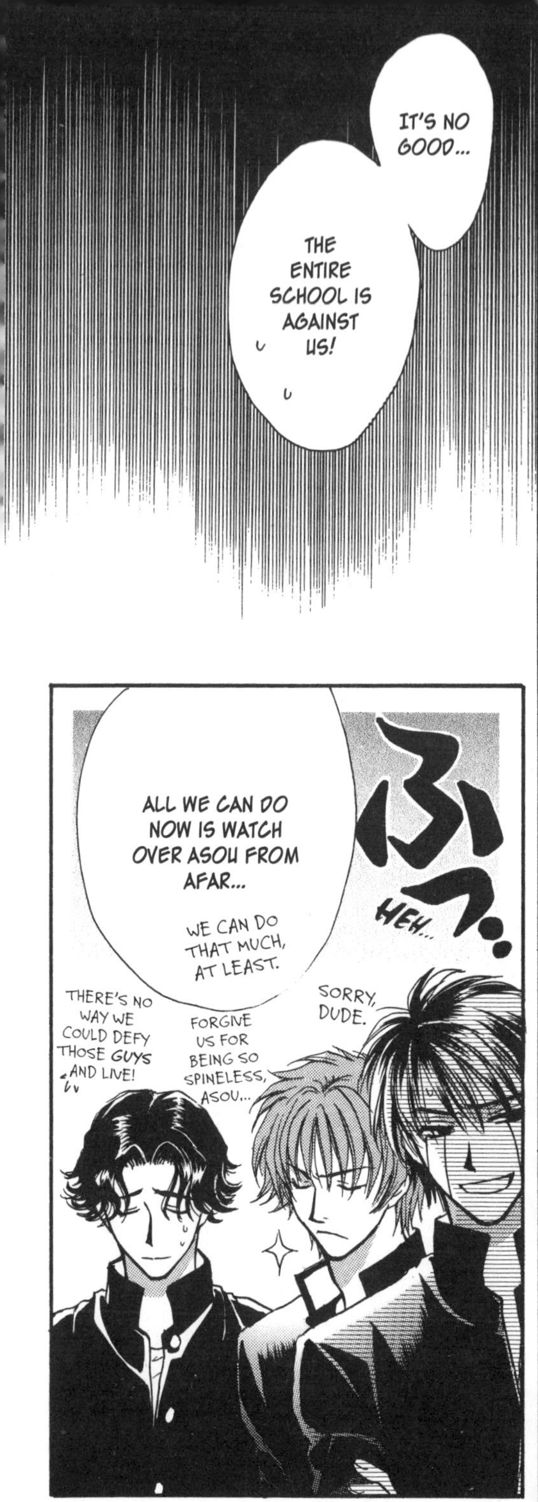
IT'S NO GOOD...
THE ENTIRE SCHOOL IS AGAINST US!
ふっ
HEH...
ALL WE CAN DO NOW IS WATCH OVER ASOU FROM AFAR...
WE CAN DO THAT MUCH, AT LEAST.
SORRY, DUDE.
FORGIVE US FOR BEING SO SPINELESS, ASOU...
THERE'S NO WAY WE COULD DEFY THOSE **GUYS** AND LIVE!

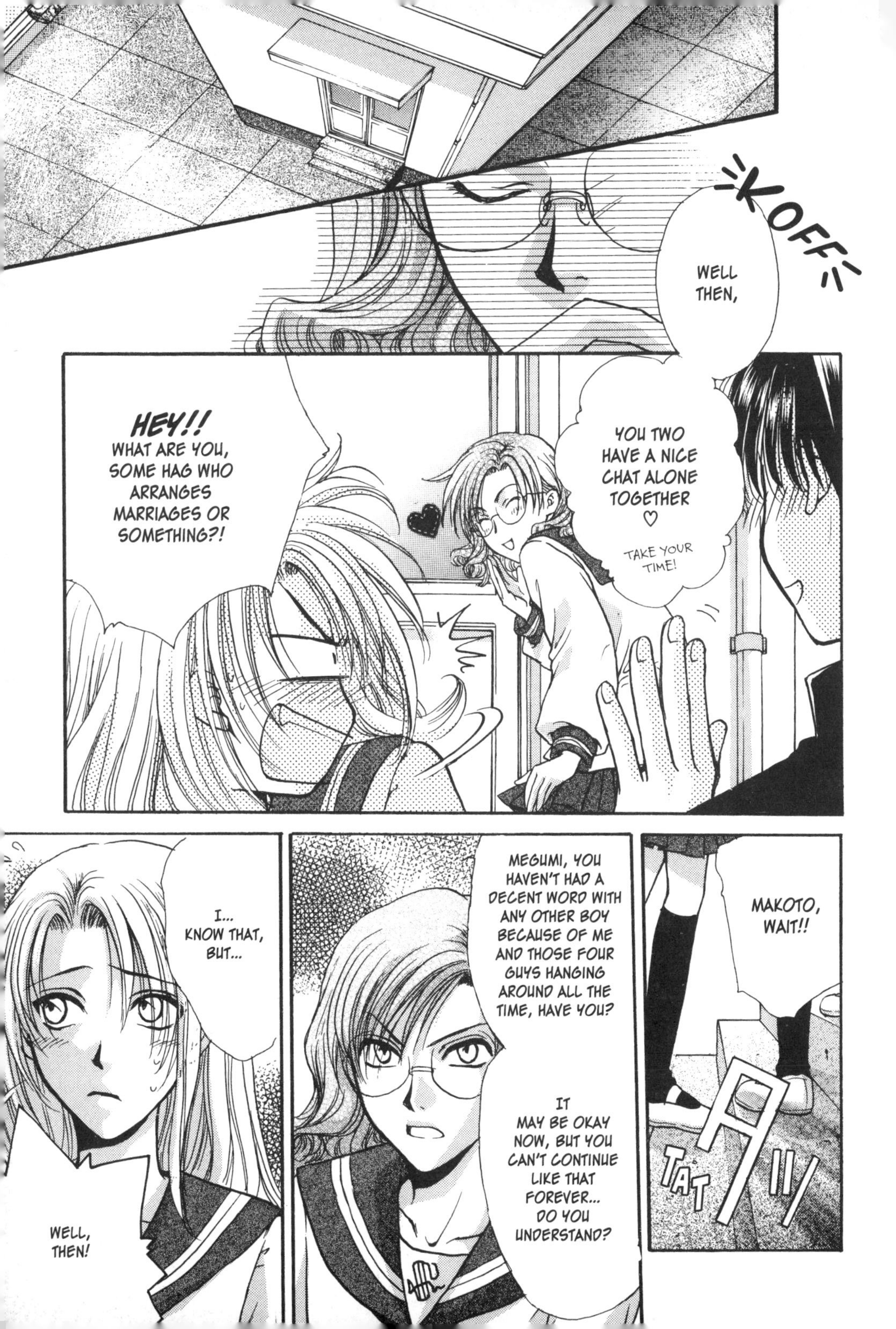
KOFF
WELL THEN,
YOU TWO HAVE A NICE CHAT ALONE TOGETHER ♡
TAKE YOUR TIME!
HEY!! WHAT ARE YOU, SOME HAG WHO ARRANGES MARRIAGES OR SOMETHING?!
MAKOTO, WAIT!!
TAT
MEGUMI, YOU HAVEN'T HAD A DECENT WORD WITH ANY OTHER BOY BECAUSE OF ME AND THOSE FOUR GUYS HANGING AROUND ALL THE TIME, HAVE YOU?
IT MAY BE OKAY NOW, BUT YOU CAN'T CONTINUE LIKE THAT FOREVER... DO YOU UNDERSTAND?
I... KNOW THAT, BUT...
WELL, THEN!

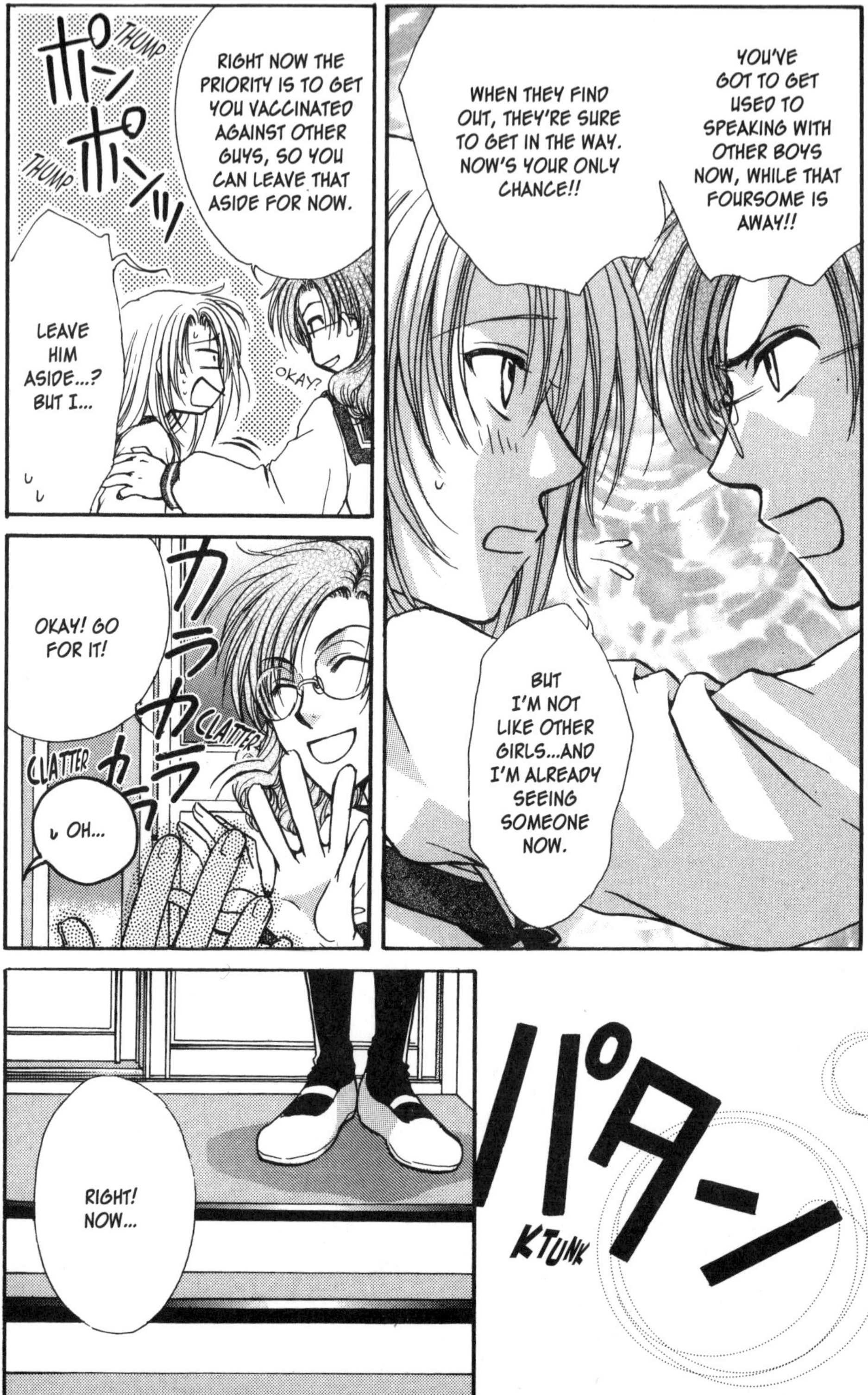
YOU'VE GOT TO GET USED TO SPEAKING WITH OTHER BOYS NOW, WHILE THAT FOURSOME IS AWAY!!
WHEN THEY FIND OUT, THEY'RE SURE TO GET IN THE WAY. NOW'S YOUR ONLY CHANCE!!
BUT I'M NOT LIKE OTHER GIRLS...AND I'M ALREADY SEEING SOMEONE NOW.
ポンポンッ
THUMP
THUMP
RIGHT NOW THE PRIORITY IS TO GET YOU VACCINATED AGAINST OTHER GUYS, SO YOU CAN LEAVE THAT ASIDE FOR NOW.
OKAY?
LEAVE HIM ASIDE...? BUT I...
カラカラカラ
CLATTER
CLATTER
OKAY! GO FOR IT!
OH...
パターン
KTUNK
RIGHT! NOW...

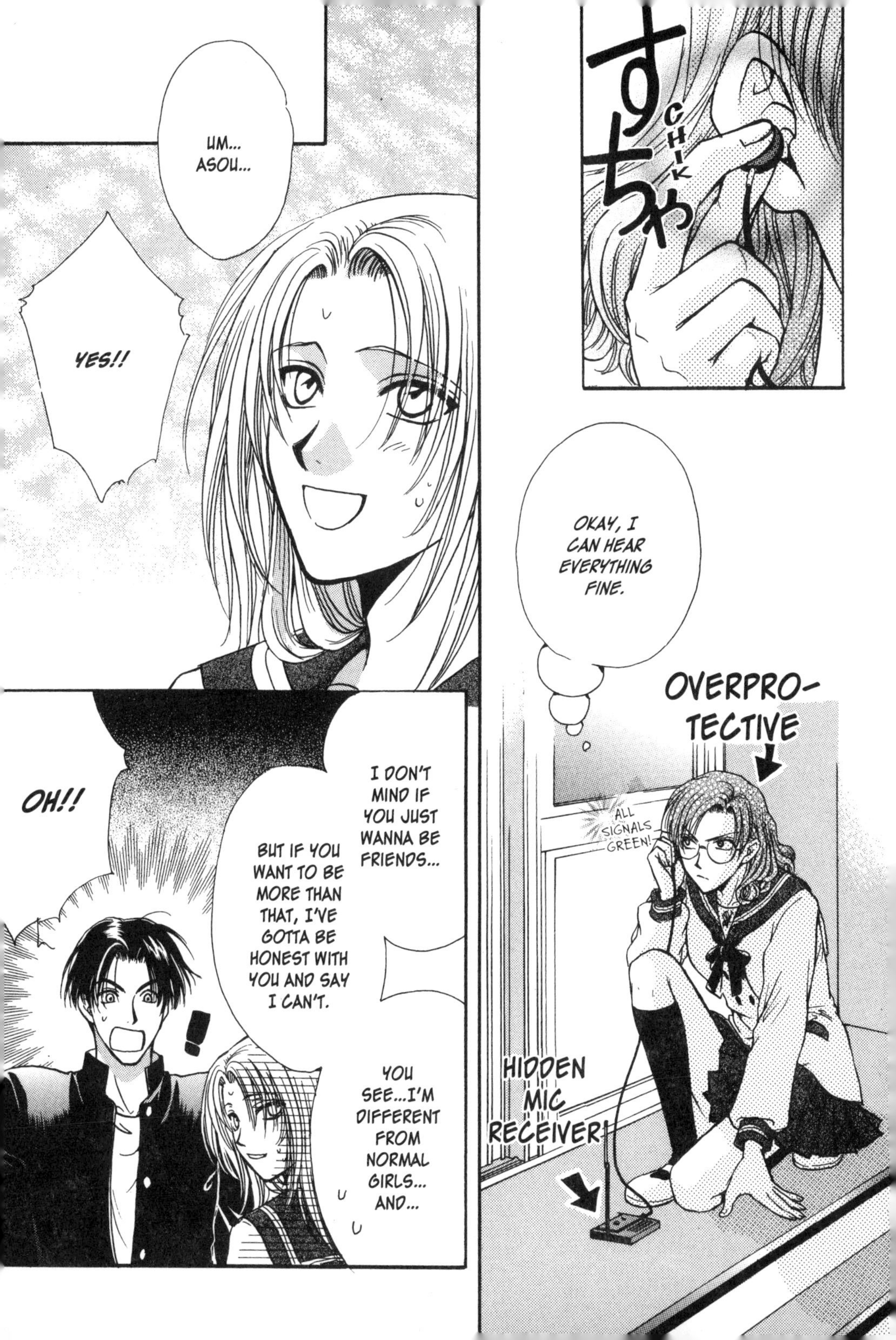
すちゃ
CHIK
OKAY, I CAN HEAR EVERYTHING FINE.
OVERPRO-TECTIVE
ALL SIGNALS GREEN!
HIDDEN MIC RECEIVER
UM... ASOU...
YES!!
I DON'T MIND IF YOU JUST WANNA BE FRIENDS...
BUT IF YOU WANT TO BE MORE THAN THAT, I'VE GOTTA BE HONEST WITH YOU AND SAY I CAN'T.
OH!!
YOU SEE...I'M DIFFERENT FROM NORMAL GIRLS... AND...

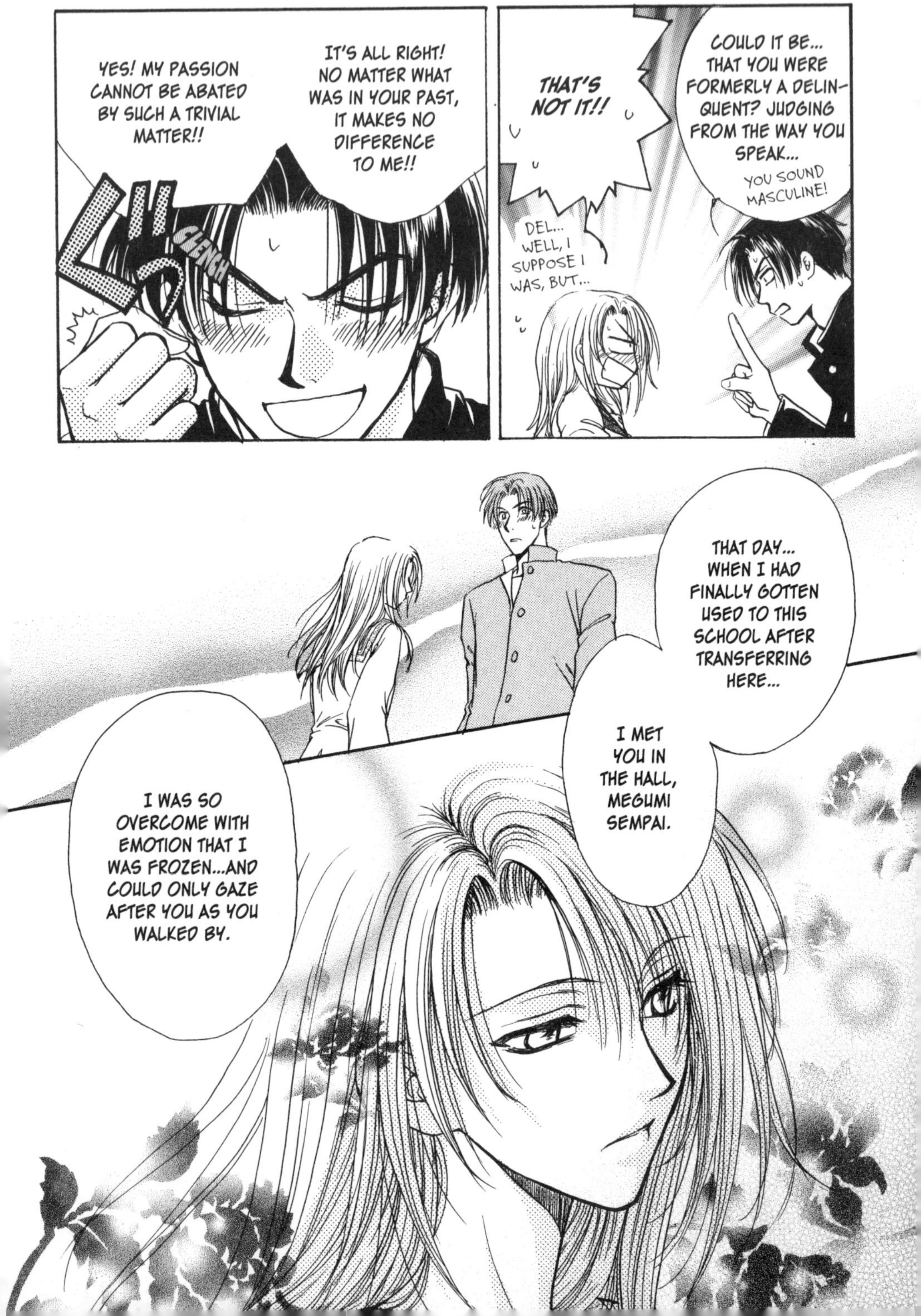
COULD IT BE... THAT YOU WERE FORMERLY A DELIN-QUENT? JUDGING FROM THE WAY YOU SPEAK...
YOU SOUND MASCULINE!
THAT'S NOT IT!!
DEL... WELL, I SUPPOSE I WAS, BUT...
IT'S ALL RIGHT! NO MATTER WHAT WAS IN YOUR PAST, IT MAKES NO DIFFERENCE TO ME!!
YES! MY PASSION CANNOT BE ABATED BY SUCH A TRIVIAL MATTER!!
CLENCH
THAT DAY... WHEN I HAD FINALLY GOTTEN USED TO THIS SCHOOL AFTER TRANSFERRING HERE...
I MET YOU IN THE HALL, MEGUMI SEMPAI.
I WAS SO OVERCOME WITH EMOTION THAT I WAS FROZEN...AND COULD ONLY GAZE AFTER YOU AS YOU WALKED BY.

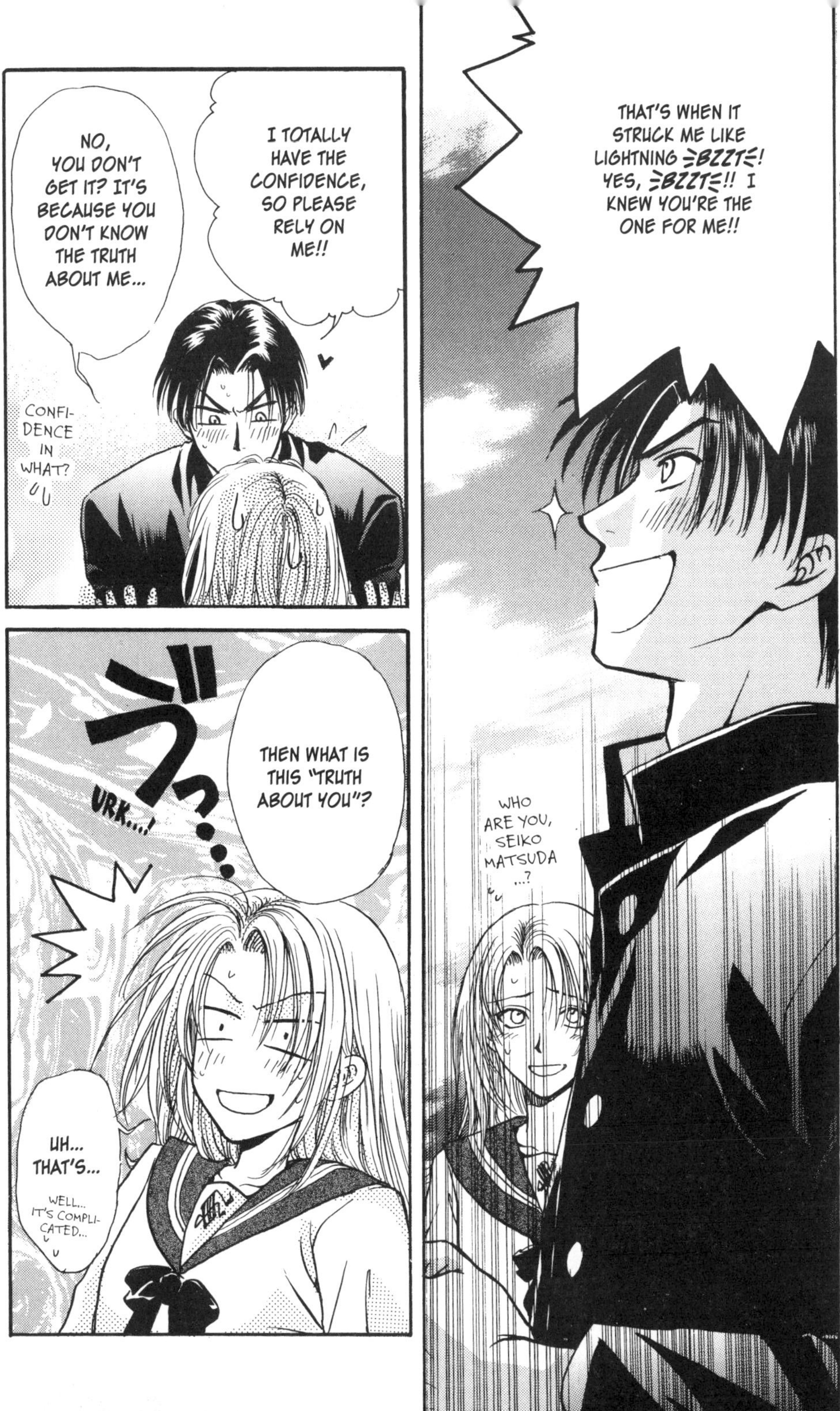
THAT'S WHEN IT STRUCK ME LIKE LIGHTNING ≡BZZT≡! YES, ≡BZZT≡!! I KNEW YOU'RE THE ONE FOR ME!!
WHO ARE YOU, SEIKO MATSUDA ...?
I TOTALLY HAVE THE CONFIDENCE, SO PLEASE RELY ON ME!!
NO, YOU DON'T GET IT? IT'S BECAUSE YOU DON'T KNOW THE TRUTH ABOUT ME...
CONFI-DENCE IN WHAT?
THEN WHAT IS THIS "TRUTH ABOUT YOU"?
URK...!
UH... THAT'S...
WELL... IT'S COMPLI-CATED...

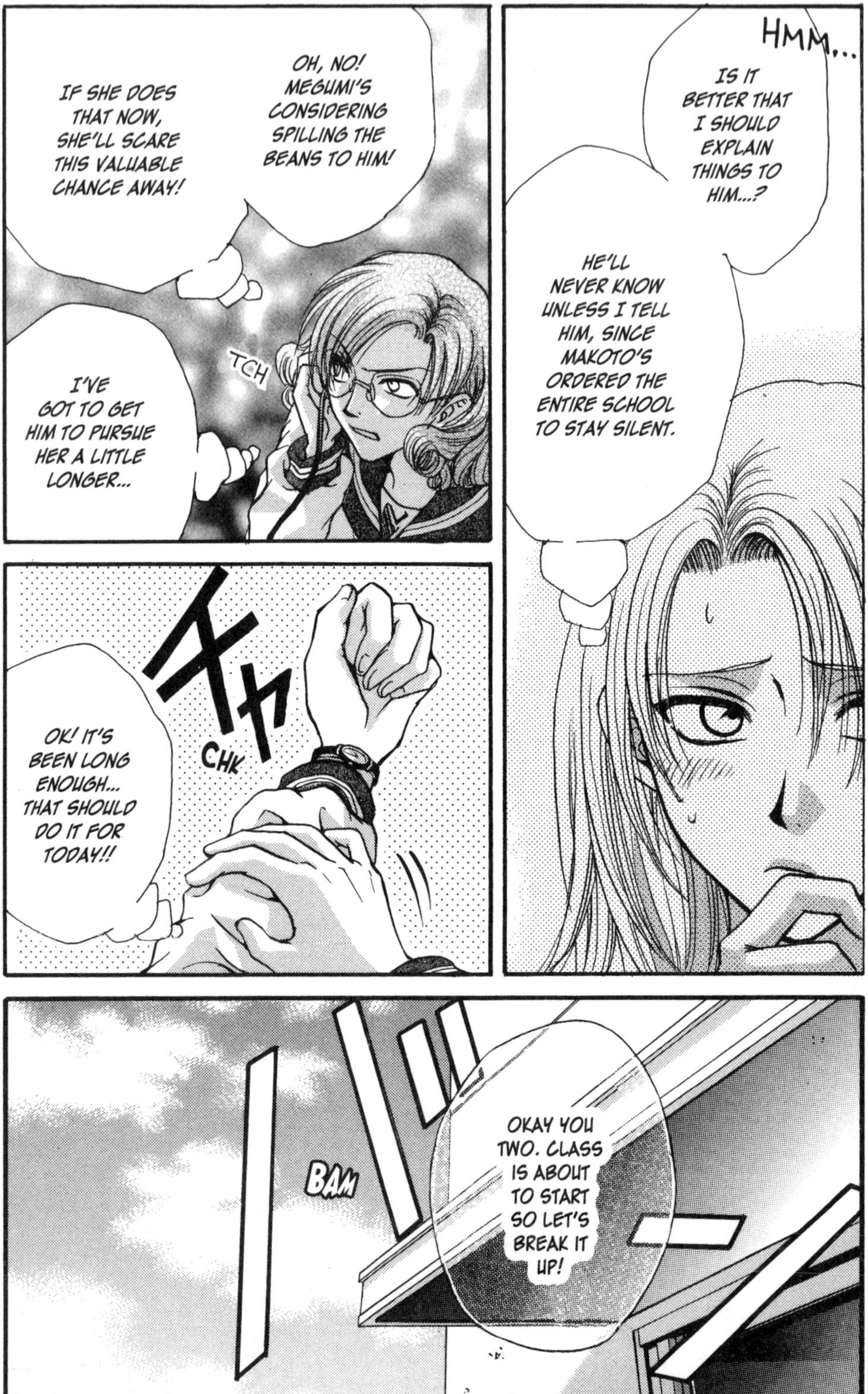
HMM...
IS IT BETTER THAT I SHOULD EXPLAIN THINGS TO HIM...?
HE'LL NEVER KNOW UNLESS I TELL HIM, SINCE MAKOTO'S ORDERED THE ENTIRE SCHOOL TO STAY SILENT.
OH, NO! MEGUMI'S CONSIDERING SPILLING THE BEANS TO HIM!
IF SHE DOES THAT NOW, SHE'LL SCARE THIS VALUABLE CHANCE AWAY!
TCH
I'VE GOT TO GET HIM TO PURSUE HER A LITTLE LONGER...
CHK
OK! IT'S BEEN LONG ENOUGH... THAT SHOULD DO IT FOR TODAY!!
BAM
OKAY YOU TWO. CLASS IS ABOUT TO START SO LET'S BREAK IT UP!

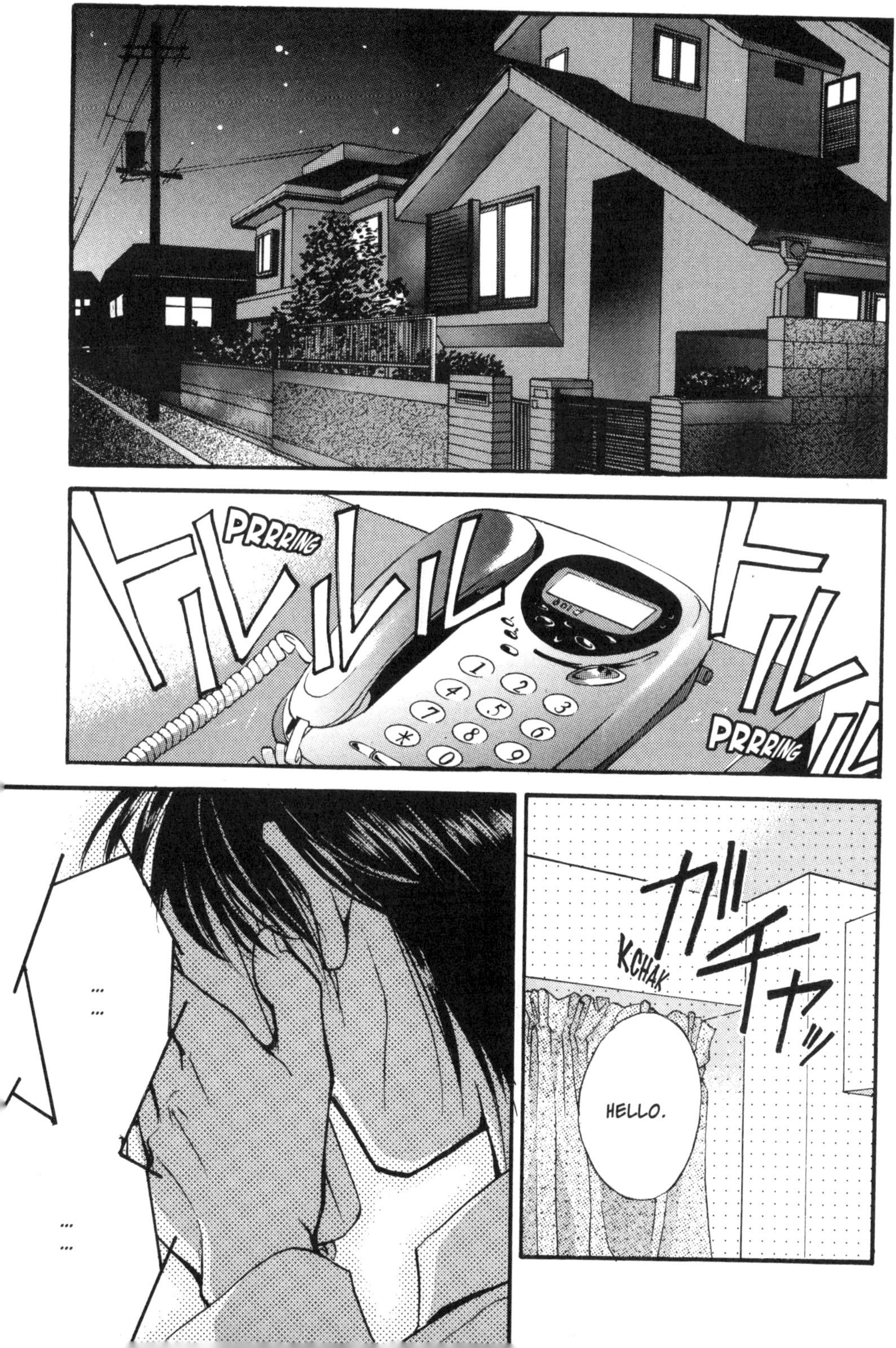
PRRRING
PRRRING
ガチャッ
K-CHAK
HELLO.
...
...
...
...

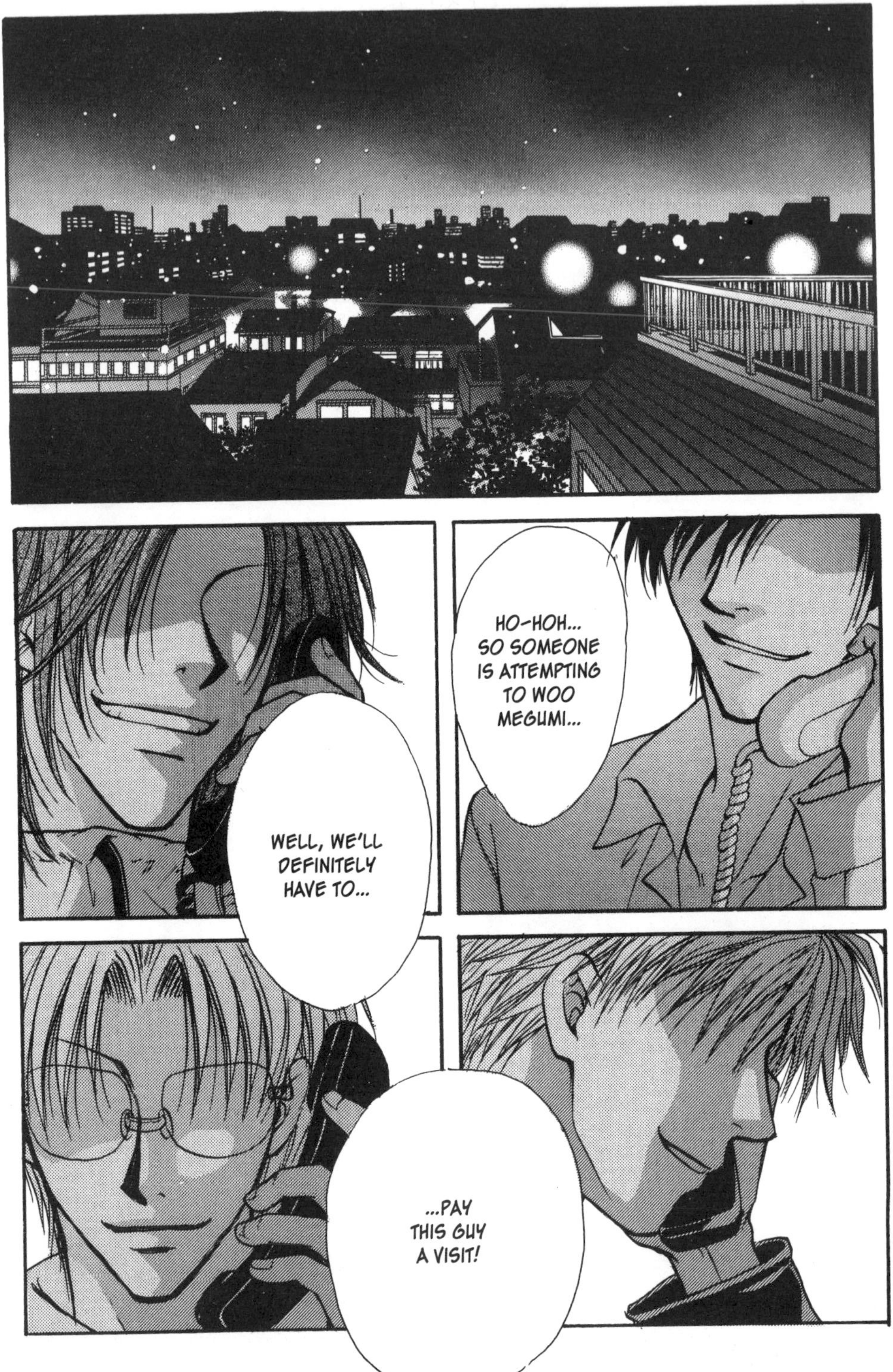
HO-HOH... SO SOMEONE IS ATTEMPTING TO WOO MEGUMI...
WELL, WE'LL DEFINITELY HAVE TO...
...PAY THIS GUY A VISIT!

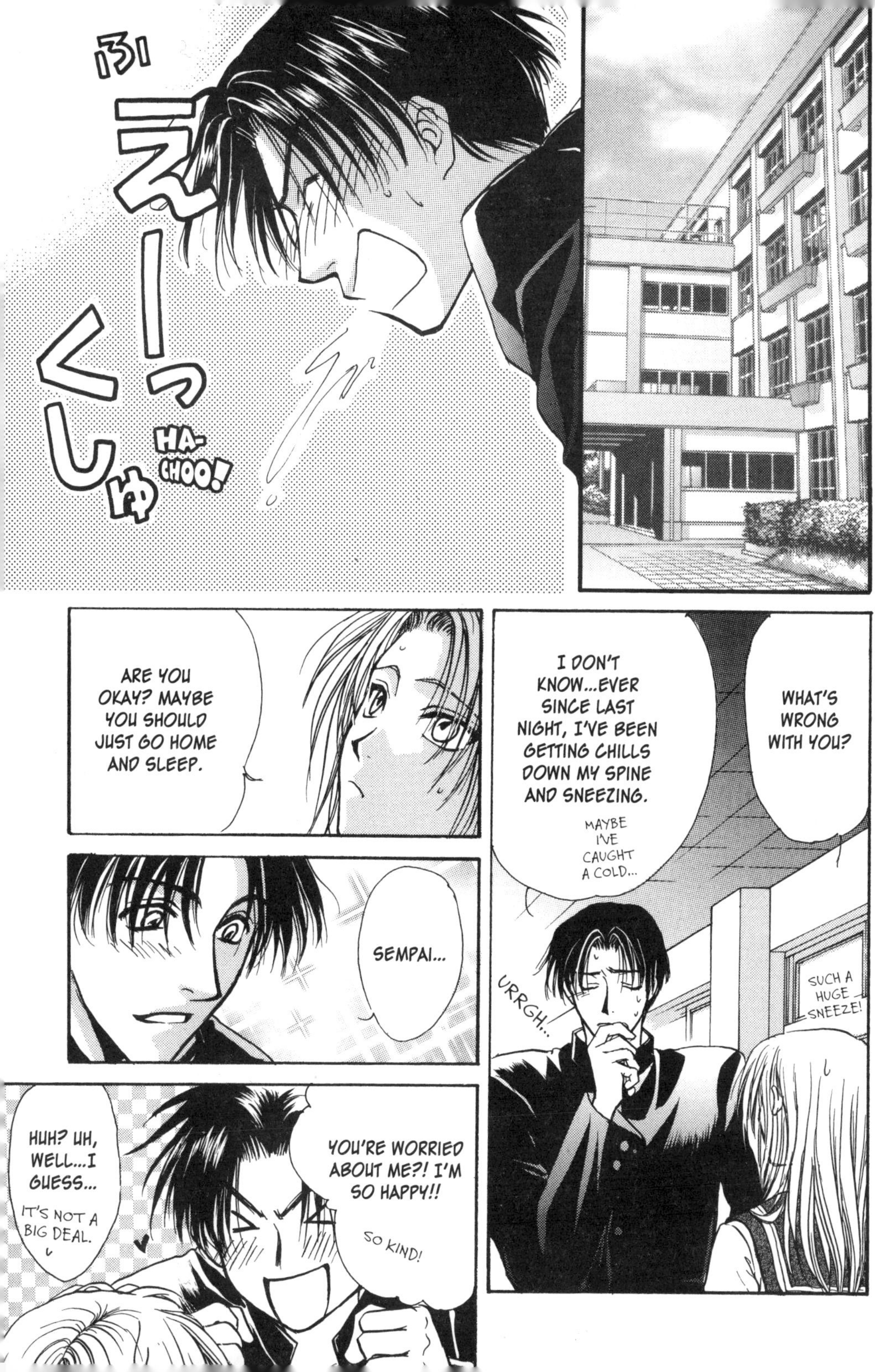
ふぇーっくしゅ
HA-CHOO!
WHAT'S WRONG WITH YOU?
I DON'T KNOW...EVER SINCE LAST NIGHT, I'VE BEEN GETTING CHILLS DOWN MY SPINE AND SNEEZING.
MAYBE I'VE CAUGHT A COLD...
SUCH A HUGE SNEEZE!
URRGH...
ARE YOU OKAY? MAYBE YOU SHOULD JUST GO HOME AND SLEEP.
SEMPAI...
YOU'RE WORRIED ABOUT ME?! I'M SO HAPPY!!
SO KIND!
HUH? UH, WELL...I GUESS...
IT'S NOT A BIG DEAL.

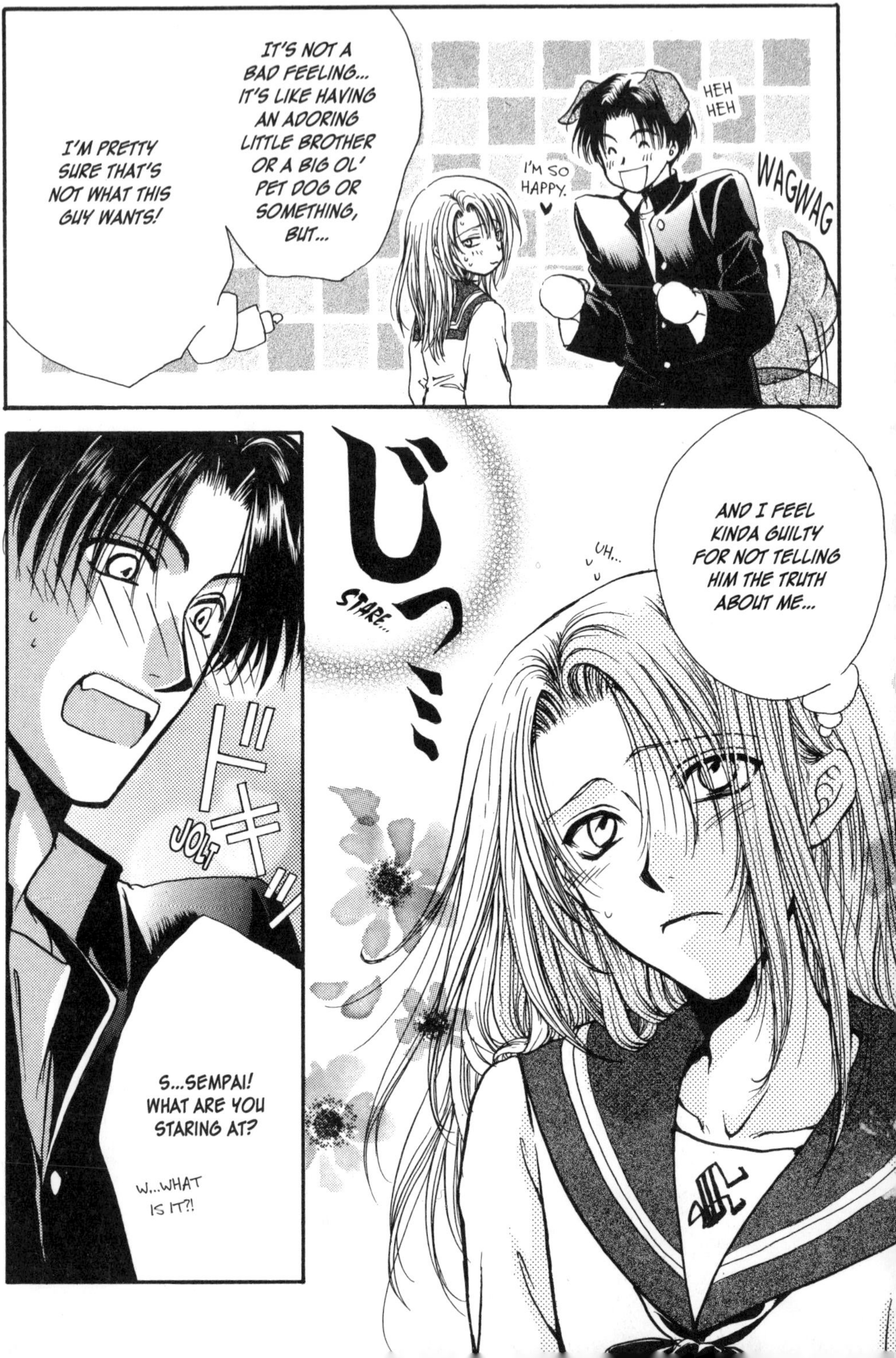
HEH HEH
WAGWAG
I'M SO HAPPY. ♥
IT'S NOT A BAD FEELING... IT'S LIKE HAVING AN ADORING LITTLE BROTHER OR A BIG OL' PET DOG OR SOMETHING, BUT...
I'M PRETTY SURE THAT'S NOT WHAT THIS GUY WANTS!
AND I FEEL KINDA GUILTY FOR NOT TELLING HIM THE TRUTH ABOUT ME...
UH...
じっ
STARE...
ドキッ
JOLT
S...SEMPAI! WHAT ARE YOU STARING AT?
W...WHAT IS IT?!

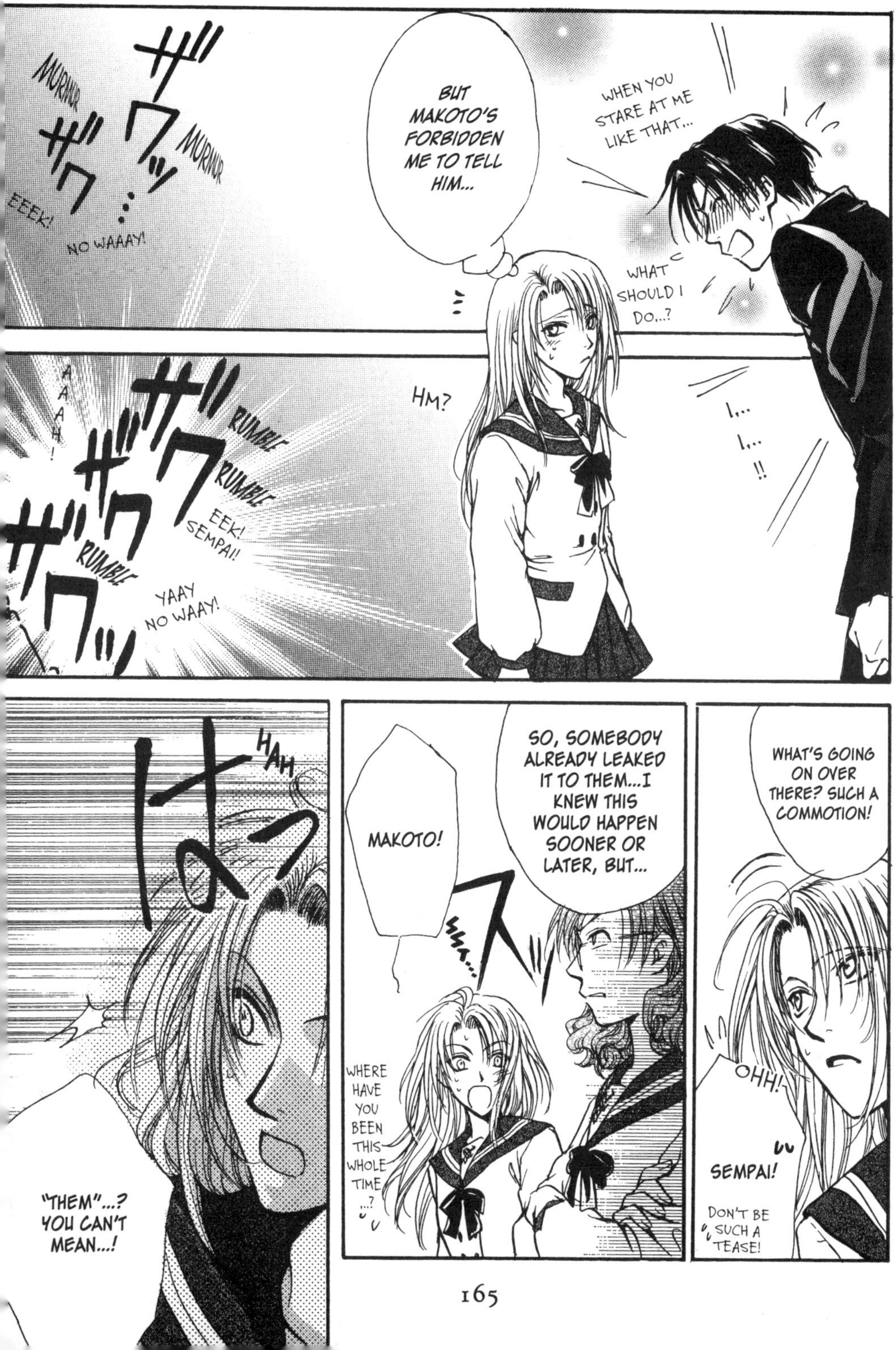
WHEN YOU STARE AT ME LIKE THAT...
BUT MAKOTO'S FORBIDDEN ME TO TELL HIM...
WHAT SHOULD I DO...?
MURMUR
MURMUR
EEEK!
NO WAAAY!
I... I... !!
HM?
RUMBLE
RUMBLE
RUMBLE
EEK! SEMPAI!
YAAY NO WAAY!
AAAAH!
WHAT'S GOING ON OVER THERE? SUCH A COMMOTION!
OHH!
SEMPAI!
DON'T BE SUCH A TEASE!
SO, SOMEBODY ALREADY LEAKED IT TO THEM...I KNEW THIS WOULD HAPPEN SOONER OR LATER, BUT...
MAKOTO!
WHERE HAVE YOU BEEN THIS WHOLE TIME...?
HAH
"THEM"...? YOU CAN'T MEAN...!

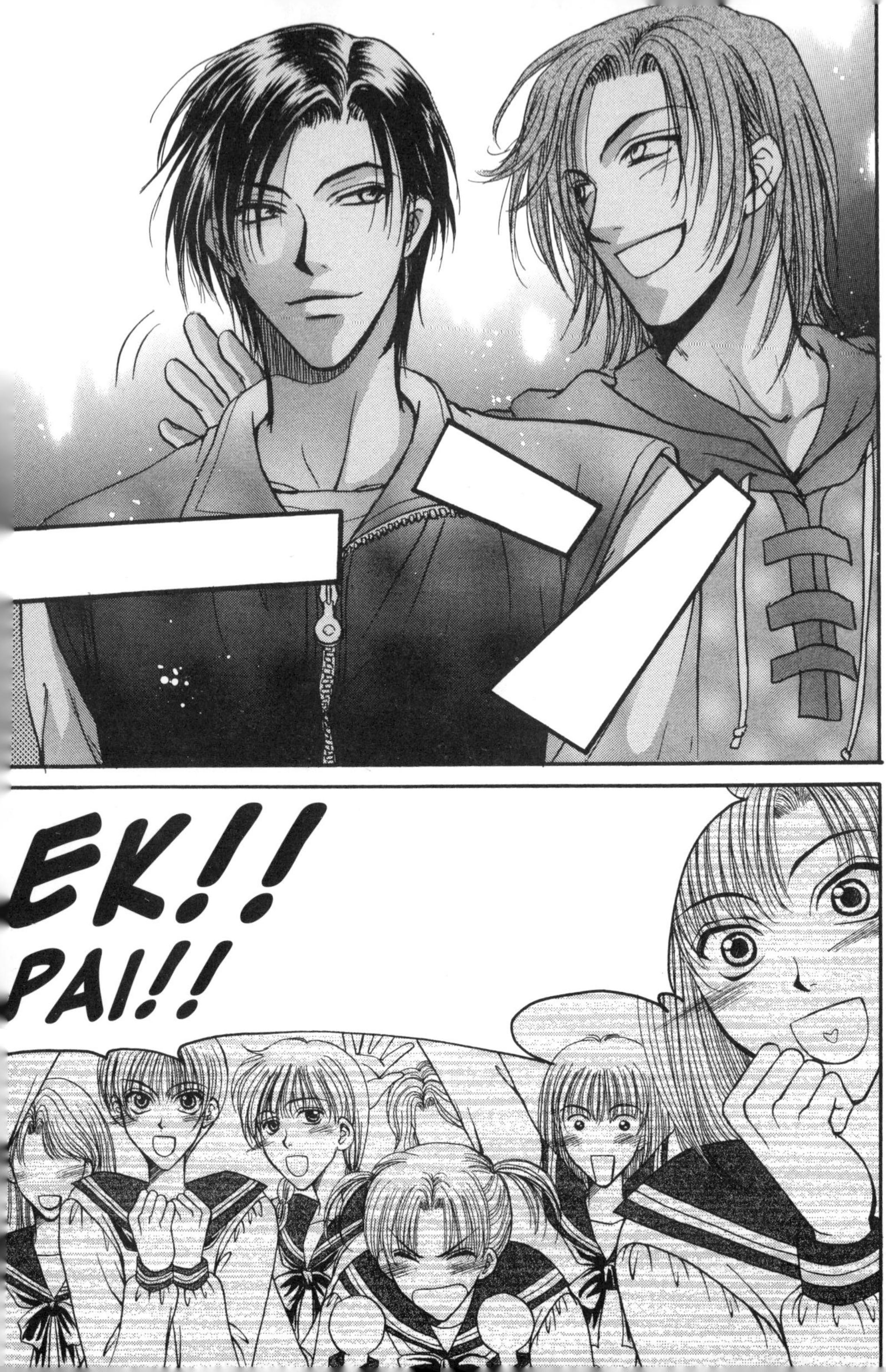
EK!!
PAI!!

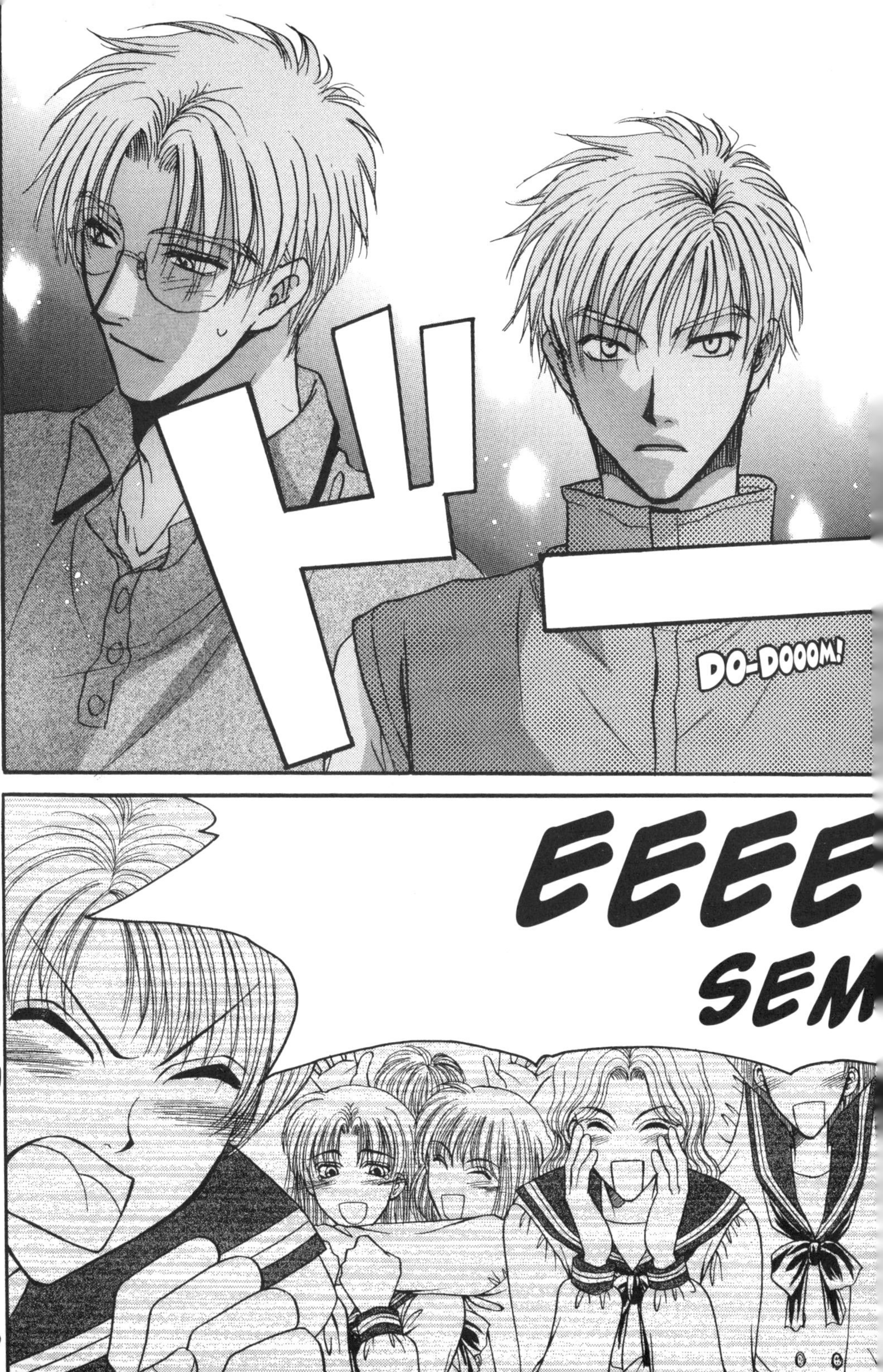
ドー
DO-DOOOM!
EEEE
SEM

WHY'D YOU MAKE ME DRAW SO MUCH? EIKI EIKI
THANK YOU SO MUCH! MIKIYO TSUDA

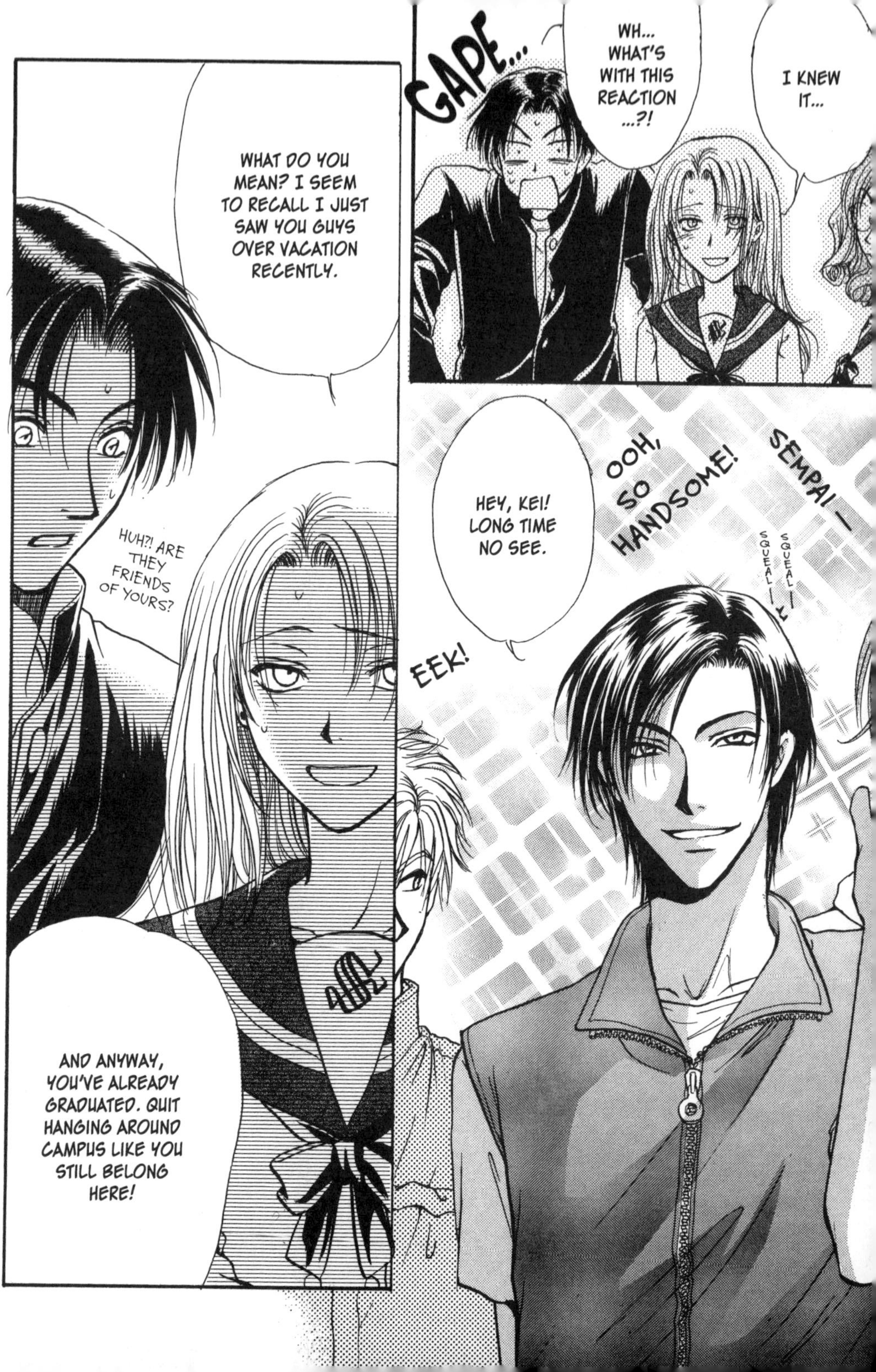
I KNEW IT...
WH... WHAT'S WITH THIS REACTION ...?!
GAPE...
SEMPAI!—
SQUEAL—
SQUEAL—
OOH, SO HANDSOME!
HEY, KEI! LONG TIME NO SEE.
EEK!
WHAT DO YOU MEAN? I SEEM TO RECALL I JUST SAW YOU GUYS OVER VACATION RECENTLY.
HUH?! ARE THEY FRIENDS OF YOURS?
AND ANYWAY, YOU'VE ALREADY GRADUATED. QUIT HANGING AROUND CAMPUS LIKE YOU STILL BELONG HERE!

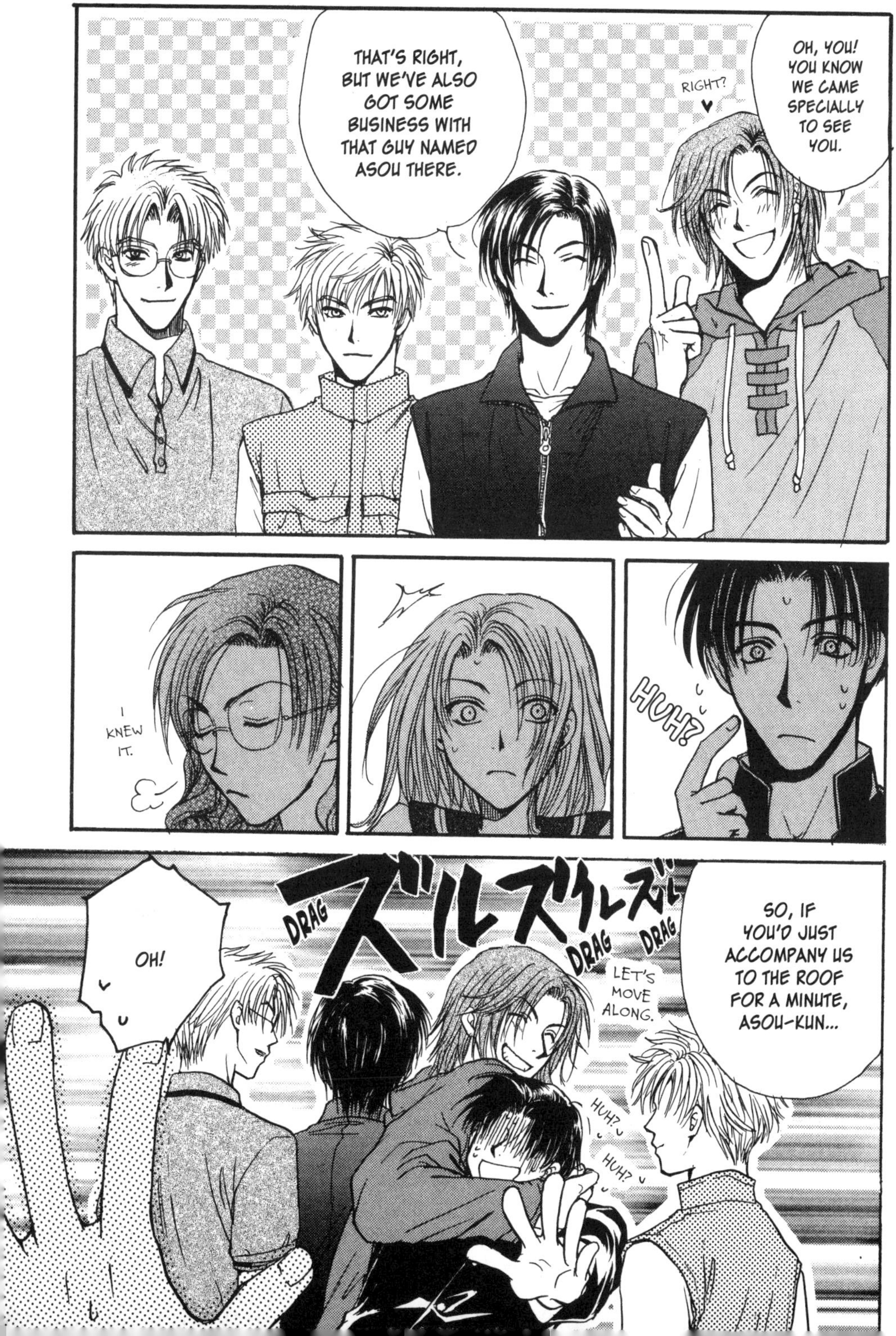
OH, YOU! YOU KNOW WE CAME SPECIALLY TO SEE YOU.
RIGHT? ♥
THAT'S RIGHT, BUT WE'VE ALSO GOT SOME BUSINESS WITH THAT GUY NAMED ASOU THERE.
HUH?
I KNEW IT.
SO, IF YOU'D JUST ACCOMPANY US TO THE ROOF FOR A MINUTE, ASOU-KUN...
DRAG
DRAG
LET'S MOVE ALONG.
HUH?
HUH?
DRAG
OH!

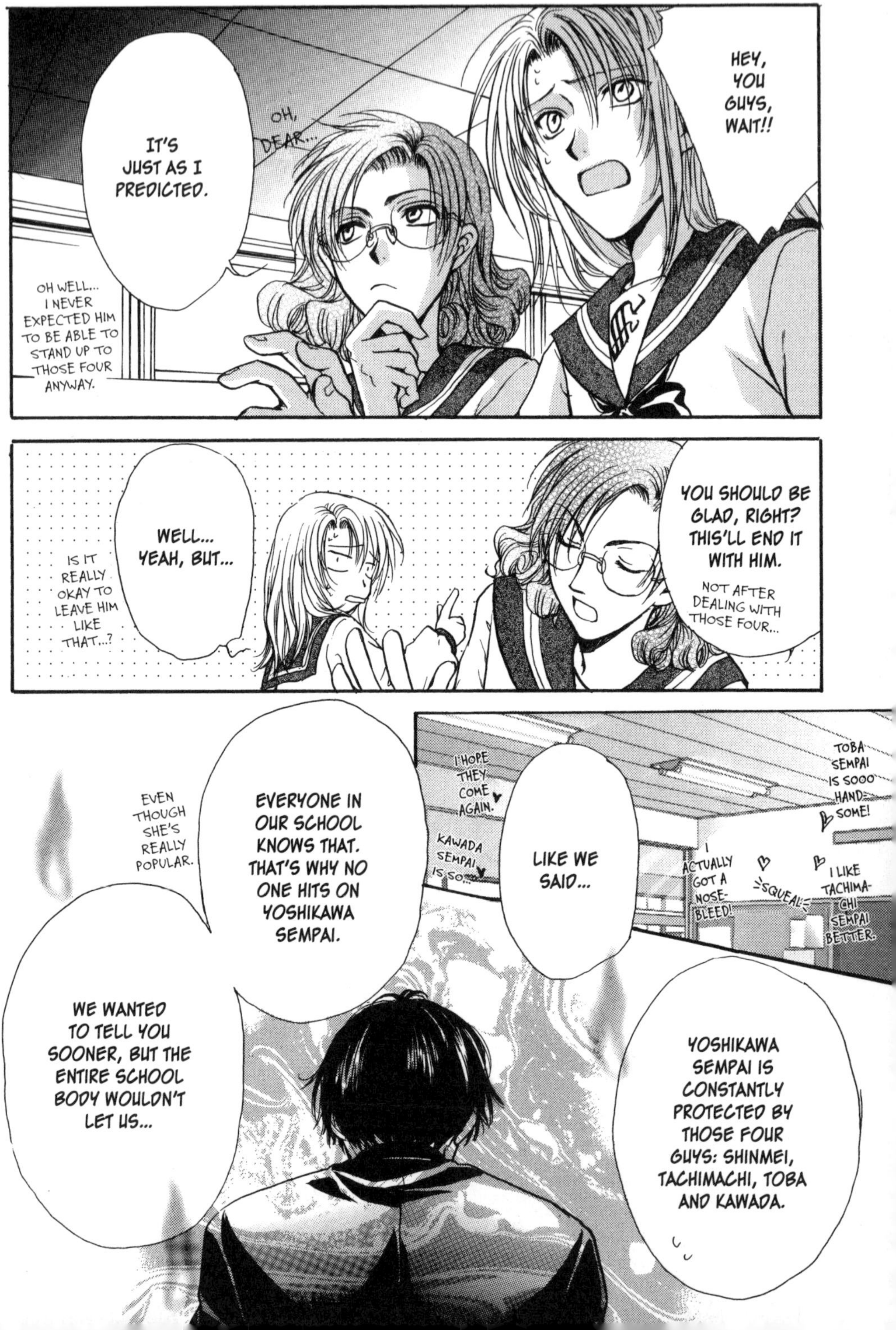
HEY, YOU GUYS, WAIT!!
OH, DEAR...
IT'S JUST AS I PREDICTED.
OH WELL... I NEVER EXPECTED HIM TO BE ABLE TO STAND UP TO THOSE FOUR ANYWAY.
YOU SHOULD BE GLAD, RIGHT? THIS'LL END IT WITH HIM.
NOT AFTER DEALING WITH THOSE FOUR...
WELL... YEAH, BUT...
IS IT REALLY OKAY TO LEAVE HIM LIKE THAT...?
TOBA SEMPAI IS SOOO HAND-SOME!
I LIKE TACHIMA-CHI SEMPAI BETTER.
SQUEAL
I ACTUALLY GOT A NOSE-BLEED!
I HOPE THEY COME AGAIN.
KAWADA SEMPAI IS SO...
LIKE WE SAID...
YOSHIKAWA SEMPAI IS CONSTANTLY PROTECTED BY THOSE FOUR GUYS: SHINMEI, TACHIMACHI, TOBA AND KAWADA.
EVERYONE IN OUR SCHOOL KNOWS THAT. THAT'S WHY NO ONE HITS ON YOSHIKAWA SEMPAI.
EVEN THOUGH SHE'S REALLY POPULAR.
WE WANTED TO TELL YOU SOONER, BUT THE ENTIRE SCHOOL BODY WOULDN'T LET US...

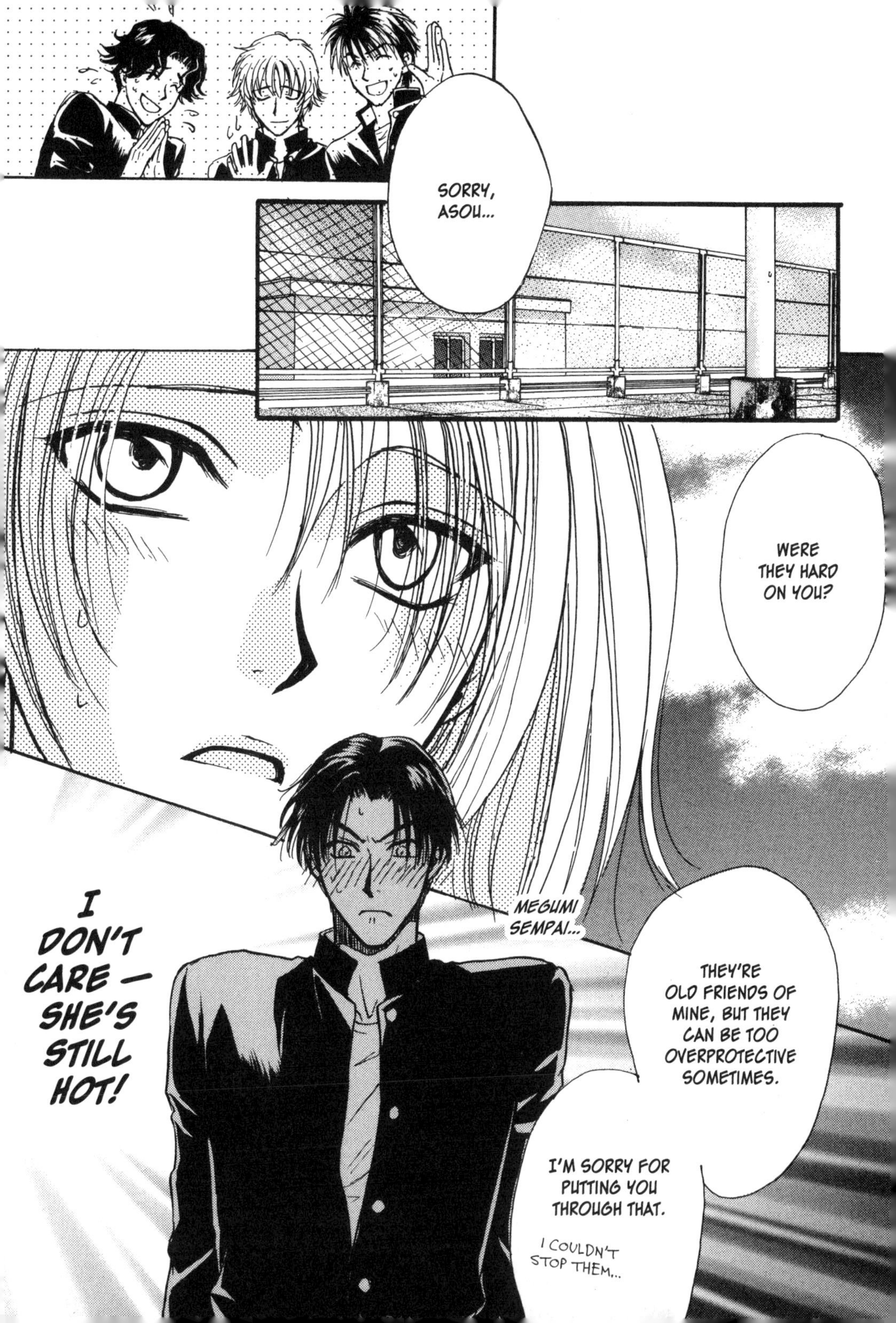
SORRY, ASOU...
WERE THEY HARD ON YOU?
MEGUMI SEMPAI...
THEY'RE OLD FRIENDS OF MINE, BUT THEY CAN BE TOO OVERPROTECTIVE SOMETIMES.
I'M SORRY FOR PUTTING YOU THROUGH THAT.
I COULDN'T STOP THEM...
I DON'T CARE — SHE'S STILL HOT!

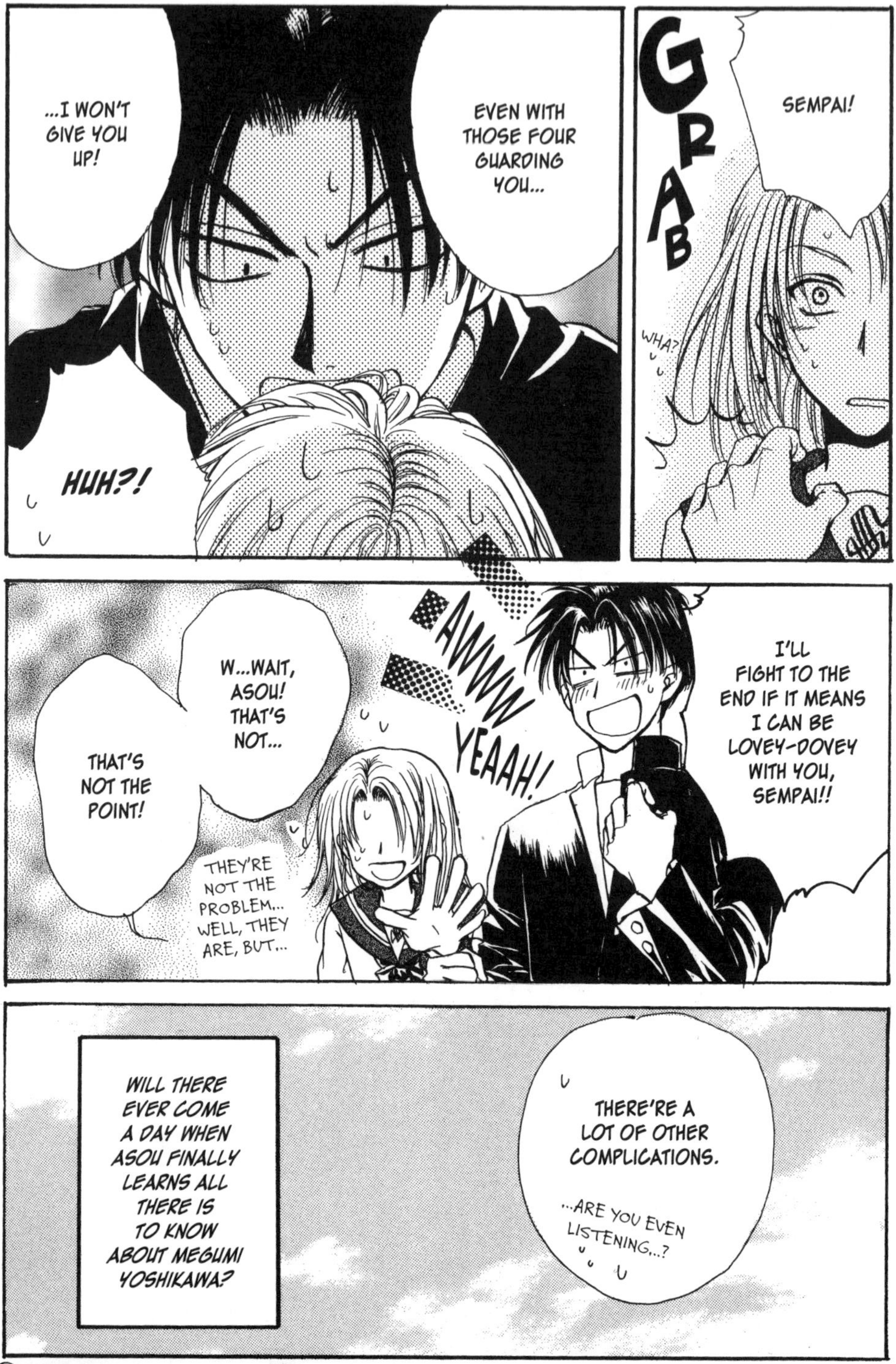
GRAB
SEMPAI!
WHA?
EVEN WITH THOSE FOUR GUARDING YOU...
...I WON'T GIVE YOU UP!
HUH?!
I'LL FIGHT TO THE END IF IT MEANS I CAN BE LOVEY-DOVEY WITH YOU, SEMPAI!!
AWWW YEAAH!
W...WAIT, ASOU! THAT'S NOT...
THAT'S NOT THE POINT!
THEY'RE NOT THE PROBLEM... WELL, THEY ARE, BUT...
THERE'RE A LOT OF OTHER COMPLICATIONS.
...ARE YOU EVEN LISTENING...?
WILL THERE EVER COME A DAY WHEN ASOU FINALLY LEARNS ALL THERE IS TO KNOW ABOUT MEGUMI YOSHIKAWA?

THE DAY OF FATE ✸ END

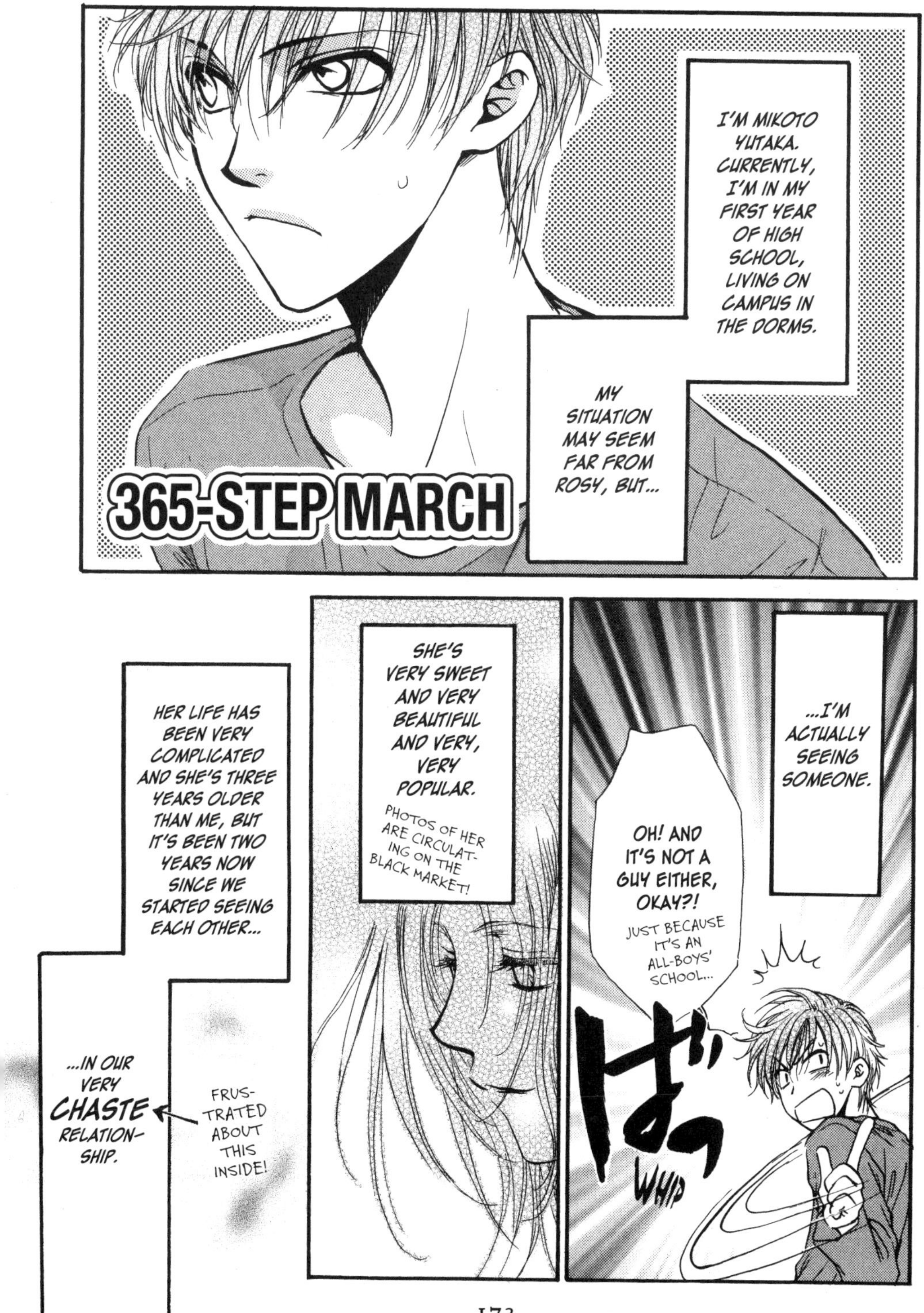
365-STEP MARCH
I'M MIKOTO YUTAKA. CURRENTLY, I'M IN MY FIRST YEAR OF HIGH SCHOOL, LIVING ON CAMPUS IN THE DORMS.
MY SITUATION MAY SEEM FAR FROM ROSY, BUT...
...I'M ACTUALLY SEEING SOMEONE.
OH! AND IT'S NOT A GUY EITHER, OKAY?!
JUST BECAUSE IT'S AN ALL-BOYS' SCHOOL...
WHIP
SHE'S VERY SWEET AND VERY BEAUTIFUL AND VERY, VERY POPULAR.
PHOTOS OF HER ARE CIRCULATING ON THE BLACK MARKET!
HER LIFE HAS BEEN VERY COMPLICATED AND SHE'S THREE YEARS OLDER THAN ME, BUT IT'S BEEN TWO YEARS NOW SINCE WE STARTED SEEING EACH OTHER...
...IN OUR VERY CHASTE RELATIONSHIP.
FRUSTRATED ABOUT THIS INSIDE!

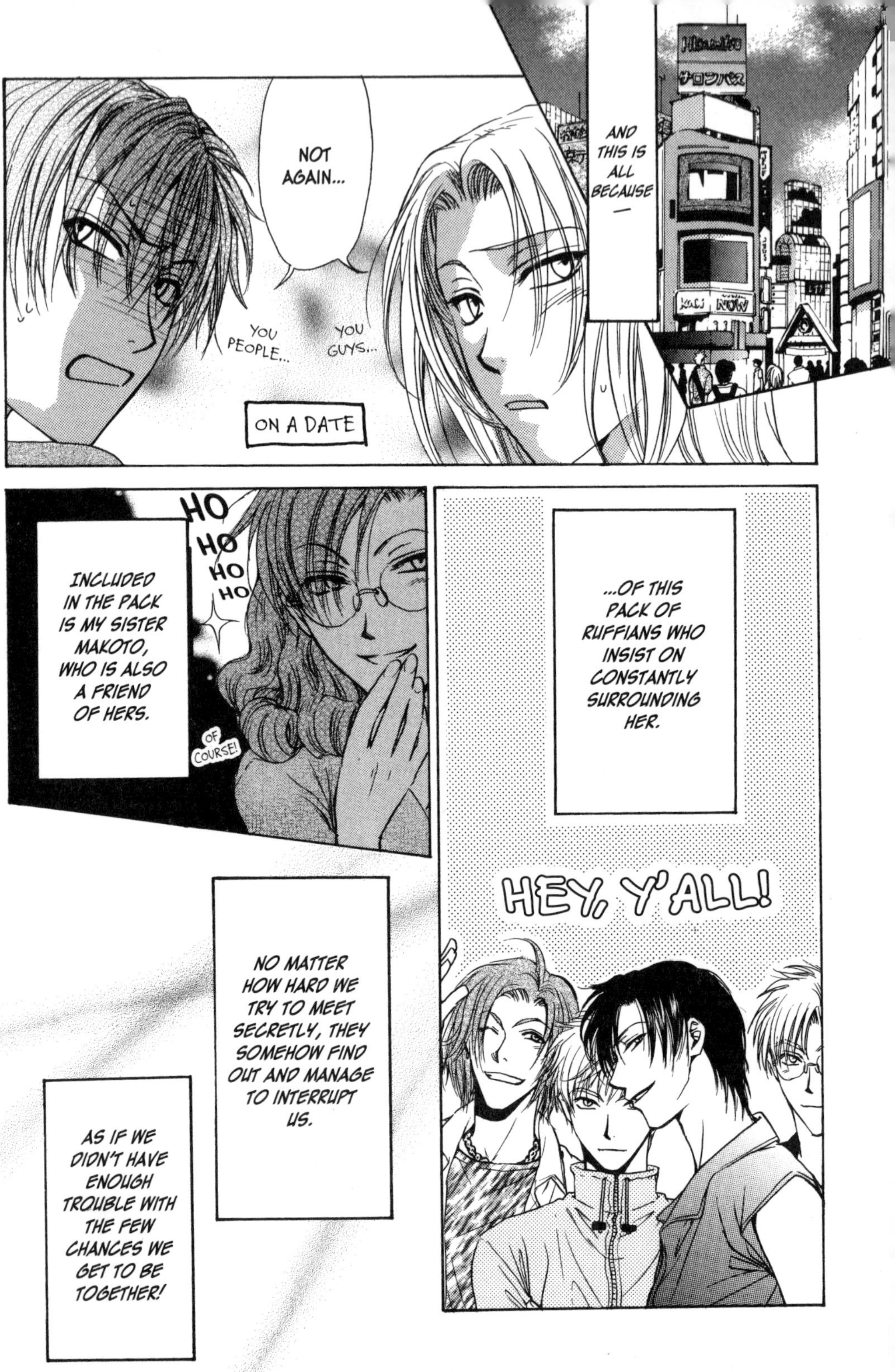
AND THIS IS ALL BECAUSE —
NOT AGAIN...
YOU GUYS...
YOU PEOPLE...
ON A DATE
...OF THIS PACK OF RUFFIANS WHO INSIST ON CONSTANTLY SURROUNDING HER.
HEY, Y'ALL!
HO HO HO HO
INCLUDED IN THE PACK IS MY SISTER MAKOTO, WHO IS ALSO A FRIEND OF HERS.
OF COURSE!
NO MATTER HOW HARD WE TRY TO MEET SECRETLY, THEY SOMEHOW FIND OUT AND MANAGE TO INTERRUPT US.
AS IF WE DIDN'T HAVE ENOUGH TROUBLE WITH THE FEW CHANCES WE GET TO BE TOGETHER!

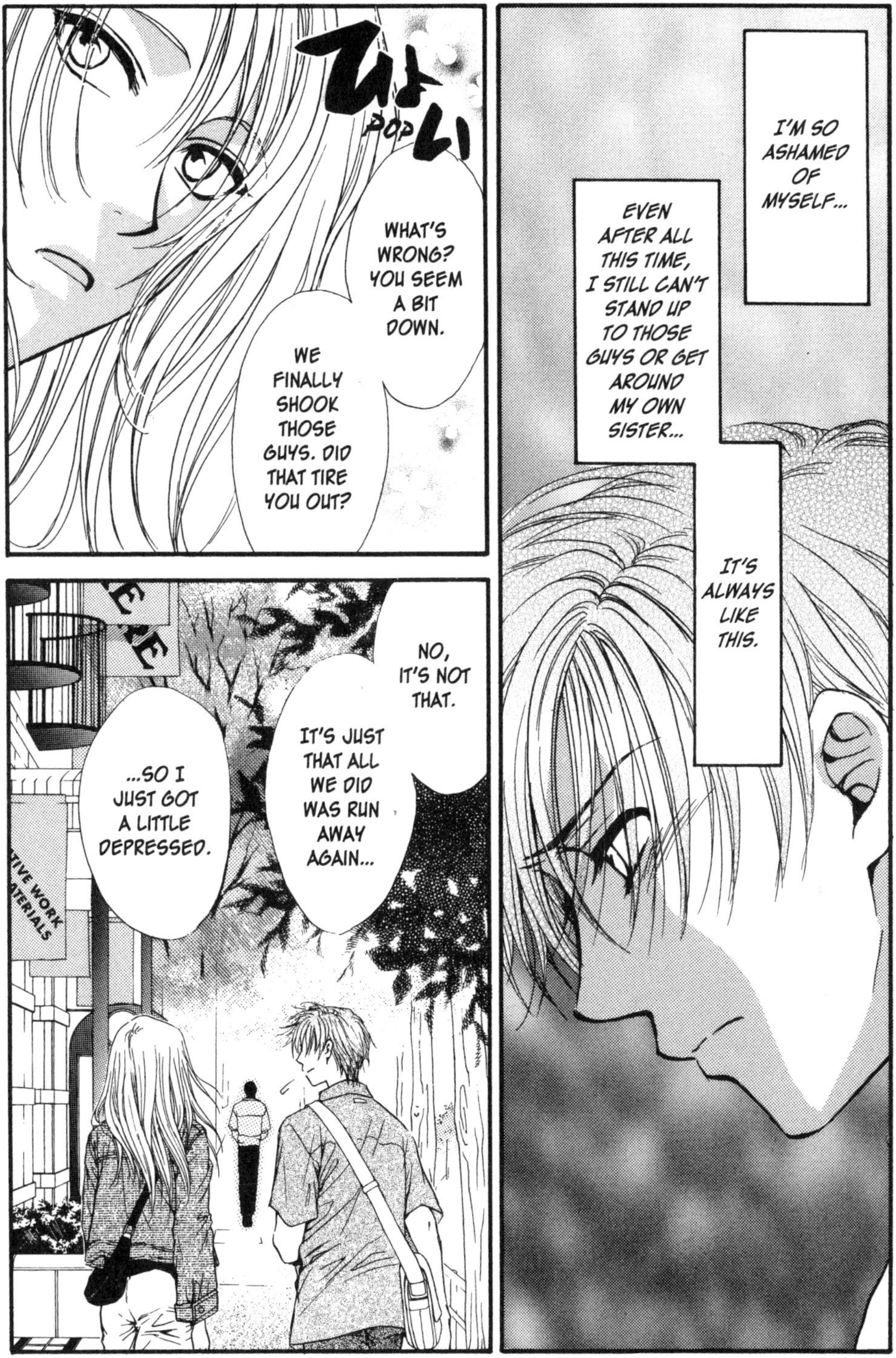
I'M SO ASHAMED OF MYSELF...
EVEN AFTER ALL THIS TIME, I STILL CAN'T STAND UP TO THOSE GUYS OR GET AROUND MY OWN SISTER...
IT'S ALWAYS LIKE THIS.
ひょい
POP
WHAT'S WRONG? YOU SEEM A BIT DOWN.
WE FINALLY SHOOK THOSE GUYS. DID THAT TIRE YOU OUT?
NO, IT'S NOT THAT.
IT'S JUST THAT ALL WE DID WAS RUN AWAY AGAIN...
...SO I JUST GOT A LITTLE DEPRESSED.

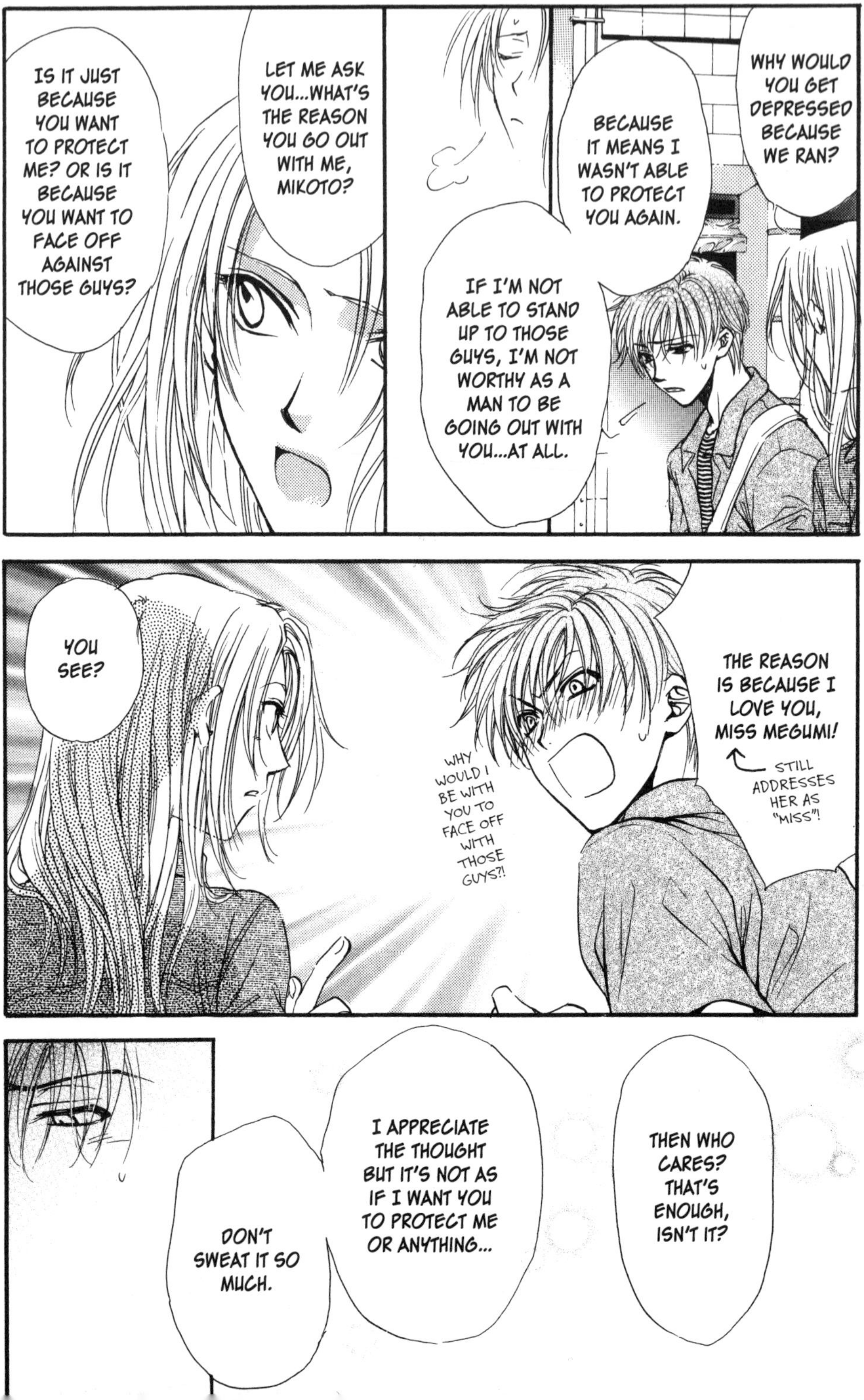
WHY WOULD YOU GET DEPRESSED BECAUSE WE RAN?
BECAUSE IT MEANS I WASN'T ABLE TO PROTECT YOU AGAIN.
IF I'M NOT ABLE TO STAND UP TO THOSE GUYS, I'M NOT WORTHY AS A MAN TO BE GOING OUT WITH YOU...AT ALL.
LET ME ASK YOU...WHAT'S THE REASON YOU GO OUT WITH ME, MIKOTO?
IS IT JUST BECAUSE YOU WANT TO PROTECT ME? OR IS IT BECAUSE YOU WANT TO FACE OFF AGAINST THOSE GUYS?
THE REASON IS BECAUSE I LOVE YOU, MISS MEGUMI!
STILL ADDRESSES HER AS "MISS"!
WHY WOULD I BE WITH YOU TO FACE OFF WITH THOSE GUYS?!
YOU SEE?
THEN WHO CARES? THAT'S ENOUGH, ISN'T IT?
I APPRECIATE THE THOUGHT BUT IT'S NOT AS IF I WANT YOU TO PROTECT ME OR ANYTHING...
DON'T SWEAT IT SO MUCH.

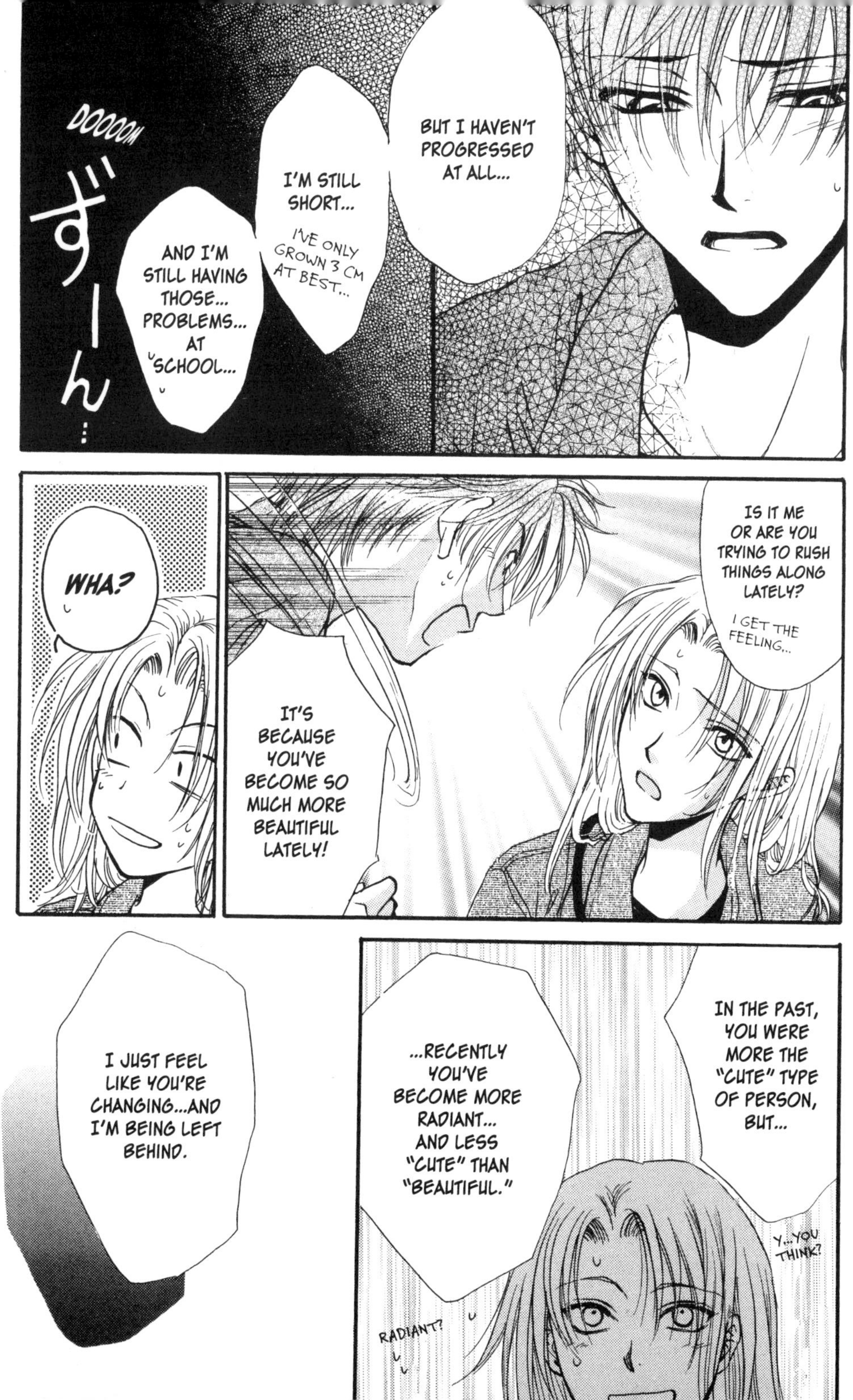
BUT I HAVEN'T PROGRESSED AT ALL...
I'M STILL SHORT...
I'VE ONLY GROWN 3 CM AT BEST...
AND I'M STILL HAVING THOSE... PROBLEMS... AT SCHOOL...
DOOOOM
ずーん…
IS IT ME OR ARE YOU TRYING TO RUSH THINGS ALONG LATELY?
I GET THE FEELING...
IT'S BECAUSE YOU'VE BECOME SO MUCH MORE BEAUTIFUL LATELY!
WHA?
IN THE PAST, YOU WERE MORE THE "CUTE" TYPE OF PERSON, BUT...
...RECENTLY YOU'VE BECOME MORE RADIANT... AND LESS "CUTE" THAN "BEAUTIFUL."
Y...YOU THINK?
RADIANT?
I JUST FEEL LIKE YOU'RE CHANGING...AND I'M BEING LEFT BEHIND.

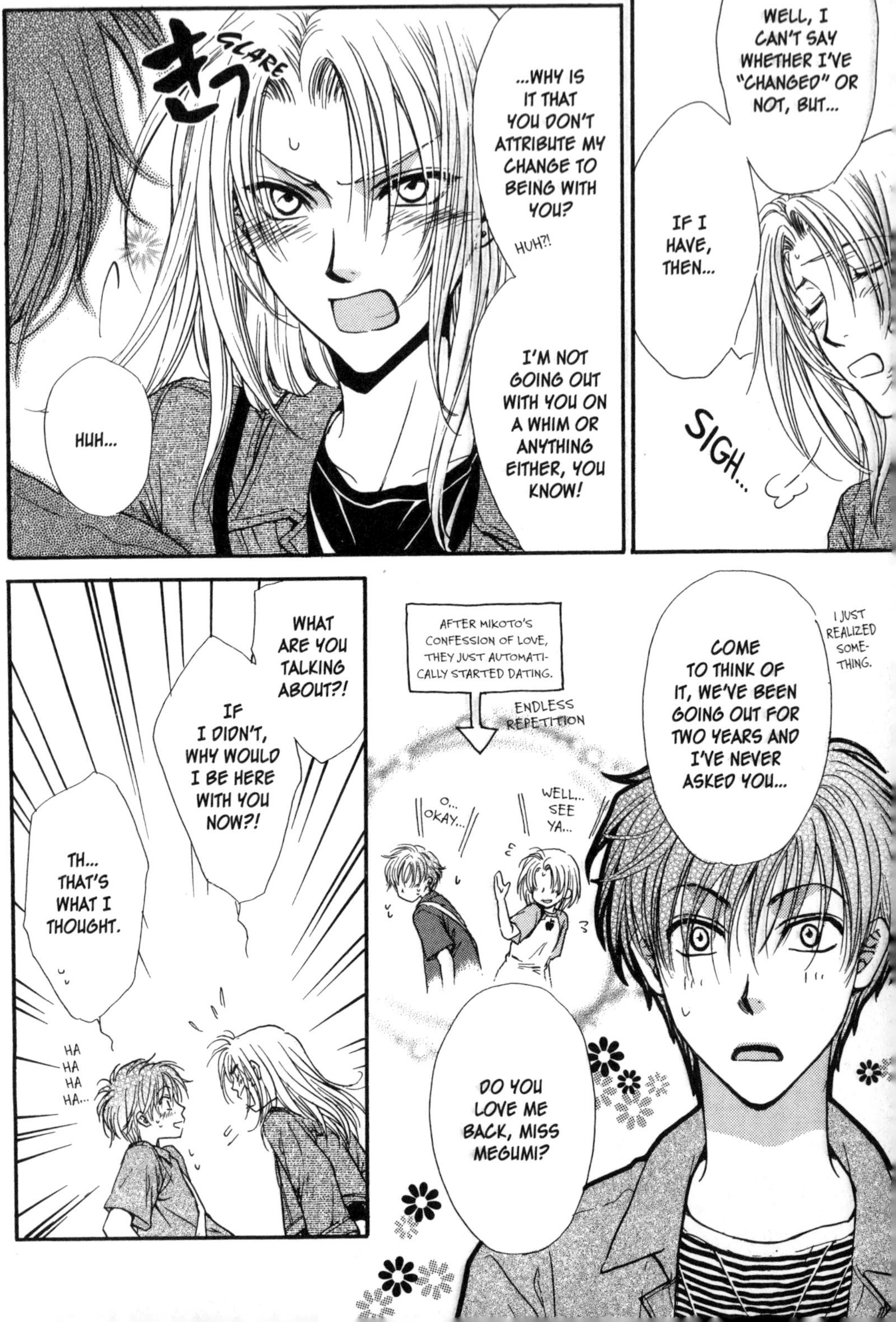
WELL, I CAN'T SAY WHETHER I'VE "CHANGED" OR NOT, BUT...
IF I HAVE, THEN...
SIGH...
きっ GLARE
...WHY IS IT THAT YOU DON'T ATTRIBUTE MY CHANGE TO BEING WITH YOU?
HUH?!
I'M NOT GOING OUT WITH YOU ON A WHIM OR ANYTHING EITHER, YOU KNOW!
HUH...
I JUST REALIZED SOMETHING.
COME TO THINK OF IT, WE'VE BEEN GOING OUT FOR TWO YEARS AND I'VE NEVER ASKED YOU...
AFTER MIKOTO'S CONFESSION OF LOVE, THEY JUST AUTOMATICALLY STARTED DATING.
ENDLESS REPETITION
WELL... SEE YA...
O... OKAY...
DO YOU LOVE ME BACK, MISS MEGUMI?
WHAT ARE YOU TALKING ABOUT?!
IF I DIDN'T, WHY WOULD I BE HERE WITH YOU NOW?!
TH... THAT'S WHAT I THOUGHT.
HA HA HA HA...

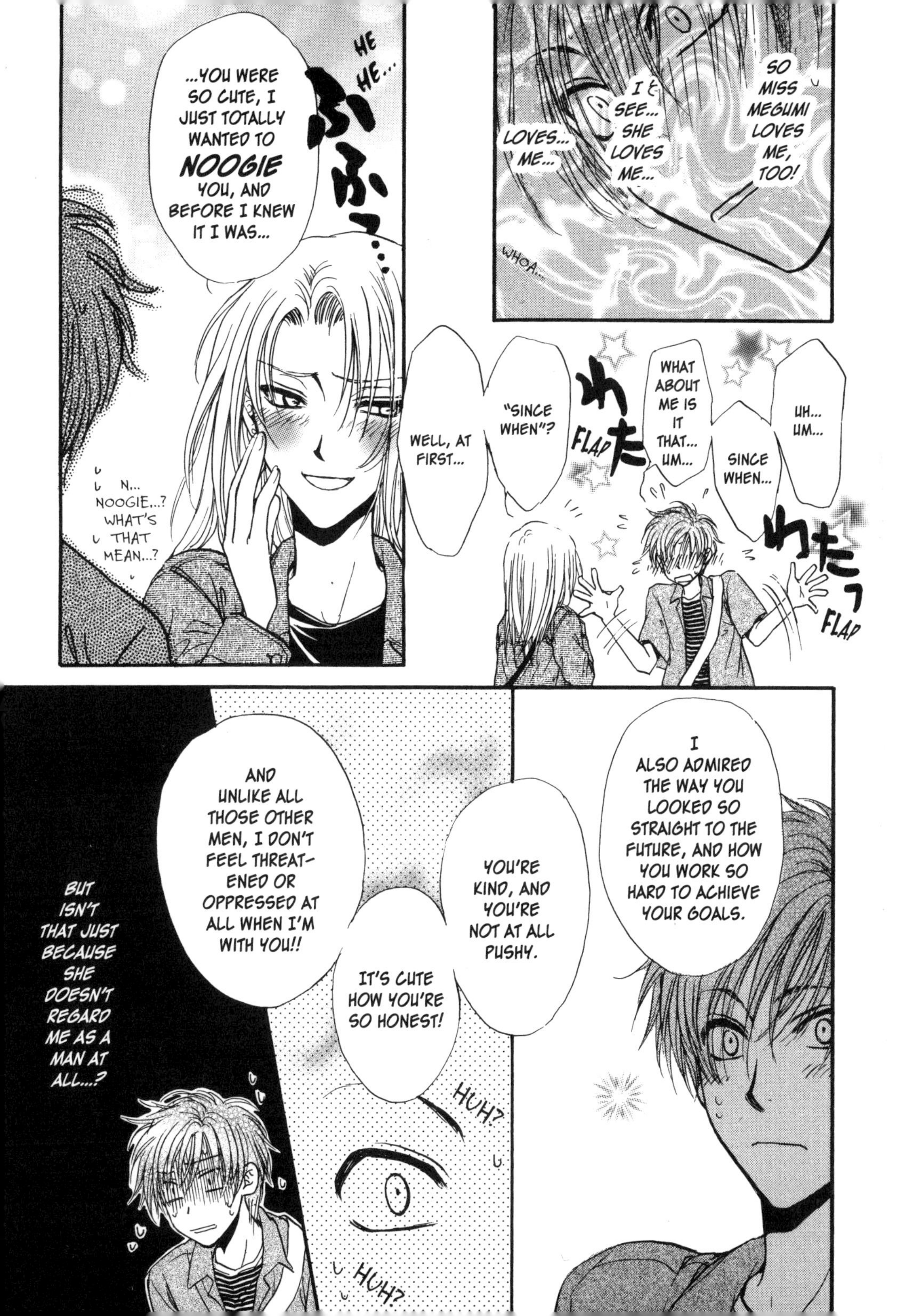
SO MISS MEGUMI LOVES ME, TOO!
I SEE... SHE LOVES ME...
LOVES... ME...
WHOA...
UH... UM...
SINCE WHEN...
WHAT ABOUT ME IS IT THAT... UM...
FLAP
FLAP
"SINCE WHEN"?
WELL, AT FIRST...
HE HE...
...YOU WERE SO CUTE, I JUST TOTALLY WANTED TO NOOGIE YOU, AND BEFORE I KNEW IT I WAS...
N... NOOGIE...? WHAT'S THAT MEAN...?
I ALSO ADMIRED THE WAY YOU LOOKED SO STRAIGHT TO THE FUTURE, AND HOW YOU WORK SO HARD TO ACHIEVE YOUR GOALS.
YOU'RE KIND, AND YOU'RE NOT AT ALL PUSHY.
AND UNLIKE ALL THOSE OTHER MEN, I DON'T FEEL THREAT-ENED OR OPPRESSED AT ALL WHEN I'M WITH YOU!!
IT'S CUTE HOW YOU'RE SO HONEST!
HUH?
HUH?
BUT ISN'T THAT JUST BECAUSE SHE DOESN'T REGARD ME AS A MAN AT ALL...?

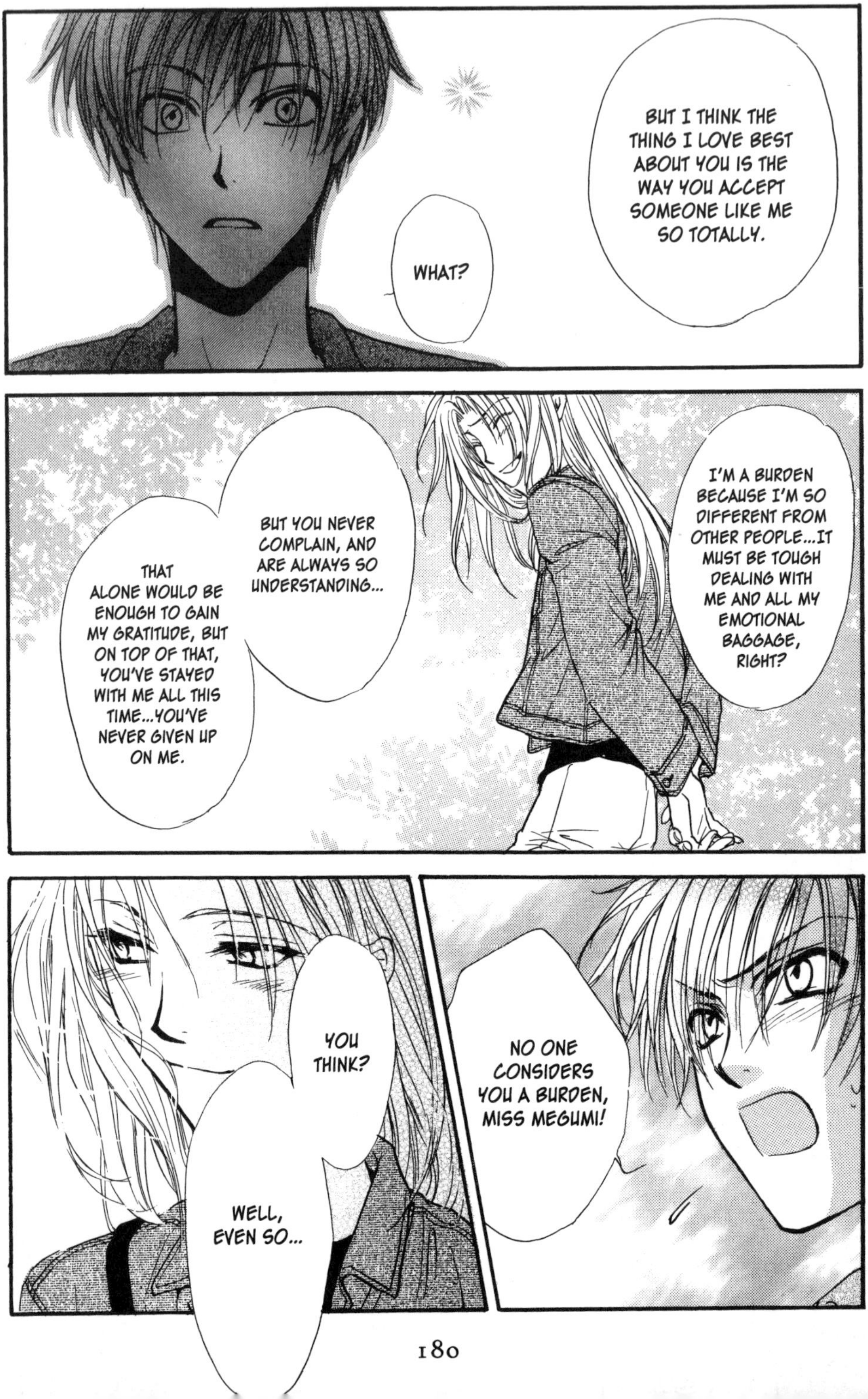
BUT I THINK THE THING I LOVE BEST ABOUT YOU IS THE WAY YOU ACCEPT SOMEONE LIKE ME SO TOTALLY.
WHAT?
I'M A BURDEN BECAUSE I'M SO DIFFERENT FROM OTHER PEOPLE...IT MUST BE TOUGH DEALING WITH ME AND ALL MY EMOTIONAL BAGGAGE, RIGHT?
BUT YOU NEVER COMPLAIN, AND ARE ALWAYS SO UNDERSTANDING...
THAT ALONE WOULD BE ENOUGH TO GAIN MY GRATITUDE, BUT ON TOP OF THAT, YOU'VE STAYED WITH ME ALL THIS TIME...YOU'VE NEVER GIVEN UP ON ME.
NO ONE CONSIDERS YOU A BURDEN, MISS MEGUMI!
YOU THINK?
WELL, EVEN SO...

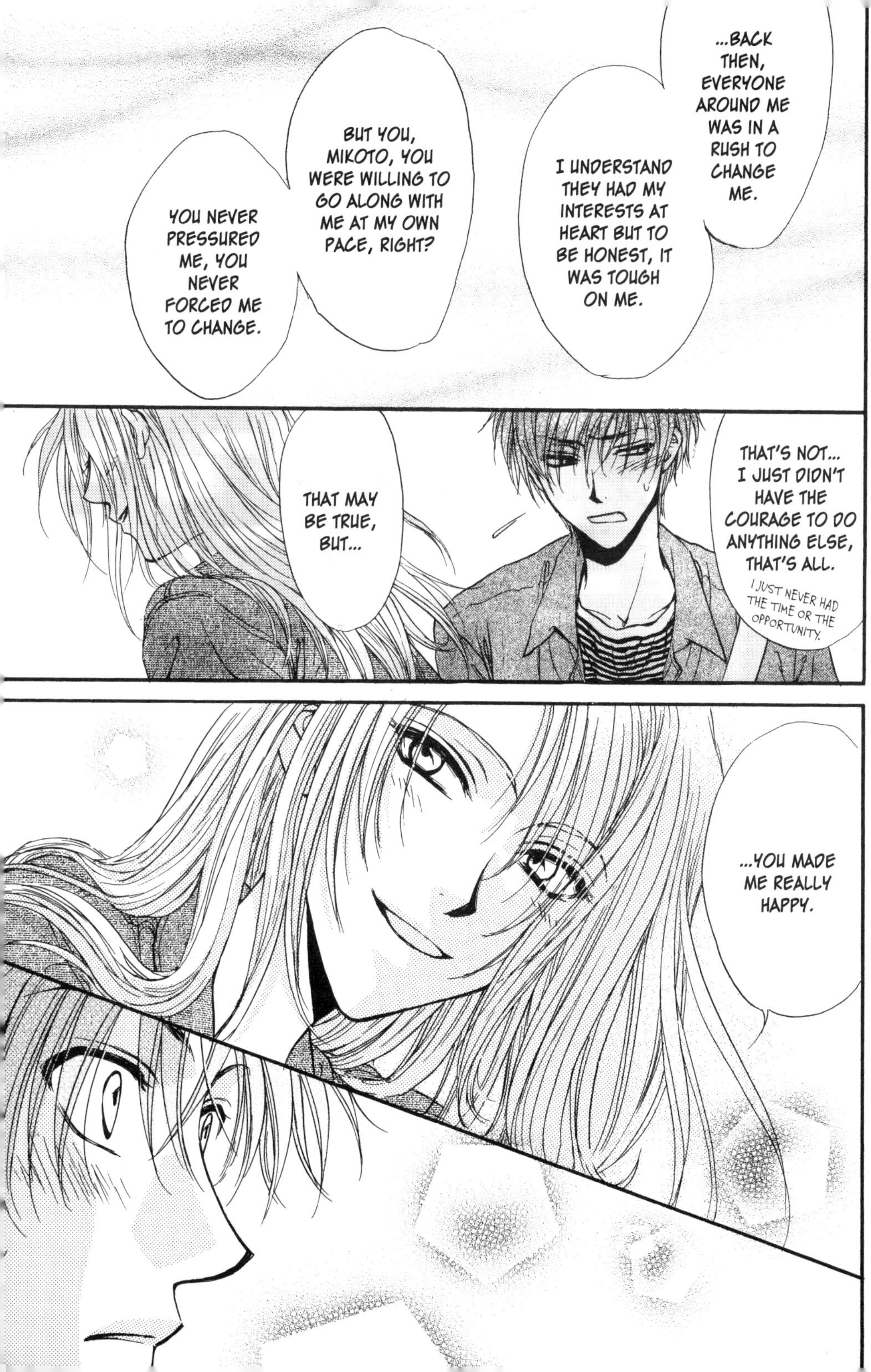
...BACK THEN, EVERYONE AROUND ME WAS IN A RUSH TO CHANGE ME.
I UNDERSTAND THEY HAD MY INTERESTS AT HEART BUT TO BE HONEST, IT WAS TOUGH ON ME.
BUT YOU, MIKOTO, YOU WERE WILLING TO GO ALONG WITH ME AT MY OWN PACE, RIGHT?
YOU NEVER PRESSURED ME, YOU NEVER FORCED ME TO CHANGE.
THAT'S NOT... I JUST DIDN'T HAVE THE COURAGE TO DO ANYTHING ELSE, THAT'S ALL.
I JUST NEVER HAD THE TIME OR THE OPPORTUNITY.
THAT MAY BE TRUE, BUT...
...YOU MADE ME REALLY HAPPY.

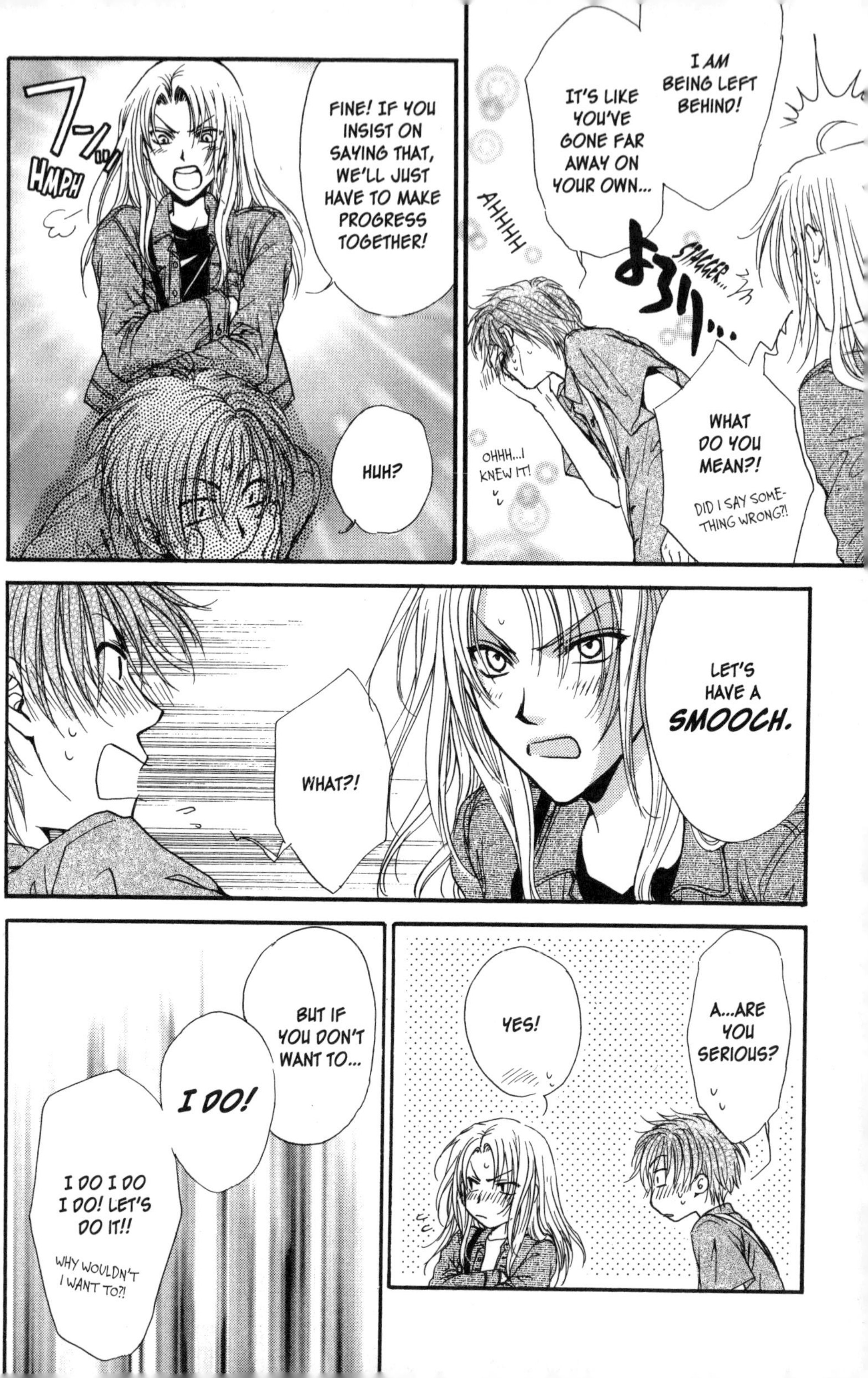
I AM BEING LEFT BEHIND!
IT'S LIKE YOU'VE GONE FAR AWAY ON YOUR OWN...
AHHHH
よろり…
STAGGER...
WHAT DO YOU MEAN?!
DID I SAY SOMETHING WRONG?!
OHHH...I KNEW IT!
FINE! IF YOU INSIST ON SAYING THAT, WE'LL JUST HAVE TO MAKE PROGRESS TOGETHER!
HMPH
HUH?
LET'S HAVE A SMOOCH.
WHAT?!
A...ARE YOU SERIOUS?
YES!
BUT IF YOU DON'T WANT TO...
I DO!
I DO I DO I DO! LET'S DO IT!!
WHY WOULDN'T I WANT TO?!

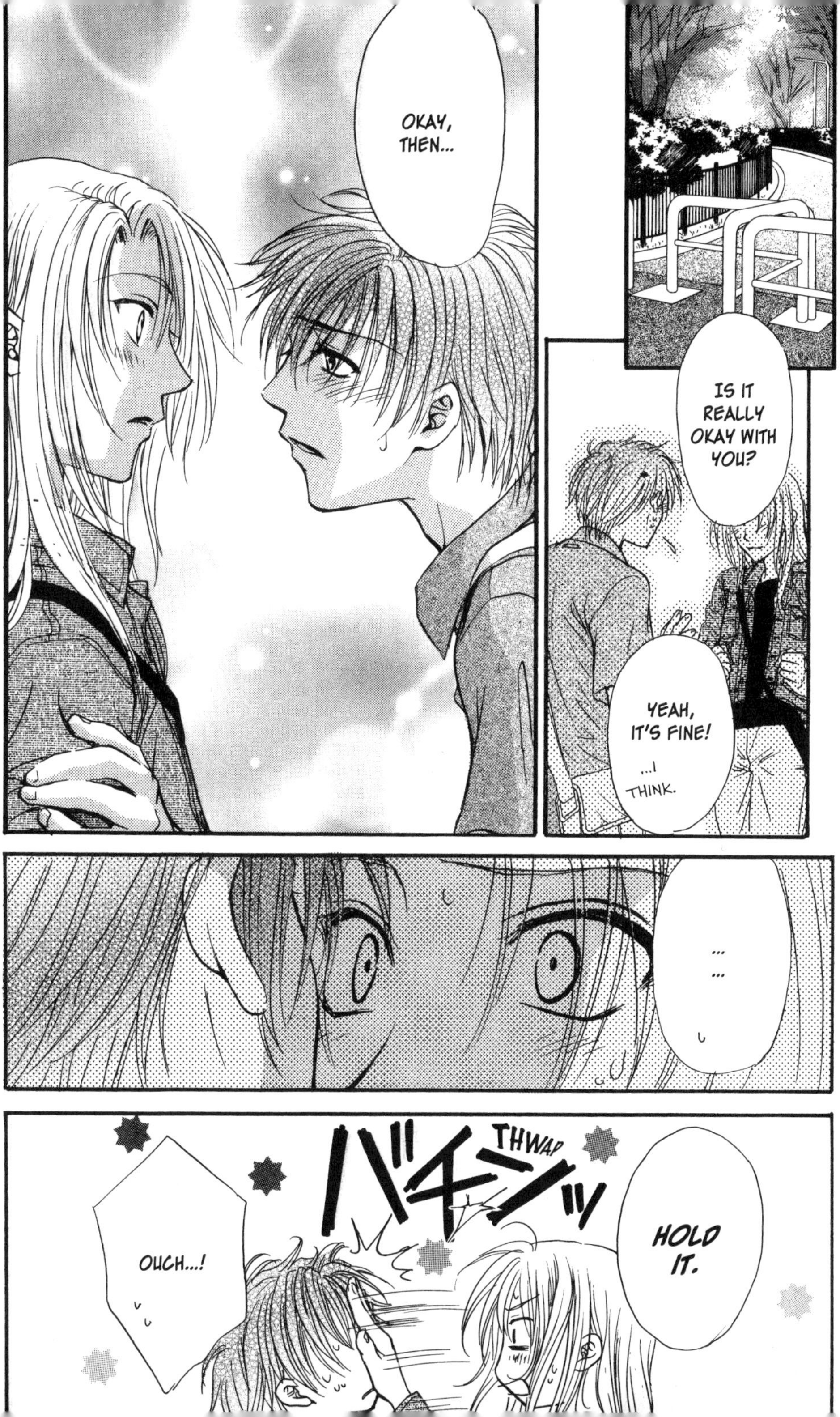
IS IT REALLY OKAY WITH YOU?
YEAH, IT'S FINE!
...I THINK.
OKAY, THEN...
...
...
HOLD IT.
バチンッ
THWAP
OUCH...!

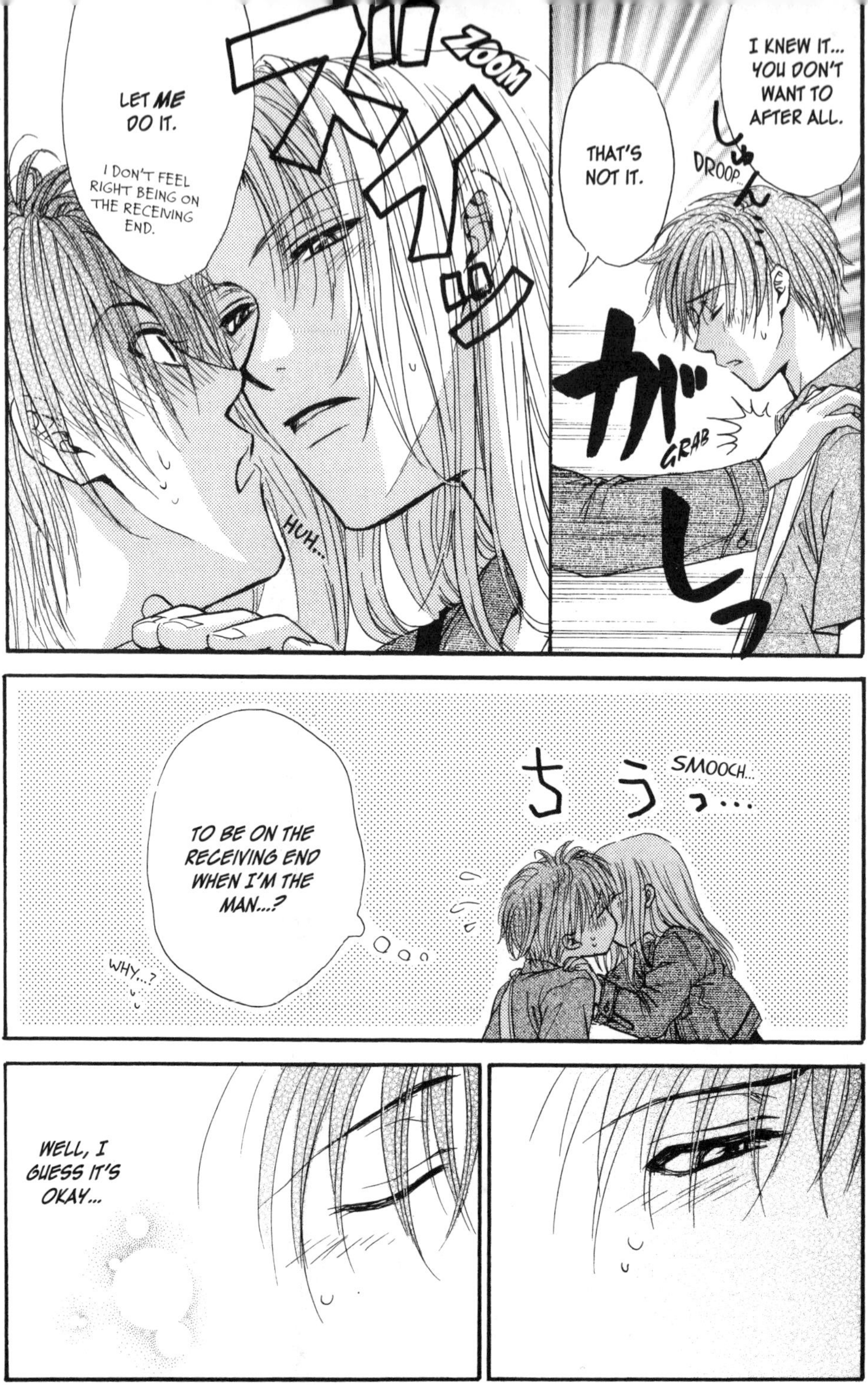
I KNEW IT... YOU DON'T WANT TO AFTER ALL.
DROOP...
THAT'S NOT IT.
がしっ
GRAB
ZOOM
LET ME DO IT.
I DON'T FEEL RIGHT BEING ON THE RECEIVING END.
HUH...
ちうっ...
SMOOCH...
TO BE ON THE RECEIVING END WHEN I'M THE MAN...?
WHY...?
WELL, I GUESS IT'S OKAY...

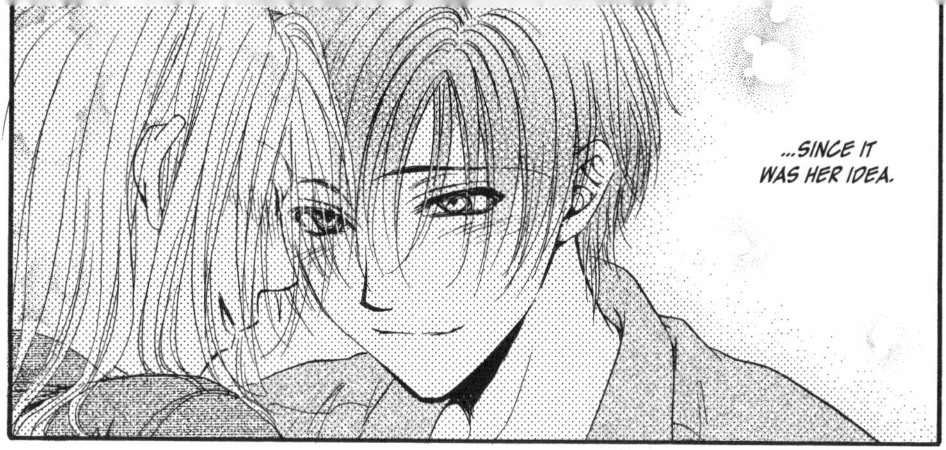
...SINCE IT WAS HER IDEA.

AND DON'T THEY SAY THE ONE WHO FIRST LOSES HIS HEART LOSES THE GAME?

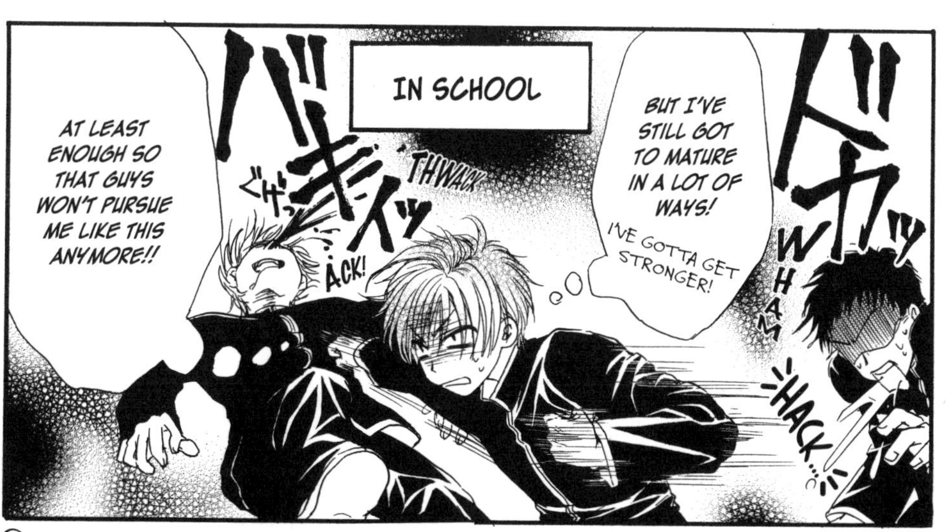
IN SCHOOL
ドカッ
WHAM
BUT I'VE STILL GOT TO MATURE IN A LOT OF WAYS!
I'VE GOTTA GET STRONGER!
HACK...
バキイッ
THWACK
ぐげっ
ACK!
AT LEAST ENOUGH SO THAT GUYS WON'T PURSUE ME LIKE THIS ANYMORE!!

365-STEP MARCH ✱ END

4-FRAME THEATER

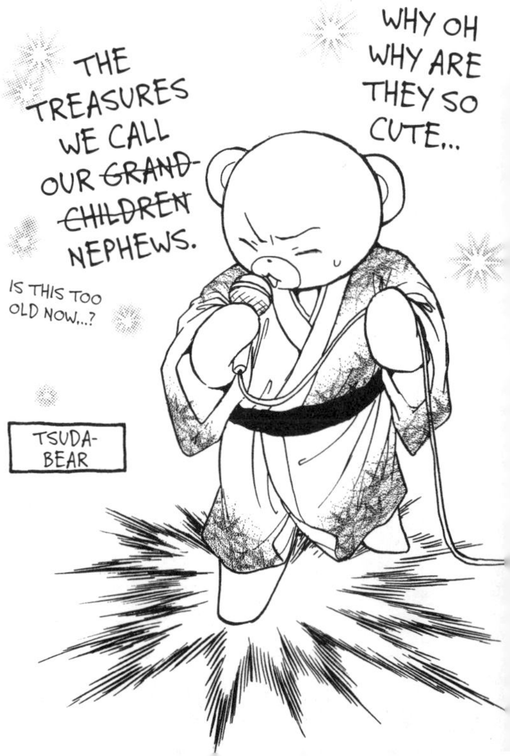

WHY OH WHY ARE THEY SO CUTE...
THE TREASURES WE CALL OUR ~~GRAND CHILDREN~~ NEPHEWS.
IS THIS TOO OLD NOW...?
TSUDA-BEAR

MY ADORABLE NEPHEW

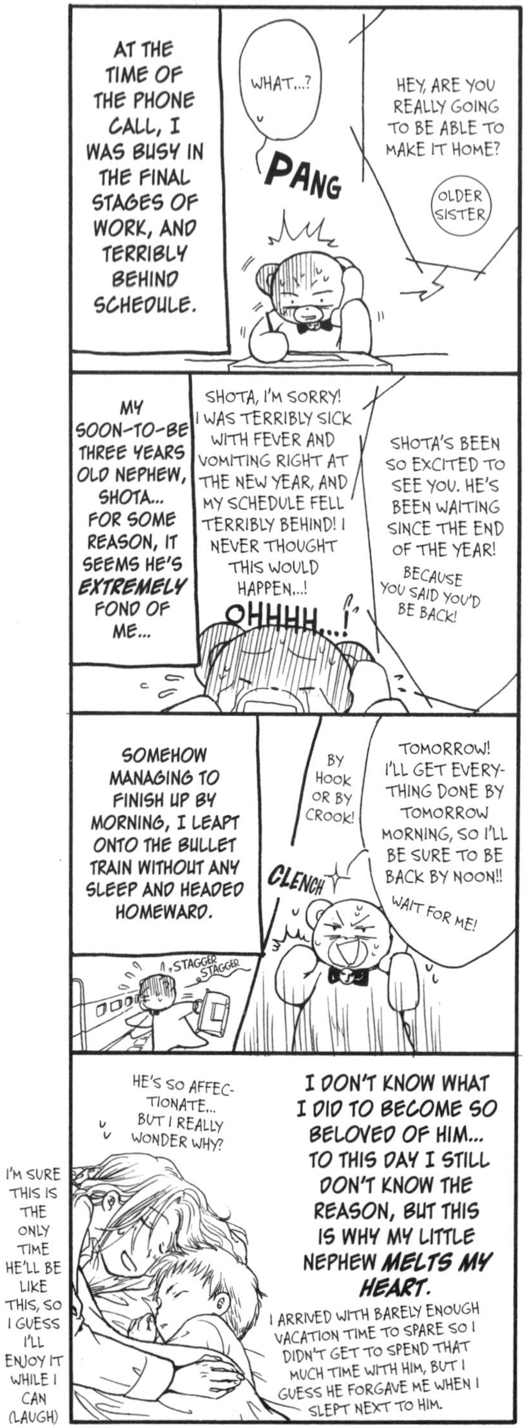

HEY, ARE YOU REALLY GOING TO BE ABLE TO MAKE IT HOME?
OLDER SISTER
WHAT...?
PANG
AT THE TIME OF THE PHONE CALL, I WAS BUSY IN THE FINAL STAGES OF WORK, AND TERRIBLY BEHIND SCHEDULE.
SHOTA'S BEEN SO EXCITED TO SEE YOU. HE'S BEEN WAITING SINCE THE END OF THE YEAR!
BECAUSE YOU SAID YOU'D BE BACK!
SHOTA, I'M SORRY! I WAS TERRIBLY SICK WITH FEVER AND VOMITING RIGHT AT THE NEW YEAR, AND MY SCHEDULE FELL TERRIBLY BEHIND! I NEVER THOUGHT THIS WOULD HAPPEN...!
OHHHH...!
MY SOON-TO-BE THREE YEARS OLD NEPHEW, SHOTA... FOR SOME REASON, IT SEEMS HE'S ***EXTREMELY*** FOND OF ME...
TOMORROW! I'LL GET EVERYTHING DONE BY TOMORROW MORNING, SO I'LL BE SURE TO BE BACK BY NOON!!
WAIT FOR ME!
BY HOOK OR BY CROOK!
CLENCH
SOMEHOW MANAGING TO FINISH UP BY MORNING, I LEAPT ONTO THE BULLET TRAIN WITHOUT ANY SLEEP AND HEADED HOMEWARD.
STAGGER STAGGER
I DON'T KNOW WHAT I DID TO BECOME SO BELOVED OF HIM... TO THIS DAY I STILL DON'T KNOW THE REASON, BUT THIS IS WHY MY LITTLE NEPHEW ***MELTS MY HEART***.
I ARRIVED WITH BARELY ENOUGH VACATION TIME TO SPARE SO I DIDN'T GET TO SPEND THAT MUCH TIME WITH HIM, BUT I GUESS HE FORGAVE ME WHEN I SLEPT NEXT TO HIM.
HE'S SO AFFECTIONATE... BUT I REALLY WONDER WHY?
I'M SURE THIS IS THE ONLY TIME HE'LL BE LIKE THIS, SO I GUESS I'LL ENJOY IT WHILE I CAN (LAUGH)

SORRY THIS WAS SO PERSONAL (LAUGH)

THE BIRTH OF MIKOTO

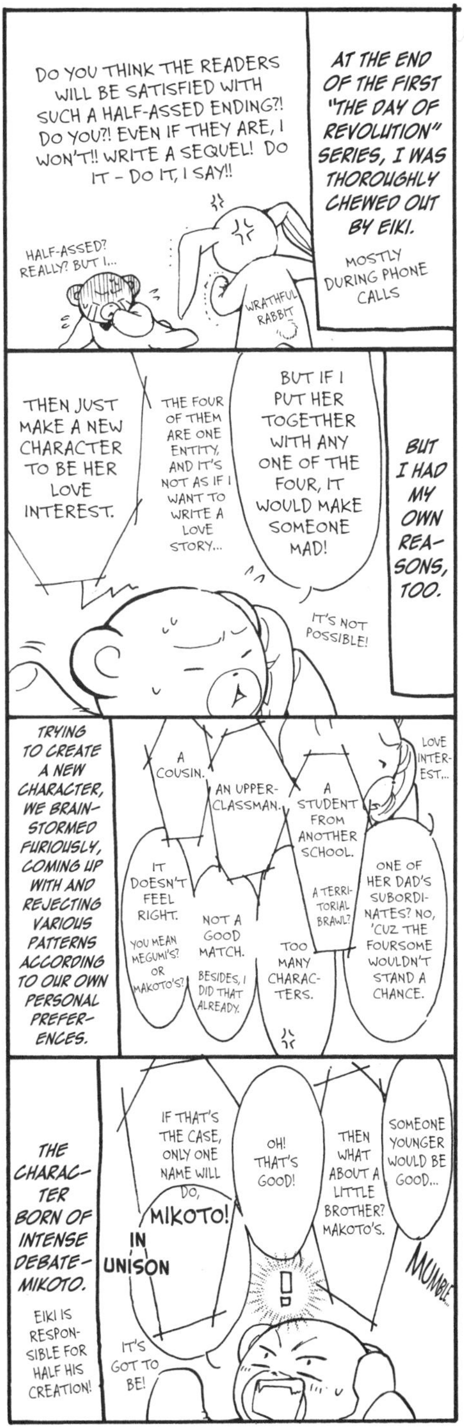
AT THE END OF THE FIRST "THE DAY OF REVOLUTION" SERIES, I WAS THOROUGHLY CHEWED OUT BY EIKI.
MOSTLY DURING PHONE CALLS
DO YOU THINK THE READERS WILL BE SATISFIED WITH SUCH A HALF-ASSED ENDING?! DO YOU?! EVEN IF THEY ARE, I WON'T!! WRITE A SEQUEL! DO IT – DO IT, I SAY!!
WRATHFUL RABBIT
HALF-ASSED? REALLY? BUT I...
BUT I HAD MY OWN REASONS, TOO.
BUT IF I PUT HER TOGETHER WITH ANY ONE OF THE FOUR, IT WOULD MAKE SOMEONE MAD!
THE FOUR OF THEM ARE ONE ENTITY, AND IT'S NOT AS IF I WANT TO WRITE A LOVE STORY...
THEN JUST MAKE A NEW CHARACTER TO BE HER LOVE INTEREST.
IT'S NOT POSSIBLE!
LOVE INTEREST...
ONE OF HER DAD'S SUBORDINATES? NO, 'CUZ THE FOURSOME WOULDN'T STAND A CHANCE.
A STUDENT FROM ANOTHER SCHOOL.
A TERRITORIAL BRAWL?
AN UPPERCLASSMAN.
A COUSIN.
TOO MANY CHARACTERS.
NOT A GOOD MATCH.
BESIDES, I DID THAT ALREADY.
IT DOESN'T FEEL RIGHT.
YOU MEAN MEGUMI'S? OR MAKOTO'S?
TRYING TO CREATE A NEW CHARACTER, WE BRAINSTORMED FURIOUSLY, COMING UP WITH AND REJECTING VARIOUS PATTERNS ACCORDING TO OUR OWN PERSONAL PREFERENCES.
SOMEONE YOUNGER WOULD BE GOOD...
THEN WHAT ABOUT A LITTLE BROTHER? MAKOTO'S.
OH! THAT'S GOOD!
IF THAT'S THE CASE, ONLY ONE NAME WILL DO,
MIKOTO!
MUMBLE
!
IN UNISON
IT'S GOT TO BE!
THE CHARACTER BORN OF INTENSE DEBATE–MIKOTO.
EIKI IS RESPONSIBLE FOR HALF HIS CREATION!

I'M SORRY, MR.EDITOR

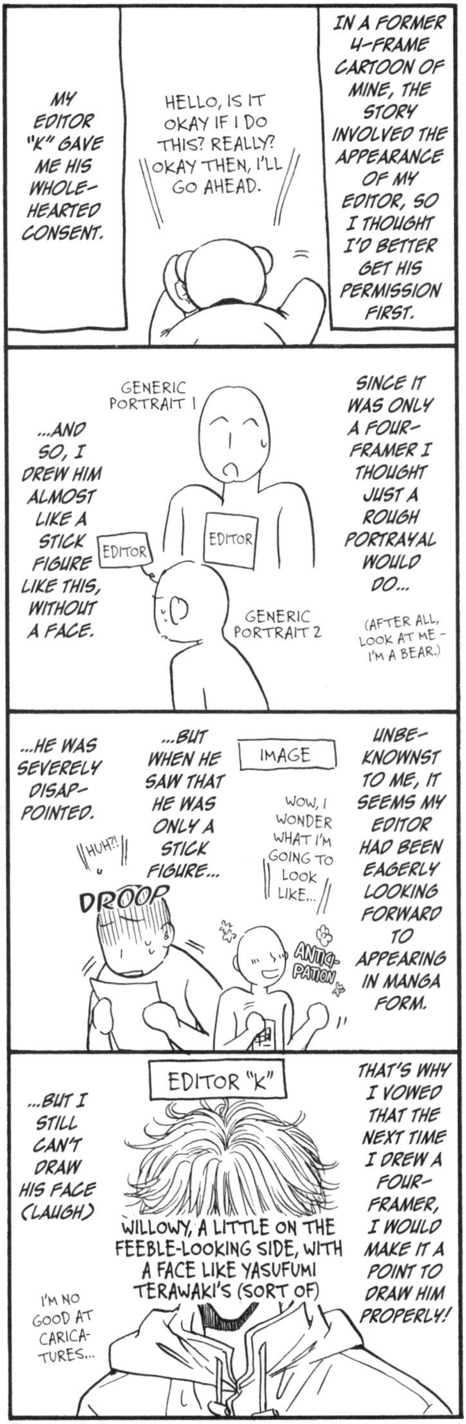
IN A FORMER 4-FRAME CARTOON OF MINE, THE STORY INVOLVED THE APPEARANCE OF MY EDITOR, SO I THOUGHT I'D BETTER GET HIS PERMISSION FIRST.
HELLO, IS IT OKAY IF I DO THIS? REALLY? OKAY THEN, I'LL GO AHEAD.
MY EDITOR "K" GAVE ME HIS WHOLE-HEARTED CONSENT.
SINCE IT WAS ONLY A FOUR-FRAMER I THOUGHT JUST A ROUGH PORTRAYAL WOULD DO...
(AFTER ALL, LOOK AT ME – I'M A BEAR.)
GENERIC PORTRAIT 1
EDITOR
EDITOR
GENERIC PORTRAIT 2
...AND SO, I DREW HIM ALMOST LIKE A STICK FIGURE LIKE THIS, WITHOUT A FACE.
UNBEKNOWNST TO ME, IT SEEMS MY EDITOR HAD BEEN EAGERLY LOOKING FORWARD TO APPEARING IN MANGA FORM.
IMAGE
WOW, I WONDER WHAT I'M GOING TO LOOK LIKE...
ANTICIPATION
...BUT WHEN HE SAW THAT HE WAS ONLY A STICK FIGURE...
...HE WAS SEVERELY DISAPPOINTED.
HUH?!
DROOP
THAT'S WHY I VOWED THAT THE NEXT TIME I DREW A FOUR-FRAMER, I WOULD MAKE IT A POINT TO DRAW HIM PROPERLY!
EDITOR "K"
WILLOWY, A LITTLE ON THE FEEBLE-LOOKING SIDE, WITH A FACE LIKE YASUFUMI TERAWAKI'S (SORT OF)
...BUT I STILL CAN'T DRAW HIS FACE (LAUGH)
I'M NO GOOD AT CARICATURES...

4-FRAME THEATER ✹ END

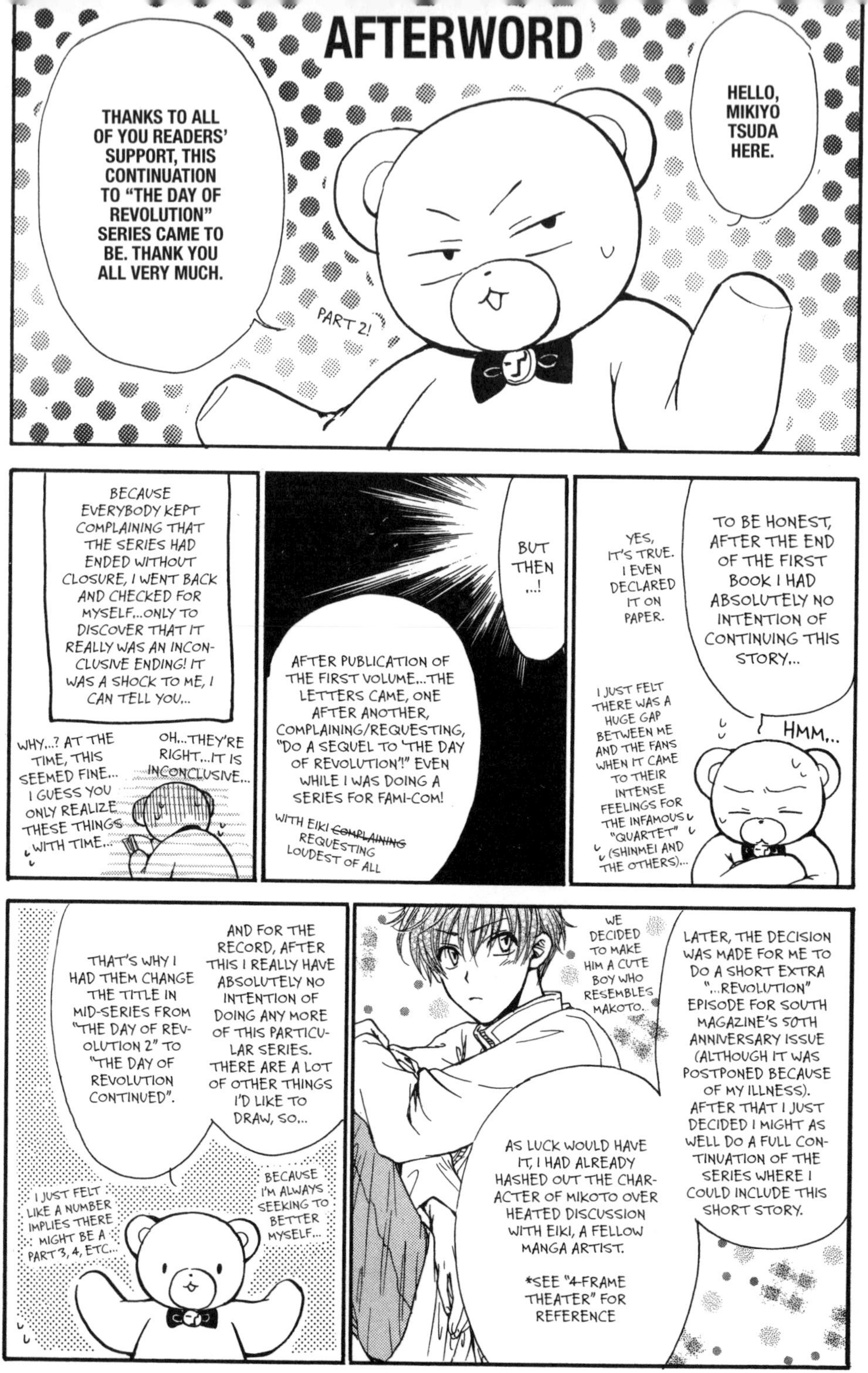
AFTERWORD
HELLO, MIKIYO TSUDA HERE.
THANKS TO ALL OF YOU READERS' SUPPORT, THIS CONTINUATION TO "THE DAY OF REVOLUTION" SERIES CAME TO BE. THANK YOU ALL VERY MUCH.
PART 2!
TO BE HONEST, AFTER THE END OF THE FIRST BOOK I HAD ABSOLUTELY NO INTENTION OF CONTINUING THIS STORY...
YES, IT'S TRUE. I EVEN DECLARED IT ON PAPER.
HMM...
I JUST FELT THERE WAS A HUGE GAP BETWEEN ME AND THE FANS WHEN IT CAME TO THEIR INTENSE FEELINGS FOR THE INFAMOUS "QUARTET" (SHINMEI AND THE OTHERS)...
BUT THEN ...!
AFTER PUBLICATION OF THE FIRST VOLUME...THE LETTERS CAME, ONE AFTER ANOTHER, COMPLAINING/REQUESTING, "DO A SEQUEL TO 'THE DAY OF REVOLUTION'!" EVEN WHILE I WAS DOING A SERIES FOR FAMI-COM!
WITH EIKI ~~COMPLAINING~~ REQUESTING LOUDEST OF ALL
BECAUSE EVERYBODY KEPT COMPLAINING THAT THE SERIES HAD ENDED WITHOUT CLOSURE, I WENT BACK AND CHECKED FOR MYSELF...ONLY TO DISCOVER THAT IT REALLY WAS AN INCONCLUSIVE ENDING! IT WAS A SHOCK TO ME, I CAN TELL YOU...
OH...THEY'RE RIGHT...IT IS INCONCLUSIVE...
WHY...? AT THE TIME, THIS SEEMED FINE... I GUESS YOU ONLY REALIZE THESE THINGS WITH TIME...
LATER, THE DECISION WAS MADE FOR ME TO DO A SHORT EXTRA "...REVOLUTION" EPISODE FOR SOUTH MAGAZINE'S 50TH ANNIVERSARY ISSUE (ALTHOUGH IT WAS POSTPONED BECAUSE OF MY ILLNESS). AFTER THAT I JUST DECIDED I MIGHT AS WELL DO A FULL CONTINUATION OF THE SERIES WHERE I COULD INCLUDE THIS SHORT STORY.
WE DECIDED TO MAKE HIM A CUTE BOY WHO RESEMBLES MAKOTO..
AS LUCK WOULD HAVE IT, I HAD ALREADY HASHED OUT THE CHARACTER OF MIKOTO OVER HEATED DISCUSSION WITH EIKI, A FELLOW MANGA ARTIST.
*SEE "4-FRAME THEATER" FOR REFERENCE
AND FOR THE RECORD, AFTER THIS I REALLY HAVE ABSOLUTELY NO INTENTION OF DOING ANY MORE OF THIS PARTICULAR SERIES. THERE ARE A LOT OF OTHER THINGS I'D LIKE TO DRAW, SO...
THAT'S WHY I HAD THEM CHANGE THE TITLE IN MID-SERIES FROM "THE DAY OF REVOLUTION 2" TO "THE DAY OF REVOLUTION CONTINUED".
BECAUSE I'M ALWAYS SEEKING TO BETTER MYSELF...
I JUST FELT LIKE A NUMBER IMPLIES THERE MIGHT BE A PART 3, 4, ETC...

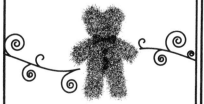

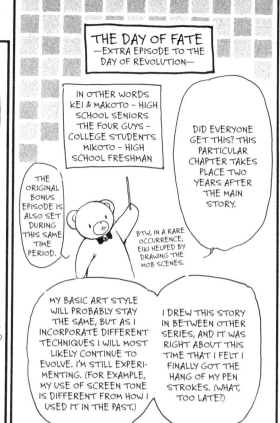

THE DAY OF FATE

—EXTRA EPISODE TO THE DAY OF REVOLUTION—

DID EVERYONE GET THIS? THIS PARTICULAR CHAPTER TAKES PLACE TWO YEARS AFTER THE MAIN STORY.

IN OTHER WORDS
KEI & MAKOTO - HIGH SCHOOL SENIORS
THE FOUR GUYS - COLLEGE STUDENTS
MIKOTO - HIGH SCHOOL FRESHMAN

THE ORIGINAL BONUS EPISODE IS ALSO SET DURING THIS SAME TIME PERIOD.

BTW, IN A RARE OCCURRENCE, EIKI HELPED BY DRAWING THE MOB SCENES.

I DREW THIS STORY IN BETWEEN OTHER SERIES, AND IT WAS RIGHT ABOUT THIS TIME THAT I FELT I FINALLY GOT THE HANG OF MY PEN STROKES. (WHAT, TOO LATE?)

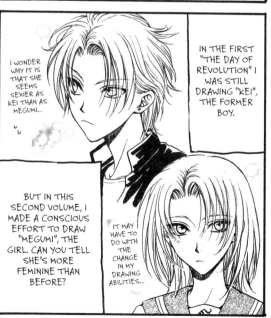

MY BASIC ART STYLE WILL PROBABLY STAY THE SAME, BUT AS I INCORPORATE DIFFERENT TECHNIQUES I WILL MOST LIKELY CONTINUE TO EVOLVE. I'M STILL EXPERIMENTING. (FOR EXAMPLE, MY USE OF SCREEN TONE IS DIFFERENT FROM HOW I USED IT IN THE PAST.)

IN THE FIRST "THE DAY OF REVOLUTION" I WAS STILL DRAWING "KEI", THE FORMER BOY.
I WONDER WHY IT IS THAT SHE SEEMS SEXIER AS KEI THAN AS MEGUMI...
BUT IN THIS SECOND VOLUME, I MADE A CONSCIOUS EFFORT TO DRAW "MEGUMI", THE GIRL. CAN YOU TELL SHE'S MORE FEMININE THAN BEFORE?
IT MAY HAVE TO DO WITH THE CHANGE IN MY DRAWING ABILITIES...

I'M FAIRLY SURE THAT THIS SEQUEL WILL PROVOKE STRONG REACTIONS FROM BOTH SIDES.

I'M SURE PEOPLE WILL SAY MEGUMI SHOULD HAVE PAIRED UP WITH SO-AND-SO (PREFERRED CHARACTER OF CHOICE), OR COMPLAIN ABOUT HER GETTING TOGETHER WITH MIKOTO...OR CONVERSELY, THAT THEY ENJOYED IT, THEY LIKED IT, THEY WERE GLAD SHE AND MIKOTO GOT TOGETHER...OR MAYBE GO FOR THE DARK HORSE AND INQUIRE ABOUT NAKAGAWA SEMPAI? (LAUGH)

OR PERHAPS I'LL GET YELLED AT AGAIN FOR ANOTHER INCONCLUSIVE ENDING!!

↑

UM...BUT I DID DRAW ANOTHER EPISODE ABOUT HOW THEY FARED AFTERWARDS...

BUT THAT'S OKAY, BECAUSE EVERYONE SHOULD HAVE THEIR OWN OPINION AND PREFERENCE.

I CAN ONLY DRAW IN ACCORDANCE WITH MY OWN OPINIONS. TO PUT IT ANOTHER WAY, THIS STORY IS WHAT IT IS BECAUSE I DREW IT ACCORDING TO MY PREFERENCES. THAT IS WHY I FIND READING THROUGH EVERYONE'S DIFFERENT OPINIONS VERY ENTERTAINING AND INSPIRATIONAL. IT ALWAYS MAKES ME APPRECIATE ANEW HOW VARIED AND MULTICOLORED PEOPLE'S PREFERENCES REALLY ARE. AND IF EVER MORE PEOPLE SHOULD FIND MY WORK ENTERTAINING, THAT WOULD MAKE ME HAPPIEST OF ALL.

I DON'T KNOW IF I HAVE SUCCEEDED IN ACHIEVING THAT WITH THIS LATEST STORY OF MINE, BUT I WILL CONTINUE TO MOVE FORWARD WITH THIS GOAL AND HOPE IN MIND.

TO THAT END, I WOULD GREATLY APPRECIATE ANY AND ALL COMMENTS AND OPINIONS ABOUT MY WORK.

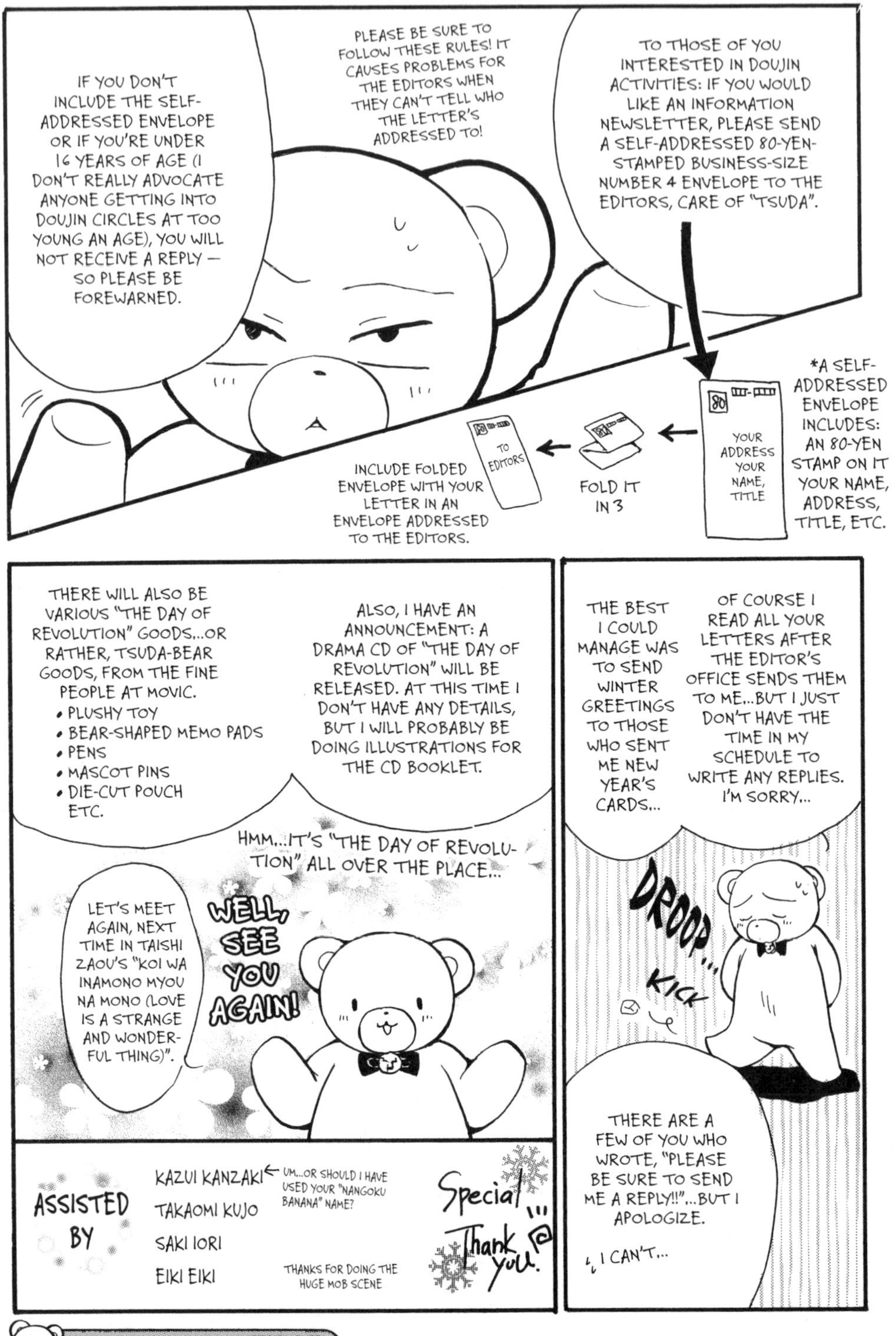
TO THOSE OF YOU INTERESTED IN DOUJIN ACTIVITIES: IF YOU WOULD LIKE AN INFORMATION NEWSLETTER, PLEASE SEND A SELF-ADDRESSED 80-YEN-STAMPED BUSINESS-SIZE NUMBER 4 ENVELOPE TO THE EDITORS, CARE OF "TSUDA".
PLEASE BE SURE TO FOLLOW THESE RULES! IT CAUSES PROBLEMS FOR THE EDITORS WHEN THEY CAN'T TELL WHO THE LETTER'S ADDRESSED TO!
IF YOU DON'T INCLUDE THE SELF-ADDRESSED ENVELOPE OR IF YOU'RE UNDER 16 YEARS OF AGE (I DON'T REALLY ADVOCATE ANYONE GETTING INTO DOUJIN CIRCLES AT TOO YOUNG AN AGE), YOU WILL NOT RECEIVE A REPLY — SO PLEASE BE FOREWARNED.
*A SELF-ADDRESSED ENVELOPE INCLUDES: AN 80-YEN STAMP ON IT YOUR NAME, ADDRESS, TITLE, ETC.
80
YOUR ADDRESS YOUR NAME, TITLE
FOLD IT IN 3
TO EDITORS
INCLUDE FOLDED ENVELOPE WITH YOUR LETTER IN AN ENVELOPE ADDRESSED TO THE EDITORS.
OF COURSE I READ ALL YOUR LETTERS AFTER THE EDITOR'S OFFICE SENDS THEM TO ME...BUT I JUST DON'T HAVE THE TIME IN MY SCHEDULE TO WRITE ANY REPLIES. I'M SORRY...
THE BEST I COULD MANAGE WAS TO SEND WINTER GREETINGS TO THOSE WHO SENT ME NEW YEAR'S CARDS...
DROOP...
KICK
THERE ARE A FEW OF YOU WHO WROTE, "PLEASE BE SURE TO SEND ME A REPLY!!"...BUT I APOLOGIZE.
I CAN'T...
ALSO, I HAVE AN ANNOUNCEMENT: A DRAMA CD OF "THE DAY OF REVOLUTION" WILL BE RELEASED. AT THIS TIME I DON'T HAVE ANY DETAILS, BUT I WILL PROBABLY BE DOING ILLUSTRATIONS FOR THE CD BOOKLET.
THERE WILL ALSO BE VARIOUS "THE DAY OF REVOLUTION" GOODS...OR RATHER, TSUDA-BEAR GOODS, FROM THE FINE PEOPLE AT MOVIC.
• PLUSHY TOY
• BEAR-SHAPED MEMO PADS
• PENS
• MASCOT PINS
• DIE-CUT POUCH
ETC.
HMM...IT'S "THE DAY OF REVOLUTION" ALL OVER THE PLACE...
WELL, SEE YOU AGAIN!
LET'S MEET AGAIN, NEXT TIME IN TAISHI ZAOU'S "KOI WA INAMONO MYOU NA MONO (LOVE IS A STRANGE AND WONDERFUL THING)".
Special Thank you!
ASSISTED BY
KAZUI KANZAKI ← UM...OR SHOULD I HAVE USED YOUR "NANGOKU BANANA" NAME?
TAKAOMI KUJO
SAKI IORI
EIKI EIKI
THANKS FOR DOING THE HUGE MOB SCENE

AFTERWORD ✸ END

Princess·Princess

By MIKIYO TSUDA

Peer pressure...
has never been this intense!

When students need a boost, the Princesses arrive in gothic lolita outfits to show their school spirit! Join Kouno and friends in this crazy, cross-dressing comedy.

DMP

**DIGITAL MANGA
PUBLISHING**
www.dmpbooks.com

PRINCESS · PRINCESS 1 © 2002 Mikiyo Tsuda. Originally published in Japan in 2002 by
SHINSHOKAN Co., Ltd. English translation rights arranged through TOHAN Corporation, Tokyo.

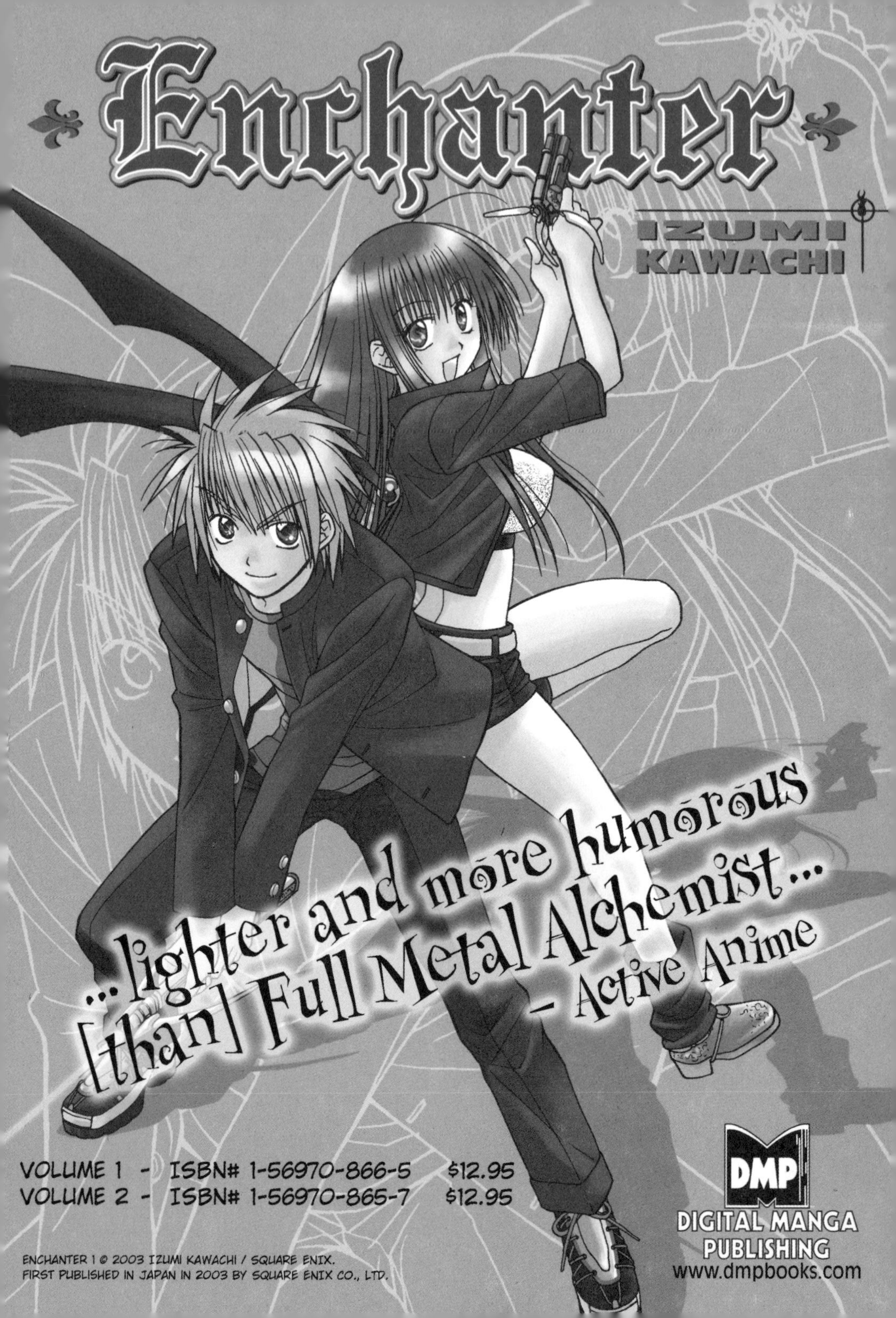

Enchanter

IZUMI KAWACHI

...lighter and more humorous [than] Full Metal Alchemist...
— Active Anime

VOLUME 1 - ISBN# 1-56970-866-5 $12.95
VOLUME 2 - ISBN# 1-56970-865-7 $12.95

DIGITAL MANGA
PUBLISHING
www.dmpbooks.com

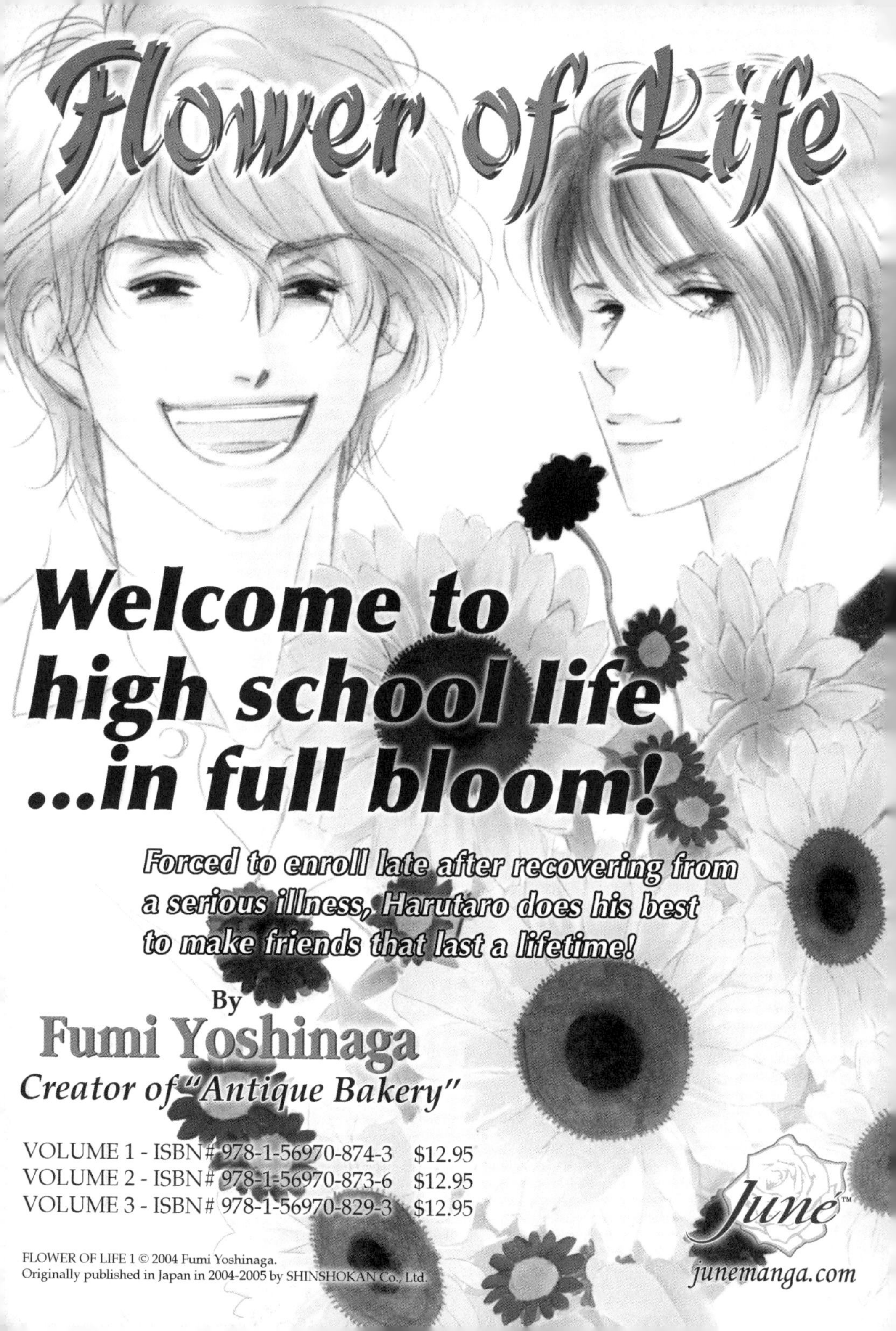
Flower of Life
Welcome to high school life ...in full bloom!
Forced to enroll late after recovering from a serious illness, Harutaro does his best to make friends that last a lifetime!
By
Fumi Yoshinaga
Creator of "Antique Bakery"
VOLUME 1 - ISBN# 978-1-56970-874-3 $12.95
VOLUME 2 - ISBN# 978-1-56970-873-6 $12.95
VOLUME 3 - ISBN# 978-1-56970-829-3 $12.95
June™
junemanga.com
FLOWER OF LIFE 1 © 2004 Fumi Yoshinaga.
Originally published in Japan in 2004-2005 by SHINSHOKAN Co., Ltd.

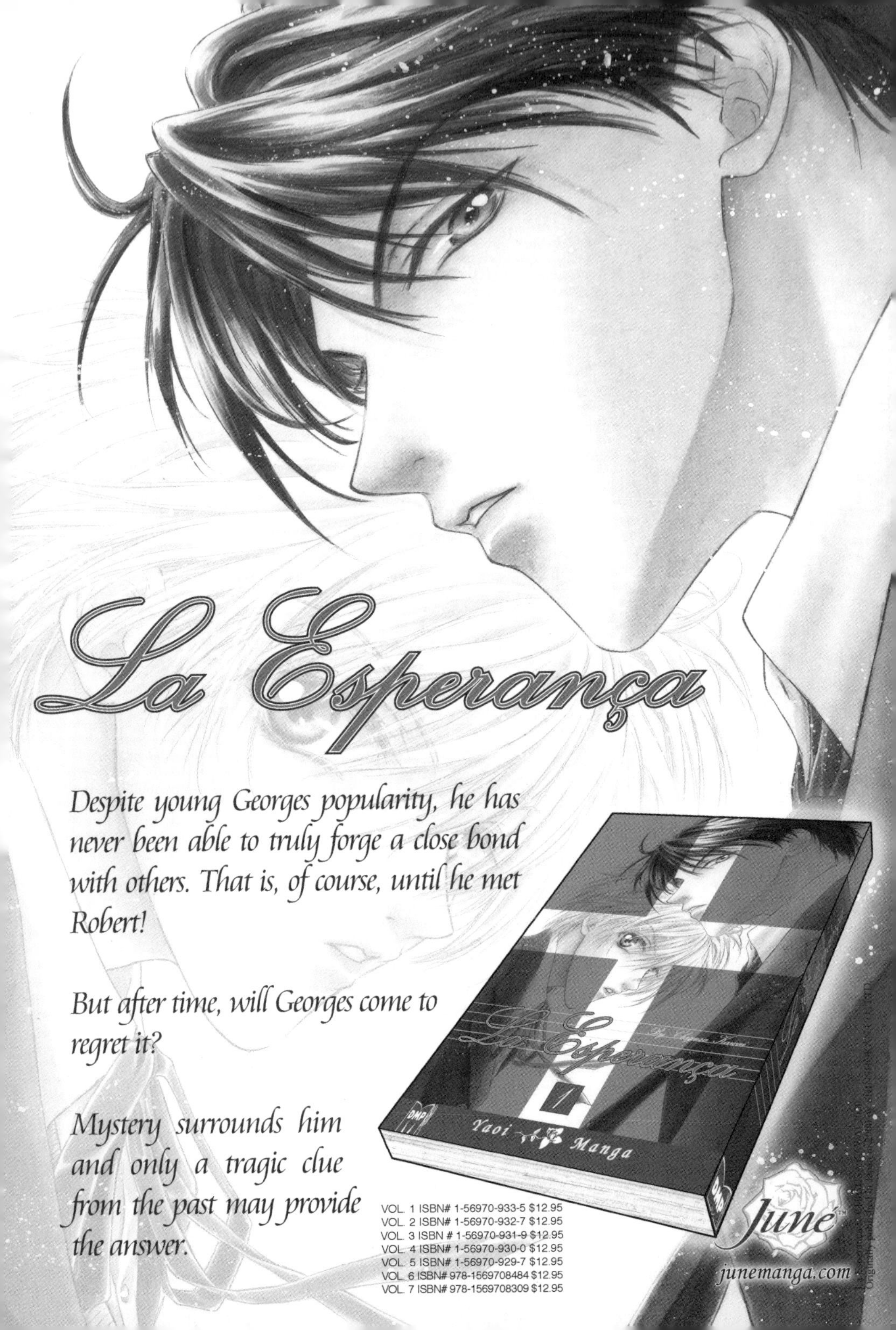
La Esperança
Despite young Georges popularity, he has never been able to truly forge a close bond with others. That is, of course, until he met Robert!
But after time, will Georges come to regret it?
Mystery surrounds him and only a tragic clue from the past may provide the answer.
La Esperança
1
Yaoi Manga
DMP
VOL. 1 ISBN# 1-56970-933-5 $12.95
VOL. 2 ISBN# 1-56970-932-7 $12.95
VOL. 3 ISBN # 1-56970-931-9 $12.95
VOL. 4 ISBN# 1-56970-930-0 $12.95
VOL. 5 ISBN# 1-56970-929-7 $12.95
VOL. 6 ISBN# 978-1569708484 $12.95
VOL. 7 ISBN# 978-1569708309 $12.95
June™
junemanga.com

Café Kichijouji de 1

"Irrasshai!"

"Welcome!" to the hilarious and most unruly café in all of Kichijouji...

...With its charming staff of five who's largely conflicting personalities usually result in even **larger** repair bills!

A new manga based on the popular Japanese Radio Drama!

DMP
DIGITAL MANGA
PUBLISHING
A New Wave of Manga

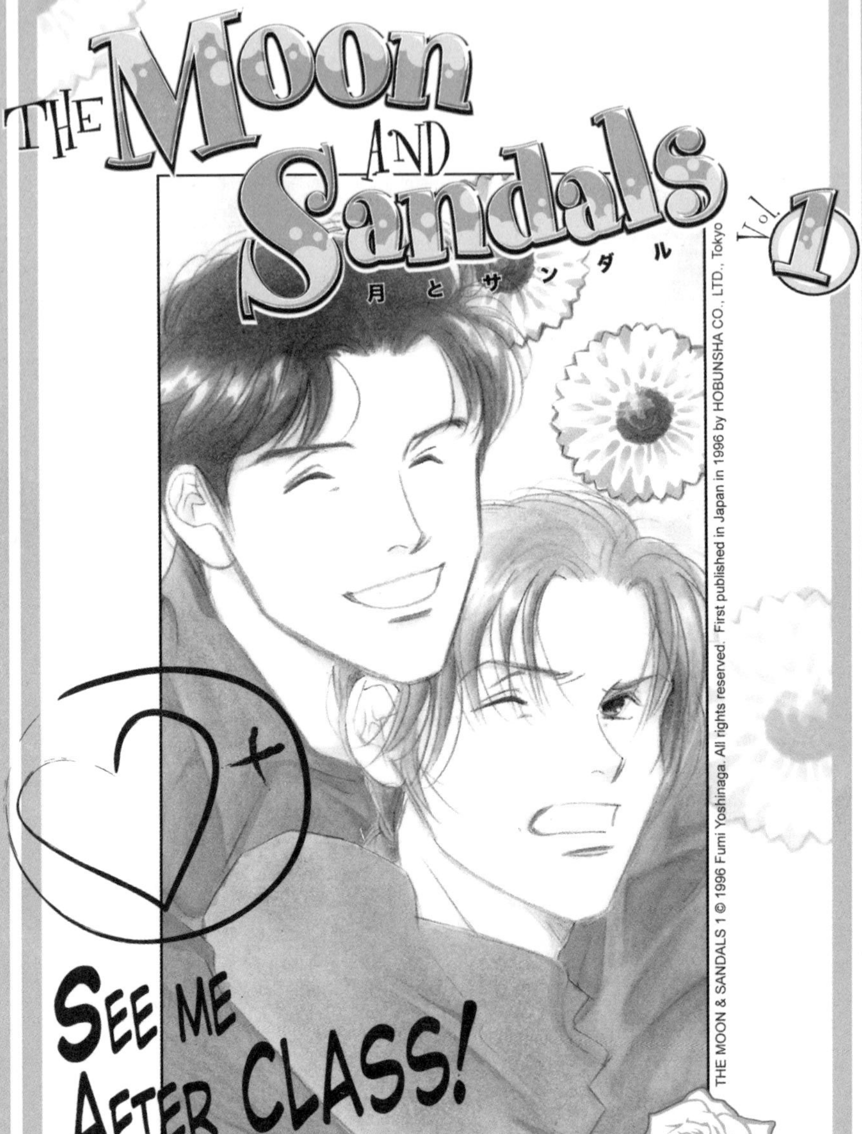
THE Moon AND Sandals
Vol. 1
月とサンダル
SEE ME AFTER CLASS!

ISBN# 978-1-56970-802-9 SRP $12.95

June™ by DMP

As a newly appointed high school teacher, Ida has yet to gain confidence in his abilities. His insecurity grows worse when he feels someone staring intensely at him during class. The piercing eyes belong to a tall, intimidating student – Koichi Kobayashi. What exactly should Ida do about it? Is it discontent that fuels Kobayashi's sultry gaze… or could it be something else?

Written and Illustrated by:
Fumi Yoshinaga

junemanga.com

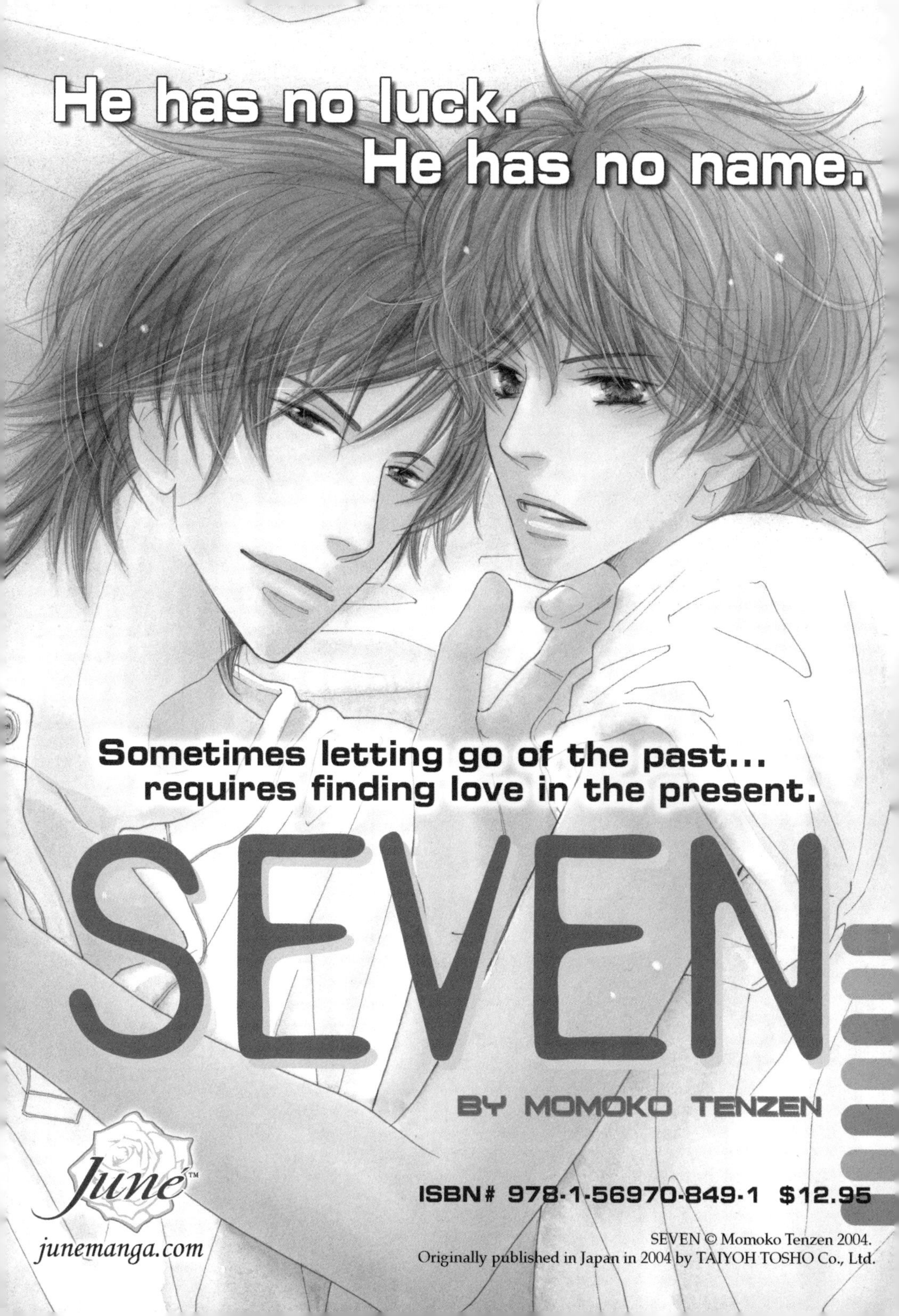
He has no luck.
He has no name.
Sometimes letting go of the past...
...requires finding love in the present.
SEVEN
BY MOMOKO TENZEN
June™
junemanga.com
ISBN# 978-1-56970-849-1 $12.95
SEVEN © Momoko Tenzen 2004.
Originally published in Japan in 2004 by TAIYOH TOSHO Co., Ltd.

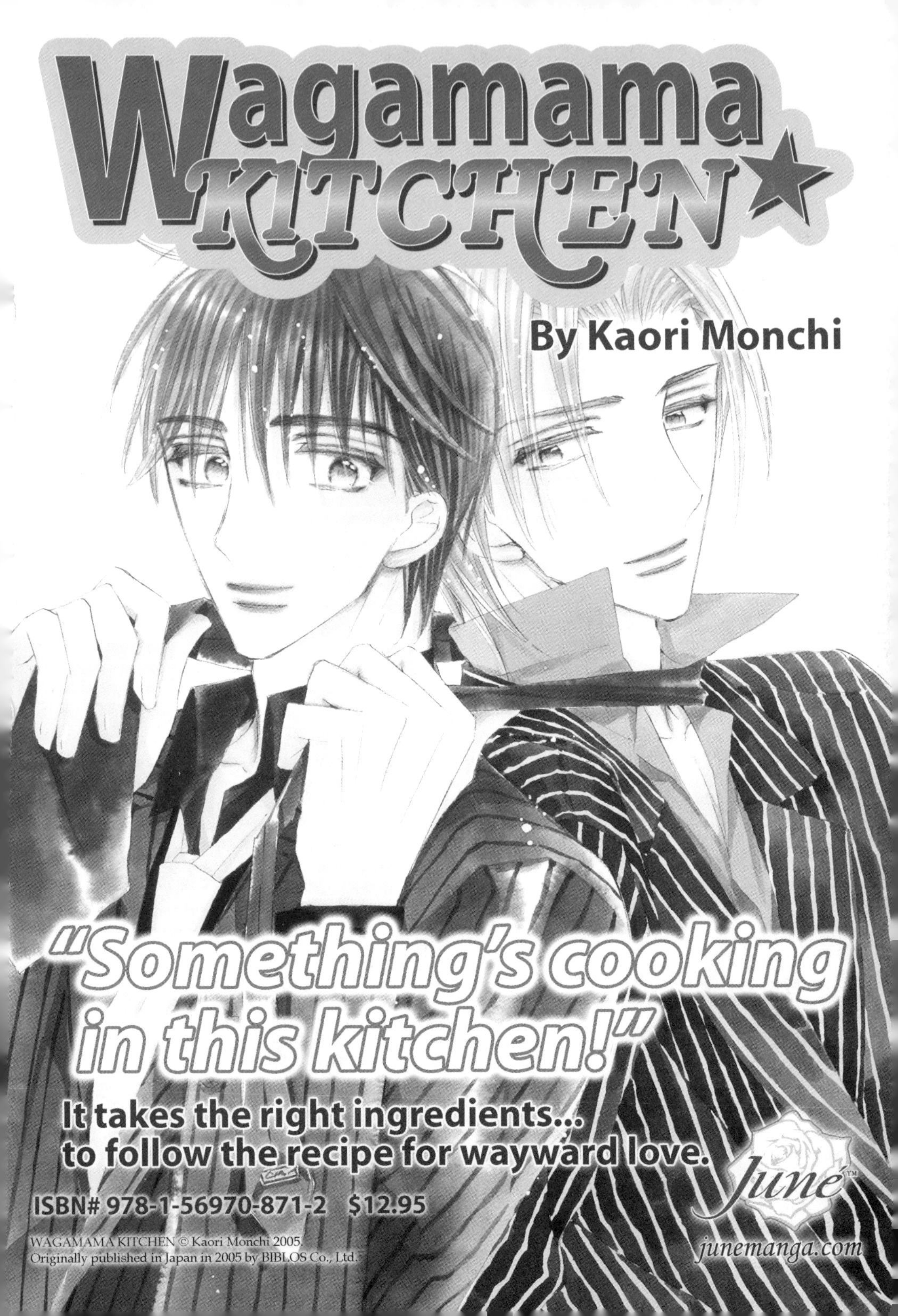
Wagamama KITCHEN★
By Kaori Monchi
"Something's cooking in this kitchen!"
It takes the right ingredients...
to follow the recipe for wayward love.
ISBN# 978-1-56970-871-2 $12.95
WAGAMAMA KITCHEN © Kaori Monchi 2005.
Originally published in Japan in 2005 by BIBLOS Co., Ltd.
Juné™
junemanga.com

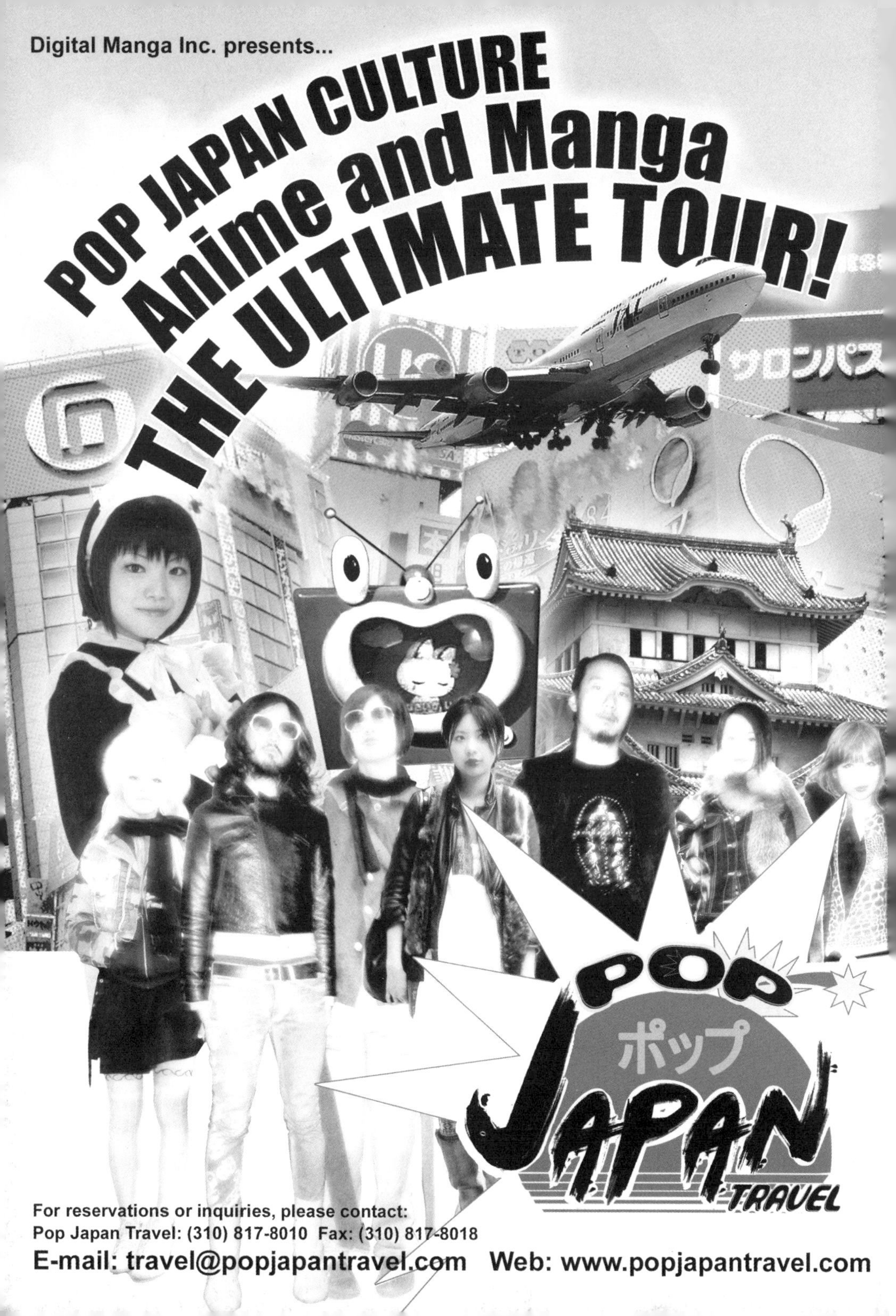
Digital Manga Inc. presents...
POP JAPAN CULTURE
Anime and Manga
THE ULTIMATE TOUR!
サロンパス
POP
ポップ
JAPAN
TRAVEL
For reservations or inquiries, please contact:
Pop Japan Travel: (310) 817-8010 Fax: (310) 817-8018
E-mail: travel@popjapantravel.com Web: www.popjapantravel.com

STOP

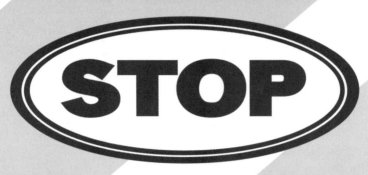

This is the back of the book! Start from the other side.

NATIVE MANGA readers read manga from *right to left*.

1
2
1
3
2
3
5
4
4
6
5
8
7
6

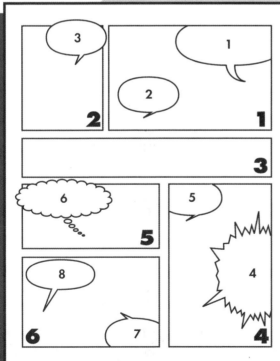

*If you run into our **Native Manga** logo on any of our books... you'll know that this manga is published in it's true original native Japanese right to left reading format, as it was intended. Turn to the other side of the book and start reading from right to left, top to bottom.*

Follow the diagram to see how its done.
Surf's Up!

NATIVE MANGA
READ RIGHT TO LEFT

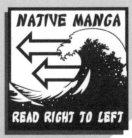